Man of Constant Sorrow

Man of Constant Sorrow

My Life and Times

DR. RALPH STANLEY

with

EDDIE DEAN

GOTHAM BOOKS

GOTHAM BOOKS
Published by Penguin Group (USA) Inc.
375 Hudson Street, New York, New York 10014, U.S.A.
Penguin Group (Canada), 90 Eglinton Avenue East, Suite 700, Toronto,
Ontario M4P 2Y3, Canada (a division of Pearson Penguin Canada Inc.)
Penguin Books Ltd, 80 Strand, London WC2R 0RL, England
Penguin Ireland, 25 St Stephen's Green, Dublin 2,
Ireland (a division of Penguin Books Ltd)
Penguin Group (Australia), 250 Camberwell Road, Camberwell,
Victoria 3124, Australia (a division of Pearson Australia Group Pty Ltd)
Penguin Books India Pvt Ltd, 11 Community Centre,
Panchsheel Park, New Delhi—110 017, India
Penguin Group (NZ), 67 Apollo Drive, Rosedale, North Shore 0632,
New Zealand (a division of Pearson New Zealand Ltd)
Penguin Books (South Africa) (Pty) Ltd, 24 Sturdee Avenue,
Rosebank, Johannesburg 2196, South Africa

Penguin Books Ltd, Registered Offices: 80 Strand, London WC2R 0RL, England

Published by Gotham Books, a member of Penguin Group (USA) Inc.

First printing, October 2009
1 3 5 7 9 10 8 6 4 2

LIBRARY OF CONGRESS CATALOGING-IN-PUBLICATION DATA
Stanley, Ralph.
Man of constant sorrow: my life and times / Ralph Stanley with Eddie Dean.
p. cm.
ISBN 978-1-592-40425-4 (hardcover)
1. Stanley, Ralph. 2. Bluegrass musicians—United States—Biography.
I. Dean, Eddie, 1964– II. Title.
ML420.S8115A3 2009
781.642092—dc22
[B] 2009021920

Printed in the United States of America
Set in Bembo Designed by Elke Sigal

For my wife, Jimmi;

In memory of my mother, Lucy;

And with gratitude to all the Clinch Mountain Boys,

past, present and future.

CONTENTS

PROLOGUE

Hills of Home

"I'd like to go back to the days of my childhood
And go to church in the village there
To meet my friends and old acquaintance
And sing again in the village choir"

—"TURN BACK," RALPH STANLEY

When I was just a little boy growing up in the mountains of southwest Virginia, singing was as natural as breathing. I was borned and raised way back in the hills, and a lot of our forefathers, our grandpas and great-uncles and so forth, were of the old Baptist faith, and they all had lonesome voices to sing out those sad old hymns.

This was a long time ago, back in the 1930s, and a long way back in steep hills and deep hollows. Where I come from, people lived spread out from one another. There was no radio or telephone. Days would pass between you seeing anybody outside your family. Singing was a way to keep yourself company when you got to feeling lonesome.

You could hear singing everywhere from church to the back porch, from the high ridgetops to the head of the creek, wherever there were chores to do or miles to walk or fields to work. You'd hear people tell about a mule that wouldn't budge unless the man behind the plow got to singing. Songs were handed down from father to son and mother to daughter. Singing gave you strength, and you needed plenty to get you through rough times. People from our mountains were used to going without, and singing didn't cost a cent. Not many things you can say that about.

Back in our little part of the world, singing was part of everyday living, one of the natural sounds all around us: the water running through the rocks on Big Spraddle Creek and the coon dogs barking down the hollow and the train whistle blowing as the freight cars hauled coal on the Clinchfield Railroad. Course, we didn't pay no mind it. When you're so used to something, you don't go around making a fuss over it.

But some voices stood out from all the rest. The way some birds stand out: them hoot owls and whip-poor-wills you'd hear when the sun went down and it got dark in the hollow. I always enjoyed a whip-poor-will come to sit on our yard gate and sing of an evening. Some people get spooked by night birds. The old superstition says when you hear a whip-poor-will, somebody's going to die. But I was always taken with the mournful song of a whip-poor-will. It made me feel like I wasn't the only one feeling lonesome.

And that's the way it was with my voice. It was lonesome and mournful and it wasn't like nobody else's. I don't say this to brag on myself but because it's true. Even today, people from all over the world tell me my voice is different—completely different—from any voice they've heard.

I tell them I've sung that way since I was a boy. I think God gives everybody a gift, and He wants them to use it. I've always done my best to honor what God gave me. I've never tried to put any airs on it. I sing it the way I feel it, just the way it comes out.

When I say I sang like this since I was just a knee-high, I mean just what I say. I'm well past eighty now, but as far back as I can remember, everyone always told me I had an old-time mountain voice: what they call weathered and lived-in, like something you'd hear moaning in the woods late of a night and not from the mouth of a young'un. They called me the boy with the hundred-year-old voice. I reckon if I make it another twenty years, maybe then I'll finally get to sound like my real age.

There's a lot of people would tell me not to even bother trying to catch up. They hear something much older than a hundred years in my singing. They say it puts them in mind of the sacred chanting at a Navajo ceremony, or the gospel singing from ancient times, way back to the olden days before the written word, when people first sung out their troubles. I don't claim to know much about chanting, but the part about gospel music, well, my singing comes right out of the church.

The first time I ever sang in public was in a little country church way out in the sticks. It was a one-room building with plank benches and an old woodstove for heat. No special occasion, just another Sunday morning. You might think there wasn't much to be nervous about, but I was scared to death because my dad put me on the spot.

It was in 1935 at the Point Truth Primitive Baptist Church in Scott County, Virginia. You just about needed a search party to find it, tucked back in Long Hollow, miles from the nearest town of Nickelsville. In our type of church, the Primitive Baptists, they don't allow musical instruments whatsoever, not a piano or even a tambourine. They sing the old Baptist hymns the old-time way, a cappella–style, just the voices alone.

You may have seen in the Bible where it says "make a joyful noise unto the Lord," and that's what a lot of Pentecostals and Holiness churches do around these mountains, and they play guitars and anything else handy and they get pretty rowdy. It's got a good beat to it, it makes you happy, and it makes you want to move.

But the Primitive Baptists are different. They're strictly business when it comes to their hymns. It's more sad and it's more mournful and it fits my voice like nothing else. Usually the preacher or one of the elders will line out the songs for the congregation, which means the leader sings a verse and everybody joins in and sings it right back.

On this Sunday morning, my family was sitting all bunched together on the pew-bench like usual: my dad, Lee, and my mother, Lucy, and my older brother, Carter, and me. There was a song my dad wanted to lead on. It was from the old Goble hymnbook: "Salvation, O! The Name I Love." It was one of his favorites, but he never could remember how the song started out. So he laid his hand on my shoulder and he called on me to start the song, to line it out for the congregation.

Here we were, the church-house packed and everybody waiting on me. I couldn't even look up I was so scared, just a-trembling from head to toe. I like to stare a hole in the floor and crawl inside and hide. These people were friendly enough, but this was a new church from the one I was used to, the McClure Primitive Baptist Church, close by the hollow I was from back in Dickenson County. We'd moved for a while to the neighboring county, where we lived in an old log house in Long Hollow while my dad worked a sawmill job in the area.

When you traveled mostly by foot or by horse or mule, another county—even the next county over—might as well have been another world. To give you an idea of the distances back then: About twenty-five miles from our home place, in the coal town of West Norton in Wise County, lived the singer and banjo player Dock Boggs, who worked in the mines and made some phonograph records in the 1920s, real old-time ballads like "Pretty Polly." Well, I didn't know a thing about Dock Boggs until I met him at the Newport Folk Festival in the 1960s. Nothing against Dock, it just shows you how the world was a whole lot bigger place back then, especially in the mountains of southwest Virginia.

So it felt strange and different to me, this little church in a new county filled with folks I didn't rightly know. Even if they were Primitive Baptists like us, they were more like strangers. Here I was, barely eight years old, sitting there in the pew, worried and shaking like a leaf, after my dad called me to lead that hymn. Trapped.

I turned to my mother, but she paid me no mind. She was silent and somber, her head bowed down. Much as she wanted, she couldn't help me. In our church, it had to be a man lining out the songs, the preacher or an elder like my dad. I never did hear of a woman leading on a song. And it was unheard of for a child. So Carter couldn't rescue me neither, not even with a funny face he'd usually pull to cheer me up.

Ever since I was born, I was in the shadow of my big brother. Carter was just eighteen months older, but that was like dog years for me, because he was my idol. I was a real shy, bashful boy—"backwards" is what they called it in the mountains. I just never could mix well with people. And what was so hard for me came easy as pie to Carter, the Stanley brother everybody loved. He took after our dad, tall and handsome with a million-dollar smile and a joke for any occasion. Carter was game for anything. Me, I was a mama's boy, and there wasn't much I wasn't scared of.

But it wasn't Carter my dad called on to line out that song. He called on me. Early on, he noticed I had something God-given and unique. He reckoned my voice could carry a hymn as well as any man's in the churchhouse. And now he was going to let everybody get a good listen. It's the sort of thing fathers do. Besides, he was in a bind, forgetting how to start that song.

Scared as I was, I knew how the song went and that was what probably saved me. The melody stuck with me from the first time I'd heard it. I was always taken by the sad old Baptist hymns we sang at our home church down by the river in McClure. I can remember singing those hymns to myself around the house when I was four or five years old. I don't know why. I just had a feeling for those songs and I still do today. So I took a deep breath and sung out the opening line the best I could:

Salvation, O! The name I love, which came by Christ the Lord above

The words come out of me and hung in the air and then faded to nothing. The silence was only for a second, but it seemed to last forever. I thought maybe I'd messed up somehow and failed my dad. Then the whole congregation joined in and sang the verse back, tracing the melody just the way I done it, and the church filled up with one big voice. I could feel my heart swell up like to bust. It was a feeling I never had before, and I jumped on the next verse before the feeling got away.

Surprising wisdom, matchless grace which regarded my low and helpless case

Just like before, everyone sang back that mournful melody in a booming voice so strong the walls of the little building like to shake down to the ground. I was too young to know what all the words really meant, but I can tell you now the hymn told my story, plain and simple. I looked up at my dad and his face was a-beaming. He finished out the hymn, and I stood there in wonder, listening to the song I had started all by myself.

Well, let me tell you, that was worth a lot to me. If it hadn't gone well, I might have run off a big cliff somewhere. It lifted me up to a place I'd never been before. Here was my dad, calling on me to lead that song and knowing I could do it. I knew then I had something special nobody else had, not even Carter. I felt proud that my dad had faith and confidence in me, because I was the boy with the hundred-year-old voice.

Another thing, too. Leading on that hymn, I learned you could be afraid and still get the job done. Fear ain't nothing to be afraid of; you just need to face it down. It's helped me a lot in my life because I've been scared many a time since that Sunday morning and I've never let it stop me.

In my sixty-odd years as a professional musician, I've sang my music all around the world. I've played over in Germany and as far away as Japan. I've played for the Queen of England and at the President's Inaugural in Washington, D.C. At all these fancy venues, I can perform with no stage fright at all, but I still get nervous when I have to line out a song in church. I feel more pressure in our Primitive Baptist church-house than I do in the spotlight at Carnegie Hall, because in church the congregation is depending on me to lead them and that's where I really don't want to foul up.

A friend of mine says he hears more grief in my singing down through the years, and I think he's right. I mourn out my songs more than I did as a young man. Like anyone my age, I've had my share of sorrows, losing people closest to me, one by one, first my dad and then my brother, Carter, and then my mother. They were all with me at Point Truth Church on that Sunday morning so long ago, and they're all gone now.

Brother Carter and I started our band, the Stanley Brothers and the Clinch Mountain Boys, in 1946, and we traveled together for twenty years. On December 1, 1966, Carter passed away and I've carried on the band ever since. Even though I've been on my own for twice as many years now, I still miss him when I get on stage. There have been so many other losses along the way. Two of my best lead singers who replaced

Carter were cut down in their prime. Roy Lee Centers was shot and pistol-whipped and left to die in a creek in Breathitt County, Kentucky, where he was from. Roy Lee's replacement was Keith Whitley, another eastern Kentucky boy. Keith was just a kid when he joined up with me, and he could sing like an angel. Just when he finally reached the top of the country charts, he overdosed on alcohol. Keith and Roy Lee were both good men and great singers—and just like Carter, taken away from us too soon.

I sung at so many funerals. I sung when we buried my fiddler, Curly Ray Cline, who worked with me for more years than I spent with Carter. When I lost one of my best friends, Bill Monroe, the father of bluegrass music, I sung over Bill's casket, the same way Bill sung over Carter's casket in 1966.

So many funerals. So many friends and family gone. Through the years, you never stop missing them. And I wish they could hear me now, because, strange as it is and as old as I am, I believe I'm a better singer now than when I made my first records in the 1940s. I can put more into it now, not as much holding back as I used to. I'm not afraid to let all the feeling out, everything I've lived for eighty-two years. And not only the experiences I've been through, but my experience as a singer. I've worked at it more the last few years. Had to, really, because I can't lean on the banjo anymore.

Now, I won't lie to you. My voice ain't what it used to be. My tenor has thinned out some. It's got more cracks in it and it can get mighty rough around the edges and I can't hit all the high notes anymore. But it ain't all tore down just yet, and I know how to use my voice better. I can put a lot more feeling in now. I started adding some crooks and turns and I can worry those lines like I never could before.

It's just me and my voice onstage these days, just like it was when I first started singing as a little boy, long before I got a banjo. Every show I still feature a clawhammer song the way my mother taught me, but I haven't played three-finger banjo for years. As you get older, your fingers don't work as good. Now I've got arthritis, too, so I don't fool with the five-string much anymore. But it's been a blessing in disguise. Instead of doing two things, I can focus on the one. Without the banjo, I don't have a thing to think about but just to mourn out that song.

I'm always working to be a better singer, always learning new ways. Some nights my voice is not as strong as I'd like it to be, especially if I get choked up with a cold. Other nights, I'm singing the best I ever have. It's something I can't control, and that's what gets me nervous sometimes. I ain't afraid to die, but I am scared of what would happen if my voice was to fail me. That's something I think about a lot. It's right hard to face up to, because singing is really all I've got to give anymore.

Now I want to tell you something I've kept to myself. Back in the 1960s, when Carter knew he wasn't long for this world, he said something in secret to George Shuffler, one of our band members. George was like family to us, the third Stanley Brother. He called my mother "Ma" Stanley and we called him Uncle George. One time Carter and George were listening to a Stanley Brothers record of me singing my signature tune, the old mountain ballad "Man of Constant Sorrow." Carter turned to George and said, "That voice of Brother Ralph's will go somewhere. It may not be in this lifetime, but I believe you're going to hear a lot more about that voice someday."

Now, this wasn't just my brother talking. This was the man Bill Monroe called the best natural lead singer he ever heard, and Bill wasn't one to hand out compliments. So singing was something Carter knew something about. Course, Carter would have never told me such a thing to my face. He didn't want his little brother to feel too sure of himself and get puffed up in the head.

Well, Carter's prediction has come true, and it came in this lifetime, even if took a good long while. The voice that Carter and my daddy put so much stock in has carried me all over the world.

If you want to find my place, you can get you a map of the Southern Appalachians and have at it, but it won't do you much good. I tell people wanting directions that the best thing to do is to go until you get to the last mountain. And then, the next mountain over yonder, well, that's where I'm at.

I live eight miles from where I was born and five miles the way the crow flies from where I'll be buried, up on Smith Ridge, where my mother, Lucy, and my brother, Carter, are waiting on me. The family cemetery sits on the highest knob of the ridgetop, in the heart of the Clinch Mountain range. This land belonged to my grandfather, Noah Smith. All around, as far as you can see, are mountains and mountains and more mountains: "the deep rolling hills of old Virginia." That's what Carter called 'em in his song "The White Dove."

Rough mountains, that's what I call 'em. There's always been a lot of murder and a lot of death and lot of heartache in these mountains. When Carter and I were coming up, life was real hard here. It was something you had to live to really know about. It was all you could do to get through it. The old songs I sing are all about that, about the hardness of life and the hope for something better beyond. I reckon that's the quality in the music that people respond to. They feel kin to it even if they've never been here.

My wife, Jimmi, is a die-hard Stanley Brothers fan, just like her daddy was. She loves to listen to me and Carter sing together. She thinks my own stuff is fine, but she likes the Stanley Brothers best. I can't say I blame her. There's never been a sound like the Stanley Brothers and there never will be. It was just God's gift. When I leaned my voice next to Carter's, there was something natural in that blend, like it was meant to be, the way a couple of mountain laurels come out of the same rocky ground and grow into one.

Through the years, people have asked me where my music and the music of the Stanley Brothers comes from. How come it sounds so dark and deep and soulful, so different from all the rest? Well, I can't hardly explain it real good, but I can tell you where you can find out for yourself: right here on top of Smith Ridge.

It's where Carter and I grew up, a couple of barefooted boys running those hills wild and free, stubbing our toes on rocks. It's where we first saw death, our uncle Emery Smith laying in the field after he shot his wife, Lena, and done the same to himself. It's where our daddy up and left us boys behind for our mother to raise all by herself and to make do from a vegetable patch and whatever we could bring home to help out. It's where we first started singing and playing music together, where we done our learning and rehearsing round in the barn, out in the cornfield, in the shade of the apple tree.

Smith Ridge is where the dream started. The dream of making music our full-time work and devoting our lives to it. The same way the miners got coal from the ground and the sawmill men got lumber from the woods, we aimed to gather that old music we found in these hills and hollows and take it out to people all around our territory.

It was mostly Carter's dream at first, but I came to believe in it just as much as he did. Together we lived the dream for twenty years, until the cold winter night in 1966 when he passed on, I believe, from the heavy price he paid to keep it alive in the hard times. Until the end he never did give up on the dream that finally done him in.

But I'm still here, bringing the old-time mountain music to people all over the world. I just wish Carter could be here, too. After all he done for the music, he died a poor man. It still hurts me he never got to share in the success and get a decent payday.

When I get to feeling a certain way, I go to the cemetery to be with Carter and my mother. I walk through the front gate, under the sign I put up that says "Hills of Home Cemetery: Let Me Rest on a Peaceful Mountain," the name of a song Carter wrote. There's a pair of white doves on the sign, and sometimes I think of the words to Carter's "White Dove" we sung together so many times:

As the years roll by I often wonder if we'll all be together some day
And each night as I wander through the graveyard
Darkness finds me as I kneel to pray

At the top of the cemetery, close by a pair of big cedar trees planted by my aunt many years ago, my grave is ready for me when it's my time to go. It's next to the graves of Carter and his wife, Mary. Before Mary died, she said she didn't want to be put underground. So we took Carter up and now the whole row of tombs are raised aboveground like theirs.

On Carter's there are etchings of the rising sun and a guitar and the words "Farewell, Carter, For a Little While." I wrote the inscription myself and meant every word. Come one of these days, I believe we'll all be together in a better place. I don't know how long it'll be, so I just said farewell until that time finally does come.

My tombstone has an etching of a banjo on the front, and it sits in between my mother's grave and Jimmi's. All ours are needing are the final dates carved into that granite slab. But I'm not ready to go just yet, not by a long shot, not as long as I can sing. Just like the words say in "O Death," the song I won the Grammy for: *Won't you spare me over for another year?*

I've had a few close calls. I've had open-heart surgery, and it's pretty rough when they have to saw you in two and stitch you back up. But I got through it. I was back on the road in seven weeks. Ever since I was nineteen, I've sung and picked a banjo for a living. I stay on the road playing shows because it's my job and, to tell you the truth, it's really all I know how to do. I ain't much good for anything except music.

It's been eighty-two years now, and I've been spared to go on. I don't rightly know why I've been allowed forty years more than Carter. I can't question what I believe has been preordained. My wife, Jimmi, says the Man Upstairs has let me stay around because he has more work for me to do.

I used to go to the cemetery a lot. I don't go up there as often anymore. When you get to be my age, you figure you'll be there soon enough for good. But it's still a place where I can spend time and look around and linger awhile. In a way, it makes me sad. In a way, I like to go. It puts me in mind what my granddaughter Amber Dawn said to me one time. I had been on the road for a tour. She was around five years old and she'd been missing me something awful. When I walked in the door, she looked at me and said, "Pa-Paw, if you ever die, I want to lie right down with you." You hear something like that, well, it makes you feel good and bad at the same time.

It's more than memories that draw me to Smith Ridge. It feels peaceful up on the high knob there with nobody else around. It's somewhere I can always go when I need to. I reckon everyone should have such a place, and I feel blessed to have it. You can see a long ways from up here, some days clear to Kentucky. It's a view you'll never forget and it puts you in your place. You feel like your troubles ain't so bad.

Sometimes I walk down the road a few hundred yards to the house where my mother lived. It's standing right there: the old home place. It's still furnished today, same as it was when she died in 1973. I keep all the furnishings and everything in there neat as a pin and shiny as a new dime, and it's setting down below the cemetery. Nobody lives in it. I don't want anybody in there. I want the house just like it was when she lived there.

Sometimes I like to go to the house and sit in there and stay awhile and reminisce. There's a rocking chair by a window where my mother sat alone for hours at a time. She'd just rock in her chair and look out the window up the hill to Carter's grave. It was her way of grieving: A cemetery, a house, a window to see a grave—there are some things you need to keep around so you know where you been and where you're headed.

I'm not the only one who likes visiting the cemetery. Loads of pilgrims come to Smith Ridge every year to pay their respects. Many have told me they think it's the prettiest spot on God's earth. I know what they mean. It suits me just fine.

When Carter and I first started out, we never thought our music would ever get past the three or four states around our home. Now, thanks to the *O Brother, Where Art Thou?* album, I'm more popular than the Stanley Brothers ever was. It still surprises me, and I know it surprises people here in Dickenson County. When Carter died, not many around here reckoned I had what it takes to be a front man. People figured I was the little brother just along for the ride. Even now, they still can't quite believe I was able to make it without him and go on to make a name for myself. If you'd known me in the early days, a backwards kid who could barely hand over a howdy, you'd be surprised, too.

And after all the places I've been, I haven't changed much from that shy mountain boy. Now, I'm nowhere near as backwards as I was. I like to meet the people at my shows. I know they're the ones who made me what I am. But it's still hard for me to converse and make small talk; I never could learn to mix as well as Carter. All those years, I was happy to let Carter do the talking for us both, and he done a good job. And in the time I've been on my own, I've mostly let my singing do my talking for me.

It's been so long since Carter passed away. I haven't talked much about it, or even tried to think much about it. It hurt too much to remember, so I tried to let it go to the past. But I've lived so long, the past has caught up with me, and I believe it's time to face it down. There were a lot of things I never got to tell Carter when he was still around, and tell my mother and so many others who've passed on as well. There are a lot of things I haven't said to a lot of people, and it's time to change that. I think it's time for me to look back and remember, the good memories along with the bad. As for time, I don't know how much I've got left. This book is my way of saying all the things I haven't been able to say, before it's too late.

It's funny how we look to other people. A famous photographer once took some pictures of me. She traveled all the way here to Dickenson County. Said she wanted to get me in my natural setting: laying around the house, walking down by the railroad tracks, standing at the old church-house where I sang as a boy. She was a nice lady, but I don't care much for the photos. Made me look freakish, I think, more like Mr. Death than Dr. Ralph. That's maybe the way she saw me, but I don't see myself that way.

Another time a painter done a portrait of me. He had the same sort of notion she did, and he set me out in the countryside, picking the banjo, Clinch Mountains in the distance. The mountains look fine, but the banjo player don't look a bit like me. "Now, who in the world is that old fellow?" I thought to myself.

I know they were just doing their job, but neither one got close to the man I am. Same with writers. A lot of words been written through the years, and there's even been a play for the stage. But they played me pretty dumb in that play, made me more backwards than I ever was. The writers told me they done that to sell more tickets, and I can understand, because in a play you can make your story any way you want. It was a good play, I enjoyed watching it, but it really wasn't me up on that stage.

I'm just an old hillbilly, and proud of it, too. Plain as an old shoe, same as a lot of us mountain people. I think it's best to try to tell your own life. What people want is to hear the words out of my mouth, and I'm going to do the best job I can, to tell you what I remember. Some politicians and preachers, they'll talk at you and not to you. The one thing I can promise is to talk to you in plain old words. I know correct and proper English just fine, but I don't use it because that's not the way I was raised. I talk natural the same way I sing, so I'm gonna give you my story like I was talking to you across the table.

I'm a man of few words, but I try to make 'em count. It was Carter with the gift for words, not me. But I'll tell you something I never told Carter, because I wouldn't have wanted to hurt his feelings. A promoter once said something to me in private, and I've never forgot: "Carter's a lot better talker than you are. But three words from you mean more than a hundred from Carter."

So this here is the memoir of a man who don't much like to talk unless he's got something to say. I've kept my mouth shut more than most, but I've kept my eyes and ears open all the while. I've been paying close attention. I believe that's how you learn things, by looking and listening.

I know a lot of you are coming to me late, maybe only in the last few years since the *O Brother, Where Art Thou?* album put me in the spotlight. I've seen you newcomers at the shows, and I enjoy seeing your faces out there; I can't make it without you. I remember the lean years when rock 'n' roll nearly starved us out, when if I hadn't had a crowd at a show, I couldn't have bought gas to get back home. It's the fans keeping me on the road, the new fans and the old fans like Bob Dylan and so many diehards from the early days who've stuck by me. It's their support that makes me feel I've done something worthwhile, that all the hard work and the hard miles ain't been wasted.

We've got a lot of ground to cover, most of a century by my reckoning, so I'm going to pull your ear for a good while, if you have the patience to set a spell and listen to an old man ramble on about the way things used to be. I've got plenty of stuff I've kept bottled up, and I'm ready to let it out. I give you fair warning: We're going to spend a lot of time on my early years, because those are the memories that stand out most, just as clear and strong as ever. I couldn't tell you much about the show we played last week, but I can tell you all about a summer day on Smith Ridge seventy-odd years ago, as fresh in my mind as my mother's garden after an early-morning rain.

But this book ain't just for me. It's for anybody that ever wanted to set down with their grandpa late of a night and hear what all he's been hoarding up in his memory, things he did and said but he never aired out because he figured nobody much cared. I sure wish I'd had the chance with my grandparents, but they were like so many from these mountains, who lived and died without ever getting to tell their story. Just like some of the best musicians I ever heard never made it off the back porch.

I can count on one hand the people I grew up with from around these parts who are still living. We were the last generation from these mountains to live from the earth. It was a hard life and there was a lot of suffering. But the music we made couldn't have come from any other place or time. The suffering was part of what made the music strong, and I reckon that's why it's lasted. It won't be long before we're all of us gone. I hope this book leaves behind something worthwhile to remember us by.

After I'm dead and buried, I don't know who will be around to carry on the old-time music, the way it's played and sung the old-time way. But I believe the songs will survive. When I was celebrating my fiftieth anniversary in the business, Bob Dylan sent me a surprise telegram. I will tell you more later about what all he wrote, but the last line said, "You will live forever." I know Bob wasn't talking about me, really, but about the songs I helped keep alive down through the years, "Man of Constant Sorrow" and "Pretty Polly" and others that took root here in the Clinch Mountains so long ago. Those old songs were here before me and they'll be here when I'm gone. What's real doesn't die.

CHAPTER ONE

Deep Hollow

"Mountain folks, mountain folks, everybody calls us mountain folks
Whole lot of work for a little bit of pay, everybody calls us mountain folks"

—"MOUNTAIN FOLKS," RALPH STANLEY

A lot of people like to talk about their ancestors. They'll tell you how they're descended from a line of Scottish kings and whatnot, and they'll brag on a Lord So-and-So who they say they're related to. Maybe even got 'em a fancy coat of arms framed and hanging on the wall. Funny how you never hear nobody say they come from a gang of horse thieves that got run out of the old country.

I don't know when or why my people came here. Don't know why they decided to stay. All I know for sure is we've been in these mountains as long as anybody can remember. So I can't tell you much about who our ancestors were. Never been much interested in my family line. I don't know why. Never did try to search the family tree; my dad and my mother didn't either, as far as I know.

When I was coming up, people from around here didn't mess around in the family history. They were working too hard to fool with it, I reckon. For people in the mountains, it was just get up at daylight, go to bed at dark, and in between work like a mule.

My mother's father and my dad's father, that's as far back as I can tell you about, and I don't know much about them either because they died when I was young. My dad's daddy was named Nathan Stanley and he came from a little hollow called Bold Camp near the town of Pound, Virginia, across the county line about fifteen miles away in Wise. His wife was named Stacie.

About the only thing I remember about my grandpa Nathan was, he was the first person who made me really cry. I was four years old and my dad had a brand-new 1931 A-Model Ford, one of the first automobiles ever seen in our neighborhood. And we drove to Bold Camp to pick up Pa-Paw Stanley so he could stay with us for a few days. When we made it back home, he got out of the car and he slammed the door on my thumb. Mashed it real bad and turned it blue and I got real mad at him. He couldn't help what he done; it was an accident, probably the first car he'd ever rode in, but it still hurt like the dickens.

My mother's side, the Smiths, was a prominent family in the area. Her father, Noah Smith, was a farmer and he owned the land on Smith Ridge where I later grew up. He and his wife, Louisa, raised a family of twelve and every one of them children played music. My mother's uncle John was one of the biggest preachers around here at that time. He was a minister and moderator and an elder at the McClure Primitive Baptist Church on the Open Fork of McClure River, one of the oldest churches in Dickenson County.

Uncle John was known all around these parts as Elder John Smith, or just Preacher John. Lord, he was one to ramble, sort of like a country doctor making house calls. Back then, you were born at home, you got married at home, and you died at home. Uncle John rode horseback all over the Clinch Mountain country preaching funerals and officiating weddings and baptisms. I remember him baptizing my mother in the river when I was nine years old.

Where Uncle John really made his name was as a singer. He didn't sing ballads, though. He done what they called heart songs like "You Hurt Me Lying," and hymns like "Tarry with Me, O My Savior," and "Amazing Grace," and a lot of Primitive Baptist gospel songs I've recorded through the years. People who was around back then said I sound a lot like Uncle John did when he sang them old hymns—and he's the only person who I've ever been told sounded anything like me.

Uncle John officiated the wedding of my mother and father, but you could say it was death brung them together, as much as anything else did. Lucy Rakes was a widow and Lee Stanley was a widower, both getting on in years and not wanting to be alone. My dad's first wife died and I never did know what of, because my dad never did say and I never did ask.

My mother had it rough in the way of love. When she was a young woman, still in her teens, she had a sweetheart named Gibson. He was from the little railroad town of Coeburn down the mountain from Smith Ridge, a good workingman, and they were both stuck on each other and were engaged to get married. Then he got killed in the mines, some sort of accident, and he got crushed by the falling rocks was the way I heard it. It wasn't until almost ten years later when she finally got married, to a fellow named Watson Rakes. Two years later, he died from a tumor in his head. So she'd already lost two men she loved, and that was awful hard for her, coming to grief both times.

Seven more years went by, with my mother raising her daughter, Ruby, by herself, and she was thirty-eight years old when she wed my dad, Lee. When they got married in 1924, they brought seven children to the deal. Lee had three boys and three girls and Lucy had Ruby. That made three half brothers and four half sisters for me and Carter, the only full brother I had. They were a lot older than we were, so we didn't really grow up with them after the early years. Out of all my half siblings, none of them played music, so we didn't hear too much picking around the home, except some old-time clawhammer banjo my mom did. But she had mostly put her banjo aside to raise the family. I reckon maybe that was why Carter and I come along, to bring some music back into the house.

I was borned on February 25, 1927, on what they called Big Spraddle Creek, about three miles down the mountain from the old home place on Smith Ridge. The nearest post office was Stratton and the nearest town was McClure, a lumber camp that sprung up down by the river. Big

Spraddle was one of them dark little hollows tucked back in them steep mountains, hard to find even when you're looking for it. Don't let the name fool you. Big Spraddle was just a little creek running by our little house, nothing you'd ever see on any map or postcard. Not much at all there besides us, really, just three or four neighbors' houses down the way.

We lived at the very end of the hollow, backed right on the creek. You could hear the creek water right outside the bedroom window. Running water's got a good sound, and it was a real comfort to hear it, especially when it rained and the creek got up; it would put you off to sleep real gentle and peaceful-like.

My mother had bought the place after her first husband died, and when she married my dad, they moved in there together. It was a little four-room, clapboard job, tin roof and stone chimney, no better or worse than a thousand other mountain cabins you'd find at the time. My dad built an extra room on the back after I came along, and that's where me and Carter slept. There were cracks in the walls, and I remember waking up in the wintertime and there'd be snow that blowed in overnight on top of the quilt.

Carter was only eighteen months older than I was, and he didn't give me any warm welcome. Saw me as competition, I reckon. He didn't like his new brother at all and he let everybody know it. Especially me. My mother told me that when I was only a couple of days old, Carter hit me on the head with a potato, and he wasn't playing around, neither. Gave me a good hard whack with that tater.

Down in Big Spraddle, we were on our own, nobody to bother us. We had a half acre there next to the house, against the woods and the mountain, where we had a little yard and a garden. There was a spring from a high place on the hillside that dropped down in the hollow and this is how we got our water. We had some gourds we raised and we'd hollow them out for drinking gourds. So we always had fresh water to drink and wash with. It was pure mountain springwater, and it was always so cold it'd put goose bumps on your arm, and I don't think I've ever tasted better.

We always had enough to eat from what we raised. My mother was a cook that couldn't be beat. She made everything from scratch, all the best things a boy could want, like big ole cathead biscuits, which get the name from how big and rounded they are, and homemade sausage gravy, and hog jowls, and sometimes grated cornbread, which is from field corn before it matures. One thing I liked best was her cream corn; she'd shave the kernels off the cob and cook it up with home-churned butter.

She could make anything taste good. It didn't matter what my older brothers dragged in from hunting. Once in a while, they'd bring back a live possum they trapped when they was out in the woods. You probably know possums will eat anything dead or alive. Well, my mother would put the possum under an upside-down tub, and prop up that tub just enough to let in some air, then she'd put a rock on top to weigh it down. She'd keep the possum like you would a pet and she'd feed it table scraps for two weeks and clean all the trash out and plump it up nice. And she'd make us a good possum dinner out of that.

For me and Carter, Big Spraddle was our very own playground. All around were woods where we could get outside and get lost together. Carter would run those woods like a rabbit. I don't think he was scared of anything. But I was scared all the time. I don't know what of. Snakes, the dark, whatever was out there, I reckon.

There was a lady we called Old Mother Hubbard; she lived down in Clinchco, near the coal camp. She was an old widow and lived by herself, no friends or family to speak of; she dressed in rags and had strange ways about her. The grown-ups would say, "If you do this or that, we'll take you to see Old Mother Hubbard." All us kids were real scared of her; we thought she would do something terrible to us, who knows what. There was other widow women like her, and you'd hear people say they were witches.

Snakes and witches wasn't nothing next to what worried me most, and that was the coal mines. All of my half brothers worked in the mines, down the mountain at the Clinchfield Coal Corporation, the biggest operation in these parts. They told about how hard it was in the mines, slaving away in mud up to their knees and higher sometimes, cold, dark water all around. I heard their stories and seen their faces black with soot, and I knew it wasn't for me. I never did think I could stand it. I had asthma and I figured I'd smother down there. I swore I'd keep both my feet above the ground.

Let me say right here that coal miners are some of the finest people you'll ever meet, and they were some of the best Stanley Brothers fans there ever was, from our earliest days when we first played the camps on payday. We could always draw a crowd in those coal towns, and they were faithful to the end. Patty Loveless, one of my favorite singers in the world, was raised by her coal-miner daddy across the Kentucky border in Elkhorn City, Pike County. Patty told me her dad was listening to a Stanley Brothers album on the record player when he died of a heart attack.

When I was growing up, coal was king. Now, the Clinch Mountains are pretty to look at on top, but it was underneath where the real prize was, and these were no ordinary chunks of coal. We had the best coal for burning there was and more of it that could be dug out the fastest and the cheapest. Whether it was a blessing or a curse, I don't rightly know. Probably a little of both.

One thing's for sure. It was the coal put us on the map. A study by the Virginia Geological Survey from 1916, "The Coal Resources of the Clintwood and Bucu Quadrangles," lays it on thick, with a bunch of fancy words and big numbers that like to give you a headache just to see 'em. To tell it to you plain, we was setting on top of ten billion tons of high-grade coal. "Distinctly superior" was the way the report rated the kind we had in the Virginia coalfields compared to other areas, so you can see why I'm bragging a bit on our coal.

The 1916 survey map shows a bull's-eye right in our neck of the woods. The railroad town of Dante, just down the road from where I still live today, is in the dead center of that bull's-eye. The year before, the Carolina, Clinchfield and Ohio Railway had been extended from Dante a ways across the Kentucky border to Elkhorn City. They blasted mile-long tunnels through the rocky ridges and they laid trestles across the deep gorges; and by the time they finished, the CC&O was the most expensive stretch of railroad track ever built in the U.S.

It was worth the money to the big investors, because the CC&O

busted open the Virginia coalfields. For centuries, we'd been cut off from the outside world because of the rough terrain. The new railroad was all the big companies needed to make their move. Now there was a way to get the coal out of our mountains, all the way down to Spartanburg, South Carolina, and points north and east.

The coal companies from up North bought up most of this land in one big grab. They paid a nickel an acre and they've made billions of dollars. The biggest was the Clinchfield Coal Corporation. It owned huge stretches of coal and timber lands, with all the mineral rights, not only in Dickenson but counties all around: Wise, Russell and Buchanan. They built Clinchco just about overnight, where Mill Creek runs into the McClure River. Clinchco was biggest, but there were other company towns, too, like Trammel, built by Virginia Banner Coal Corporation, and Splashdam and Bartlick and Vansant.

The company towns had rows and rows of those little shotgun shacks and the bosses packed 'em full of workers who poured out of the mountains and hollows looking for steady jobs. Many a one later wished they'd never left.

The company bosses all got rich and the people stayed poor like they've always been. That's the way it's been and it's still like that. There's still a lot of coal in this ground, and they're still getting it out. Nowadays they haul it by truck as much they do by train. Even today, the coal companies own almost half the land in Dickenson County, and they have mineral rights to 75 percent.

Yeah, buddy, I'll tell you what, the coal trucks are keeping the roads around here hot. They've deep-mined right under my house, five miles down or more, and there's some closer to the ground easier to get at. They tell me there's $60,000 worth of clean coal right under the property here, and that's only about three feet down. I used to think if the music ever went bad on me, I could get the coal.

They can cut through the hard limestone and sandstone like it was nothing; nowadays they've got to where they're cutting the mountains down, too. They just lop the tops right off to get to the coal. Around Dickenson, they've pretty much stripped the countryside clean. I don't like the strip mining. It tears up the land, but everybody's got to make a living somehow. And it's a lot safer for the workers than it used to be.

Back when I was a boy, it was digging coal with a pick and shovel and hauling it out with mules. Men worked seams no more than three feet high for twelve-hour shifts, flat on their backs, take lunch breaks laying sideways, a big swig of water to make it go down. There was an old song they'd sing: *O Lord have mercy on a miner's soul, down on my knees in thirty-inch coal.* My brothers said the trick to loading coal was to bounce a shovelful off the top of the mine shaft into the coal car. You'd load twenty cars a shift and never stand up once. I remember a neighbor came out of the mines one night and swore he'd had enough. "I don't care if I have to starve," he said. "I ain't never going back in there no more." The next day, he was back in the mines.

There was a mine shaft in McClure that was real dangerous. Anytime you get below the riverbed, the mine gets real gassy, what they call "hot." This one stayed hot too long, and something ignited all that gas and it blew up and killed a bunch of miners. There are memorials all around Dickenson and Wise and Buchanan counties, stone monuments with the names of the men who died in the mines. Some people say the reason so many young boys from around here went off to war is because they figured fighting had to be better than coal mining.

Down the mountain, along the little two-lane dirt road between Clinchco and Tom's Creek, you'd see the coke ovens by the side of the road where they burned the coal. Great big open-air fires. They'd be a-burning all the time. It was a mighty fearsome sight, especially at night with those big blue flames shooting into the black sky. Like the whole world was on fire. And the trains ran that coal night and day, steam whistle screaming.

Back up at the head of the holler, you felt protected. It was two worlds, really, and they were separate: the mining towns and lumber camps with all that commotion, and our little hideaway at Big Spraddle with our little house bounded by a creek and a green hill and the woods. I'd say it was paradise next to Clinchco and Dante and those scary places full of fire and smoke where the men and the machines worked night and day digging and sawing and hauling.

My dad never did mess with the mines. He was a sawmill man, and I'll tell you more about that later, because this early on, all I knew about my daddy was he was the best singer I'd ever heard. I can close my eyes right now and hear his voice a-ringing out, loud and clear like he was here beside me. He had a real old-time lonesome voice, down to earth like he dug it right out of one of these mountains.

My daddy didn't play music, but he sung a lot around home. He sung for himself; he wasn't out to impress nobody. He sung when the feeling hit. He didn't often sing a whole song from start to finish, mostly just snatches of sad old ballads that caught his fancy. I reckon he picked up a lot of what he knew when he was out in the woods cutting timber with men from Kentucky and Tennessee and North Carolina and other places I'd never heard of. In them days, people swapped songs as fast as they would pocketknives or anything. My dad knew a lot of songs. He sung "I Am a Man of Constant Sorrow," "Pretty Polly," "The House Carpenter," "Wild Bill Jones," "The Brown Girl," and "Omie Wise."

Far back as I can remember, I'd lay awake in my room late at night listening to my dad sing alone out on the porch after a long day at the sawmill. It'd be dead silent and I'd be drifting off to sleep and then he'd light into a string of verses that hung like wood smoke in the night air and lingered in my mind long after he'd gone to bed. Some kids get lullabies and nursery rhymes. I got my daddy moaning "Man of Constant Sorrow" to himself out in the dark:

You can bury me in some deep valley for many years where I may lay
Then you may learn to love another while I am sleeping in my grave

My mother didn't do much in the way of singing except in church. But there were my half sisters from my dad's first marriage and they were good singers like he was. They were a lot older than me and the songs they liked were old as dirt. They sung around the house while they did chores and when they was resting, too, just to pass the time, real sad old-timers like "Barb'ry Allen" and "Tragic Romance." They were better at remembering the words than my dad was, and I'd listen close to find out what happened. Seems like in every song somebody always come to a bad end. There was cruel Barb'ry Allen and her man, Sweet Willie, buried side by side in the churchyard, a green briar and a red rose growing out of their graves. I'd hear my sisters close out the song, and I'd be hanging on every word:

They leaned from the top and locked in a true lovers' knot
The rose run around the briar

There must have been a hundred verses, but the last lines always stuck with me. I liked the stories and I liked the melodies even more. For me the words and the melody were always joined together, like the briar and the rose. Most people just listen to the words in a song. I listen to the words and melody both, but I like the melody best because that's where your feeling is, I think. It's the way I hear music and the way I sing it, too.

Those songs helped pass the time and made the chores go by easier, because there was always a lot to do. At our house, my mother always kept everything in order, from the kitchen to the garden, everything in its proper place and neat as a pin, too. There was a hook for every utensil and a can for every preserve. You'd seldom see her without a broom or a mop or dishrag.

I've always tried to be neat and tidy because that's how my mother raised us. Some people don't care what their place looks like; they leave everything laying around the house and the yard in an awful mess. Some people got no pride, I guess, but I do.

There were no books I can recall, save for the family Bible. There wasn't much in the way of toys and playthings like children have today. My parents wouldn't allow even a deck of playing cards in the house, because it could lead to gambling and all kinds of trouble. For Christmas, we'd get an orange, one for Carter and one for me, and handful of rock candy. Maybe a cap gun, too. It wasn't till years later that I got a bicycle of my own and I had to trade a dog to get that bike.

There was only one what you would call "modern convenience" in the whole house. In the corner of the living room there stood a nice Victrola, one of those windup jobs they had back then. You didn't need electricity; you'd just crank it by hand and it would play those old 78-rpm phonograph records, one song on each side. I remember having to change the steel needle all the time. In the bottom shelf of the Victrola there was a pile of records, and Carter and me wore 'em out. It was the first music we heard from the outside world, on phonograph records; we never heard of radio until several years later.

Our favorite records were by the Carter Family, and Grayson and Whitter, and Fiddlin' Powers and Family; they came from places that weren't so far away, less than a hundred miles. They sounded familiar to us, like people we knew back in our mountains.

G. B. Grayson was from near Mountain City in eastern Tennessee, a little hollow called Laurel Bloomery. Grayson was blind, so he couldn't do regular work. He earned his livelihood at barn dances and pie suppers and fiddle contests and on street corners, wherever he could. He played the prettiest lonesome fiddle and he was a good singer, too, which was rare for a fiddle player. Grayson sang a lot of the lonesome ballads my dad sung: "Omie Wise" and "Rose Conley." In 1930, he got killed in a wreck out near Damascus, Virginia, when a log truck hit the car he was hitching a ride on and he got thrown off the running board. So we never got to see Grayson play, but we had his records and we couldn't get enough of 'em. The way some boys studied schoolbooks, we studied these old 78-rpm records, and we learned 'em good.

We loved the Carter Family, too, Maybelle, Sara and A.P. They were from down in Scott County, just a few mountain ranges to the south of Dickenson. We liked when they sang "My Clinch Mountain Home" because that was our home, too. They were masters of pure harmony and they sang about heartache and hard times and heaven and how you got to walk that lonesome valley. By then, the Carters were big stars; they got famous the same year I was born, after making their first records for Victor Talking Machine Co. in Bristol. It was the beginning of country music as a big business, and my life'd be a lot different thanks to their success.

I would have never dreamed, when I was laying on the floor and listening to the Victrola, that in a few years, me and Carter would first make our name in Bristol, too, following in their footsteps. And that we'd make friends with A. P. Carter and we'd get known all around these parts. It would have seemed like the impossible.

And there wasn't much stock put in the impossible back then. What mattered was just surviving and that meant either the mines or the sawmills. There was coal under the ground and timber above it. If you didn't go digging, you'd be out logging. They'd get you one way or the other.

The biggest timber operation was the W. M. Ritter Lumber Company in McClure. They had two big mills on the river. They had a planing mill, where they sawed the logs, and they had a banding mill, where they dressed the logs and smoothed 'em. Then they'd send the logs down the McClure River out to Big Sandy through the Breaks, just like the coal went out by the railroad. You'd see the Ritter men everywhere, cutting down timber and hauling logs with horses.

In the summer of 1932, there was a shooting up at Smith Ridge. It was about three miles from Big Spraddle, up the mountain, where my uncle Emery Smith and his wife, Lena, lived at the old home place where my mother was raised.

When we got there, we found Uncle Emery laying dead under the apple tree behind the house, his shotgun right next to him. In the garden by the porch out front, Lena was dead on the ground, too. It was before the sheriff got there, and everything was real quiet and still. The whole ridge was hushed, no breeze, no birds, no nothing—that's how I remember it, anyhow. The grown-ups were talking low to one another. I couldn't catch much of what they were saying, but it wasn't hard to figure out Uncle Emery had shot Aunt Lena and then killed himself.

We never did know exactly what was behind all of it. There was no arguing or cheating or fooling around that anybody ever heard. All we ever knew for sure was Lena was stringing beans in front of the house that afternoon. Emery was out hoeing in the garden close by her. He put down the hoe, went in the house and got his gun. Then he walked over to where Lena was and shot her down. He went behind the house down below the apple tree and shot himself. They said he needed the tree to rig up the shotgun to be able to shoot himself. Had to stare right down the barrel before he done himself in.

You just never know what triggered it. Don't know the situation, whether he and Lena weren't getting along or what. Emery had got caught making liquor and did a year or so in the federal penitentiary, but a lot of people in the mountains did time for bootlegging. There was no shame in it. You had to make a living some way; you had to survive. The shooting happened a little while after he came back home from prison. So maybe something happened when he was locked up, I can't say. He wasn't the only suicide on my mother's side of the family. Some of her other brothers, and there was a bunch of Smith boys, done themselves in the same way Emery done, with a shotgun. Maybe it run in the family. I heard one of 'em, Ory Smith, was asked why that was and he just shook his head and said, "Hell, we're all just crazy, I reckon."

We were there for a while before the sheriff came and his men moved the bodies. I saw Uncle Emery laying bloody in the grass under the apple tree. I'd never seen a dead person before; neither had Carter. I don't think we had seen anybody laid out in a casket even. I was only about four-and-a-half years old, but it seems like I remember everything about that day. It was rough for a boy to see, and it worried me for a long time.

Nobody talked about it; me and Carter never asked any questions about it. Emery and Lena were buried side by side in the family cemetery on Smith Ridge, just the names and dates on the granite headstones, and that was that. It was just something that happened. Back then, folks didn't talk about a lot of things in public like they do now. People took all their troubles and sorrows to the church.

For our family, that meant the McClure Primitive Baptist Church, where my uncle John Smith moderated and preached for years. It was built by the congregation in 1876, on the bank of the McClure River. It was a plain, one-room church-house set on cinder block, wood-framed with white clapboard, homemade plank pews. There were hundreds like it hugging the sides of creeks and hillsides: no steeple, no sign, and not much to look at, but always a whole lot going on inside.

Early on, there was a nasty split in the church when a member got in trouble for shooting a neighbor's hog. They took the matter to the congregation and there was a lot of arguing and finally the fellow stood up and said, "All who want to follow the Lord, follow me." Some of the members went with him and they built a new church of their own down near Nora, below the forks of the river.

A lot of little mountain churches sprung out of disputes such as that. Most of the time, though, when they had problems, they was able to iron things out. The church was where you could get some justice without having to go to the courthouse in Clintwood. It was sort of like a trial they'd have in church, where they'd take it up with the brothers and sisters of the congregation.

In most ways, the Primitive Baptists weren't as strict as the Old Regular Baptists, who didn't believe in women wearing pants or showing off their ankles or cutting their hair short and whatnot. But the Primitives were awful strict on how you behaved. They could what they call "turn you out" of the church, depending on something you done, like getting drunk or spreading gossip or using God's name in vain or if you lay out so long a time and didn't go to church. If one church member did another church member wrong, they'd take action on it. After the singing and the preaching, they'd get down to business. An elder would say, "Are all in love and fellowship?" and then they'd take up a case and maybe turn a member out. Now, that didn't mean it was permanent. Later on, they'd take up the case again, and the member was allowed to give an account of himself and admit he'd done wrong and he could get restored as a member in good standing. There was mercy and forgiveness, as long as there was repentance by the wrongdoer.

There's an old book of the Minutes of the McClure Primitive Baptist Church from the 1860s, not long before my uncle John took to preaching there. A church member typed up the business from the meetings, and you can dip in for a few pages and see just how busy they were turning out and restoring church members: "The case of Sister Mary Holbrook for reporting and swearing scandalous talk" and "the case of Brother J. Blare for false statement in the behalf of his son and following after Brother G. W. Smith with his guns and threatening to spill blood" and "the case of Brother William Green for getting drunk and fighting and he made his acknowledgement and was restored."

You have to remember, there was no clubs or organizations like nowadays; the church was the only group outside your family there was in the mountains. Fellowship in the church counted for a lot. So you didn't want to get turned out, and as far as I know, nobody from our family ever was turned out. Nobody on the Smith side, anyhow.

These cases were still common when I started going to the McClure church, but I didn't pay attention to it. I thought it was a whole lot of grown-up fuss over not much at all. What I liked about going to church was the singing, and that's still what I like best about church today. As kids, we didn't sing very much in church. The time I led the hymn for my dad, it was special because it was so rare. For years, all I ever did at service was listen, and that was enough for me.

I told you how we don't use instruments in our church. I don't know exactly why that is. It's not from the Bible; it's just a tradition that's been handed down for years and years. I believe part of the reason is that it used to be musicians didn't have a very good name. They thought musicians was mean and low-down and not fit for church, and the same with musical instruments.

So the Primitive Baptists stuck with the singing and shut the door on everything else. The way they sung in church is the same way they do today. Everybody sung together, the men and the women both, and the women would come in an octave higher and they really blended well. Like I told you, the men would always lead on the hymns, meaning the preacher or an elder like my dad would line out the songs.

There's a joke about the old Primitive Baptists and their way of lining out the hymns. A man asks the preacher, "Don't you folks have good memories or what?"

"I reckon we do," the preacher says. "Just as good as anybody."

"Well," the man says, "you all have been singing these songs for years and you still have to tell 'em the words—seems like they'd know 'em by now!"

There's a good reason behind this tradition. Back in the early days, in the Primitive Baptist churches around southwest Virginia and eastern Kentucky, there was an awful lot of hymns to sing—I mean, hundreds and hundreds—and not a lot of hymnbooks around. Not too many could read much, and people were so poor they didn't have but one songbook, and that was the preacher's. They didn't know what words to sing, and the old preacher, well, he'd get up there and line out songs from the book and spit his tobacco juice right out, and that was doing something. The people would sing the words back, and they had the feeling to it. And the feeling grabbed me and it's never let go. I reckon I was about the only boy in Dickenson County who looked forward to church.

School was different. I never did care much for schooling, and neither did Carter. School just tied us down, really. Music was what we liked and there weren't no classes in that. Just the three R's—reading, writing and arithmetic—and we didn't see much use for all that scribbling.

Big Oak was the first school we went to, a one-room schoolhouse over on Ramsey Ridge. It was originally a horse stable and they converted it into Big Oak School. It got its name from a great big hollow oak that stood close by. It was a few miles up the mountain from Spraddle, and we made the walk back and forth every day. We'd leave before dark and get home after dark, sometimes climbing half-blinded through those dark woods in more than eighteen inches of snow. The first year Carter went to Big Oak, he'd make the walk alone; I wasn't old enough for school yet. One time he got caught in a blizzard and he lost his way, and he'd've probably died if the Ritter men hadn't found him before dark, wandering in a snowdrift out by a logging road.

Big Oak was for students who lived walking distance for miles around; it went from primer, what they now call kindergarten, all the way to the seventh grade. There was but one teacher for all the grade levels and that was Mr. Sydney Stanley, a third cousin to me. He was the educational supervisor for Dickenson County Elementary Schools, a fancy way of saying he ran things his way.

On the opening day of classes, when I started in primer, the very first thing Mr. Stanley done that morning was, he took all the children outside the schoolhouse, under the oak tree. He had us all stand next to a little water hole by the side of the school. Then he took out a homemade rag doll, an itty-bitty thing he put together from pieces of cloth and stuck on marbles for eyes and whatnot. He held it up so we could get a good look, sort of cuddling that cute little doll like he was real special: "This here doll, his name is Cant."

We all sort of giggled, wondering what this was all about. We thought Mr. Stanley was going to put on a show for us, and maybe have Cant say funny things about how much fun school was going to be. Then Mr. Stanley took the doll and throwed him down in the water. He dunked poor little Cant like he was punishing him or something bad, and he let him lay there in the muddy puddle. We didn't know what to think, but Mr. Stanley was as serious as could be. "We just drowned Cant," he said. "Now don't never tell me you can't do nothing when I ask you to do it."

Those were the first words Mr. Stanley said to us the first day of school. It was the way he started every year, drowning the little rag doll in the water hole. It was to show us he meant business. Thing was, we sort of liked what he done; even if it was a little scary, it was kind of funny what happened to Cant. It got our attention, though. When Mr. Stanley might say, "Write me ten pages of words," it made you think twice about saying, "I can't do that."

I was a little scared of Mr. Stanley at first. Then I learned to respect him, because he had a way about him so that you couldn't hate him. He was the best teacher I ever had. He made you afraid of him, but you loved him, too, even if you didn't love school.

Mr. Stanley was my teacher again when I was in the seventh grade and I still respected him then. But when I was still real young, in some years in between, I had some teachers I didn't care much for. There was an old woman teacher who was strict and mean and always had a sharp word. One time I caught her sitting on the commode in the outhouse behind the school. I decided it'd be a lot of fun to pull a prank on her. I closed the door and pushed her over when she was in there, knocked the outhouse down. She was hollering and it was a big mess. I was well pleased with what I'd done.

I went home that day and my dad was waiting for me. He had heard all about it, and he had him a switch ready when I got there.

I said, "Dad, you mean you're gonna whip me for that?"

He said he sure was.

"Now, I'm gonna own up to it," I said. "I done this and I'm sorry."

He didn't say a thing. He just tightened his grip on the switch, so I figured I could maybe wiggle my way out of a whipping by bringing up a history lesson I'd learned in class: "George Washington, he chopped down the cherry tree and he told his daddy the truth about it, and his daddy didn't whip him. What's the difference?"

"Well," my dad said. "That teacher of yours wasn't in the cherry tree." He went ahead and gave me a good whipping.

Carter used to pull some pranks, too. He'd always be cutting up, causing trouble and yanking the pigtails on the girls. He was always pretty mischievous, a lot more than I was. I sort of sneaked 'em through. Carter, though, he didn't care who seen him do it or what. He did whatever he felt like doing.

Carter made me braver than I could ever be on my own. He was always taking chances, always up for any kind of adventure. My dad's brother had a little country grocery store, and the back window was big enough so we could get through. On Sundays, when the store was closed, we'd crawl through the opening and get us cans of Vienna sausage and potted meat and crackers. We'd hide our supplies under a dry stump so we'd have us a little snack on the long walk to Big Oak.

Now, don't think we ever starved or nothing. We raised our own food from our garden, so we always had something to eat, even if we had to forage a little once in a while. A nice vegetable garden and fresh springwater was plenty compared to some. We felt lucky to be up on Smith Ridge. I'm glad I was raised there instead of down in the coal and lumber camps.

In the boom years, all the mountain people who didn't have farmland like we did, well, they came out of the hills and hollows down in those little camps and company towns. The families there mostly lived out of the company store. If they needed money in advance, they got paid in scrip, which was company coin to buy goods at the store. They lived in houses built by the mining company, all crowded and close together with no garden. The company pretty much owned their workers, lock, stock and barrel. It was a bad exchange, I thought, to trade your freedom for a job in the mines.

They didn't have land but they did have the money to buy produce from us. We'd peddle vegetables and fresh produce that they couldn't raise like we could, and I will tell you more about this later, because when I was a little older, after our daddy left us, we did a lot more peddling so we could get by on our own. What I'm trying to say for now is that, as little as we had on our little mountain farm, we had it pretty good.

We knew all about the Depression, but it didn't really affect us the way it did people in the other parts of the country. I remember going with my dad to a mining camp in Jenkins, Kentucky, where there were families standing in a soup line, and that's the only time I saw anything like that. The worst of it was over by the time I was old enough to remember much. Franklin Roosevelt was elected president in 1932, when I was five and already in school. So we had the Works Progress Administration and other government welfare programs coming in to help people out. Our family was never involved in that, either with the work or the welfare. We didn't pay much attention to what they was doing or what they was all about. We'd see the WPA crews by the roadside, leaning on their shovels and smoking cigarettes. They always looked to be taking breaks and goofing off. We was more used to hard work, and we thought they was soft and lazy. We had our name for them: the "We Piddle Around" Boys.

To tell you the truth, we didn't worry too much about the Depression 'cause people here was busy working. My dad was one of the busiest workers around. He ran a sawmill operation; he was an independent. His work kept him on the move.

He'd buy what they called boundary timber, which was trees on a property you'd cut for lumber. Where the boundary timber was, he'd move the sawmill there and set up the operation; he had a crew working for him, and they'd work that boundary, cutting big trees all the way down to ones with eight-inch-diameter trunks. So he sawed the lumber and hauled out the logs with a team of horses.

This was wilderness country, way out in the woods; you had to have what they called a swamping road, which was a road for the horses to haul the wood out. The timber cutters would have their logging road cleared, but you still had to cut out your own road to get to the swamping road. So you're cutting more trees down just to make a way to get the logs out of there. And that's how my dad took the logs to the mill. He sold lumber for railroad ties and mining timbers and houses and buildings and whatever people needed. If they wanted whole logs, he'd give 'em whole logs. If they wanted 'em sawed, he'd saw 'em. Cut to order. Then they'd load the lumber on trucks and head 'em to the market.

There was poplar and oak and ash and locust and all kind of hardwoods; it was virgin timber, some of the tallest and widest old-growth trees you ever saw. We heard about a giant poplar so big around, it took a whole crew to use dynamite on it. There used to be a lot of timber and a lot of sawmills around here, but you don't see it anymore because they cut everything they could use and the big trees are scarce now. They've timbered all the good timber and it's mostly scrub trees left now, not even big enough or straight enough to get you one board of decent lumber. When it rains the water just washes away; it don't linger like it used to when there was big tall trees to catch it, and you get some awful winds now, too, blowing off the mountain. The land is all tore up. If you've lived here all your life like I have, you can really tell the difference and see what's been lost. It's not near as pretty in the fall no more, and it's a pity when I think about all the fine timber that's gone.

My dad moved wherever the timber was. He'd take his sawmill from boundary to boundary; he'd be in Buchanan County one month and maybe over in Russell County the next, then across the border into eastern Kentucky. He'd work out a patch of woods here and a patch there, setting up his sawmill where the work was. That's how we ended up moving for a while to Scott County, where he worked a job for nearly a year. He thought it'd be best to bring the family close to his work, and we lived in a log house there in Long Hollow and that's when I helped him lead the hymn at Point Truth Church. This was in 1935, and after the job was over we headed back to Big Spraddle.

Not long after we moved back to Dickenson County, there was some news about the old house up on Smith Ridge, the one Emery and Lena had lived in. Somehow it went vacant and the county was putting it up for sale; it could have been to finally settle on Emery's debts. I can't remember if anybody had been living there. I don't know what went on up there in the years that had passed. I know that neither Carter or me had gone for a visit at all since the killing.

Anyhow, we heard the house was going up for public auction at a county sale. I believe my mother had been waiting for a chance like this. She'd had her eyes on the property all along, biding her time until the right moment came. She wasn't about to let the old home get sold to somebody outside the family. Somehow or other, she and my dad scraped some money together and bought the house, and I'm sure glad they did. It was surely moving up in the world in every way. It was a bigger house than the one down in Big Spraddle Creek, with six rooms and an old-fashioned wraparound porch; and it was a bigger piece of land than down in the hollow. The ridgetop had grassy fields where cattle could graze and you could run around. The best thing was, it was where my mother had been raised, and she was happy to be going back to the old home place. And if anything made my mother happy, well, I was happy, too.

Chapter Two

Smith Ridge

"I'll go back to old Virginia where the mountains meets the sky
In those hills I learned to love you, let me stay there 'til I die"

—"Think of What You've Done," the Stanley Brothers

At first, we hated to leave Big Spraddle. We felt safe and sound in our little hollow. The way baby birds feel protected in the nest. It was a big change moving up to Smith Ridge. There were more open fields on that high knob, nothing but mountains for miles all around and the sky so big and blue it made you feel dizzy to take it all in. You'd see the red-tailed hawks wheeling way up high, hunting for their supper, maybe even snatching away a small boy just about my size.

We loaded up a wagon to haul our things, pair of mules leading the way, and we followed a dirt road that snaked its way up the ridge. From over the edge of the road, the view would take your breath away, it was so steep, a straight drop to treetops two miles down. That road's only been paved in recent years, and they widened it and took some of the curves out down through there, and they really improved it. It's still a test if you don't know what you're up against, though. Now I drive those turns like it was nothing. You can get used to anything, I reckon.

But when you're just a boy and the only thing ahead of you is the backside of a mule, you get to looking over the edge and thinking the worst. You'd hear stories of people who wrecked off the side of the mountain and come to an awful end. You'd hear the old-timers say, "There's been two or three starved to death before they reached the bottom." You'd wait for them to laugh, but they didn't even crack a smile, because that would ruin the joke.

I'm a lot like those old-timers, always have been. Smiling and laughing and cutting up never did come easy to me, anyhow, so I'm a natural straight man. I've always liked to play the straight man onstage when we do our comedy routines. Even my wife, Jimmi, can't hardly tell when I'm pulling her leg. She says she's never learned how to read me. She calls me Poker Face. I don't mean to confuse her. I can't help it. It's just the way I am. I hate to mess up a good laugh by laughing. It just ain't right.

Anyhow, in spite of my fears, it didn't take long for me and Carter to get used to things up on Smith Ridge. After a while, we didn't miss Big Spraddle at all. On the ridge, we had more room to run around and play. Seemed like nobody had a better perch than we did, and after a short while it started to feel like it was our mountain.

And with all the land we had on Smith Ridge, which was sixty-five acres of good ground, a lot of it grassy pastureland, we could have us a real farm now. Now we were able to have some livestock and lay out some crops. We used to keep three or four workhorses, two or three milk cows, and some hogs, too. We raised some hay and field corn and an acre or so of tobacco. And my mother had her a nice vegetable garden, a lot bigger than the little backyard patch she hoed down in Big Spraddle.

One of the first things my dad did after we moved was, he had a barn built. At the time, it was one of the best, if not the best, barns anywhere in this part of the country. He sawed all the best lumber himself and he hired out some carpenters from Kentucky to do the job, and they did it up special. It had a great big loft and six or seven stalls, and we kept our horses and cows in there.

Every morning about four o'clock, way before daylight, we'd have to get up and do the chores. We'd bring an old lantern, the kind that burned kerosene, to light the way in the dark, and we'd walk to the barn and milk the cows and feed the horses and slop the hogs. We called it "doing up the work" and it took some doing. After we were done, we'd get some breakfast, go to school, come home and sleep. Then we'd get up and do the same thing the next morning.

Once I was in the stall feeding out hay to the animals with the big ole pitchfork we used, which was about as long as I was tall. I was still half-asleep, eyes barely open. I got down nearly to the bottom of the pile, and I could feel something moving around. When I scraped the fork next to the ground, there was a weird rustling at my ankles, and I found myself smack in the middle of a nest of copperheads squirming around right under me. Well, I dropped the hay fork and run out of there fast. That woke me right up.

I was pretty handy with that hay fork when there wasn't no snakes to mess with. Back in them days, we didn't have balers or any machines such as that; we mowed and raked it and stacked it all by hand. We'd take the forks and throw the hay up around the pole, and pile it twenty feet high in tall pointy stacks, some folks called 'em peak bales, and that was the way we kept it to dry in the fields before we'd take it to store in the barn.

We had an old milk cow named Pied. She was black and white and most of her tail had froze off one winter. It was just a stub and it hung down about halfway. Sometimes, when you was milking her, why, when she'd swish her tail back and forth, she'd take that stub and hit you in the head. It was just long enough to get you right in the face, and it didn't feel too good, especially when you're barely awake and you ain't in the mood for any foolishness. She was playful, Pied was; she just couldn't behave. When we was gone all day at school, she'd run out in the woods and we'd have to hunt her down every evening and bring her in and milk her. Pied was a good old heifer; she had to be to get away with all the mischief she done.

In the cold months of the year, we'd go cut some kindling and build a fire to warm the house. Back then, we had an old-style woodstove in the living room to get the fire going. Part of the time, we had just a grate there, like an open fireplace, and we'd bake potatoes in the hot ashes.

We'd let the taters bake till they was smoking and dust 'em off good. Then we'd eat breakfast and head off to school.

During the long winter months, we never saw daylight at home except on weekends. When we got sick, we had home remedies like sheep's tallow, which was the lard you rendered into a little waxy ball. For a fever or a bad flu, my mother would rub the bottom of my feet with that tallow and she'd hold my feet right up to the fireplace. The heat would soak the tallow right in and it would really help me feel better and get well. My mother did all that sort of thing for us; whenever we needed help, she's the one we turned to. My dad was too busy with work so he wasn't around like my mother was.

We didn't know there was such things as electric lights and flush toilets and refrigerators. We didn't have running water or an indoor bathroom until the last part of my teenage years. The first electricity we had was powered by a Delco gasoline engine; for years we got by with kerosene lamps and lanterns. There were things we'd liked to have had that we didn't, like new shoes once in a while or a change of clothes every day.

Of course it was rough, but we didn't suffer too much, and we didn't know nothing else. I think about it sometimes, about the early years up on the ridge when we was young and barely scraping by. I'd hate to have to go back and live that way now because I've had so much better since. At the time, though, we didn't pay no mind to it, 'cause we didn't have anything different and never seen anyone who did.

And there was a lot of good in those hard times. Sometimes I think I'd like to go back to them early days for a month or so, and then just switch it right back to the way it is now. It would be a nice visit, I reckon. To see the morning dew on my mother's garden again and smell the fresh-cut hay stacked in rows in the field. But you know you can't go back, and it wouldn't be like you remembered it anyhow.

You can't really know how it was unless you lived it. Young people nowadays don't know what it was like, staggering sleepy-headed and stomach growling into the cold dark mornings and doing chores before school. None of my kids never had to do any of that. They've had it very easy. In a way, I think that's bad and I've failed my kids somehow by letting them off so easy. I believe every child, by the time they get to a certain age, should have some responsibilities and duties. Not as hard as I had it, but enough to get them ready for the world.

I don't say we suffered too bad, though, not compared with a lot of our neighbors. We may not have had many modern conveniences, but we finally got the one that mattered most to Carter and me: a battery-operated Philco radio my dad brought home one day in 1936. It was one of those big console models with wooden legs, like a nice piece of furniture, one of the first radios ever seen in our neighborhood. We wouldn't have swapped that Philco for a hundred electric refrigerators.

While we were fixing the fire and waiting on breakfast, we'd have the radio on. The music we heard filled us up like nothing else could. There weren't many radio stations we could pick up, as far back as we were in the mountains. But the ones we did get on the Philco came in loud and clear, and it was all country music.

The nearest to where we lived was WHIS, out of Bluefield, West Virginia. That's where we first heard people like Molly O'Day. On a Louisville station we listened to Cousin Emmy and Her Kin Folk. She had an early morning program, a bigmouthed, laughing gal who could frail on the banjo as good as any man.

Then there was WSM, out of Nashville, home of the *Grand Ole Opry*. It had fifty thousand watts, and that was something powerful back then. Roy Acuff was King of the Hillbillies and he sang "Wabash Cannonball" and one we really liked, "I Called and Nobody Answered." That's when we first heard Charlie and Bill Monroe, brothers from bluegrass country out in western Kentucky. They did "Nine Pound Hammer" and "Sinner, You Better Get Ready," and they played fast as lightning and could really lay down the harmonies, tight as a tick. They were our favorite of the brother duets; and there were so many great brother teams: the Delmore Brothers and the Bailes Brothers and the Blue Sky Boys, Earl and Bill Bolick, later good friends. Then there was Fiddlin' Arthur Smith and Uncle Dave Macon—the Dixie Dewdrop, they called him—and Sam and Kirk McGhee, who played with Uncle Dave in the Fruit Jar Drinkers. And there were singers you never heard much about later on, but they were known in their day, like the Poe Sisters, who could really sing the old-timey style. I never did know what happened to them.

One of the strongest signals came from farthest away. That was XERA, a clear-channel station from down in Villa Acuna, Mexico, across the border from Del Rio, Texas. The Mexican border stations like XERA didn't have to follow the rules set down by the U.S. government. They were outlaw operations and they could crank up the broadcast power to 500,000 watts and Uncle Sam couldn't do a thing to stop them. People said the signal was so strong you could pick up a border station off a barbed-wire fence or a bedspring. I don't know about that, but what we heard on our Philco beaming all the way from Mexico was like someone talking to you across the table.

We listened to a real early morning show on XERA, and that's where we first heard Mainer's Mountaineers, from North Carolina, J. E. Mainer fiddling and his brother Wade playing a two-finger banjo style I liked right off. They did "Maple on the Hill" and "Little Maggie" and tragic songs where J.E. sang, *That train ran back for miles from town and killed my girl. Her head was found in the driver wheel, her body I never could find.* If the mines didn't get you, the railroad would.

XERA was where the Carter Family worked for years during the Depression. There was nobody else like Maybelle and Sara and A.P. Like I told you, they came from Scott County near Bristol, not far from where we lived. They put everything into singing; they had a way with song that made the melody stand out.

Country music was like a great big family back in them days. The groups were mostly kin to each other, they grew up playing together, and the closeness came through in the music, especially in the singing. There wasn't no pretentions put on, people could be themselves. Listening to the radio was like eavesdropping on a family gathering, like they were singing from their home right into ours.

This was important for Carter and me, because we were brothers singing together, just like Charlie and Bill and all the rest. It gave us hopes maybe we could make it big someday, too. We'd listen to the stars on the *Grand Ole Opry* and we'd imagine how we'd like to be people like that, entertaining over the radio. We wanted to have that life, if it could be arranged. It made our dream into something real to shoot for, and it was always on our minds from then on. We went through a lot of batteries on the Philco, let me tell you.

Most mornings, we'd be in the living room waiting on breakfast and listening to the radio while we cut chestnut kindling and wood shavings for the fire. We'd take those kindling sticks and pretend we had a fiddle or banjo and beat on the sticks and sing along to the music we heard on the Philco. We were one of the first families around to have a radio, and on Saturday nights some of our neighbors would come by the house to listen to the *Grand Ole Opry*. Me and Carter would grab our kindling sticks and start our little routine. Of course, we couldn't get any real music out of those pieces of wood, but the neighbors would clap and holler for us. They enjoyed it.

Now Carter, he ate up the applause like apple pie, but I didn't much like the attention. I was so shy I'd make Carter come with me in the kitchen and play while the grown-ups listened from the living room. He didn't mind because he knew I was too bashful to perform out in front of an audience. When you're a brother team, you have to stick together, and we did that right from the start.

It wasn't too long before we had a craving to swap the kindling sticks for the real thing. Now, back then, there wasn't many stores around selling musical instruments, outside the commissary at the mining camps. Where we lived, it was make 'em yourself or send away for 'em by mail.

I knew right off I wanted a banjo. My mother was the first person I saw play a banjo and I liked the sound she got. It made me feel good. There's always been something about a banjo ringing out; it cheered me up. Maybe it run in the family, too. Lucy was one of twelve children, and every one could played banjo, the old clawhammer style, and the girls were every bit as good as the boys. It's not true what I've heard some say, that the banjo was frowned on and forbidden in proper homes. At least it wasn't in our neck of the woods. It's true playing fiddle was mostly for men, but picking banjo was for anyone, and there was nothing bad about it.

My mother had what they called a thirty-nine-bracket banjo, the brackets being how you tightened up the head. The more brackets a banjo had, the better it was. These were fretless, backless banjos, and there were a lot of homemade banjos around then. They used to make 'em out of animal hide; old-timers would skin a groundhog and use the skin. Nowadays they use plastic on the head of the banjo, but for years and years I played 'em with the skins and hides and they sounded fine. The only problem was, the hide would loosen up when it got damp and it'd get tight when it was dry. So if it rained, the head would loosen up on you and you'd have to tighten it. Then when it got sunshiney, if you didn't watch out, it'd get too tight and the hide would burst on you. I've bursted many a head on a banjo because of a change in weather.

Back before she was married, my mother used to entertain a lot in the neighborhood. She played banjo at old-time square dances and house parties, what she called barn dances, and at bean stringings and corn shuckings. Somebody'd have a whole field of beans to string, or maybe thirty or forty bushels of apples to be peeled for winter canning, and the neighbors would come over to help out. They'd put a half-gallon can of moonshine on the ground, pile those bushels of apples or beans over it, and they'd say, "Ain't nobody get a drink till we get to the can." That got the work done fast, let me tell you. Then they'd get to drinking the whiskey and playing music and dancing, and they didn't quit till the sun came up the next morning. It was hard work back in them days, maybe, but never too hard for people to sing.

My mother would tell me how much fun she had picking banjo while the people danced. She played the old drop-thumb, clawhammer style that was handed down for years and years. She was much in demand. Her timing was good as anyone back then. Your timing is so important; you don't want to play too fast or drag behind neither.

At that time, if you had a fiddle and banjo, you had enough for a band. There weren't guitars in the mountains yet, not too many anyhow. My mother might play all night and then she'd walk back home, sometimes five miles or more, and get right back to work planting her garden or hoeing her corn, whatever needed to be done. Making music and having fun was something you squeezed in when you could.

After my mother got married and started raising kids, she put her banjo away. But she always remembered how good it made her feel. She saw music as something precious, a reward for a hard life, and when she saw how keen Carter and I was to sing and play, it really tugged at her heart. She wanted us to feel the same way making music had made her feel. So when I was eleven years old, she was going to let me have my own banjo. She'd seen that her sister's banjo had caught my eye.

I was due for a present, and she said I could get a banjo or a pig. You might think I'd go straightaway for the banjo, but it wasn't easy to choose. I liked music, but not as much as Carter. He was already burning to be onstage, where I had other things besides music that interested me. I was taking agriculture classes at school and I had farming on my mind. I was liking the farmwork a lot more than Carter; he'd rather be running wild than slopping hogs. Me, I liked the looks of pigs. I thought they was pretty.

My mother's sister Roxie lived close by; she had a banjo and she raised hogs. She had a fine sow that had a litter of pigs, and there was a little sow pig, and I had my eyes on that one. Well, Roxie had the banjo, too. Nothing fancy, it was an open-back banjo, tattered, with a fraying skin, but I thought it was pretty, too. Roxie wanted $5 for the pig or $5 for the banjo. That was a lot of money back then.

"Now, you make up your mind," my mother told me. "I can't buy the both of them. So do you want the pig or the banjo?"

I took the banjo, and I'm mighty glad I did. I don't think I'd have made much of a pig farmer. My mother had a little grocery store where she peddled her produce, and she traded out in groceries with Aunt Roxie so I could get the banjo.

My mother taught me my first banjo licks. I remember her tuning up my banjo and putting it into my hands where I could hold it myself. It felt right, like it was made for my hands. It was a tool to me, something to make your living with, that's how I looked at it. I wanted a banjo for my tool instead of a pick and shovel, so I could stay out of those mines. It's the only instrument I've ever cared to play, except one summer when I backed up my mother on fiddle, and I always thought if a man could do one instrument justice, that's about all he could handle. For me, it's been the banjo.

The first tune I learned from my mother was "Shout Little Lulie," and the first time I tried I could play it pretty well, so I reckon my musical talent come natural. I believe it's a gift from God, same with my singing. I can't read a note of music and neither could Carter. We always played by ear, same as everybody did in the mountains. You can go to college or music school and learn to read and study notes, or you can sit down and hear somebody play and catch on like that. But I believe to play our type of music, real down-to-earth mountain music, it just about has to be born and bred into a man to really feel it and do it proper.

I play "Shout Little Lulie" on every show I'm able. Whenever I do, I still think of my mother and I always mention her and what she taught me so many years ago. It always peps me up hearing the clawhammer; it takes me back to when I was a boy. But that ain't the only reason. I play it because it's such a big crowd-pleaser, right up there with "Man of Constant Sorrow" and "O Death." Especially all the young people at shows nowadays; they go wild when they hear "Lulie." They get to dancing and shouting, and I know my mother'd be happy I've taken her song all over the world and it helped people forget their troubles for a little while, like it done for her. I have to admit I'm a little selfish about that song; I play it for my own pleasure, too. I'll tell you what, I'll take "Shout Little Lulie" over "O Death" any day.

After I got the hang of "Lulie," my mother showed me other songs she used to play at barn dances: "Little Birdie," "Cripple Creek," "Chinquapin Hunting," "Old Joe Clark," "Walking in the Parlor," and "Cluck Old Hen." These old banjo tunes come from the same hills where I come from. The traditional ballads my daddy sung, a lot of those were brought over by the early settlers from England and Ireland and Scotland, but the banjo songs are different. They're homegrown in these southern mountains and played at barn dances and passed down for generations. People around here didn't have no jewelry or fancy things to hand down, just these old-time songs. If you'd asked my mother, she'd a-told you "Shout Little Lulie" was given to her, just like she give it to me.

I tried to play like her at first, but I ended up doing my own way. The style she had was different from what I do. She dropped her thumb on the strings when she played, which is the way most old-timers do it. I never did care much for the drop-thumb. What I do is scrape my fingers up and down on the strings. But both styles are clawhammer to my way of thinking. Some people call it frailin' but that's not really right to say that. Now, frailin' is when you use a straight pick. I use my fingers like I'm clawing those strings. That's why I think clawhammer's the right word.

What I learned about most from my mom's playing was her sense of timing. She picked up her timing from playing those barn dances and watching the fiddler play and the people dance when she picked. She wasn't just playing for herself, she was paying attention to the fiddler. She wasn't out to show off but to fit in with the music. I believe most good pickers have fast fingers maybe, but the best players are the ones with the good ears. Listening's what makes a good musician over one who's just in it to hear themselves and show off.

My mother didn't do much singing, except in church, when she'd help out on the hymns. Singing was my dad's department, and he was one of the best I ever heard. He was a big strong man and he had a big strong voice. He had one of the strongest voices at the McClure church, and many a Sunday he would lead on the Primitive Baptist hymns like "Village Churchyard," "Tarry with Me, O My Savior" and "Amazing Grace."

Besides church, my dad never did sing in public, just around the house, strictly for his own amusement, whenever he got the notion. He always sang a cappella. He couldn't play any instrument, but he didn't need one to carry a song. He had a voice that could really carry, and the songs he sung fit his voice. Like I told you before, he done ballads and sad tunes he heard his men sing on a sawmill job. He had a brother, Jim Henry Stanley, who worked for him, and they'd come home and sit out on the porch late of a night. I'd be in bed listening; I couldn't sleep. I didn't want to miss out.

Pretty Polly, Pretty Polly, your guess is about right
I dug on your grave the best part of last night

A song like "Pretty Polly" sounded real to me, like it happened. In them real old ballads like "Pretty Polly," the words mean a lot; they tell a story where you can imagine what it would be like. When I heard it, I could envision how it'd feel if it happened to me. There was one song my dad always sung by himself when he was all alone in the dark. He sang it all the time, and it became a favorite of mine. It was the story it told, the way the words and the melody worked on my imagination and preyed on my mind.

I'm a man of constant sorrow, I've seen trouble all my days
I bid farewell to old Kentucky, the place where I was born and raised

Like I already told you, my daddy knew a lot of songs but hardly any all the way through. He'd pare down the verses to fit his mood and find the heart of the song, same way he'd saw a straight plank out of a rough crooked log. That helped me and Carter later on, when we'd have to cut three-minute songs for those 78-rpm records. That was all the time you had back then, and you had to make every word, every second count. You learn how to keep it simple and straight to the point. The other thing I learned from my dad was to pick songs to suit your style. So many singers don't understand this. It ain't no use trying to sound like other people or do songs that don't suit you. It's best to find your own voice and stick with it, no matter what. It was from my dad that I got so many old ballads I've done through the years, like "Man of Constant Sorrow" and "Pretty Polly," which I still play every show. I reckon they were made for my voice somehow, mine and my daddy's.

About the same time I got my banjo, Carter got himself a guitar even though guitars weren't very popular back in the sticks where we lived. Fiddle and banjo was about all you heard. But he always wanted to sing lead, and the guitar and the lead singer fit together more than the banjo and the lead singer.

And something else got him interested in guitar. It was our mailman, Woodrow Owens. He was the only mail carrier we had in those days, and he'd bring the mail by horseback. He'd start out from Stratton post office down near our old house in Big Spraddle Creek, and he'd make the eight miles or so back and forth in a big wide circuit, taking his own sweet time. We'd watch for him every day; it gave us something to look forward to. He was just a slim little fellow, but he had a big voice like to knock down trees, and we could hear him a-coming up Smith Ridge. You could tell just how he was feeling from a mile down the mountain, especially if he'd been a-drinking,

Woodrow would make the top of the ridge around lunchtime, loaded down with two leather mail sacks hanging off the saddle, a beat-up guitar slung over his shoulder, his old horse tuckered out from the climb. He took a liking to us, especially Carter, and he'd stop for a while and play. He picked guitar and played a mouth harp the best. He blew an awful good harmonica, real bluesy, and he done old-time mountain tunes like "Lost John" and "The Fox Chase." I can still see Woodrow, head reared back and a-wailing on his harmonica, so carried away he'd nearly be falling off the saddle.

One day, here come Woodrow riding up the hill carrying a long box along with the regular mail. Carter had ordered his very own guitar by mail from the Montgomery Ward catalog, and here it was, special delivery courtesy of Woodrow. I remember how excited we was tearing at the brown wrapping paper. The guitar cost $3.55. Only trouble was, Carter had no idea how to tune it. Woodrow sat down like there wasn't nothing more important in the world than to get the guitar to sound just right. He tuned it and showed Carter a few chords, some real simple ones to get him started. Then he handed it over, and Carter held the guitar like he'd been borned to it. He started picking out a tune right off, just like I did with my banjo.

An instruction manual came with the guitar, but Carter threw it away. Books and formal training wouldn't do any good; it just don't apply to the style of music in the mountains. Old-time music and old-time singing ain't something somebody teaches you in a class. It's bred into you; it comes out of the way you live. For us it was a lot of hard work and rough times and suffering. Practicing, too. And all that's in our music.

It wasn't long after Carter got his guitar, I wanted my own mail-order banjo. My uncle Dewey Baker had an account with the Spiegel catalog and he let me order a banjo in his name. It was a real nice model, a lot better than the one I got from my aunt Roxie. It cost more than a hundred dollars, a fortune in those days. I paid Uncle Dewey five dollars a month on it in installments, from money I made doing odd jobs, like picking up rocks that cropped in the spring and plowing out my older sister Ruby's field.

We were in clover. To us, the guitar and banjo were worth a million dollars, especially because we paid out of our own pockets. When you're growing up without much to call your own, it means more when you earn what you get.

We practiced just about anytime we could, mostly on Sundays and at night before we'd go to bed. There wasn't much free time with school and chores. Our mother always encouraged us. She understood we were trying to learn the music and improve our playing. She'd always say, "That's good, boys," and of course it was long before we were much good at it. She grew up in a house filled with music, and to her it was natural to hear her two little boys banging away on banjo and guitar. She welcomed it. She was the first booster we ever had. I think she was planting a seed and wanting to help it grow, same as she did in her garden. She'd drop comments sort of dreamy-like: "Someday I'd like to see you boys broadcasting on the radio," she'd say. "Now, wouldn't that be something?"

My mother was in favor of our playing, but my daddy didn't see it that way, at least not at first. Music wasn't something you made a living at. Besides, he had business to take care of. He worked men in his job, and he had to figure his accounts and his paperwork. The noise of our rehearsing made him nervous and he couldn't stand to hear us playing in earshot, so he'd run us out of the house. He had a lot on his mind from work; it seemed we was always bothering him. Now that I'm older, I can see his point on that. I understand what he was going through. When my grandson Nathan was learning how to play his mandolin, he drove me crazy with it, too.

"You boys get out of here!" my dad would shout. "Scat!"

Most times he didn't have to say anything. All he had to do was stamp his feet three times, and we'd grab our instruments and be out the door, running as fast as we could. We'd go out to the coal shed or up to the barn or out by the woodshed. We'd go anywhere where we could practice by ourselves so we wouldn't bother nobody. Sometimes we'd sit under the shade of the apple tree where Uncle Emery died, and we'd practice with a neighbor friend of ours, Richard Nunley. He played the fiddle and he'd chime in when he could, and we'd take a break and eat on the apples when they fell off the tree.

I don't know if playing outdoors so much did something to the way we sounded or not. I did hear one time somebody say Stanley Brothers sound like the wind in the woods, and maybe that's not too far off. I do know that our singing just come natural. I sang tenor behind Carter's lead, right from the start. The church singing influenced us a lot, but we had our own style that come from growing up together and being around each other so much of the time. We spoke our words alike and we liked the same things as far as music went, so it just fell into place.

These were some happy times, but not like some people see as happy. Most times I remember like that was when my parents were still together. But I have to tell you that nothing bothered me too much as long as Carter was around. He made things seem better than they maybe were. He was always game for some fooling around; only he didn't like it much when he was the one who was getting pranked on.

One time, we were riding a mule down near the tree line by the coal shed. I was sitting in the saddle and Carter was back on the hind end. I noticed the lope of that ole mule was putting Carter to sleep, so I decided to have a little fun. I gave the mule a good kick and slapped his flanks with my hands up front. Course that made the mule pick up his trot quick, enough to make Carter fall off the back on the hard, rocky ground. There wasn't many a soft spot on Smith Ridge, outside of our mother's vegetable garden.

Well, that got Carter wide awake and he jumped up fighting mad. He came after me swearing and throwing rocks and trying to catch me. I kicked the mule out of there fast, and Carter was running hard but he couldn't keep up. I got away, but I knew I wouldn't be safe with him after me. He was some kind of mad, hotter than I'd ever seen him. I laid out for a long while in the woods, and I could hear him hollering and swearing at me through the trees. It was almost dark before I could come to the house safe. But it was all worth it, just to see the look on Carter's face when he hit the ground.

There must have been something about that mule that brought out some mischief in me. I played a pretty good joke the very same day I bought him. This was when I was about fourteen years old. Back then if you were growing up on a mountain farm and you came of a certain age, instead of getting a car or pickup like nowadays, you'd get you a mule.

I had to go to Clintwood to buy the mule. Paid thirty-five dollars, and I was starting back home, which was about fifteen miles by road. Now, there was also a shortcut where you could come through the mountain and that would shorten it into a five-mile trip. After about thirty minutes on the road, I was going to take that shortcut when a farmer came by hauling livestock he'd bought in Clintwood. He stopped and said, "Just load that mule on the back of the truck and we'll take you a few miles of where you're going."

So I got a ride for a good long stretch, then the farmer dropped me off and I rode the mule by taking the shortcut the rest of the way. When I made it back home, I passed by my uncle and gave him a big wave. He hollered for me to come over. He knew I'd gone to Clintwood and he couldn't understand how I'd managed to ride the mule all the way back so early in the day. It had only been a few hours since I'd left to buy the mule, and here I was with the mule. I just kept a straight face and told him the mule wasn't no ordinary mule and left it at that. My uncle looked at me, then at the mule, then back at me again. I didn't crack a smile. I just patted the mule and said, "After a ride like that, I reckon I'll keep him." Well, my uncle about went crazy. He was amazed and started telling everyone how his nephew had rode a mule back from Clintwood in two hours. He was so proud he used to tell that story to everyone he met.

I never did tell my uncle any different. Now, you may say it was cruel not to tell him the truth, but I don't think so. It was something he was always proud of. I believe when he told the story about me and the mule hightailing it across the mountains, it made him happy and maybe got him feeling amazed all over again. Life's rough enough without a little boost now and then.

Most of the time, me and Carter just tried to have fun as best we could. Even at a funeral, we'd try to find something funny to get a laugh or two. At these country funerals, they'd get to preaching and singing by the grave and really get carried away. One time, this woman got into the spirit and got to shouting and she knocked an old lady beside her down into the open grave. They hadn't lowered the coffin yet, and a couple of men went down in there and got her out of the fresh-dug grave. When they lifted her up on the ground, the old lady had dirt all over her dress and she was a mess. But nobody made a bit of fuss at all. The woman who'd shoved her in went right back to her shouting and the preacher went on with his preaching like nothing had happened.

We had a game called fox and dogs. Somebody would be the fox and everybody else would be the dogs trying to catch the fox. There was a lot of woods back then to hide in if you was the fox. You'd think it might be more fun to be the dogs, but I always liked to be the fox, because I knew the woods real good, and there were a lot of places where I knew to hide.

I've been telling you a lot about some pastimes we had as children, just some of the ways we had fun. And we did have fun. But, you know, it wasn't too much of that stuff went on. It was always pretty much business. There wasn't too much foolishness in them days.

Chapter Three

Down from the Mountain

"Tell me why Daddy don't come home
I know that I am much too big to cry
Why don't he come and play with me again
Why oh why did Daddy ever say good-bye?"

—"Tell Me Why My Daddy Don't Come Home,"
the Stanley Brothers

In 1939, my daddy one day up and left us. He didn't say a word to me and Carter. All I know is, one day he was with us, and the next he was gone. I never did find out how long it was coming or what finally drove him to do it. You probably may have guessed it was another woman, and it was. He left my mother for a younger woman named Louisa, and they got married and started raising their own family in the next county over, Russell County.

He kept on working as a sawmill man, and he was still good ole Lee Stanley to everyone else, only he'd traded in for a new wife and a new family. He just started out fresh and left his old life behind back on Smith Ridge. For Carter and me, just hitting our teen years, it was tough. We'd lost our dad when you need one the most, and he never even said good-bye. For our mother it was the worst, and I couldn't hardly stand to see her hurt so bad.

My mother never did get over our dad leaving. She'd already had her first two men taken from her, and that was plenty enough heartbreak for anybody to bear. When Lee left for a younger woman, she never wanted no one no more, and she never wanted to remarry. She just took care of her boys and done without. From then on, the only men that mattered in her life were Carter and me.

Not long after Lee was gone, my mother got some even worse news. It came from a fortune-teller. She took it for the gospel truth, and I believe it weighed on her for years.

Fortune-tellers were common in our area, especially down by the coal and lumber camps, and people believed the things they told. There was one named Vertie Gibson, who told fortunes on the street corners in Coeburn. Nothing fancy or big time; she'd make maybe a quarter or two in tips, just some extra money to get by. Vertie was an old woman been working the corners for years, and my mother had known her since they were both young. There was nothing shady about old Vertie. With my dad gone and my mother alone with two boys on her own, Vertie would come stay with us at Smith Ridge every once in a while, to keep my mother company and help pass the time.

Vertie told fortunes with a deck of playing cards, same as you had in poker or bridge or what have you. It tells you how much my mother trusted her friend, because she didn't usually allow cards in the house. A deck of cards laying around was as dangerous as a book of matches. But Vertie used her cards for serious business, not for fun and games and foolishness.

Every night after supper, Vertie would tell our fortunes. She knew the whole deck like it was her own family, and every one of the fifty-two cards meant something. Me, being fair-haired, I was the king of hearts, and Carter, being dark-haired, he was the king of spades, and so forth. Most times, she'd hand out the cards and they didn't amount to much. She was smart that way, playing it safe so whatever she said would likely come true. The first thing she might say was "You're going to get a letter," and then she might say, "You're going to take a trip." And of course, it wouldn't be long before you got a letter in the mail, and maybe you'd take a day trip into Clintwood and that'd be that.

One night, Vertie was telling my mother's fortune, laying the cards out on the table same as she always done. Well, this time, the cards come up a certain way. She just let 'em lay there and she didn't say a word. Then she got a real sad look on her face and she told my mother, "You're going to lose one of your sons." She said he couldn't be sure which one it would be, Carter or Ralph. She said the cards were never wrong on matters of life and death: One of us would be gone before my mother passed away.

Now, let me tell you what. Hearing what Vertie told her, well, it really hit our mother hard. She'd already had her first sweetheart get killed and then her first husband die on her and then Lee walking out. And here was Vertie telling her she was going to lose a son. She believed the fortune because she put stock in the fortunes Vertie told. She didn't question it, and I know it preyed on her mind and worried her all the time.

Carter and me didn't pay much attention to the fortune. We weren't old enough yet to worry about things like that. We already had our own fortunes in mind. We was going to make it as professional entertainers.

Right around the time our dad left, we saw a show at Ervinton High School. It was a hillbilly-music package show, where they had different acts on tour. That night we saw Clayton McMichen and his Georgia Wildcats, an old-time string band, and the Delmore Brothers, Alton and Rabon, one of the best brother duets around. The headliner was Bill Monroe and His Bluegrass Boys.

It was the first stage show we ever saw, and it really got me and Carter excited. I can still remember how it felt to be in the crowd. The only way I can explain is to say it was like a jolt to your whole system, head to toe. It took you to a different place.

When the curtain come up and the Georgia Wildcats started playing, we felt like it was the best thing we'd ever seen. It was all the commotion and excitement and the action up on the stage, watching the Wildcats whip up the crowd. McMichen had started out as an old-timey country fiddler back in the twenties, but when we saw him, he'd been all around the South and soaked up every style there was, and he could do it all, from hoedowns to western swing to jazz.

We liked the Delmores, too, but Bill Monroe was the one that stood out. He was our favorite on the *Grand Ole Opry* and here he was in person, up on the stage right there in front of us. It was almost beyond our wildest dreams. Now, some musicians will disappoint you when you see them play live. They don't measure up to your expectations. With Monroe, he was more than we could have ever hoped. This was only a few years after he and his older brother, Charlie, had split up, and Bill was out to set the world on fire; he played like a man with something to prove.

The band with him was one of the best he ever had. Bill had just got Clyde Moody the day before in Bluefield, West Virginia. Clintwood was the first show he worked with Bill. And they had Art Wooten on fiddle and Stringbean on banjo, and I believe it was Cousin Wilbur on bass.

We just loved Bill's sound. He put some overdrive to the music. The energy grabbed us, and the precision, too, every note ringing out crisp and true. This was music with some juice to it. Monroe held his mandolin like his life depended on it, and the band followed every move he made. Clyde was a powerful lead singer, and Bill's tenor was kind of rough around the edges, but it was right for his music. He had a pearl in his voice. When the band ganged around the microphone, and Bill hit those high notes, it raised the hair on your arms.

And the Bluegrass Boys looked as sharp as they sounded. They dressed formal the way a Kentucky colonel did, in foxhunting outfits with hats and riding boots and jodhpurs. There was no doubt Monroe was the leader. He stood tall and proud; he left the clowning for Stringbean. I don't remember seeing Bill smile the whole night, but Carter and me couldn't stop grinning at each other.

Here we were a couple of wide-eyed country boys, barely in our teens. Monroe was a dozen years older and he was bigger than life to us. It made an impression, especially on Carter. When your daddy ain't around no more, you may be needing a hero, somebody to look up to, and that night Bill became ours. That show was it. We decided that someday we'd tear up the crowd the way Bill and the Bluegrass Boys did.

There were other Nashville acts coming through our area, too. Some of the best package tours stopped in Clintwood. It was some big goings-on when they came to town. The miners and sawmill workers and farmers would come pouring in there to see the entertainers they heard on the *Opry*. I still remember Fiddlin' Arthur Smith and his Dixieliners, along with Uncle Dave Macon.

Arthur Smith was everybody's favorite fiddler back then, at least he was in every part of the country where people listened to the *Opry*. He was so popular with the miners around our area they petitioned to have his show moved up an hour so they could hear him between shifts. He was best known for his fiddling, but he could play a mean banjo. He picked a two-finger style common in Dickson County, Tennessee, where he was from, not far out of Nashville. He did one called "Bound to Ride" he learned from a tent-show man out West; I used to do clawhammer on that one. Uncle Dave Macon was another one we loved. He was a real self-made man, one of the best entertainers I ever saw. He got his start on the vaudeville circuit, and it seemed like he knew every song.

Not long after that, we saw Molly O'Day put on a show at a ballpark down in Clinchco. She's not so well known today, but she was one of the best singers around back then. In the late forties, she was very popular on the radio, when they called her the Mountain Fern. She had hits like "Tramp on the Street" and "Drunken Driver," with her band the Cumberland Mountain Folks. Hank Williams used to say Molly was his favorite female country singer, and that's saying something. Molly later got religion and quit the music business. She decided it wasn't right to make money off what she believed belonged to God.

When we saw Molly play in Clinchco, she was just starting out. She was sixteen years old and she went by the stage name Dixie Lee. She didn't have her own band yet, and she picked her banjo real backwoods mountain-style. The leader was Gordon Jennings, and Molly's brother Skeets Williamson played fiddle. I always liked Molly's singing. It's the way I think a woman should sound, natural and no frills. She was just a plain ole country girl straight out of the mountains. She didn't wear makeup and there was no put-on about her. She just got up there and throwed her head back and sung the way she felt.

Molly's show gave Carter and me another boost of confidence. She was from McVeigh, a coal town close by Pikeville, just over the state line in eastern Kentucky, not far from us. She was only a year or so older than we were, too. Here she was, a local girl, singing her own way and drawing big crowds. If Molly could make it, we figured the Stanley Brothers could, too.

It was time to take our music off the ridge. We started to play a few dances around the neighborhood, some little get-togethers with family and friends. I never did like to play dances. It wasn't much fun. It was really more like work, because everybody'd get to dancing, and you'd get tired playing a song for so long. That wasn't our style, really, the hoedowns and such.

We was always singers more than pickers, right from the start. We always liked the old ballads and the heart songs with the sad stories. We'd sing "Hills of Roane County," "I Called and Nobody Answered," "When I Lay My Burden Down" and "A Month of Sorrow." Mostly songs we heard at home. We took a shine to the sad and lonesome songs, and we always did, till the very end.

I believe the first time we really played out before the public was at a local political rally. It was a convention, a fund-raiser, held by the county Republicans at the Greenwood Grade School in Greenwood, Virginia. It was the first public gathering we ever played. Course, we weren't even old enough to vote; we were just hired for entertainment by the party officials. They came by the house and we rode in the back of a pickup truck to the school and naturally we thought it was about the best thing in the world. They had their meeting and made their speeches and we played our music and they brought us back home.

Now, as far as politics goes, I've been a Democrat all my life, ever since I voted for Harry Truman in 1948. I've played at political fund-raisers and rallies through the years, and I'll play a show for any party wants to hire me out, as long as the price is right and I get paid. When you have a band, you take the jobs you can.

But I don't mix the politics with the music. Some entertainers stand onstage and tell you who to vote for or how they got saved. When I'm playing a show, I don't try to pull anybody nowhere, not with politics or religion neither. There's as many Republicans in my audience as Democrats, so you've got fans on both sides.

Now, an endorsement is different. Last year I campaigned for Barack Obama when he was running for President. I didn't know if I was going to endorse him or not, but he called me several times and he was real nice to me. He told me he had to have Virginia to win the election, and he asked would I put in a good word for him. I said I was glad to help in my own little way. About two months before the election, I went out to Russell County and joined him there for a rally. That's a den of Republicans down there, but I got a big reception from the crowd. I enjoyed meeting Obama; he's a look-you-in-the-eye fella and he's as impressive in person as he is on television; he's young and he's sharp as a tack.

I also did a radio ad for his campaign, and I think it stirred up some support for Obama in the coalfields, where people didn't know him too well and where I have some name recognition. Maybe I made a little difference in his favor. A lot of people weren't happy I done all that; some of my fans even called me a dirty traitor and a senile old fool, but I didn't let none of it bother me. I felt like I had to do it and I'm glad I did. It's my right.

Anyhow, the little Republican rally me and Carter played at Greenwood School didn't pay a dime, and I've since learned the hard way that politics never does pay unless you play dirty, and I'll tell more about all that later.

What I wanted to tell you now is how the very first people who paid to see the Stanley Brothers perform was the people who could afford it the least, and they were the coal miners. We'd go down to the coal camps in Clinchco and Dante and play for the miners on payday. Sometimes we'd climb on the back of a flatbed truck. Most times, though, we'd just stand on the corner and draw a crowd. We used to go a lot on Saturday afternoons, too, and the miners would pass by on their way into the commissary.

Carter would stand out front, and I'd be behind, which is how we sang, him on lead and me backing him on tenor, and we'd sing everything we knew. You can't find a better audience than coal miners who just got paid. They worked hard and they liked to play hard, too. Die-hard music fans, and mighty generous, too, poor as they were. They'd pitch dimes and nickels to us and holler out for favorites. They'd toss a quarter or more, and that's a song that would stick in your head. We could make $25 or $30 between us on a good day and that would be worth $500 now.

We were getting a name for ourselves. We started to win at local fiddlers' contests, and we were beating out bands more than twice as old as we were, or at least playing to a draw, like it says in an article from the *Dickenson Forum* newspaper from 1941: "The honors for the best string band music was divided between Roy Reed and His String Band and a pair of youthful Stanleys, Ralph and Carter, of the Sandy Ridge section." I don't have the foggiest idea what became of Roy Reed, or of the fella who won the fiddle contest with his rendition of "Dixie," a preacher from Clintwood named Reverend L. D. Perkins.

It wasn't long before we got a chance to play on the radio. There was a popular Saturday morning show called *Barrel of Fun* on a station out of Elizabethtown, Tennessee. In the spring of '41, we auditioned and were chosen to be special guests on the program. I was fourteen years old and Carter was almost sixteen, and we reckoned this was our big break. The station was a couple of hours' drive south across the Virginia border.

My dad had a car and he came by to carry us to the show. We didn't see him much anymore, but he'd always try to lend a hand whenever it come to helping us with our music, especially now as he saw we had a knack for it and maybe a shot at a career. On the way down, we was real nervous, thinking about how people would be hearing our voices on the radio like we listened to country stars back home on our Philco.

We got to the station and we knew the number we wanted to sing, "When I Lay My Burden Down," because it was such a hit with the miners in Clinchco and Dante. Now, Carter was already quite a showman and all-around entertainer and he liked to cut up a little bit when we played. He'd add his own whoops and hollers and whatever popped into his head and he'd always get a reaction from the crowd. Well, we lit into the song, but Carter was uptight and scared so bad, this being his first time on the radio, that when he tried to holler, it wouldn't come out. Nothing. I was as nervous as he was, but it turned out just fine after that and we got some good experience singing on the radio, which came in handy later when we had to do it regular for our first professional job.

Course, we weren't ready to go professional yet, so we had to make money to help our mother in other ways. To let you know how it was back in the mountains: We could make more money hauling moonshine than just about any other kind of job.

One of our uncles, Dewey Baker, made some of the best whiskey around, and he needed us to deliver it. It was too risky for grown-ups, so they had us kids do it. We'd get up around three in the morning and carry the liquor in jugs a mile or so down the mountain. We'd walk along the Clinchfield Railroad tracks a ways, and then cross over the creek to an old house where we delivered the whiskey. We'd bring it in gallon jugs and they'd sell it in pint bottles. We thought it was the best adventure we'd ever had.

We didn't know it at the time, but the deputy sheriff would see us come by of a night. He lived in a house along the route we took and he'd stay up late waiting on us. He'd set by his window and watch us jump the rocks to cross the creek. He knew our daddy and our uncle Dewey and I reckon he liked us, because he never did arrest us. He just let us go and do our little job. He never gave us trouble. Never said a word to nobody. Years later, we got to talking at one of our shows, and he said it touched his heart to see young boys hauling liquor out in the dark so late. "I was watching you," he told me, "but I wouldn't bother you."

The deputy sheriff understood we were just doing a job. He knew bootlegging was just another way to make a living. A lot of people have a misunderstanding about moonshiners. They think they're a bunch of outlaws like you see in the movies. Some may have been, but not in our area. Most every family had somebody in the bootleg liquor business. On the Smith side of my family, one of 'em made whiskey and another worked for the sheriff and somehow or other they fell out. The brother that was the law went to the woods and shot up the brother's moonshine still so he couldn't make whiskey for a while.

About the only killing I can recall related to bootlegging was the murder of the Rose brothers, over on Rabbit Ridge. I'm just going by hearsay, you understand, because I was just a boy when it happened. Alvin and Bennie Rose went to a party one night up on Rabbit Ridge, and they disappeared. The way I understand it, they were murdered in the house and they were dragged off somewhere down in the woods. Nobody ever saw them again. Come summertime, a lady was out picking blueberries and come up on the bones, a pair of skeletons laying by a fence; some animals picked 'em clean. It turned out bootlegging was at the bottom of it, bootlegging and women both, and a fellow named Harrison Hale went to the pen over it.

A killing was rare, though. Bootlegging was mostly just hard work and drudgery like any other manual labor. It was illegal, but there's no more honest labor outside the law I know of. I helped out a few times, and I'll tell you, making liquor is a hard job. You put fifty-pound bags of sugar or cornmeal on your shoulder and start through the woods a mile or more; see, you had to get way back out of the way in some deep hollow or you'd get caught. Then you had wait and cook that mash; then you had to carry the liquor back out of the woods, and that's heavy, too. Everything was done by hand, and on foot, and you mostly had to do it at night.

We'd get paid $12 a gallon carrying a couple of jugs in old Kroger grocery sacks. We could make almost $25 each on those runs, and that was good money in them days. Maybe you needed a shirt or some shoes or a good workhorse, and that extra money was the only way you could get those things. My mother may have suspected what we were doing, but we never told her. We'd say we were heading off to school and change into work clothes at my uncle's house, then back into our school clothes, so I don't think she ever knew for sure.

Some of the boys running the liquor off that still would sample the stuff. And they'd take more than just a drink or two. Carter had a taste for it right from the start. He made friends with moonshine and he always loved it. Years later, we'd be staying on Smith Ridge with our mother, a-laying up for a few days' rest from playing shows. Before we'd head back on the road, Carter set up in the front seat and got a gleam in his eye. He'd tell me to pull the car around and head down the mountain and stop by our uncle's. "Gonna get me some of Dewey's finest," he'd say.

Back then, I never cared for the moonshine much, not the taste or the way it made me feel. Some of that stuff could take the hide off you. Even if I had liked it, at that time I wouldn't have fooled with it. I felt like I knew I'd be letting my mother down if I'd a-gotten drunk. We was all she had.

We knew we couldn't fill our daddy's shoes, but I helped my mother more than Carter did. I was always more of a homeboy than Carter was. I didn't care to go to places and meet with the public and maybe get to drinking like he did. Carter was more forward about meeting people and he liked to get out and go to parties and have a good time. I never was much for that; I never wanted to run around like that. But it didn't bother me a bit that Carter done it. That was his business and his right, I reckon. I always liked to stay with my mother and be with her around the farm; I knew she needed help with the chores. She couldn't do it all alone.

Up on the ridge, things could get awful slow and we always looked forward to the times we'd go into town. The biggest town close by was Clintwood, the county seat. It wasn't more than a few hundred people, but it had a main street with a soda shop, pharmacy, and a movie house.

The Mullins Theater was where Carter and I would go to the Saturday afternoon matinees and watch a double feature, usually a couple of cowboy movies that was popular then. The Mullins Theater was where we saw our first Hollywood picture, *Jesse James*. Tyrone Power played Jesse, and Henry Fonda played his brother Frank. Westerns have been my favorite ever since, and this being the first one, it had a big effect on us. We could really identify with the James brothers, not so much wanting to be outlaws or desperadoes or nothing like that. It was the way Frank and Jesse stuck up for each other, no matter what, like when Jesse came to bust Frank out of jail. That's how Carter and me felt, too: us against the world. Instead of robbing banks and trains, though, we were going to make our fame and fortune in music.

Years later, the Jesse James movie helped me get a new song. People always ask me how I write songs and I tell them I don't rightly know. I can't do it on my own, that's for sure. Songs come to me like dreams. Something from that movie stuck with me. It just crossed my mind one night, and I wrote "Jesse James Prayed." I've always thought there's some good in every man. I don't care how mean he is, there's some good in him. The image come to me, when Jesse gets shot at the end, there's a "Home Sweet Home" sign on the wall and he'd quit his robbing and was trying to do right, back with his wife and family. That's why I was defending him in the song: *Before every raid, Jesse James prayed/Maybe Jesse was a God-loving man.* It was my way of giving Jesse James some credit. I believe there was some good in him, even if he was an outlaw.

Most of the time we went to Clintwood on Saturdays, which was court day, a big draw for people from all around these parts. There was all sorts of cases and trials, and you'd have folks crowding into the Dickenson County Courthouse to watch the lawyers go at it. Carter and me would sit there all day while our mother did her shopping and run errands. There was always something interesting to watch, from chicken stealing all the way to murder and rape. Carter really enjoyed listening to them sweet-talking country lawyers, the way they'd befriend a jury and defend a man who nobody else would. I reckon he picked up a few pointers he used later onstage as an MC; he saw how words can touch people's hearts.

I can still recall the faces of people sitting in the jury box, the local men and women come to court in their dusty overalls and homespun dresses. Working folk from places like Caney Ridge and Dog Branch and Lick Creek. These were the people from the far deep hollows, the ones scratching out a living on the steep hillsides and way up the creek branches. Not the town fathers and the coal company owners, but the mountaineers. Along with the miners, they were the first Stanley Brothers fans. These were our people, the people in the songs and the people we'd sing to. It was only ten years or so later that we'd be playing our music for 'em in one-room schools and theaters and union halls and even in courthouses like this one, wherever we could draw a crowd.

Anyhow, Carter done his best to help out in other ways, to bring some money in. One time he helped his friend, Carl Hammons and Carl's dad, try to start their own coal mine; they dug a hole in the side of a hill and took a mule in there and made a go of it and then quit. Said it felt like a rat to be crawling in the dark. They'd seen enough to know they wasn't cut out for mining.

Good thing for us there was plenty aboveground to keep us busy. We had some timber on our land, and Carter and me would get out and cut what they call mining timbers, four-foot-long planks they used in the mines to hold up the top of the shaft. We'd go in the woods on Smith Ridge and we'd take a two-man saw and cut a pile of timbers and sell 'em to the mines to make a little extra money.

We took odd jobs anywhere we could; we even worked for a while at my dad's sawmill business. Since he'd moved to the next county over in Russell and started another family, he was doing good for himself. We didn't see him much at all, but he'd always give us work if we needed it. He worked us good, too. Me and Carter were a couple of green boys, maybe fifteen and sixteen years old at the most, and we just did what we were told. I never had to work in a mine, but the sawmill was enough for me. It was brutish.

Back then they didn't have buzz saws and chain saws to help you out. They just had the old crosscut saws, the kind with one man on each end. Now, that was a job, let me tell you. But that wasn't the job I done. My job was what they called rolling dust. It was supposed to be the easy job, but there wasn't nothing easy about it, to my way of thinking.

Here's how we did it. They had what they called a skidway that they'd haul the logs on. They had a man who rolled them logs up on a carriage, and the carriage ran through a triple saw, and they had a man pushing those logs into that saw. Then they had a sawyer who handled the saw and there was a whole lot of dust everywhere. So you had a hole to get rid of all the sawdust, and you had to have a man for that. And that was my job, rolling that dust as the logs rolled across that hole where the saw blade ran. I had a wheelbarrow and I'd pick the pile of sawdust off there with a shovel and then roll it off.

It wears you out fast. The logs keep coming and the dust pile keeps rising and it never stops, not until quitting time. I only done that for a few days; I didn't like it a bit. They put way too much dust in that hole.

When my dad left, there was just the three of us, Carter and me and my mother. And he left my mother high and dry on Smith Ridge, without a penny of help. He never did give any money to my mother, for child support or for anything. My mother could have tried to get it, I reckon, and taken him to court over it, but she decided not to go that route. I do know there was hard feelings on both sides. And my daddy even tried to come back to Smith Ridge and get a team of horses. My mother wouldn't let him have the horses. When my dad came back from a trip to Texas he took with his new wife, why, my mother had sold the horses, and he wasn't a bit happy about it.

You can see what my mother was up against. Here she was left by herself with two growing boys to feed. "Ralph, it's just you, me and Carter now," she told me. "We've got to make it on our own." And so we did. She was determined and that counts for a lot. She raised her garden and she raised us boys. Somehow she always found a way to make ends meet and I never heard her complain.

We couldn't have gotten by without my mother's garden. She'd hoe corn and take one or two bushels to the mill and trade it out in groceries. She had a scrubboard to wash our clothes and she made soap from boiling lye and meat rinds. The garden was our saving grace, along with our milk cow, Pied. We always had plenty of butter and eggs and vegetables, tomatoes and turnip greens and Irish potatoes and Hanover beans, not only for us but enough to peddle at the lumber camps, where there were people down the mountain worse off.

The nearest camp to us was at Fremont, where the W. M. Ritter Lumber Company had built a band mill at the mouth of the Big Branch of McClure River. There was another band mill about a mile south on the river. This is where they'd haul the lumber from all parts of Dickenson County and they'd dress it at the band mills. At the time, Ritter was one of the biggest hardwood lumber companies in the world. They had a contract to clear all the mining properties for Clinchco Coal Company, and they were cutting the forests down like there was no tomorrow.

The workers at the Freemont camp were our best customers. It was a hard life they had. They didn't have a house to live in or land for garden. They were logging men with their families, and they lived out of railroad cars near the sawmill operation by the river. There'd be twenty railroad cars pulled over on a siding, one family to a car. When the garden came in, we'd take down whatever we had and peddle to them. We'd peck on the door of the rail cars and ask what they needed. We'd sell them fresh fruit and vegetables. Then we'd take the money we made to the commissary and get flour and baking soda and such, all the things we couldn't raise up or make ourselves.

We always got by, but it wasn't the same without our daddy. I knew how it hurt my mother, but I never thought much about how it affected Carter and me. When you're young, you don't think about what you're going through. You don't dwell on it. You just live from one day to the next.

Thinking back on it now, though, I believe Lee leaving hit Carter harder than it did me, him being older and so much like my dad in his looks and his ways. So he just set aside how he was feeling, and the way he handled the hurt was by leaving the scene that made him sad, and to go out and have his fun. He was more freewheeling than I was. Me, I was quiet, kept to myself. He liked to get out and have a good time and he didn't worry much about nothing. He'd go play poker and hunt coons and fight chickens with friends like Carl Hammons, who lived on Flat Top Ridge about a mile from us; they'd do just about anything you could think of without hurting anybody. They'd bet like the devil on those roosters, down the mountain close by Tom's Creek.

Coon hunting was about the only sport where I'd join Carter. It's a real adventure when you're a boy out at night, running the woods with the dogs and your big brother. It was a way to get out of the house and forget about our family troubles for a while. Takes your mind off everything to see a big coon up in a tree.

Outside of coon hunting and music, though, I didn't fool around much. I was more levelheaded as a boy than Carter. I thought more about our situation at home with our dad gone, and I knew I had to help my mother because she didn't have nobody else. So while Carter'd be out fighting chickens, I'd be back home feeding chickens with my mother. We'd milk the cows and churn the butter, and I'd help her hoe out the garden, put in the crops and bring in the harvest. Pick beans and corns and stuff, whatever I could do. When we were canning, she needed help getting those lids on good and tight. You have to keep that lid airtight, with the metal piece in there that's got the seal, and the lid would pop when you'd tighten it up right. I split wood and plowed and picked up the big rocks that cropped up in the fields come spring; all the heavy work around the farm, the things you have to have a man take care of.

Helping my mother didn't bother me. When you're needed, you know what you're doing is important. You know it makes a difference. By now I was going to high school and I didn't like it any better than at Big Oak. At school, it didn't make a bit of difference if I was there or not. Nobody missed me, and I didn't miss nobody there.

It was a long trip to school, and that was another reason I wasn't there sometimes. Ervinton High School was in Nora, several miles down the mountain the way the crow flies, and by road, it was a lot longer. There was a little back road winding down Smith Ridge that went to Nora, and that's the way Carter and me went to school. We lived on a dirt road, and we had to walk two-and-a-half miles to the paved road. It would be just about daylight when we'd catch the bus to the high school, because we'd see it coming and the driver would shut off the headlights about the time it pulled up to where we got on. Well, we never did have a school bus exactly. The last couple years I was in high school, a neighbor took a pickup truck and built some benches across the back, and that was how we rode to and from school. We didn't care much about getting there at all, and the only subject that I was interested in was agriculture.

One thing we did like at school was the theater plays they used to have; it gave us a chance to perform our music in front of an audience, and it was good training. They'd have a junior or senior class play in the auditorium, and the school drama club would give us a spot or two during the intermissions. Between the acts, they'd pull the curtain down to change the scenery and the sets, and we'd step out in front of the curtains and play a few numbers, maybe "Branded Wherever I Go" or maybe a song we heard on the *Opry*. A friend named Jewel Martin joined us onstage sometimes; he played the mandolin a little and he helped us out. We went over pretty well, and your classmates can be a tough crowd. But I reckon they liked the Stanley Brothers as much as they liked the Shakespeare.

One day, after we'd come off the stage, the school principal took us aside and gave us some advice: "When are you boys going to throw down that old music and get you a good education so you can make a decent living and make something of yourselves?" He wasn't trying to get nasty, just trying to be helpful. He was being honest with us; he didn't believe in music as a career. He didn't think we could make it with music, and that's how everybody felt back in them days. We knew he meant well, but all it did was make us more determined to make it as professional musicians. Carter told the principal we was going to be famous no matter what it took, and one day we'd come home wrapped in glory. And not too many years later he did come back in glory, when thousands of Stanley Brothers fans gathered around Carter's coffin in the very same school auditorium where we stood that day. He'd made his dream come true but it cost him everything.

At high school, Carter was as popular as ever. He was smart so he didn't have to study hard to get by. Classes didn't much hold his interest; his favorite subject was the same one as in elementary school, pranking, and he got straight A's in that. He'd tease the girls and pinch 'em in the rear. He'd steal the chalk pieces from the blackboard when the teacher wasn't looking; then he'd break 'em into little pieces and he'd fling 'em at the back of your head, and when they hit, he'd play innocent. He'd burn you up and then swear for all his life that it wasn't him that done it.

Now, if anybody else done that, it wouldn't've been tolerated; Carter could get away with it because he was Carter. He'd go out at recess and smoke cigarettes and pitch pennies with the other boys. They were tough to beat at penny flipping. They had a system worked out. Carter would rub his head to give a signal so his friends would know if it was going to be heads or tails; they'd win a few pennies and go buy a bag of hard candy.

He'd have a thousand ways to have fun and make trouble; he thought school was a waste of time because he was already set on being a professional musician. Much as he goofed off, he made pretty good grades. And much as he teased everybody and stirred up trouble wherever he could, he was everybody's favorite. That's because he had personality. He was president of his class and head of the local chapter of the Future Farmers of America. The girls liked him and the boys loved him.

Uncle Sam liked Carter, too. Right after his graduation, he was called into the service. It would be almost two years before I'd see him again.

It was lonesome without Carter. He may not have been around as much as before my dad left, but he was still my big brother and my singing buddy. That was probably the worst, not having him around to play music with. No matter how different our personalities were, music was something I could count on to bring us together.

I don't know how I'd a-made it without him if hadn't been for Patsy. She had big sad eyes and she was just as sweet as sugar. Next to Carter, she was about the best friend I had growing up, and when he went into the Air Force, me and Patsy spent just about every day together.

Now, you may be asking, just who is this Patsy and what made her so wonderful? Well, I'm about to tell you. She was an old spotted gray mare, and she was the best horse I've ever known.

We had owned plenty of horses and mules, and there were plenty not worth two cents for all the trouble. We got hold of one horse that was so mean you couldn't do nothing with him. So Carter and me, we wanted to whip him, but we was afraid to stand on the ground next to him where he could get after us a-kicking and a-biting. We tied him to the trunk of the apple tree and we climbed up on the branches so he couldn't get to us, and we really poured it on him and whipped him good. It didn't help, though. He was still mean and ornery as ever, so we finally swapped him for a nicer horse; but before we did we got to give him a couple of good whippings.

So you can see it wasn't very easy to find a good-tempered workhorse like Old Patsy. She was special, not only because she was mine but because she understood me so well. I believe she could just about read my mind. She was iron gray with dark specks on her coat, a real pretty color. When I bought her, she was seven years old and still in her prime.

My uncle knew about Old Patsy from a neighbor. He'd heard good things about her habits, and he helped me find her. The man who sold her to me said she made a good workhorse, one of the best he'd ever seen, and he wasn't lying. He was a straight shooter, and me just a boy, he didn't want to cheat me.

Getting a fair deal was no sure thing. I'd seen a man get rooked at the jockey grounds outside Clintwood, where they'd gather at a certain place and have horse swaps every Saturday for the locals. The called it jockey-ground trade day. This fellow loved horses and he loved to socialize, too. Well, this time he drank more than his share and got too much whiskey in him. He had a good horse but he wanted a better one, and he saw a real good-looking brown mare prancing in the sunshine he thought was a real find. She was pretty and she could really step. Now, this horse belonged to a professional horse trader, and the drunk fellow made the swap straight up, one horse for the other, and he shook the dealer's hand like he'd won the lottery.

But when he took the saddle off her, he saw there was a great big sore on that horse's back. He didn't like the looks of it and he said so, but it was too late to change his mind, so he figured there are worse things than a sore. We headed back in high style anyhow, this fellow leading the way on his new horse like he was off to the Kentucky Derby. On the ride home, though, the horse started falling behind, and by the time we made the ten miles all the way back, her head was a-dragging the ground and she could just barely go. What happened was, some of the shady traders, they used special narcotics, real strong stuff, that would pep up a horse. It could fool anybody until that dope ran out and then the horse wouldn't be good for nothing. The fellow got to cursing and the horse just stood there, tail too limp to swat a fly. I felt bad for him, and I felt worse for the horse.

You have to watch out for the professional traders; that's where the other man is smarter than you. You need to look over whatever you're trading for or you'll get taken bad. Like with cattle—you can judge cows by their bag, you know, where they give milk, and their titties need to be smooth or you're asking for trouble. Now, the first thing a horseman will do is check a horse's teeth; I used to tell their age looking at their teeth. There's a lot of things about a cow or a horse you have to look at.

I've got cheated myself several times, but I had better luck on my first horse deal than that poor fellow, thanks to my uncle looking out for me. Patsy didn't come cheap. I paid $175 for her, and that was a high price, but she was worth it. She wasn't only a good workhorse, she was my companion and she never done me wrong.

There ain't a horse ever lived could listen better than Old Patsy. She never nickered or balked, always did what she was told, even when she was tired. You didn't need any cinch lines on Old Patsy to make her go this way or that way. All you had to do was talk to her gentle-like and she knew exactly what to do. If I wanted her to go right, I'd say, "Gee," and if I wanted her to go left, I'd say, "Haw," and if I wanted her to stop, I'd say, "Whoooah," and that was all there was to it.

Lord, Old Patsy was one to work; she'd pull a plow or wagon sled, haul logs or brush, whatever you needed done. She'd do it, and then she'd be waiting on you when you were finished, to start on the next chore. One time, me and Old Patsy plowed the garden for my half sister Ruby, and we done so good, Ruby gave me a chocolate pie. I ate that whole pie myself, but I reckon I oughta've shared it with Old Patsy, seeing as she did most of the work.

Come Sunday, when every work animal around was getting their rest, Old Patsy was ready for more. Rain or shine, she'd take us to Sunday morning prayer service, which was more than a mile of rough mountain road called Rush Branch down to the McClure Primitive Baptist Church. Many a time I'd saddle Old Patsy and my mother'd crawl on back and set in the saddle, her bonnet pulled on tight. I'd walk alongside, whispering to Patsy to keep her calm all the way down Rush Branch. My mother was no spring chicken, but Old Patsy made that ride as smooth as she could, like she knew the woman riding on her back meant more than the world to me. Old Patsy wouldn't let my mother get hurt for nothing.

I've had some fine horses in my day. Back in the 1970s, I had a Tennessee walking horse, and I've still got a couple of fine-looking mares out back now. But I've never had a horse I loved as much as Old Patsy.

As hard as Old Patsy worked, I have to tell you my mother had her beat. Nobody worked more than Lucy Stanley, especially after our daddy left. She buried the hurt and went to scraping by for us the best she knew how. She wore holes in her stockings and dresses, so she could buy us school clothes and whatnot. She'd barter for whatever we needed, the things we couldn't raise ourselves, like sugar and flour. No matter what it cost her, she went without so we could have a little something.

The way she kept going puts me in mind of the woman who at eighty finally caught herself being idle and said, "This is the first time in my life I've sat down with folded hands." In my mother's case, the only thing that could ever quiet those hands was her arthritis. I remember how sad she looked when she told me the arthritis had finally took hold so bad she couldn't make biscuits from scratch anymore.

Whatever good in Carter and me come from her. She was our touchstone, not just growing up, but later on, too, when we were full-grown men and traveling musicians. We'd always come back to Smith Ridge for a home-cooked meal from our mother's kitchen. So much of our music comes from our mother, not just in the singing we heard in the church, but what she meant to us, and it came out in so many songs Carter wrote, like "Memories of Mother" and "Visions of Mother."

If I'm putting her on a pedestal, I reckon she deserves it, after a life scrubbing floors, hoeing the garden and beating out clothes on the washboard. "We've got to save all the money we can," she'd tell me. "We've got to pinch pennies, we can't waste nothing." And I watched her scrape and barter and stretch every dime. She taught me to use judgment with my money, and it was a good lesson to have when you're young. It helped me out later on, especially running my own band for all these years. I've heard musicians pass up on a show they had booked, and they'd say, "I don't believe I'll go on Sunday to play because there's a ball game on, and I'm going to lay around the house and watch it on TV." But I never did that; I always put my work before pleasure. I have my mother to thank for that.

Even my mom needed a break sometime, so I came up with a plan. There was a company that gave you a premium if you sold so many garden seeds. So I went out in the neighborhood and sold enough seeds so I could get a little fiddle they offered as a premium. And I tried to learn the fiddle so my mother'd have somebody to play banjo with. That got her back in music a bit, just for fun and to go see people and to pass the time. Some neighbors would invite us on weekends and we'd go around and play for them. We did old-time dance songs she used to do: "Boil the Cabbage Down," "Cindy," "Cripple Creek" and "Old Joe Clark," and of course her favorite, "Shout Little Lulie."

I couldn't do much on fiddle, to tell you the truth, but nobody could tell the difference and I was decent enough so my mother could get out and enjoy herself and be sociable again. I remember watching her play at these little dances and gatherings and how good it made me feel. What tickled me so much was seeing how happy it made her to play her banjo and feel like young Lucy Smith again. It took her back to her courting days. For a little while anyway, playing music give her some joy.

Carter used to write us a letter every week or so; he'd always say pretty much the same thing: Doing fine and be home soon. But he'd been gone for more than a year and we ain't seen him. Most of the time he was stationed out West for the air force, somewhere in Texas or it may have been Colorado. He was tail gunner on an airplane and he had it pretty good. He never did see any combat, never went overseas at all. He'd always say he was doing well and the military life was treating him just dandy and so forth.

No matter what, he'd always make a mention of our music and what we had planned. It gave us both something to look forward to. He said for me to be ready to start up a band when he got back. The Stanley Brothers was still a team, even if we were separated by the war.

Then came the day both me and my mother had been dreading. I got my call from Uncle Sam, and I had to leave Smith Ridge. I was going into the army.

Chapter Four

Banjo Man

"You ask me, stranger, why I made this journey
Why I crossed three thousand miles of rolling waves
Like many others, my love was killed in action
So I'm here searching for his grave"

—"Soldier's Grave," the Stanley Brothers

When I went overseas for the army, I was just a scared mountain kid. Until then, I had never stayed away from home but maybe two nights. I hadn't been anywhere, not far anyhow, and I didn't know red lights from green lights. I didn't really know nothing, to tell you straight, and I was afraid of the big wide world outside our mountains. Here I was in Germany, thousands of miles and across the ocean from Dickenson County, for more than a year. Those were some lonesome days for me. It wasn't much fun at first, but in the end it done me a world of good.

Going to serve your country was nothing special where I come from. It was what you did if you could, and it's still that way today. The "Fighting Ninth" congressional district, stretching from the far southwestern tip of Virginia through my home county of Dickenson all the way to Roanoke, got its nickname from all the men from there who've fought for their country.

Mountains make fighting men. No matter where in the world you go, you'll find that's true. It's a fact the Appalachians have always made some of the best soldiers. Been that way for generations and for many a war. They've won more Medals of Honor than men from other parts of the country, and most were born and raised in the mountains of eastern Kentucky and eastern Tennessee and southwest Virginia. Some say it's because so many are old-time Baptists who believe in predestination and because of that they believe God has it all ordained from on high no matter what they do. So maybe they're braver in battle and put their life on the line and do dangerous things that ordinary men wouldn't do.

Some of that may be right, but I don't think it tells why so many mountain boys, all those ones who aren't Baptists or believers, are so willing to stand up and fight and die for their country. I'd say it comes down more to honor and duty. There used to be a saying, "upon your honor," you'd hear a lot back in the mountains, but you don't hear it nowadays. It meant your word was as good as the truth in your dealings with other people. And that goes for your country as much as your neighbor or anybody. So you uphold your honor and you do your duty, and when Uncle Sam calls you, you go. Seems like for a lot of men borned in the coalfields, nothing comes easy no matter what you do.

I'll never get to find out what I'd have done in combat. By the time I went into the army, the war was over. It was May of 1945, two weeks after my high school graduation. I did my basic training in Camp Gordon, Georgia, then I shipped out to occupied Germany. I'd never seen much more water than McClure River, and the ten-day boat ride across the Atlantic seemed more like ten years. About all I remember was the smell from all the seasick soldiers throwing up down in the hold.

When we got to Bremerhaven, I went into the infantry with General Patton's Third Army. The fighting was done with, but there was a lot of work to do because the whole country was tore up from the Allied bombing. We were there to try to restore some order or, to put it plain, to start cleaning up the mess.

We mostly did a lot of what they called disarming missions. We'd go on search parties through the villages and go house to house and get up all the guns. We didn't find much, because the German people were pretty much down to nothing. On one raid, I got a .32 Walther pistol from the duffel bag of a German soldier who'd been killed. I'm not much into guns, but that was a fine pistol. You were allowed to bring one gun back as a souvenir and so I picked the .32 Walther.

Now, we didn't have to dodge bullets on the front lines, but it was some dangerous work. The fighting was over, but we were still in enemy territory. We didn't know what we were going to turn up in those quiet little houses in those little towns and villages. Your nerves would get on edge because you didn't know what to expect. Sometimes I seen the soldiers break down the door with the rifles and knock the men and women down and just take everything they had.

The disarming duty didn't last long, because I got promoted pretty soon. It had nothing to do with what kind of a soldier I was, though. It was all on account of my old-time banjo picking.

Not long after getting to Germany, I got hold of a banjo from Special Services. It was nothing much, but I was happier with that than any weapon you could have put in my hands. One night, it must have been four in the morning, I was feeling lonesome and couldn't sleep, so I started fooling around on the five-string. Then I hear a knock on the door. It's a lieutenant colonel and a captain wanting to talk with me. Here I was, just a private. I figured maybe I was making too much racket and disturbing the peace.

But Captain White and Colonel Lorenz liked the sound of my banjo and they had come by my room to hear more. Back at that time, banjos had gone out of fashion. Course, way back in the mountains, they stayed popular as they always had been. For these officers, a banjo was something different, especially the backwoods way I played. So they were excited to have a real banjo man in the barracks, especially this Colonel Lorenz. They asked me to play a tune or two for them. I picked a few old standbys, "Cripple Creek," "Shout Little Lulie," and they really enjoyed it, especially when I lit into "Lulie." You know, I have yet to meet the man, woman or child who don't get happy when they hear me play "Lulie."

Anyhow, I didn't think any more about it. I was just happy I wasn't in any trouble. A few days later, they called me into headquarters and made me a mail clerk, what they called a T-5. That's about the same as corporal but it's office duty. So I had my own room, no bed check, no nothing. My banjo gave me privileges and saved me many a morning from having to get up early and answer reveille.

So I'd play banjo for them once in a while. I wasn't that good yet, but they didn't know any different. At that time, I was still learning how to pick the two-finger style, so I done a lot of old clawhammer tunes my mother had taught me. So many people back then thought of the banjo as a comedy instrument, something silly. I wanted these top officers to hear what a banjo could really do. Then I'd throw in some lines you used to hear at a corn-shucking late of a night:

Wish I had a big fat horse and corn to feed him on
And a pretty little girl to stay at home and feed him while I'm gone

Those officers really got a kick out of those old dance tunes. I'd see the feet start a-tapping, and that's when I could see that behind those uniforms with all the fancy stripes, they were regular folks like anybody else. I remember the captain, he was from California, and Colonel Lorenz was from some other big city out West. It made me feel good to know people outside the mountains enjoyed the banjo as much as I did. A banjo was something different to them, and it really put me up in their eyes. It was the first time I saw old-time music as something to be proud of.

A few months later, they called me for another promotion, this time down at headquarters. I was made an S-2 sergeant in intelligence, a tech sergeant, which was more office duties. Now I really had it made. We were stationed in a little town called Bad Aibling, about sixty miles from Munich, and I had an office of my own, and a lot of classified, top secret information went through there. I'd ride a jeep with the mail on deliveries every week, rain or shine. I had no idea what was in those mailbags and didn't want to know.

One time I made a run across the border into Austria close by the Alps. I saw those great high snowy peaks up against the sky, jagged as a bunch of daggers. They looked dangerous to me, and I didn't want no part of it. It just made me homesick for the Clinch Mountains I was used to back home.

I'll tell you how good I had it over there, all because of my banjo. One time, I was in the office and Colonel Lorenz busted in with some big news.

"Sergeant Stanley! Guess what. Orders just come in that soldiers that's been in the army eighteen months and served a year overseas are eligible for a discharge. You can go home, Sergeant Stanley!"

I was so surprised, I didn't know what to say, so I just let it rip: "You're a big fat liar!"

That's how good I was in with the top brass like Colonel Lorenz. If anybody else talked to them like that, they'd a-been locked in the brig for thirty days. The colonel didn't want to see me in the brig or discharged; he wanted me to go to officer training school. "If you stay in with us, the sky's the limit," he said. "We'll move you to second lieutenant in three weeks and then after a while we'll make you a first lieutenant. We'll send you right on up."

It sounded all right, but I kept thinking about the plans me and Carter had made. So I told him I wasn't interested. I was going home.

Now, the army was good to me and it was good *for* me, too. I learned a lot of things. Even with the privileges I had on account of the banjo, I still had to toe the line same as the other men. The military taught me discipline and responsibility and what it was to put the many ahead of the one. But the best thing was that I had got some confidence. When I first come into the army, I couldn't hardly speak to anyone, I was so bashful. But the way I was treated by those officers helped me break out of my shell. They made me feel I was worth something.

Yes, sir, I had a right good time in Germany; I learned some of the language and saw some of the country. And I was proud to wear the uniform, but I didn't want to make a career out of it. I already had a career in mind: playing music with my brother back in Virginia. So I said thank you to Colonel Lorenz for all he'd done for me and I played him a farewell song. He wished me good luck, and I knew deep down that he was going to miss my banjo more than he was going to miss me.

The trip back seemed longer than it took to get there. First I had to catch a train to Bremerhaven. Then I got a ship and sailed to New York, and after a few days I got my discharge out of Camp Shanks. It wasn't until I got on a Greyhound bus heading south to good ole Virginia that I knew I was finally going home, and all the way down I was thinking of how great it was going to be back home.

Carter had got out of the service six months before me, and straight away he got a job in a professional hillbilly band. It happened that quick and easy, like most things did for Carter. He was getting his discharge at Fort Meade when he met with another local boy heading back to southwest Virginia. He was a fiddler by the name of Roy Sykes, and they hit it off. Sykes was from the little town of Haysi, a few miles from Smith Ridge. He had his own band, the Blue Ridge Mountain Boys, and he invited Carter to join up as lead singer and guitarist. They had their own daily radio program on WNVA in Norton, and things were looking up.

They played shows all around the area, and they'd take anything they could get, from store openings to Elks Lodge halls. They even played a basket picnic sponsored by the High Knob Rod and Gun Club of Norton, where they shared the bill with a professional bait-and-fly caster. After Carter joined, they started to get more of a real following; Sykes was needing a full-time banjo player, and Carter had told him about me.

Riding the bus home, I already had my first paying music job lined up. Here I was, still in my teens and I was on my way. When the Greyhound rolled into Bristol, Carter and my dad were waiting at the bus station. Carter looked like a million dollars. His time with Uncle Sam had done him good. He was lean and hale, like my dad, Lee, in his prime. When he saw me get off the bus, he hollered and ran over to me there and took my bag off my shoulder. He lit into a big grin and showed off his a gold tooth. "There were two things I wanted when I went into the service," he said. "A gold tooth and some tattoos. And now I've got 'em!"

He pulled up his sleeve to show me the tattoo running down his forearm. It was the "DEATH BEFORE DISHONOR" dagger insignia a lot of men get when they're in the military. Then he pulled up his other sleeve.

It was a heart with an arrow going through it, with the word "MOTHER" alongside. Carter loved our mother something fierce and he had missed her a lot, and that's why he got her name tattooed on his arm. But I also think he done that because he figured she couldn't get too mad at him for getting some tattoos if he used some of that ink to remember her by.

I reckon he had enough tattoos and gold teeth for the both of us. I never went in for that sort of thing. Any gold on my person I would rather keep safe in my pocket. And I never did want a tattoo. To my way of thinking, all a tattoo does is make you a marked man. You might want to leave the scene and go somewhere, and a tattoo is a dead giveaway. The police or anybody that wants to can find you too easy.

I was so busy having my reunion with Carter, I almost forgot about my dad. Standing next to Carter, Lee was like a stranger, mostly because of how much he'd aged. He was pushing sixty, and all those years working sawmills in the woods had worked on him good. Whatever hard feelings I had about him leaving my mother and us boys didn't much matter right then. I was just glad he was here to give us a ride to the station. I reckon maybe he was making up for lost time.

Seeing my dad made me think of our mother, all alone back up on Smith Ridge. I'd been gone from the old home place for so long, and I know how bad she'd missed me. I was thinking I should be headed home just now, to check on her and help with some of the chores and make sure she was doing all right. My mother maybe was needing me. Or maybe it was me needing her. Carter must have seen the worried look on my face.

"Ma's doing fine," he said. "She's just as happy as can be that we're both finally back home now, and she's all the way behind us to go sing on the radio."

Then he looked me straight in the eye, and he was serious.

"Don't you be worrying about her," he said. "Just worry about yourself. Are you ready to play some music or what?"

The band was playing their radio show at three o'clock that afternoon. We drove straight to the station, where I changed out of my uniform and strapped on my banjo, and I sang a song with Carter before I even got home. Then we played a show that night. And I hadn't even had a chance to see my mother, after more than a year overseas. That's how my life in the music business started and I've been at it ever since.

I worked three weeks with the Sykes band. We put on a good show, with comedy and the whole works. I didn't sing much, just picked the banjo. That suited me fine, because I was still bashful when it came to stepping up to the microphone. I'd rather stand back and let somebody else do the singing. Carter did some old-time brother duet numbers with the mandolin player, Pee Wee Lambert. He and Carter sounded good together and I liked Pee Wee as a man right off.

The thing was, though, I didn't like the setup with Roy Sykes. There was two reasons: musical and personal. Sykes was the fiddler and leader, but he liked to mess around with the banjo some, too. On most of the songs, I'd pick the banjo and that was fine. But if there was a special banjo tune featured, Sykes would walk across the stage and take the banjo from me and strap it on and then he'd play the banjo while I'd have to stand there and watch. I didn't like a man taking my instrument and stealing the spotlight and making me feel a fool. I don't think he took me or my banjo serious enough, and I didn't see much of a future in that.

Besides, I didn't go for the way Sykes ran things. It was too much fooling around after the shows. All the boys in the band would sit around until one or two o'clock in the morning having their fun and wasting time and me sitting around and waiting on them to call it a night. I wanted to get home and get some sleep. I'd been in the army and I was used to being on time and getting to bed early and getting up early and getting things done right. All through my career, I play the show and then I like to go hit the sack, no matter where I'm at. Maybe that's why I'm still playing at eighty-two years old, because I got my proper rest all those years.

The biggest reason was, I didn't want to work in another man's band, not this one anyhow. I wanted to have my own band with Carter, like the way we'd always planned it. I was more business about it than I was about the pleasure, right from the start. It was a job to me. Music was what I wanted to do and I wanted to make a living out of it. I wanted to find out if I could do that. If I couldn't pull it off, I wanted to pursue something else. So for me, it was now or never. That's just the way I was at that age, stubborn as an old mule. I couldn't change for any man, not for Roy Sykes or nobody else.

I didn't talk to Sykes about it. I got Carter aside and told him I was leaving the band. I said if he wanted to start our own band with me like we'd always talked about, I was ready to do that. If not, then I was going to do something else. Do the GI Bill and enroll in veterinary school and try a career doctoring animals. I was pretty firm, and it sort of surprised me that I had that in me, he being my older brother and all.

"If you want to organize our own outfit, we'll do it," I told him. "If not, I'm just going to step out on my own and you can go ahead and do what you want to do."

Now, Carter liked working in Sykes's band and he was having a real good time, and he had nothing to complain about. He never had any notion of pulling out until I told him how I felt. I didn't know how he would take it. But he was with me all the way. He'd made his mind up we were going to make it as professional entertainers, and we were going to stick together no matter what, and nothing was going to stop us. Now was as good a time as any to see what we could do.

"I'm ready to do that," he said. "If you're not happy and well satisfied, we'll give notice right now."

And that's what he did. And naturally, when Pee Wee Lambert found out what were planning, he was ready to come right along with us.

"Wherever you boys go," said Pee Wee, "I'll go, too."

Let me tell you a little about Pee Wee Lambert. Without Pee Wee the story of the Stanley Brothers would have been a lot different than it turned out. We would probably still have made it sooner or later, but it would've been probably a lot later, and it would've been only half as fun if he hadn't been right there from the very beginning.

Pee Wee's career started on the road. He was hitchhiking from his hometown of Thacker, West Virginia, on his way over the mountains to Matewan. Hitchhiking was very common then because cars were still rare and too expensive for most people living back in the hills. This was in Mingo County, close by the Kentucky line. There was a lot of trouble there in 1920, when the coal miners tried to unionize and there was a big shoot-out and there were people laying dead in the streets. The big coal bosses crushed the strike and the miners lost.

Pee Wee was of the same mind as me and Carter about the mines; he didn't want to spend his life down in those dark holes. He wanted to see the country and breathe the fresh air and play music. He'd got his start playing his brother's mandolin, and after he heard Bill Monroe on the *Opry,* it was the only sound he really loved.

On this Saturday morning, Pee Wee was walking along the highway, carrying his mandolin and trying to catch a ride. When you're a musician, waving your instrument is better than trying to use your thumb, because a band might be driving by and be in need of a man, and that's what happened. When Sykes saw that mandolin in Pee Wee's hand, he pulled his car over and said, "Hop on in." By the time he got out of the car, he was already a Blue Ridge Mountain Boy. What got him the job so fast was not only could he play the mandolin like Bill Monroe, he could sing high tenor, real lonesome, just like Bill, too. He even tried to dress like Bill, but he didn't look too much like him. He was a little fellow, maybe five foot five at the most, almost short as I was, and that's how come everybody called him Pee Wee. I don't ever remember anyone calling him by his given name, which was Darrell.

Pee Wee and Carter became close friends in Sykes's band, and Pee Wee took to me right off, too. Me and Carter were so different that if Pee Wee was tired of one brother he could always start fresh with the other. Some people become just like family when you first meet and they stay that way, and that's how it was with Pee Wee. So when Carter and I were ready to leave Sykes, he knew he was going with us. We gave our two weeks' notice and commenced to start our own group.

We put the word out and got us a fiddler, a young boy out of eastern Kentucky named Bobby Sumner. He was from a hollow near Vicco, a little mining town that got its name from the Virginia Iron Coal and Coke Company. He was another one running from the coalfields as fast as his fiddle could take him. Bobby could really tear it up on them old breakdowns like "Blackberry Blossom." Carter used to love the "old greasy fiddle" Bobby played. He gave our music a real kick and he was a pistol on and off the stage.

Right off, we got our own daily program on WNVA in Norton, which was only twenty-five miles or so from Smith Ridge. It was a coal town on Route 23 in Wise County, and you could drive through it in less than five minutes. For us, it was perfect; we could drive out there and do our shows and be back home in the evening.

We had a fifteen-minute show at 7 A.M. every morning. It wasn't the best time slot, and the station only had 250 watts, so the signal wasn't too strong, but it was good enough for us. In those days, it wasn't enough to have your own radio show, you had to have a sponsor, too, to help get your name out to the public. Our first sponsor was Kennedy's Piggly Wiggly chain of grocery stores. A lot of bands used to take their name from their sponsor, but this wasn't the right sort of name to use, much as I liked pigs and all.

Well, we couldn't hardly think of what to call the band. Pretty soon, we got another sponsor, the Clinch Valley Insurance Company, and that gave us the idea for a name. After that, we called ourselves the Stanley Brothers and the Clinch Mountain Boys. It was a good name because it told it just like it was.

In those days, there were a lot of funny names for hillbilly bands—Roy Acuff and the Crazy Tennesseans and so forth—and I think a lot of those boys had the names pushed on them by promoters and record companies to make a stir. One time I heard Roy explain all about that when he was on a country music show on TV and he was talking about the early days, and he said he never did care much for the name "Crazy Tennesseans." When he joined the *Grand Ole Opry,* some big shot in Nashville told him the name was sort of a slur on the state of Tennessee and people might not take kindly to that. "Well, you boys are from the Smoky Mountains, ain't you?" the fellow told Roy. "Why don't you call yourselves the Smoky Mountain Boys?" And that's why Roy changed it.

We were lucky to get the proper name for our band right from the start. The Clinch Mountains was where we came from and who we were. It was straightforward and fit our style. We never tried to be something we weren't. We carried that name around the world and we always tried to do it proud.

CHAPTER FIVE

Farm and Fun Time

"Rolling along, singing a song of home sweet home
Come on along, join in our song, singing our troubles away"

—THEME SONG FROM WCYB'S *FARM AND FUN TIME* SHOW,
THE STANLEY BROTHERS

We were doing fine at the Norton station and played the area for about a month. Then we heard about a radio station down in Bristol, on the Virginia-Tennessee border, not far from where our daddy lived near Lebanon. Now, here was some news we could use. WCYB was a brand-new station, and it broadcast a powerful ten-thousand-watt signal over five states; it was clear-channel 690 and you could really get it strong over hundreds of square miles in Virginia, Tennessee, North Carolina, West Virginia and Kentucky. Back then, that was pretty much the whole world as far as we were concerned.

Our dad went over to the station to find out the details. He was a good businessman and he wanted to help us on our career and get us the best opportunities. He found out they were going to start an hour-long program called *Farm and Fun Time*. It would go on the air every day at noon for an hour and they were looking for some fresh talent to get it started with a bang. Curly King and His Tennessee Hill Toppers had a half-hour Saturday show and he was doing mighty fine on that slot, with weepers like "Whisper Softly, Mother's Dying." He was afraid to chance the new show, and it's hard to blame him. There was no telling how a daily program might do. Maybe the people wouldn't take to it. If the show tanked, the performer would sink along with it.

We were game because we didn't have anything to lose like Curly did. We were green as they come, and we'd never been heard of outside our home territory. Carter was gung-ho from the start. He'd just got married the month before, to Mary Magdalene Kiser from St. Paul, a little railroad town down the tracks from Coeburn over in Russell County. Her parents gave her that name because she was born on Christmas Day. Mary was the sister of a girl who'd married Roy Sykes, so even though we'd left his band, Sykes was still family and there were no hard feelings.

Now Carter had a new wife and new band and he was ready to make his name. He really believed in our talent, and he made us believe, too. I was feeling pretty cocky in my own right because I had got me a new banjo, a real beauty that sounded as good as it looked. At that time, when I wasn't much of a ladies' man, a "banjer," as folks in the mountains liked to call it, was all I really needed to make me happy.

Here's how I found the banjo. Down the mountain at Tom's Creek, there was a commissary for the miners to trade in goods and supplies, and it had most everything you ever wanted. Well, a man had brought in a Gibson banjo, and it was unique, the only one I ever saw like it. It had a bright yellow fingerboard and the sound it made was just as bright as that yellow. The man had got it for $125 but now he was in need of some money, so he let me have it off him for $50.

I had a little bit of cash I'd squirreled away from my army days. In the service, every man was allowed so much in cigarettes and so much in whiskey per month. I didn't smoke and I didn't drink then, so I could sell my rations to my buddies, and I had some savings from that and that's how I bought the banjo.

It was the first real professional banjo I ever had, and it gave me a real boost. We needed every bit of our confidence, because the station had put the word out all over about the new show. Seemed like everybody and their brother from miles around was heading to Bristol to take a shot at the big time. This was a way out of the coal mines and the lumber camps and the mill towns, a chance to make a real job out of music.

An article in *Billboard* magazine reported that WCYB was holding auditions for more than thirty-five "rustic string bands." We thought we had as good a chance as anybody, maybe better. We could do the old-time hoedowns and banjo breakdowns, like any band worth its salt. But we believed we had something else to offer. We could render them old songs people knew but in a new style, the Stanley Brothers style. A lot of groups could out-pick us on a bet maybe, but we had something these string bands didn't have, and that was our singing. With Carter leading the way, and Pee Wee's and my tenors coming behind him, we had a sound with something extra.

When we went to the studio for our audition, we were all pretty nervous, even Bobby, who usually took everything easy like he didn't have a care in the world. Carter tried to calm us down with his usual wisecracking, but I could tell he was nervous, too, because he couldn't set still. He kept fidgeting around while we waited our turn.

Finally the station manager came in. He was in a big hurry and he gave us a tired look, like he'd heard enough hillbilly bands for one day, maybe for a lifetime for all he cared. "Okay, boys," he said. "Let's hear what you got."

We gave him the same stuff we did every day at the radio station in Norton, only now we put on a little more mustard. We ripped into "Cotton-Eyed Joe," Bobby's fiddle tearing it up, Pee Wee's mandolin a-shredding the notes like a band saw, and my bright yellow banjo a-ringing in that tiny studio. And then Carter got to leading us in an old-time spiritual.

From a stomping hoedown to the hush of a gospel quartet, we gave 'em everything we had. It wasn't long before the station manager stopped us, and we didn't know what to think. He looked at us with a big wide smile, but we weren't rightly sure if that was good or what; maybe he was just happy to get some peace and quiet after all the music he'd put up with. "You boys are hired," he said. "You go to work right away." It sounded too good to be true. There had to be catch, and there was.

The station's vice president, Fay Rogers, called us into his office and he got right to the point. We had the job, but there was no salary or money for meals or nothing like that. The only thing WCYB was offering was the chance to make our name.

"We won't promise you nothing," Fay said. "And I'll tell you straight out you might starve to death up here."

He was dead serious and I believe he meant well. He just wanted us to know what we were getting ourselves into. It was a gamble.

"We won't even give you a dose of medicine if you get sick," he said. "The free advertising is all you get from us, so folks out yonder can hear your music. You make your audience from playing our show and then you can make it out on the road on your own. Now, you go out and make it."

So that's what we did, and I'm glad to tell you that we did make it. One thing I want to say right up front. It's been said WCYB made the Stanley Brothers, and it's true it was our first break. But we made WCYB as much as WCYB made us.

Well, we had our own band, and we had our own radio show. Now all we were needing was a car. We didn't have much in the way of ready cash. I still had some of the savings from the army, but not much after I'd bought my Gibson banjo. We borrowed some from our daddy and some more from our half brothers, and our mother gave us a little, too.

We pooled the money and bought a 1937 Chevrolet from our brother-in-law, Slemp Armes, who lived in Buchanan County. He was a sawmill man and he worked for the Ritter Lumber Company. Slemp had owned that car for years, but he kept it in fine running condition and he was real proud of it. We paid him a good price for that ole Chevy. He was family, but it was all business when it come to things like that.

Buying the car from Slemp just about broke us, and there wasn't much money coming in at first. The first time we played a personal appearance, it was about a week after the show went on the air, the day after Christmas 1946. I believe it was in Belfast, over in Russell County; all I know for sure is we split the proceeds between the four of us, and I remember we each made $2.25. But that was plenty, because we were drawing crowds of a couple hundred right from the start. The next night we played a fairly good-sized school, between Big Stone Gap and Pennington Gap, close by the town of Appalachia. It was our first Saturday night appearance and there were so many come to see us we had to play two shows for two packed houses. From then on, we just couldn't hardly find buildings and auditoriums big enough to take care of the crowds.

We were all business, and we expected every man to be the same way. Playing music was our job and we took it as serious as any lawyer or doctor took their practice. Bobby was a good fiddler but like a lot of fiddlers he was a wild seed. He was always homesick and wanting to see his friends and go carousing.

After a while we got to realize Bobby was a boy you couldn't depend on. He'd come up and stay with us and play a week, and then after a show he'd slip off into the night and he'd leave us high and dry. We liked Bobby fine as a fiddler, but we didn't know where he'd go or how to reach him to make sure he'd show up the next time. Once he disappeared like he always did. Only this time he took his change of clothes with him, so we figured he wasn't planning on coming back and we was right.

Years later, we heard that he got burnt up when his house trailer caught fire. With Bobby gone, we went out and got us another fiddler, Leslie Keith. I call him the first real fiddle player of the Clinch Mountain Boys because he stayed with us regular and we could always count on him. We'd heard Leslie on a radio station out of Bluefield, West Virginia, and we liked his style of playing. He had an old-time lonesome sound that people loved and that fit in with our music. Leslie was working on the other side of Virginia, down in Tidewater. We really wanted Leslie to join up with us, so we got our dad to contact him.

Business deals was what my dad did best, and he really helped out in situations like this. He was a good talker, same as Carter, and he was a good persuader. Lee Stanley made things happen. He called Leslie and told him about the *Farm and Fun Time* show and the big crowds we'd been having at our personal appearances. He played us up pretty good, but he didn't forget to play up Leslie either. He told him since he was such a big draw in his own right, together we could really make it. Leslie had a young wife and a baby girl and he was sorely needing some money. Dad told Leslie that if he didn't think he was making enough after a week or so, Dad would make up the difference out of his own pocket.

Well, my dad called on a Friday, and the next day, Leslie took the bus on Highway 58 across the state and made it in time for the noon radio show. It wasn't just his fiddle that made Leslie so valuable to us. He was twenty years older than we were, and he'd been in the business a good while. He was experienced and he could show us things he'd learned. What to do and what not to do. He was an old-timer and he knew the tricks of the trade, like his songbook said: "27 fiddle tricks."

Then we got a bass player, Ray Lambert. He was no relation to Pee Wee, but he had been in Roy Sykes's band with Pee Wee and Carter. Like most bass men back then, he also handled the comedy for Sykes when he went by the name "Pickles." When he came on board with us, Ray became our first comedian, Cousin Wine-Sap.

It was Carter who thought up the name, winesap being a type of apple common in the mountains, and we billed Cousin Wine-Sap as "The Nit-Wit of All Nit-Wits."

Ray would wear a funny costume and put dots all over his face and black out his teeth. He had baggy pants way too big, a patched-up shirt stitch, and a hat with a hole on top with some hair pulled through. He had a big pair of glasses with no lenses, so he could scratch his eyes right through the glasses. That's how Ray would turn into Wine-Sap.

Cousin Wine-Sap was your typical country bumpkin, only he'd say and do all the things people might have the urge to do but don't because it ain't considered polite behavior. He'd be onstage and commence to scratching his leg below the crotch like a dog might do when he had fleas. Carter would play the straight man. "Wine-Sap, don't do that, it don't look good." Cousin Wine-Sap would scratch even harder at whatever was itching him and say, "Yeah, but it sure feels good!"

Wine-Sap was a character. He'd be acting like he was drunk onstage during the show and Carter had to call him out: "Wine-Sap, you're coming around here drinking again; that ain't gonna get the job done. I guess I'm gonna have to fire you."

"No, sir, Mr. Stanley," says Wine-Sap. "I ain't been drinking nothing."

"Yeah, I think so," Carter says. "I want to ask you something, Wine-Sap. I've got this little jar here and you know what, we're gonna pretend it's full of whiskey."

"Okay."

"Now, lookie here. You see this little worm? I got a worm here."

"Yes, sir, Mr. Stanley, I sure do see that."

"I'm going to drop this little worm in this jar of whiskey and you tell me what you see now."

"Uh-oh, the worm is dead."

"Now, don't that teach you something?"

"Yes, sir, it sure does," says Wine-Sap. "Drink a whole lot of whiskey and you won't have no worms!"

The crowd really got a kick out of Cousin Wine-Sap. They were country people and this was old-time country comedy. These jokes had been around for years; we made skits out of these routines and featured them onstage to give the crowd some laughs. We didn't invent nothing; we just made it work for us. Like the old-time songs, these old corny jokes had been around the mountains, handed down and so forth.

Another thing come to mind while I was thinking about Wine-Sap. The people loved him, but I reckon we loved him just as much. When you're tired and hungry and on the road so much, you need some silly stuff to get you through sometimes. Take the edge off. I think Carter especially took a shine to Cousin Wine-Sap. Made him belly-laugh sometimes when nothing else could.

Wine-Sap was something else, but the biggest showstopper we had was Leslie Keith. He had one of the best bullwhip acts around. He said he learned it from a comedian named Shorty Aluff, but he put his own twist on the act. He was part Irish and part Indian, I believe it was Cherokee, and he had long black hair that he combed straight back. When he'd start his routine, he'd pull that hair down over his brow and put a headband on and he looked just like an Indian brave. He'd take his whip and crack it good, loud as a rifle shot, and he could snap a lit paper out of any man's mouth and put that fire out at twenty feet. The crowd would really go for that. Wine-Sap was usually the one who had to hold the paper in his teeth, and I sure was glad he was around because I was afraid to be a part of Leslie's act. Wine-Sap said you could feel the rush of air from the end of that whip. Leslie was pretty good, though, and I don't recall he ever hit anybody.

Leslie told us stories about his early career. He was from Pulaski County, not far out of Roanoke, but he'd been all around the South, and he picked up a lot of songs when he worked as a prison guard back in the 1920s. During the war, he was sent to fight with the infantry in North Africa, but because of his fiddle playing he got transferred to Special Services and he said that weren't the only time the fiddle saved his hide.

One time he and another fellow held a fiddler's contest in Glenwood Park in West Virginia. They had a crowd of nine thousand paying customers and a few dozen fiddlers come out of the mountains from everywhere. Fiddlin' Arthur Smith came in all the way from the *Grand Ole Opry* in Nashville for a hundred dollars and bus fare, which was peanuts for a big star. That tells you right there how much pride went into it for these fiddlers. They wanted to keep their reputation as the best and they'd take on anybody to prove it. Before the contest, they'd work those crowds like politicians, shaking hands and slapping backs. Arthur was national champion at the time and he had the *Opry* fans cheering him on. Leslie had all the locals busting the applause meter for him. Leslie hit Arthur with his "Black Mountain Blues," his signature tune, and he and Smith tied four times and they finally called it a draw.

"Black Mountain Blues" was one we featured a lot on our show. That was the song we had heard him play on WHIS out of Bluefield. Whenever somebody asked Leslie what type of fiddle he played, he'd always say, "old-time," and that's why it worked so well in our band. He was a pro all right, but he never got too fancy with his fiddling, always kept it backwoods. I'd say next to "Orange Blossom Special," Leslie's "Black Mountain Blues" was the most popular fiddle tune going for years.

Leslie had made up a songbook for "Black Mountain Blues" with some notes and a photo of himself. He sold the hell out of those songbooks for ten cents apiece. That gave us the idea to put out our own songbooks, which I'll tell you about later.

Just now, I wanted to fix in your mind what you'd have seen barreling toward you if you found yourself driving some back road in the mountains, close by the Kentucky border, late at night. A big black '37 Chevrolet sedan, bass fiddle strapped on a rack top, a portable PA system and a few instruments in the back trunk. It's the Stanley Brothers and the Clinch Mountain Boys, coming to a town near you.

In the backseat, crammed in the middle, is Pee Wee. Onstage, we call him the Coal Miner from West Virginia, but he's good old Pee Wee to us, and every band needs a Pee Wee to keep the peace. Next to him is Ray. That's his bass fiddle on top of the car. Then there's Leslie, a bullwhip curled in his lap,

Up in the front passenger seat sits Carter, smoking and talking nonstop. Behind the wheel is a short, stubby fellow in no mood for foolishness. That's me, brother Ralph, and I'm trying to see the road in the darkness, so we don't go flying off yonder into a cow pasture.

Two Stanley Brothers in front, three Clinch Mountain Boys in back, and just enough gasoline for a round trip: That's how we made the miles in the early days. We'd travel fifty or one hundred miles and more, six nights a week and sometimes seven. We didn't have much time for things like eating and sleeping.

It wasn't too long before we were pulling in enough money to trade the Chevrolet for a '39 Cadillac. After all these years, that first Caddy is still my favorite car of all the ones I've had. It was a real beauty, long and sleek and gleaming white, just a sight to see. But most of all, it was a good car with a good engine inside, and that's what we needed. It had low mileage, so it was like brand-new when we got it.

I believe we paid close to $1,000 for the Cadillac, and it was worth every penny. Just like now, the name Cadillac meant a lot—the best of the best, the epitome of excellence. You didn't see many Cadillacs around then, especially not back in the mountains. People really noticed our car; a white Caddy with a big bass fiddle on top stood out on them back country roads. Then we went ahead and hired a man to stencil "Stanley Brothers and the Clinch Mountain Boys" across the sides, so people knew who we were. It was important to look good, on the stage and off. A lot of people didn't think much of musicians, which I'll tell you more about shortly. So we wanted to show we were professionals and we meant business. We wanted to make those hard miles the best we could, and the Cadillac was a way to travel in the best style we could. She lasted us many a year, and she gave us a touch of class even when we were feeling dog tired.

All around the broadcast area, we were getting to be well-known radio personalities. We happened to hit at the right time and we did real well because our music was the right blend of old and new. People were hungry for it, and there wasn't many radio stations back then. The show was aired live from WCYB studio in the lobby of the General Shelby Hotel on State Street. It was named for Confederate general Joe Shelby, the last Rebel leader to surrender in the Civil War. It was an eight-story building, one of the tallest in town. Down in the basement was Johnnie Campbell's barbershop.

One thing you have to understand is that back then, radio was the biggest thing going, like the way TV is now, and if you were on the radio, you were as popular in your little broadcast areas as a Hollywood movie star.

The best thing about the radio show was the more popular we got, the more the girls started to notice us. There'd be crowds outside on the sidewalk, watching through the lobby window while we broadcast the show, and a lot of 'em were girls. Seeing their pretty faces made me sing better, and behind the plate-glass window, I still felt safe. And then we'd see girls come to the shows at the little schoolhouses and the VFW halls and they'd come up to us afterward and get an autographed picture or songbook. I was still too bashful to say much, but it gave me a real boost that girls liked our music.

The *Farm and Fun Time* show was a big hit right from the start, bigger than we could have dreamed. Our main sponsor was Honaker Harness and Saddlery, and we had some flour companies, too, General Mills and White Lily, where we'd get on the air and brag on their flour. After six months, we had more sponsors lining up to get a piece of the action, but the station didn't have any more time to sell. They added another hour to the program, and they still had a waiting line of sponsors.

It was nice to have all the sponsors, but that was how the station made money, not us. It was the mail that made us a living. We really got the mail, a big pile every day. In the bunch, we'd get twenty-five or fifty letters wanting us to come to a school or a church or a theater or a miner's union hall. And we got so many we had to throw handfuls in the trash. They'd say, "When do you want to come and play?"

So we'd send them a date and there wasn't enough days in the week to take care of them. We had shows usually six nights a week, and we still couldn't take care of all the requests for personal appearances. We thought we had it made, and we thought it'd be that way forever.

The mailbags were also loaded down with song requests. The ones people were really wanting bad were the "old-timers" we liked to do. Sadder the songs, the more people liked them. Seems like country people are the most happy when they hear sad songs. Some were by Grayson and Whitter, ones we used to hear on our parents' old windup Victrola, "Short Life of Trouble, "Poor Ellen Smith."

The most popular requests were for songs we heard around our house when we was boys, the ones our dad used to sing, "Man of Constant Sorrow," and "Pretty Polly."

One of our biggest mail pullers was "Little Maggie." I heard Steve Ledford do that on an old 78-rpm record, I believe it may have been with the Carolina Ramblers. He was later the fiddle player with Wade Mainer and Zeke Morris in the thirties and he featured "Little Maggie" a lot then, too. I don't know where he found the song, but it had been around the mountains for a good long while. I took to Little Maggie right off and I still play the song just about every time I'm onstage. People holler out for her wherever I play. She's always a real show-stopper.

The old mountain songs were what really got me started as a singer in my own right. My old-time singing just fit the style, and I'd step up to sing lead, a solo showcase for the boy with the hundred-year-old voice. And it also gave me a chance to bring my banjo to the forefront, to shoot off the new forward rolls I was working out, and let Carter stand back for a change and then, after I finished up the song, he could brag a little to the listeners about "Brother Ralph and his fancy banjo."

I reckon I had something to prove with my music. See, I was still so shy I couldn't get up the nerve to help Carter read out the mail over the air. Singing's a whole lot different than talking over a live microphone beaming out ten thousand watts of clear-channel signal to five states and Lord knows how many people tuned in and a-hanging on every word.

Back in the early days, I believed in my music a lot more than I did in myself. It was the backward nature I was borned with and that was bred into me those early years on Smith Ridge, not seeing or needing to see too many people; it was tough to shake. I'll tell you what, in the mountains where I grew up, there were a hundred like me for every one like Carter. A whole lot of folks were just more accustomed to being by themselves a lot instead of socializing.

Anyhow, the old-time songs helped me break out of my shell as a singer, and helped me find out what I could do on my own, just me and the song. I got a real boost stepping up to the microphone by myself and taking lead vocals. I started to look forward to the part of the radio show when I could sing "Man of Constant Sorrow" or "Little Magpie" and then get a sack of mail from people wanting to hear it again and again.

Every singer needs to find the right songs to fit his voice, and for me, it was them sad and lonesome traditional mountain ballads.

Chapter Six

Hit Men

"They fold their arms around each other, they cast their eyes into the sky
'Oh God, Oh God, ain't this a pity, that we both true lovers are bound to die.' "

—"Little Glass of Wine," the Stanley Brothers

When I come up in the business after the war, it was every musician's dream to get an offer that was hard to refuse. It wasn't more than a few simple words, but when you were young and hungry and just starting out, those words sounded sweeter than any other: "Do you want to make a record?"

I don't know of many musicians back then who turned down that offer. And when we heard those words, we didn't say no, either.

The man who made us the offer we couldn't refuse was Hobart Stanton. Everybody called him Hobe, and he called his record company Rich-R'-Tone. You don't hear names like that nowadays, for people or for record labels.

Hobe was a hunchbacked fellow from Johnson City, Tennessee. He fell into the record business and we fell in right along with him. I don't want to call Hobe a crook, but we never saw any money from the records we did for Rich-R'-Tone. I will tell you that when it came to hillbilly music, Hobe didn't know beans from apple butter. But that was all right.

When it came to the record business, we didn't know nothing. So you might say we were even. Hobe knew how to make and sell records and that's all we cared about. He never paid us a dime in royalties, but we were just glad to get on record.

Hobe didn't have any overhead to worry about. He ran the whole operation out of the back of his 1939 Oldsmobile. One thing you need to know—they made big wide trunks for cars in those days, and you could fit a lot of records in the trunk of a '39 Olds. And Hobe did, too, and he probably drove a million miles all over the Southern Appalachian mountains, with nothing but the suit on his back and a trunkful of Rich-R'-Tones. It was what you call a drive-by-night sort of business.

What we liked about Hobe was, he was local. Johnson City was just down the road from Bristol, part of the Tri-Cities along with Kingsport. Carter always said the reason we went with Hobe was, we knew where he was if we ever needed to hunt him down.

To put it plain, Hobe was a jukebox man, and that's all he ever did really know, was what made the nickels fly. He got his start in the business from the distribution end of things. When he was still in high school, he went on runs with a jukebox operator into Tennessee, Virginia and Kentucky. Hobe's job was to stock the records and collect the coins from the machines. He got to know what people in the little towns liked when it come to hillbilly music. Hobe came to realize that a lot of customers in the juke joints, they liked the big country stars like Red Foley and Roy Acuff just fine, but they'd just as soon spend a nickel to play a record by one of their favorite local musicians they heard on stations like WCYB.

There were only four major labels at the time, and they had their roster of stars based in Nashville. They could afford to ignore all the regional talent out in the sticks where we were. So Hobe decided he was going to start his own label and stock the jukeboxes with his own records. He didn't care much about hillbilly music, I don't think. A lot of "corn" is what he called it. What Hobe heard was a market nobody else did.

Now, Hobe did have a real love for making and selling records, I'll give him that. He started Rich-R'-Tone in the fall of 1946, around the same time we were starting out at WNVA. He didn't have a studio, but he didn't need one. There was plenty of recording equipment ready to use at the radio stations, so he cut all his Rich-R'-Tones at radio stations in the Tri-Cities of Bristol, Johnson City and Kingsport. There was no recording tape at that time; they used disc cutters. Hobe would make what they called an acetate pressing off a disc cutter at the station and send off the master to get pressed on shellac at record plants in Philadelphia and St. Louis. Then he'd get a shipment of 78-rpm records and go hawk those shiny new Rich-R'-Tones wherever he could find a taker.

Hobe was lame from childhood polio and he had a limp, but he didn't let that stop him. He'd load boxes of 78s into his Oldsmobile and hit the road, peddling records out of the trunk of the car. All the while he'd be twisting the radio dial, checking all the local stations for talent to get on Rich-R'-Tone. It's a wonder we didn't have a wreck with Hobe head-on when he was making his rounds, since we were traveling the same back roads he was around the Bristol broadcast area.

You have to admire the sweat and gumption he had. He worked hard and he done it by himself, a one-man company if there ever was. He scared up a lot of down-home music that might not have ever been recorded; he got the real sound, right off the back porch, and not something all slicked up for a national audience. You can listen to those old Rich-R'-Tones and hear exactly what a hillbilly band sounded like at the firehouses and taverns and legion halls in those years right after the war.

Like us, they were local musicians proud of who they were and where they were from. If you tried to go big time, the big record company bosses would make you change your name from Leonard Slye to Roy Rogers, or Ruby Blevins to Patsy Montana. Polish you up for the mainstream audience. But Hobe didn't want to change nothing about the singers or the bands. The rougher the better, as long as they had a following. The names on the Rich-R'-Tone labels tell you how far he searched the hills and hollows for talent: Glen Neaves and the Grayson County Boys from near Galax, Virginia; Curly King and His Tennessee Toppers; Cecil Surrat and His West Virginia Ramblers; Ernest Martin and the Kentucky Mountain Boys. Some were close by our neck of the woods, like Buster Pack and His Lonesome Pine Boys, from near St. Paul.

I don't reckon there were many counties in the Tri-Cities area where Hobe didn't poke his neck into. He listened for bands that already had a big following on the local radio stations, like Curly King on WCYB. If they were popular in their area, he figured they'd be popular in other areas, too.

There were hundreds of hillbilly bands Hobe never got to record, but what he did get was the cream of the crop. The way they judged your popularity back then was how many sponsors you had and how much mail you pulled in every week, all the cards and letters people sent in for song requests. All these groups would be needing was a record to find even more of a following. So Hobe kept track of the mailbags and the sponsors.

Most Rich-R'-Tone bands never did amount to much. Maybe a record or two and it was back to the farm or the mine or the mill. But some made it, not only us but real fine outfits like Wilma Lee and Stoney Cooper. Now, we didn't have any notion of the business, but we knew a record was a way to get a foot in the door, and Rich-R'-Tone was our stepping-stone to the major record companies. Hobe was about the first of the independent labels, and he blazed a trail that helped make a way for so much that came later. Rich-R'- Tone proved there was other ways to skin a cat, and Nashville wasn't the only place for a hillbilly band to cut a record.

One day in February 1947, Hobe contacted us at the WCYB radio station. We didn't know anything about him or his record label, but he knew all about us. He'd heard the *Farm and Fun Time* program and he knew we were the biggest mail pullers in the Tri-Cities area. He'd heard about all the mailbags filled with requests for "Little Glass of Wine" and other songs we did on the radio every day.

"Come on down and see for yourself," Carter told him.

Next day, Hobe came by the station, with a salesman's big smile and a big handshake to go along with it. I'd say he looked pretty sharp: dark business suit and hair slicked back as shiny and black as his shoes, and you didn't barely notice his stoop. One look and you could tell this fellow was cagey. You could understand how he'd weaseled some of these hillbillies to pay *him* to cut a record.

We emptied the sacks of mail out on the floor, and that was all Hobe needed to see: "You boys want to make a record for Rich-R'-Tone?"

Course, he knew the answer. He'd sized us up and knew we'd a-made a record for nothing, which is just about what we did. We never did sign a contract with Hobe. It was what you call a gentleman's agreement, but we never did agree on what the money was supposed to be. There was some mention of royalties and other promises that were never put on paper. It didn't matter to us, because we were young and dumb and didn't know any better.

We did our first recording session for Rich-R'-Tone in spring of 1947. It was only a few months after we'd become a working band, but we were ready because we played music just about every waking hour. It was at the studio of WOPI, the rival station of WCYB, right down the street but on the Tennessee side of town. Hobe used WOPI as his home base in Bristol. He had made buddies with the engineer there and the studio had nice acoustics and a disc cutter as good as any you could find. It was a thrill to be cutting our first record here, like making a raid in enemy territory.

There wasn't anything fancy about the session. It was done in the time today's recording engineers take to fire up all the computer equipment and get started. All the boys in the band ganged around the microphone, like we did on the *Farm and Fun Time* program. Hobe was over in the corner, bent over the cutting machine, watching the needle cut into the soft wax acetate disc. If you've seen the movie *O Brother, Where Art Thou?* when the blind man at the little roadside radio station records the Soggy Mountain Boys on "Man of Constant Sorrow," you've got an idea of what it was like. Of course, we weren't lip-synching like George Clooney was.

Back then you had to sing and play straight into the disc cutter, so there wasn't any room for mess-ups. Making a record was a whole different thing than it is now. It was a live performance start to finish, no gimmicks, no tricks. The disc-cutting machines could only get what you played, not cover up where you fouled up. There wasn't any tape splicing or overdubbing back then. If you made a mistake, even if it was the very last word or note, you had to go back and do the whole song over again.

Nowadays, if you miss even half a word, they can fix that and make it sound perfect. You've got your multitracking now and musicians playing their own little parts, and the producers put it all together later on. The new technology has made recording a whole lot easier, but I don't know if that's really better or not. The real sound of a band is playing all together at the same time in the same room like they way we did it. I think the old-time way of recording the whole band with one microphone sounded the best then and it still does today. For our type of music it ain't about perfection; it's about the feeling.

Back then, the musicians worked harder, because there weren't no second chances. You had to really nail it. If you didn't, why, you didn't sound any good and you could hear the difference. The bands today don't have to play as well, because the producers can cover up the mistakes. With this multitracking, they spend four days fixing what the band should have done right to begin with. I think the music has suffered, because there ain't no pressure to be the best you can. They've made things too easy. The old records have stood the test of time; and I wonder if the ones they're making today will last. Anyhow, Hobe was well pleased with us, because we were so used to doing a radio show and playing shows at night. Every man in the band knew what he had to do. We did all the songs on the first try.

We were as happy with Hobe as he was with us. The best thing about him was, he left musicians alone to do their own thing. He didn't try to mess with your sound or tell you what songs to do. He was like a studio photographer you'd find in any small town, where people come in to get their portrait done. Instead of a camera, Hobe had a disc cutter.

The first record we cut was a gospel number, "Death Is Only a Dream." We always devoted a special portion of our radio programs to what we called Hymn Time. People really loved Hymn Time, and a lot of requests we got in the mailbag were songs people knew from church. We found "Death Is Only a Dream" in an old hymnbook and we worked it out as a vocal quartet. Carter took lead, Pee Wee sang tenor, Ray came in on bass, and I did the baritone:

Sadly we sing and with tremulous breath, as we stand by the mystical stream
In the valley and by the dark river of death, and yet 'tis no more than a dream
Only a dream, only a dream of glory beyond the dark stream
How peaceful the slumber, how happy the waking, here death is only a dream

It was a little bit strange, after singing such a mournful song, to see Hobe across the room with a big grin on his face. That's because he had a keeper on the very first take, and now he knew for sure he had a band that didn't fiddle-faddle around when it come to making records: We was young but we was all business. So Hobe lifted the mechanical arm on his disc cutter and got another acetate ready and said how nice it was to hear us boys do things right. We sang another gospel number, "I Can Tell You the Time," and that went fine, too. We'd just made our first two-sided record and we felt about ten foot tall. Hobe said, "Well, boys, there's time for two more tonight, so what else have you got for me?"

Carter had something he'd just wrote. As far as I know, it was his first original song, the first one he done from scratch. It was called "Mother No Longer Awaits Me at Home." Now, some songwriters get their ideas from life and things that happen to them, and they put those experiences in their songs. Hank Williams was the best at that, and his songs were all about the troubles in his life and you could hear it in his singing.

Carter wrote a lot from his experience, too, as a young man out rambling the world to find his fortune, but his gift came more from his imagination. Our mother was alive and well and she always waited for us back home when we'd come in from playing shows to rest up at Smith Ridge. He wrote about what he dreaded the most; the thought of losing our mother was about the worst.

When I left my old home way back in the mountains
I said I'd return with honor and fame
But a young reckless heart turned wrong at the crossroads

And now as I go home I bring Mother shame
When I got to the place where I spent my childhood
The silvery moon was shining so bright
When I asked my dear friends to tell me of Mother
They said she was called on to heaven last night

Leaving the mountains and losing your loved ones; it was a theme he'd come back to again and again. The last song we cut that night was another original by Carter, "The Girl Behind the Bar." He took the story from the old ballad tradition, but he cut to the chase. The singer meets a girl at a roadside tavern, and they get together for a date outside, where her boyfriend's waiting on 'em and stabs her in the back; he escapes into the night, leaving the singer to take the rap.

Our first four songs, and we had two hymns about dying and the sweet hereafter, and two ballads with a mother and a lover dead. Not the sort of songs you hear on any country station today. Too dark, I reckon, especially the ballads. Both end with a man who's lost everything he loves; one's motherless, the other's in jail. Neither man committed a crime, but they still have to pay the price.

We come out of the studio feeling sky-high. We'd made our first records. Carter was so excited he grabbed the acetate for "Death Is Only a Dream" so we could listen to it at home. We wanted to hear for ourselves what we sounded like. We put it on the record player and just about wore it out. Sounded mighty fine to us, our voices coming off a record.

When we brought the acetate record back to Hobe, he threw a fit. An acetate pressing was all you had to make a master disc to press your records, and now it had the surface noise from our record player's needle digging into the wax. Hobe was irate; he didn't call his label Rich-R'-Tone for nothing, and now he had an acetate with an awful hiss in the background. So Hobe held it from release for a good long while, a few years or so, I believe. You can still hear the surface noise on it today on compact disc.

The first Stanley Brothers Rich-R'-Tone that Hobe released was "Mother No Longer Awaits Me at Home" and "The Girl Behind the

Bar." It sold real well, especially in our area, not so much in more faraway places down South. As Hobe said later: "We could sell five thosand Stanley Brothers records in Kentucky and absolutely not give one away in Georgia." We was popular, maybe, but only in our little corner of Appalachia.

We showed our first phonograph record to our mother and dad and everybody we knew. "Well, we're on record," we thought. "We're on our way!" It especially made Carter proud. It made him feel part of a tradition, like he was carrying on from the records of the Carter Family and Grayson and Whitter we'd heard on the Victrola.

All those records we did for Rich-R'-Tone didn't make us any money, not in royalties anyhow. But what they did was make us a name. We ended up cutting a bunch of records for Hobe, but the one that done the trick was "Little Glass of Wine."

First we ever heard of the song was back in the late thirties when we were boys up on Smith Ridge, learning to play music. We had a neighbor named Otto Taylor, and he worked for the W. M. Ritter Lumber Company. He played banjo in the old drop-thumb style like my mother, and he used to sing an old ballad he called "Poison in a Glass of Wine." He only knew a few verses, but we learned the melody from him.

When we started on WCYB, we needed some songs to fill out the show, so Carter worked out some new lyrics to the melody we'd got from Otto, and we worked out a new arrangement. Well, once we started playing "Little Glass of Wine" on the *Farm and Fun Time* program, people took to it right off. That was the one that really filled the mailbags. "Little Glass of Wine" goes a bit beyond your usual murder ballad because here you've got a murder and a suicide as well. The jealous man kills his girlfriend when he poisons her wine and then he drinks it, too, and they die in each other's arms. It was popular for the same reason as *Romeo and Juliet*, I reckon. It touched people. Like it says in the last line, "True lovers are bound to die."

The way Carter sung it, you felt bad for the girlfriend and you felt bad for the man who done her in. When he sung a song, he'd make you hear the story, whether it was about a murder or someone who's homesick, heartbroke, or just hurting. Carter always used to say, "If you feel a song and sing it like you really feel it, I believe the people listening will come along with you. They'll recognize that feeling and they'll respond to it. Then you've done your job as a singer."

We cut the record back at the WOPI studio, and Carter and me sang it as a duet. At that same session we did "Little Maggie," and Hobe was fixing to put that on the flip side. We knew with the "Little Glass of Wine," we had something that could be a hit, and we gave it a big buildup on the *Farm and Fun Time* show. Our main sponsor was Honaker Harness and Saddlery in Honaker, in Russell County, about an hour's drive from Bristol. They sold all kinds of farm supplies and sundries and we were bringing them some good business. So they had us play at the store on a Saturday. They advertised it pretty heavy on our radio show the week before. They gave it a real push, to let everyone know we'd make a personal appearance and the record would be for sale that day at the store.

We showed up at the store early Saturday morning. It was a big two-story brick building, next to Dickenson Hardware, right there on Main Street in downtown Honaker, a little railroad depot on the Clinchfield line. It was one of those old coal-boom towns that had seen better days but was somehow hanging on.

The owner of the store was there waiting for us. He was a jolly fellow and it was a big day for his business, and he told us he'd ordered a thousand copies of our record to handle all the customers he was expecting. He shook all our hands like we'd come straight from the *Opry*. He looked us over and noticed that we all had some worn-out shoes. We'd all gone downtown to a men's store in Bristol and got us sport coats and some homburg hats, but we didn't have enough for matching shoes.

"Set these boys up and treat 'em right, y'hear?" he hollered to the clerk behind the counter. "These here are the Stanley Brothers!"

The clerk hightailed it back to the storeroom and came out carrying a stack of boxes, and he gave every man in the band a pair of black boots. Nothing special, mind you, but nice enough anyhow. It's a wonder what some new footwear, fancy or not, will do for your mood. So we felt like big-time stars at this little town out in the sticks, a-standing there in our shiny boots.

Outside the store, and all the way down the street, was the biggest crowd we'd ever seen. People came out of the mountains and from all over. You'd never have believed so many lived back in those far hollows, but here they were. There were families on foot, babies on their shoulders. You'd a-thought the old folks had risen up from their deathbeds; seemed like any able-bodied person with a radio for miles around had made the trip. Evrybody wanted to see if the Stanley Brothers could sound as good in person as we did on the *Farm and Fun Time* show.

Carter had to shout out to introduce us to the crowd. They gave us a big cheer and we hadn't played a note. They were already hollering to hear "Little Glass of Wine." All the people in the audience had me spooked. I didn't want to look into all those faces, so I just held tight to my banjo and kept my eyes looking down at my boots. I saw myself staring back from that shiny black leather. It was the face of a scared kid.

Once we got to playing, and the crowd stayed behind us, I felt fine. To tell you the truth, it felt like a dream come true, because we'd never heard such loud applause. It was like to be a riot in the streets of Honaker. You never forget the feeling you get when people are enjoying your music, and you never get tired of hearing the cheers. It means you've found a way to use your gift and share it with people. When you're a musician, nothing else matters.

Carter handled the audience like a pro, talking up our record for sale. Hobe drove up with a thousand copies of the record and by noon he'd sold out. He could have sold another thousand. You've never seen a man with a bigger smile than Hobe on that Saturday.

Honaker Saddlery paid us a pittance for the appearance; I can't remember exactly what we made, but it wasn't too much. So Hobe made out like a bandit, and all we made out of that "Little Glass of Wine" was some pocket change and new boots. But that was all right because that "Little Glass of Wine" turned out to be our ticket to the biggest record company, Columbia, so it did us fine.

Besides, we was having too much fun to worry about royalties. I think back on the time in Bristol, and it's the funny things that stand out. Everything was new to us then, and when you're young in a new place, things seem more comical. And when you're from the country, and you're living in town for the first time, you see things you haven't seen before.

Bristol was a big step up from the country we were used to. It was a real town, with streetcars and department stores. If you were going to Bristol, you were going somewhere. It was a border town, too, and border towns always have a hustle and bustle to 'em. The General Shelby Hotel, where WCYB had its studio, was right on State Street, the main thoroughfare in Bristol that divided the town right in half. On one side was Virginia and on the other was Tennessee, and the hotel was on the Virginia side, same side where we all roomed together in a boardinghouse. We weren't about to leave our home state if we could help it, even though the Tennessee side was wet and the Virginia side was dry; I didn't fool with nothing like that yet, so it didn't bother me a bit, but Carter and Pee Wee liked to wet their whistles over in Tennessee.

I told you earlier how the crowds would gather outside the building to watch us through the lobby window. So we really wanted to look our best, whether we were onstage or doing our radio program. We always wanted to look like professionals, and we patterned ourselves after Bill Monroe. He dressed neat and he wore a hat and he was always shaved, so he looked as sharp as his music. It means a lot to put forward your best appearance before your fans.

At that time, old-time country performers wore overalls and loud checkered shirts and straw hats, to play up the hillbilly image popular then. Now, we played what they called hillbilly music but we didn't want that look for ourselves, and we didn't want to look like cowboys, like a lot of country stars did back then. We never yodeled in our lives, not even in our sleep. Cowboy music was for singers like Tex Ritter who grew up out West. Later on, we toured with Tex and he was the real deal. There was no use trying to wear rhinestones and ten-gallon Stetsons with six-inch brims like Tex. So we never pretended to be cowboys or anything else.

We saw ourselves as Southern gentlemen form the mountains of Virginia, and that's how we presented ourselves as best we could. One way we set ourselves apart from Bill and Tex and the rest was with our hats. No matter what style we had, from the homburgs we wore early on, we always made sure the brims were never more than three inches wide and turned up so you could see our faces plain. The way a Southern gentleman wears his hat when he's out on the town and he means business.

Once we finally got some matching suits and some nice homburg hats at the men's store downtown, we went right off to get our haircuts.

There was a barbershop down in the basement of the Shelby Hotel. It was called Johnnie's and there was a Big John and a Little John who were the barbers. I never did find out which John it was named for. The first time we went in there, I got in Big John's chair, and he said, "Howdy, I reckon you want the regular?" and I said, "Well, sure, that'd be fine."

I didn't know what I was getting myself into. Big John proceeded to wet down the side of my head behind my ear with some sort of lotion, and then he stood back and I smelled butane and I felt a flash of heat and I realized he'd lit my hair on fire. I had never seen nor heard of such a thing.

Then he did it again, on the other side, like it was no big deal, like a man pouring lighter fluid on a barbecue grill. It didn't hurt or nothing, because he'd blow out the fire as soon as he lit it. He didn't use any scissors or razors, just the flame and his know-how. He'd light the area he was working on and singe whatever hair he was after. That's what he called it. "Singe-ing."

It was his own work, and nobody else did that as far as I know. It was his way of giving his customers the "short on the sides" look popular then. It was his own remedy, and it was a good haircut even if there wasn't much cutting, but we thought it was the strangest thing. All of us boys in the band got the "singe-ing" and we'd go to Johnnie's pretty regular. I've been around the world and I've never seen a barber anywhere use fire except for Big John.

We all got rooms at a boardinghouse on Moore Street, not far from the radio station. The landlord who run the place was a sort of a queer fellow. He was old and cranky and he was odd, too, and right off we didn't get along. I don't know what all set him against us, but he didn't much care for us Clinch Mountain Boys, not a one, not even Carter. I reckon part of if it was because he didn't like musicians, but I believe mostly it was just that he was borned mean.

One of the Clinch Mountain Boys had a room of his own; I won't mention no names, because of the story I'm going to tell you. The landlord had bought a brand-new mattress for the bed in that room. He always made a fuss about how much he paid for the mattress, $49.95. Well, he claimed that the Clinch Mountain Boy peed on that mattress and ruined it. He was hopping mad and he took him to court over it.

We went to the trial and the old landlord stood up to state his case. He said the Clinch Mountain Boy was a nasty, dirty, no-good musician who messed up his beautiful mattress. He told the judge all kinds of foul things and then he said he wanted him to pay the money for a new one. The man was so mad standing there, he got the words all jumbled together because his crazy old mind was stuck on the amount of money he was trying to get back. He kept saying, "He peed on my forty-nine-ninety mattress, I mean, forty-five mattress," and he'd pronounce it "mat-er-ass," and everybody in the courtroom and even the judge was laughing at how mad he was and how he said the word "mattress." By the time he sat down, he was still sputtering about the "forty-nine mat-er-ass" like he was losing his mind.

Strange thing is that I can't even remember who won the case. All I know is that the landlord made a fool of himself in public and he hated us even more after that because we had put him through that humiliation. So he became even more childish to deal with, and he was even more particular about everything. It was hard to live there, but we needed a place to stay so we went ahead and stayed there.

Not long after that, we got some revenge on the old man. We were coming back to Bristol after a show real late at night, I believe it was the little Dog Branch School not far from our home place, and we nearly hit a big ole fat possum that was out in the middle of the road. The same Clinch Mountain Boy who got in trouble over the mattress, well, he got an idea when he saw those red eyes of the possum glowing in the headlights. He had me stop the car and he went out there to catch the possum.

You know, when you go after a possum and corner him, he'll sull up on you. He'll pass out and double up and lay there like he's dead. That's what this possum did, and the Clinch Mountain Boy scooped him up and brought him on back to the rooming house. And he set the possum down in the living room, and we all went to bed to wait and see what would happen.

The next morning, we went downstairs for breakfast. The possum was a-sitting in the front window, just as cozy as a house cat. Well, we knew that we were going to get a good laugh, and we did. The old man came in and he saw the possum sitting there, and he just about had a heart attack. He fussed up and down, cussing and hollering, wondering which one pulled a prank on him like that. Nobody said a word, and the possum just sat there looking at him like it was his rooming house and not the old man's.

But the Clinch Mountain Boy wasn't done yet. He had another prank ready for the landlord. We played some shows in Florida on a stretch down South, and he bought a young alligator at a roadside stand. He got a good deal, too; he paid $5 for the baby gator. It came with a little cage and we took it back to Bristol with us.

He set the alligator loose in the boardinghouse, and the old man got pranked again. Every once in a while, that's what he'd do, turn him free from the cage, just let him wander and roam all over the place or set up on the front porch like a guard dog, anything to aggravate the old man. Then he'd put him back in the cage and keep him in his room. He took a liking to him and the gator became like his pet.

One time, I was walking in the house late one night when it was as dark as it could be. Down the hallway, I met something coming at me, and it was the alligator. He'd gotten out of his cage somehow, and I nearly tripped over him. It about scared me to death.

Gators and possums and forty-nine-ninety-five mattresses. These are the silly things that stick in your mind sixty years later. So many show dates and personal appearances and radio programs, they all start to blur together, and you remember more the little things that don't have much to do with music. And the further back I go in my mind down through the years, the more the memories seem happy. Especially in Bristol.

More than anything, those were happy years because we had no thought of the future. We were just enjoying the moment. And, early on, Carter was such a happy-go-lucky fellow, nothing could bring him down. He and Pee Wee were pals and they spent a lot of time together, drinking and carrying on. One time, Pee Wee's wife, Hazel, met them at the door of the boardinghouse when they come in real late, both about as drunk and happy as could be. She wasn't angry but she wanted to know how they did it.

"Carter, one thing I've been a-wanting to know," she said. "And that's how in the world you and Pee Wee can hold all that beer?"

"Aw, Hazel," said Carter. "We don't hold it, we drink it."

It was Carter who made the *Farm and Fun Time* show such a hit. He was a natural in front of the microphone, just as natural as I'm talking to you right now. He had a way of making friends with the listeners, just as easygoing as if he'd pulled up a chair and joined them at the supper table.

The noon time slot was a very important time for the people of that area. It was when they'd take a break from the farmwork and gather together for their midday meal. And the Stanley Brothers became as much part of that meal as anybody in the family. We were right there in their home, and we made it a special time, and Carter seemed to know his way around the house.

He'd introduce an old song, the way you'd maybe begin a story with a few friends. It was a way he had of lowering his voice so that it sounded like what he was saying was just between him and you; he didn't holler, didn't shout like Uncle Dave Macon and Gid Tanner and those old-time entertainers. Uncle Dave cut his gold-plated teeth on the medicine shows and tent shows, where to grab a listener it helped to yell.

But radio had changed everything, and now there were singers like Bing Crosby who had come into style. When Uncle Dave first heard Bing, he said, "He'll never make it." He didn't understand how you could sing soft and be able to put over a song.

Carter was like Bing in the way he made that microphone work for him. Carter learned how to speak low and mellow, sometimes almost in a whisper, to draw listeners in, just like the way he did with his singing.

Our dad helped spread the word, too. He may not have been the best father when we were boys, but you couldn't beat him as a businessman, and that's just what a couple of young, inexperienced musicians needed. All those years traveling on the sawmill circuit, he knew the places and the people around the WCYB broadcast area. It was his territory, and he beat the bushes finding Stanley Brothers fans.

He printed up handbills touting WCYB and its new *Farm and Fun Time* show starring the Stanley Brothers and the Clinch Mountain Boys. He'd drive all over the Tri-Cities area of Virginia, Tennessee and North Carolina; he'd stop in the stores and say howdy and post his handbills, to publicize our radio show. He'd hit those little towns and hunt down the school principal and set up a show date before the man had a chance to say no. You didn't need a manager when you had Lee Stanley. He really did believe in us and, of course, we did pay him a percentage, so we made it worth his while to help, too.

All the hustling worked. We got big sacks of mail, from five hundred to a thousand letters and cards a day. And there'd be a lot of requests for songs, and those sacks is what first brought Hobe Stanton down to see us.

That was how we made our name and I'll tell you that was one happy time. We started playing five, six, seven nights a week. Everywhere we'd go, we'd pack the place one or two times, people standing outside waiting for the first show to finish. There was a long stretch in 1947 when we were booked as much as ninety days ahead. One time we worked for a month straight without a single day off.

That winter, we rented a house on Carolina Avenue in Bristol, along with Pee Wee and his wife, Hazel. We had kitchen privileges, and it was a much better setup than the boardinghouse with the old landlord.

We brought our mother down to stay with us; it was so cold that winter, and we didn't want her all alone on Smith Ridge until springtime. I just wanted to get her where we had some good heat in the house. Hazel and my mother got along great, and my mother done most of the cooking for us. It was just like we were back at the old home place and we'd all eat together like family. She brought down all she'd canned, so she'd stew up mustard greens with some ham and fried potatoes and pinto beans, and she'd make the biggest and best country breakfasts we ever had since we was little boys. Her meals spoiled me, though. I gained about twenty-five pounds and got pretty heavy that winter, thanks to my mother's home cooking.

We were getting known on the radio, and my mother got to see her boys doing well. Those were some real happy days, let me tell you. We had our music and we had our mother close by, and we couldn't have asked for anything more.

That's how it is when you're young and never had nothing and don't know any better. When some good things finally come your way, you think it'll always be that way. Kind of like a hog under an acorn tree. The hog never looks up to see where they're coming from or how many are left. When the acorns fall, he just grabs however many he can and gobbles 'em down. Well, we felt like that old hog, and it took us a while before we realized that trees run out of acorns.

CHAPTER SEVEN

Friends and Neighbors

"Howdy, friends and neighbors. We're all here today, everybody feeling good. All the Clinch Mountain Boys here on hand, ready to go on Farm and Fun Time.*"*

—CARTER STANLEY, ON THE *FARM AND FUN TIME* RADIO PROGRAM, 1947, WCYB, BRISTOL, VIRGINIA

We were really on a roll. We had a popular radio broadcast beamed into the farthest hollow for hundreds of miles around, and we had more show dates and personal appearances than we could handle. There were a lot of people for us, but there was a lot against us, too. Back then, entertainers weren't accepted by the general public like they are today. Leastways, not in the mountains of southwestern Virginia.

In those days, a lot of people in our neck of the woods didn't believe in music as a profession. It was something you might do after work as a pastime, but not in place of a real job. They thought musicians were out for no good.

Especially the church people. They didn't approve of entertainment, not the type of show you charged admission for people to come and see you. They looked down on entertainers, and musicians most of all. If you was a musician, they just assumed maybe you weren't up to par and were low-down trash and a drunk just out for a big time. Lazy and no count.

And there's people right through this section of country, they still feel that way and they don't mind letting you know it, too.

Around Dickenson County, those die-hard church people never did like us and we didn't get any encouragement from nobody else, neither. Early on, all we had on our side was our mother and dad. From the time we first tried to make it in music, they was our biggest boosters. Even after they split up and went their separate ways, the one thing they were together on was supporting us in our career. They were the first fans we ever had. My mother most of all.

Our parents didn't care what some church people said against our profession. They didn't pay these folks no mind. They were real proud of our music. They always felt that religion had its place and music had its place; and neither one didn't interfere with the other. They believed it depended on the individual.

It was still hard to get respect, though. And back in the 1920s, it was even worse. Even family acts were considered suspect by some, out on the road playing shows. On the handbills advertising their shows, the Carter Family printed a special announcement at the bottom: "This Program Is Morally Good," and they meant it, too. Same with Fiddlin' Cowan Powers and Family. Their posters promised "A Good, Clean, Instructive Amusement," and there was a photo of Cowan and his son Charlie in jackets and bow ties, and his daughters in long dresses. Everyone in their Sunday best.

A man by himself with a guitar or a banjo had it rough. Fiddlers probably had it the worst. A lot of time they were seen as sinners bound for hell. I'd say some musicians may have abused the name, getting drunk and messing about and maybe a few got what they deserved. But most worked as hard at what they did as anybody else. It didn't matter, though, because entertainers were considered low-down, and they were treated no different than you would a vagrant or a drifter, not much better than a hobo. Police were all the time running 'em out of town.

Even musicians who'd made it and done pretty well for themselves could catch hell. They'd get arrested for suspicion of being suspicious.

One of the early country music pioneers, Ernest Stoneman, for years made a decent a living as a musician in southwest Virginia. He even had a hit record in 1925 with "The Titanic," but he still used to carry around a letter of introduction in his pocket that he could show to authorities if they gave him trouble. Ernest had a family friend, the town attorney for Galax, write it up for him. That tells you what a musician was up against, even a successful recording artist like Stoneman, who was real well known in southwest Virginia. You'd think he was a man just out of prison: "Mr. Stoneman is an honest hardworking straightforward young man, works at the carpenter's trade a good portion of the time and spends some time in the capacity of a professional musician. It gives me pleasure to recommend Mr. Stoneman, both as a carpenter and as a musician, because I have confidence in him and feel that he will satisfy those for whom he may work."

We didn't have any attorneys or judges to recommend us. We just had our parents—a sawmill man and a single mother—and nobody cared what they thought one way or the other. Our dad and mother didn't know nothing about the music business, only that it wasn't reckoned to be a decent way to make a living. But they were still for us trying to make it because they believed in us. They told us to be honest and straight with everybody. They said never go on the stage drinking and never do anything wrong before the public. They told us to hold ourselves in such a way to be somebody the audience would respect. We had to show the people we'd been raised up right.

It wasn't just about getting known but getting respected. The *Farm and Fun Time* show helped get our name out, and someone who helped us make a good name for ourselves early on was A. P. Carter. A.P. was one of the true pioneers of country, and he was one of our fans early on. It's not too much to say the Carter Family put country music on the map. A.P. did a lot of traveling around Scott County and all over the Clinch Mountains, and he'd stop at houses and collect songs. The Carter Family helped popularize so many songs, like "Wildwood Flower," that would have died out. A.P. and Maybelle and Sara helped make old-time country music popular and more respectable, too—something you didn't have to be ashamed of, even if the church people looked down their noses at you. They earned respect and they sold a lot of records, too, and that made the business types respect hillbilly music. The Carter Family made what we were doing possible.

A.P. was just an old-time country fellow, real dry, not too much joking around, pretty sincere about everything. He had been out of the music business for a while, after the Carter Family had broke up. He ran his little general store; he was all alone; Sara had left him for another man years ago, and I reckon he never got over that.

Not long after we first started on the *Farm and Fun Time* program, A.P. invited us to play a show at his music park. It was near where the Carter Family Fold is now in Scott County. It was a way he kept his hand in music, and he started a little festival with outdoor shows up the side of the mountain behind his store there. He called it Carter's Park. There were no seats or much of anything, just a little stage he built himself and the Clinch Mountains all around. He didn't want a fence, because he didn't want to spoil the view. It was supposed to be $1 admission, but he never turned nobody away. There wasn't even a PA system. What you call rustic. The people had to be real quiet and they had to get close to the stage.

A.P. had shows there on Sunday afternoons and he had us out as his special guests. He paid us to come play, but I don't remember how much he paid. The money didn't matter to us; we considered it an honor to be invited, and we wanted to help him make the Sunday shows a success. He got up on stage and introduced us to the crowd. I never will forget it, because it was pure A. P. Carter. He told it like it was and nothing more.

"This here is the Stanley boys, Carter and Ralph," he said. "Far as I know, they're all right. They ain't done nothing wrong yet. I never heard nothing different. Not yet anyhow."

That was the best okay you were going to get from A.P. Nowadays that sort of introduction wouldn't fly. You have to brag more on the entertainer taking the stage, even if it's a lot of bunk. A.P. didn't go with that; he wasn't a man to say a lot. No swagger or bluff in him. Words like that from A. P. Carter carried a lot of weight in southwest Virginia. He was giving his blessing to the Stanley Brothers as men, not just as musicians, and we needed all the help we could get.

I can't remember just exactly how we first met up with A.P. The best

I recall he just showed up one day at the radio station, and we saw him watching through the studio window while we played our show. He liked our music and wanted to meet us. He was a fan, but he wasn't the type who comes up and tells you that. He didn't say much, but you knew he'd taken a shine to the way we did the old songs. I think we reminded him of the Carter Family when they were starting out. We played traditional music and respected the tradition, but we put our own stamp on it, same as the Carter Family did.

Anyhow, here was A.P. himself, just him and an old guitar, a living legend to us young boys. He'd come by the station and sat in with us, and he was as down-to-earth as they come. He didn't put on any airs whatever. I'd say it was a big surprise, and we knew it was special to have him visit. It was quite a trip into town for him in them days. He'd catch a ride to Bristol from the Carter home place in Maces Springs, because he didn't drive no more.

A.P. was well past sixty by then, an old-time country man, plain as dirt. He may have had some money from royalties, but he didn't show it. I believe the only things he spent much money on was land and those portable sawmills you'd often see back then. By the way he looked, you couldn't tell him apart from any other farmer you'd see around the old potbellied stove at his store. Under his suit, he'd have on a white starched dress shirt and frayed suspenders that he pinned to his wool trousers with a nail. His hair was cut short around the sides, the shade of gray you see on a weathered old barn. I remember seeing wood shavings in his ear, and he said he'd been out doing his chores.

I've heard people say A.P. was odd in his ways. Well, we got to know him real well and we didn't find him strange. I'd say he was A. P. Carter and he was just natural. He was a straight shooter and said just what he thought. Not too much joking around for him. Sara had run off on him years before and he'd never remarried; he was alone and got used it. He stayed busy with his general store and his little country music park. But you could tell he was still wanting to be an entertainer somehow. He wanted to keep in music any way he could.

He called himself a Musicianer. He still saw himself as a musicianer even though he hadn't made a record in years. He didn't believe in retirement, and neither do I, even though I'm now twenty years older than A.P. was when we met him. Playing music keeps me going; I can't sit around the house for very long.

A.P. got himself a show on *Farm and Fun Time* and we'd see him every day. He had a fifteen-minute spot, just by himself on the guitar. He was still a fine singer and he sung a lot of old Carter Family songs. He was real fond of "Storms Are on the Ocean." That was a favorite from the first session in Bristol that had made the Carter Family famous. He could still put over a song, even without Maybelle and Sara. Just honest, simple music that touches you.

A.P. stuck mostly to numbers that worked best solo. One that sort of stuck with me was called "It'll Aggravate Your Soul." It's what I remember him doing the most on his show. It was one of the only Carter Family records where he sung lead. And it's one of the very few he wrote from his life, about when he and Sara first came to Bristol to get married. I think it was a song he was still living out, one that stayed on his mind after all those years.

Now young men take warning from me
Don't take no girl to Tennessee
For if you get married and don't agree
It'll aggravate your soul

I really got a kick out of the words to this song. That was personal for a man like A.P., and he wasn't one to get personal about his life when you were talking to him. He could only get personal like that in a song. A lot of mountain people are like that. There's only so much they're willing to say about things. Get 'em singing, though, and you'll learn a whole lot in very few words. You can get a man's whole life into a song, I reckon,

A.P. never said a word about Sara. But it must have weighed on his mind, and the way he got it out was singing that song. It was a way of telling people about what happened to him right there in Bristol. Like he was handing out free marriage advice from a fella who had to learn the hard way.

It helped us a lot having A.P. on our side in the early days. He was a good friend for us. But that only went so far as it goes. Your reputation and good name depended on who you were, and people got to know us every day on the *Farm and Fun Time* show.

The program got so popular it would just about set people's work schedule every day. Farmers would stop plowing in the middle of a furrow to run inside to hear it. People would tell us they'd be out a-hoeing corn and they'd keep checking their watch for noon to come. They didn't want to miss us one day.

The songbooks was another way we made our name to the public. I told you before that Leslie Keith gave us the idea. They were maybe eight to twelve pages long, little picture books with our photos and our biographies and lyrics to our favorite songs. We sold them for a quarter. We got a printer in Bristol to do it for us. He made a nickel or ten cents a book, and we'd clear fifteen cents a copy, and that was pretty good money back then. The songbooks and performance fees was the only way to make it financially. You couldn't make any royalties on your records the way the business was set up. We needed that money something awful back then.

Our very first songbook was a ten-pager. On the front was the title, *Greetings from the Stanley Brothers, Singers of Mountain Ballads*, and on the back were the words to Carter's first original song, "Mother No Longer Awaits Me at Home." Inside were photos of me and Carter, and Pee Wee and Ray Lambert. It was a way to get to know us better, and we gave our own little introductions, so the fans could be familiar with the Stanley Brothers and the Clinch Mountain Boys.

Carter's went like this: "HOWDY FRIENDS: It gives me great pleasure to offer to you a picture and a little history of myself. I was born August 27, 1925, on a small mountain farm on a creek known as Big Spraddle. There I stayed until Uncle Sam called me to serve our country in 1943. After receiving my discharge in 1946, I started singing on a small radio station in Norton, Va. I am proud to be broadcasting from WCYB at this time. I wish to thank my many friends for the nice cards and letters they have sent me. I hope to keep singing for you on the air. Thanks, CARTER STANLEY."

Mine went like this: "HELLO FOLKS: It makes me very happy to offer you this Souvenir folder. I sincerely hope you will enjoy reading it. I too was born on Big Spraddle Creek, February 27, 1927. There I stayed with my family until I went into the service in 1945. After receiving my discharge I too started singing on a station in Norton, Va. Leaving there we organized our own band and came to WCYB. I really appreciate the wonderful support you friends have given me here. Hoping to remain, Your Radio Friend, RALPH STANLEY.

You can see by reading these howdies how Carter was a tough act to follow, even when you were introducing yourself in a songbook. Seemed like I was always a half step behind him in word and deed, always in his shadow, almost like I was tagging along. I reckon I was, like little brothers tend to do. But I didn't mind, not at all. I was glad he could do that. He was more forward than me and he could talk for both of us, and he was good at it.

My favorite item in the first songbook was the photo of Cousin Wine-Sap, which was Ray Lambert in the funny glasses and false nose and crazy outfit. He got a chance to tell his fans about himself. His went like this: "Howdy Friends: Here's a pitcher of me and hit shore is a pleasure to know my good friends want one. I was born on Huckleberry Creek, up stairs, at home, in the bed on a pallet. My Maw was gone but my Grandmaw was there, so I guess it was just as good. I never asked where she was and I don't suppose it was any of my business. I appreciate all the mail and just keep it coming to me as you have done in the past. I thank you, WINE-SAP."

They say there is a lot of pain behind comedy, and a character like Wine-Sap was a way to tell stories about how hard it was for a lot of people in the mountains. Wine-Sap was letting the fans know he had a hard way coming up, and that he could make light of it and it wasn't going to stop him from enjoying life as best he could. That's the way he was about everything. A lot of our fans had some hardship like that, or they knew somebody been through something close to it, and Wine-Sap was a way to make fun of being from the country and going without. Maybe not ever knowing your mother.

I believe we sold about ten thousand copies of that first songbook, over a six-week period. We advertised it over the radio so people could order it and we'd mail them a copy. That was a big financial help.

The songbooks helped our fans put some faces next to the voices they heard on the radio. I guess for a lot of folks it was comforting to know we looked just the way we sounded: a couple of farm boys from the Clinch Mountains, not putting on any airs, just singing straight from the heart. We wanted the fans to know we were proud of who we were and where we come from.

We played a lot of shows at schoolhouses, and I wanted to tell you about one kind of show that you may not have heard about. They'd have what they called pie suppers at these schools, and we'd be the entertainment. These pie suppers were like fund-raisers, and here's how they worked: You'd pay all the money you could rake up for the chance to sit and eat a pie with your girl. It was like an auction, and you didn't want to see some other boy sitting with your girlfriend eating pie, so you'd bid all you had on the pie your girl had baked up and brought from home.

See, some fellows would team up on a boy. They'd pick out one boy that might be jealous-hearted or something. Two or three fellows would act up and gang up on the boy, and they'd mop up on 'im, just to get him away from his girl. They'd drive the price up to where maybe he couldn't afford it. They'd make the boy spend his very last penny to win the pie so he could eat that pie with his girl.

Schoolhouses were some of the best venues; they usually had an auditorium or a recital hall of some kind, so the acoustics were better than most places. My dad or Carter would get hold of the school principal and work out a deal. Courthouses, too. Just give the janitor a few dollars to open up and close down the place.

It was strictly percentage work. We didn't get many flat rates at all, not till years later in the 1950s. There were no guarantees. We either drew the people in or we didn't get nothing. We tried to get 70–30. That would be

70 percent for us and 30 percent for the sponsor. That was what we'd shoot for and we usually got it. Though at some places where they drove a hard bargain, we'd go 60–40.

Whatever we could get. Four hundred dollars for a show was a good payday. It wasn't too long before we started paying a regular salary to the Clinch Mountain Boys. We paid about $50 a week per man, and at that time, that was good money.

In the summer months, when the weather was good, we'd play anywhere you could think of. We'd play the stage of a county fair and the back of a flatbed truck; it didn't matter to us as long we could draw a crowd. In the afternoons, after the *Farm and Fun Time* program, we'd play a lot of auctions. Some were livestock auctions and some were real estate sales, where'd they be selling off property, mostly farms.

By having the Stanley Brothers, the organizers of the auction could get a big crowd. We'd put on a show and draw the people in, and then they'd do some auctioneering, and then we'd do some more singing. We would help business. Maybe a lot of the crowd wasn't interested in buying when they got there to hear us, but they'd hang around and the auctioneer would start reading off all the items for sale and they'd get the itch to bid on some properties or some cattle and whatnot. At night we'd play the schoolhouses and the courthouses and the drive-in theaters. It was a pretty good day's work, six days a week.

Let me tell you more about these shows at the drive-in theaters. There are not many left nowadays, but they was everywhere around the South in the 1940s and 1950s. You would have the big screen and the parking lot where everybody sat in the cars, watching a movie, and you had a concession stand and projector room, and that's where we would set up and play.

We'd have our own little sound system on top of the concession stand, just a couple of our own speakers we brought, and we also had it miked out to the theater's portable speakers you'd see hanging on the cars for the movie. So we'd play before and after the movie or maybe between the movies when it was a double feature. After we'd play a song they'd honk their car horns for applause. I remember playing a show in 1947 where they was showing the film *Devil Doll.*

The people would pay for the movie feature and get our show for free. We'd get 50 percent and the theater owner would get 50 percent. If they didn't run a movie and it was just the Stanley Brothers playing, it was usually the old 70–30 split.

Two of the things that really did draw the crowds was comedy and Leslie's bullwhip routine. Leslie had been around, so a lot of people knew his routine, but they never got tired of it. He would get Wine-Sap or somebody from the audience to hold the piece of paper, and Leslie would take that whip and cut the paper in two. There would always be a time set aside during the show for Leslie's bullwhip act. He'd put down his fiddle and pick up that whip and you'd better look out! It was nerve-racking to watch. I was too scared to ever hold that paper.

You had to have your bullwhip and your comedy routines and what have you, or you'd have a dull show. Of course, we had Cousin Wine-Sap, but we also had a lot of guests that helped us on the comedy routines. People expected the comedy just as much as the music. It was part of the deal.

Early on, we had us a wonderful entertainer, one of the best comedians in country music history, and that was Tom Ashley. A lot of people know him from his 1929 record of "Coo Coo Bird" on the *Anthology of American Folk Music*. He was a fine singer and guitar player and banjo man, too. But by the time he traveled with us, he was doing strictly comedy. All around the mountains people knew him as Rastus Jones from Georgia. He was one of the last blackface comedians on the road.

Ashley was another entertainer who'd got left behind. The records he made in the twenties and thirties run the gamut from murder ballads like "Little Sadie" to novelty songs from his days in the medicine shows. Didn't matter what the song, he was right there in your face. When he sang, *I don't want your gold watch and chain, All's I want is my .32-.20 to shoot out your dirty brain*, you believed him. He could be a cold-blooded killer on the run just as easy as he could play a drunken fool.

But after the Depression years, his old-time music had gone out of style. For a while he ran a truck business hauling anything that needed hauling. Tobacco, livestock feed, green beans, lime fertilizer, junk—whatever needed hauling, he'd do it. He'd even take used furniture from east Tennessee up to Pennsylvania.

Somehow or other, Ashley heard us on *Farm and Fun Time*, and he contacted us at the station in Bristol. At the time he was living out of a place they call Trades, which is close by Shouns, outside of Mountain City, Tennessee. He had got back in the music business touring with Charlie Monroe, not playing guitar or banjo but by going back to his roots, which was doing the old blackface comedy routines. After Charlie had moved his outfit on to another territory, Ashley wanted to join up with us and work the area close to his home. We were all for it.

If you asked him, Ashley would have told you he did comedy first and music second. He was an old pro of the skits and routines. As Rastus Jones from Georgia, he blacked his face with burnt cork and he blacked a couple teeth out and he put on a big baggy suit and got in all kind of scrapes and mischief, and he'd usually outsmart everybody in the end. He would get all the Clinch Mountain Boys to join in and help him do the little plays and routines.

We got along fine and Tom taught us a lot. He told us stories from his medicine show days. He said he'd lived like a gypsy, sleeping on the ground and setting up the tents where they played night shows under kerosene lamps. There was all kind of chores, too, like feeding and watering the horses that pulled the covered wagons from one mountain town to the next. He was sixteen when he joined up. So to him it was like some big adventure and he got enough know-how on entertaining to last him all his days.

Tom traveled most of the 1920s, first with Doc White Cloud, who wasn't a real Indian or a real doctor neither, and then with Doc Frank Hauer's Mo-Ka-Ton Show out of Knoxville, where he met up with Roy Acuff, just a teenager then, a fiddler from the Smoky Mountains who was hired to do blackface just like Tom. These medicine shows hawked tonics and remedies that were supposed to cure all kind of ailments.

Ashley said he learned his old-time frailing style of banjo from his aunts, just like I'd learned clawhammer from my mother. He got his song "Coo Coo Bird" from his mother, just like I got "Little Birdie" and "Shout Little Lulie" from my mother. The more you dig into the early days of mountain music, the more you find out how big a part women had in handing down the old styles. They could pick banjo right along with keeping house, and there was nothing bad about it.

We talked a lot about the old songs, and Carter was always asking where Tom got such and such a song. Ashley enjoyed the murder ballads I featured in our show, like "Pretty Polly." He said his most popular records were the ones with somebody dying; he called 'em those "old kill-'em-dead songs." And it's still true today. Those are the ones you hear people holler out for at my shows.

Once we even had a killing during a show. We were playing at a bar in Pikeville, Kentucky. This is the territory along the border where the Hatfields and the McCoys had their family feud, and it could get rough around there, it didn't matter what family you were from. The bar was called Marlo's, one of them beer joints where people drink too much and get to arguing. Now, most of the time, these beer joints would just have a fight or two and it wouldn't amount to much. When that happened, we'd keep playing our music right through the fight, and somebody would separate whoever was brawling. They'd break up the fight and that would be the end of it. We'd go on with our regular show like nothing ever happened. Ain't no use in making a comment on something that weren't none of our business.

But this Marlo's thing was bad business all around. We were backstage and getting ready to go on. Then we heard loud pops like somebody setting off firecrackers. It was a feller killed a man right there on the dance floor next to the stage. It was six steady shots: *POW-POW-POW-POW-POW-POW.* This feller just stood there in the middle of the crowd and emptied his pistol into the man right there beside him; so you knew he was mighty irate about something. The crowd sort of stood there too stunned to move, and nobody went after the shooter or nothing, and he just stood there, too, like he'd done what he needed to do and that was that.

Turned out it was a couple of bootleggers jealous of each other. They was arguing over business, and the man with the gun decided to settle things once and for all. The shooting closed down the show; the authorities came and they pronounced the man dead at the scene, and they arrested the killer, who didn't even try to run. He was there waiting for them, still holding his gun. And there right beside him was the dead man, just a-laying there in a pool of blood on the dance floor.

Chapter Eight

Ridin' High

"White dove will mourn in sorrow, the willows will hang their heads
I'll live my life in sorrow, since Mother and Daddy are dead"

—"The White Dove," the Stanley Brothers

Sometime in the spring of 1948, Flatt and Scruggs came into Bristol to work the *Farm and Fun Time* show. We had started out doing the hour program at noon, and as it got more popular, WCYB had sponsors lined up at the door and they had to add another hour and get more performers. Flatt and Scruggs came to do the second hour, and they was hotter than a two-dollar pistol. Lester and Earl broke away from Bill Monroe to start their own band, the Foggy Mountain Boys. They played a radio show and were really making a name for themselves. A lot of people thought they were better than Monroe and they were getting more and more followers.

Now, Bristol was a big town for us, but not so big that we didn't see Lester and Earl out and about. Matter of fact, Earl's wife, Louise, went shopping for baby clothes with Carter's wife, Mary, and Pee Wee's wife, Hazel. They'd got pregnant about the same time, and they would go to the JCPenney and socialize.

We'd already gotten to know Earl pretty good. He had been up to

Bristol after he first left Bill Monroe and before he and Lester started the Foggy Mountain Boys. Earl had stayed about a week and he went on a couple of shows with us. Earl was real friendly with me and I got to asking him about how he worked out his style, and he kindly showed me some stuff on the banjo in the backseat of the car when we were traveling. That helped me some, but I still didn't try to get the same lick Earl did.

The first three-finger banjo I heard was Snuffy Jenkins, and I heard Hoke Jenkins play that style, too. But what decided me was Earl, because he really did take the three-finger and do something new with it. He knew the neck and knew how to use his fingers in a whole new way, and he improved it so much over what Snuffy or Hoke or anybody before had ever done. Earl's always been my favorite banjo player. I loved his style, but I didn't want to sound like Earl. I'm the same with my banjo as I am with my singing. I ain't interested in copying nobody.

Now that the Foggy Mountain Boys had come to Bristol, it was a little different than when Earl was in town by himself. They was competition now. We didn't mind this at all. We welcomed it. If you don't have some competition, I don't think you can get better at what you're doing, whether it's in music or anything else.

This was business and we didn't want to get shown up by anybody. And we knew they felt the same way. We went to see Lester and Earl play a few shows around the area. We weren't there to cheer them on. We was there to get us some more material. We used to scout out new songs when Bill Monroe played, too, like when we got "Molly and Tenbrooks." All of us Clinch Mountain Boys would be there out in the audience, and each man would write down a verse on a piece of paper and we'd learn it that way. The melody we could learn by ear, but the words was tough to get down from one listen, so we'd put together all those lines from those scraps of paper, and we'd work out the song.

Flatt and Scruggs had a song Carter liked a lot, "Mother's Only Sleeping." He was always real fond of any songs about mothers sick or dying. They touched his heart, and most important, he knew they touched other people's hearts, too. We worked up our own version and started playing it on our radio program. Well, Lester didn't like that, and he tried to ground us.

One day after the *Farm and Fun Time* show, we was out on the street outside the station, and Lester came right up to us and he was hopping mad. Now, Earl was as easygoing as they come, but Lester was a different story. He had a temper. He got right in Carter's face and told him we couldn't be playing their songs. "Don't you ever be fooling around with any Flatt and Scruggs material," he said. He laid it out strong. It was a threat and he wasn't joking one bit.

Carter gave it right back to him, and they was close to blows over it. He got pretty smart with Lester and he told him a word or two. He said that suited us fine. We didn't need their songs in our show anyhow. We'd already started writing our own material and had our own songs. Then Lester said something against me, and Carter popped him.

He was always quick to defend his little brother.

The showdown with Lester was big for Carter. We'd already got in hot water with both of the Monroe Brothers, first with Charlie, then with Bill. When Charlie was at WCYB for a short spell, he'd been friendly and flattered that we did some of the old Monroe Brothers songs. He encouraged us and he said, "Go ahead, boys, you can do any of my songs you want to." But when he went to work at the station in Knoxville, he changed his tune real fast. He got irate and he wrote WCYB a letter saying, "We don't want the Stanley Brothers to sing any of my songs." Now, some of them songs were older than all of us put together, and we all knew it. This whole dispute came down to business; Charlie was just protecting himself because we were getting so popular.

Then it was Bill's turn to get sore at us Stanley Brothers. We'd heard the Bluegrass Boys play a song at shows, called "Molly and Tenbrooks," which was a real fast number about a horse race. We liked it, so we went ahead and cut our own version for Hobe at the WOPI studio in Bristol. The way we did the song, we featured Pee Wee on lead vocal, and he took his tenor higher than even Bill got, and I put my new three-finger banjo playing into overdrive, thanks to what Earl had shown me. It was really the most we'd ever sounded like Monroe's band, or ever would, but, to tell the truth, we were just having fun, letting Pee Wee step out by himself like his hero Bill. The hitch was this, though: Our "Molly and Tenbrooks" was released on Rich-R'-Tone a year before Bill's record came out on Columbia, and that really got him mad. He thought we was ripping him off like some others were doing. Thing was, he hadn't even met us in person like Charlie had; he just took us for some upstarts from the mountains; and I can't say I much blame him, even if we didn't mean any harm.

We was just so excited by Bill's music we couldn't help but emulate him early on, being so young and impressionable. But we found out right fast it wasn't no good to copy anybody, not even Bill. The main thing in music is to be original and different, and to be yourself. You need to be original to get anywhere, and you need to do your own material if you're going to make your way. We just had to learn the hard way.

The feuds with the Monroe Brothers was bad enough, but this here spat with Flatt and Scruggs was even worse. Lester was a rival calling Carter out, man-to-man, right there on the street. This was personal. Lester and Carter weren't on speaking terms for years after that.

Carter was so proud about his music that he took it as a blow to his honor. It shook him up and gave him a challenge. I believe it helped turn him into the songwriter he became. Anybody who wants someone to thank for all the classics Carter wrote through the years, they really ought to thank Lester Flatt, because I believe that's when Carter made up his mind he would outdo all the rest and make his name with his songs. From then on, we didn't fool much with anybody else's material. In the next year's time, Carter had fifty or sixty songs he wrote, and that's when we began singing Stanley Brothers songs.

What also got Carter writing was the road. The farther we played from our home base in Bristol, the more homesick we got. The more homesick we got, the more Carter wrote. All it took was a while out on the road and that was enough. He might not write a song for six months, and then he'd write ten songs in a week. He was like an old water pump. Once you'd get him primed, the songs just came pouring out.

Most of the time it happened on the road, late at night after a show, and I'd be driving. For miles and miles it'd seem like I was the only one awake in the car. I'd get to singing to keep myself from drifting off. Roll the window down and let the air hit me, slap my face a little bit, and sing gospel songs at the top of my lungs. When the road goes by, your mind starts to wander, and it usually goes back to when you were young. Many a mile, I've stayed awake behind the wheel, singing the old hymns I heard when I was a boy at McClure Primitive Baptist Church. They come to me of their own accord. After a while, even gospel songs will plumb wear you out, but you've got to do something to pass the time.

You'd think Carter was asleep, and then all of the sudden he'd raise up and ask for help on singing a verse or something he had in his head. He'd turn on the dome light so he could write some words down while they were fresh in his mind. It'd sort of make me mad, because the light'd be blinding me, and I'd be having trouble seeing the road. There'd be log trucks and tractor trailers coming at us and he'd be scribbling on a scrap of paper under the glare of that dome light; we nearly bought the farm many a time so he could get a song down. He'd write some and sing some and we'd be singing what he wrote, working out the melody and getting the harmonies down, and by the time we got to the radio station, he'd have a couple verses and the chorus worked out.

One night in 1948 we were coming back from a personal appearance outside Asheville, headed back home to Bristol. It was late, and outside was pitch black. Carter got to bustling around, first humming a melody line and then singing some words. He flicked on the dome light and I told him to shut the thing off or he was going to get us killed. I really got puffed up this time because I couldn't see the road. He did what he always did. He just ignored me and went right on with his composing. I didn't know what he was working on, but in an hour or so we were singing it right there in the car. That's the first time I ever knew about "The White Dove." After that, I didn't bother him anymore about the light. A song like "The White Dove" is probably worth getting in a car wreck.

People have asked me how it was Carter wrote so many great songs.

We never did talk much about it, so all I can tell you is, it's just a gift given by Him who has more power than any of us have. I think everybody is equal, but with a gift. Some don't find it. Some do. Carter's gift was singing and writing. His songs make you see what he's singing about, like the land around where we were raised up on Smith Ridge. That stayed on his mind like a vision that wouldn't let go.

Carter got his inspiration from visions he had riding on those lonesome back roads. He'd just get the ideas from memories drifting in his mind. Traveling so much, he'd ponder about things he missed and he let his imagination wander back home.

I don't know what caused him to think of the white dove. I only know he had been studying on it, and how it could affect you. A song like "The White Dove" is the backbone of the Stanley Brothers. If you go to Smith Ridge, and look around and study the words to "The White Dove," you can just see it in your mind. He was writing about what he dreaded most. Carter really loved our mother and daddy, and he dreaded the day when, according to nature, he'd have to give them up. He had always visioned going back home and they wouldn't be there. And that was what he visioned in "The White Dove."

There was so much driving back then, it's only natural songs would come to you on the road. And so many of the songs were about home and childhood memories. Bill Monroe wrote some of his best songs from the backseat, too. I heard that "Uncle Pen," the one song about growing up and hearing his uncle Pendleton Vandiver play his fiddle at dances, came to Bill when he was on the Pennsylvania Turnpike headed for a show.

Good as Bill was, nobody wrote more great songs in bluegrass than Carter. He wrote most before he even turned thirty years old. I remember being way out West in Montana. Up until then it was the farthest we'd ever been from home, and after a show we just kept driving through the night, and the sun was coming up on down the road. If you've ever been there, you know how it looks: Big Sky Country, they call it. It does something to you, and that morning it done something to Carter; that's when he wrote one of his best gospel numbers, "Let Me Walk, Lord, by

Your Side." It came without warning, and all he did was try to get it down before it got away from him.

When he was wasn't writing sad songs, Carter was pulling pranks and looking for kicks. He never let sad feelings take him down for long, because he was having too much fun the rest of the time. The road brought out both sides of his personality, the man who could write "Life of Sorrow," and the fellow who could spend hours telling jokes.

Mostly, he just wanted to see what would happen. I remember one time it almost got us killed. We were down in Winston-Salem, North Carolina, working out of a radio station there. It was only for a short spell, just a breather from WCYB. But we were moving back to Bristol again. During the time we were gone, the Blue Sky Boys had been filling in for us at the *Farm and Fun Time* show. They was brothers, Bill and Earl Bolick, and they was good friends. Carter called 'em the Skies for short. We had kept in touch with them, and that same day, they were headed down to Atlanta to their regular show.

It was a Saturday afternoon, I believe it was the fall of '49, with all them pretty leaves falling to make a carpet of red and yellow and orange on the road to Bristol. One of those days when you felt lucky to be a traveling musician and just blessed to be young and alive and doing what you loved. And the best thing of all was, we were headed back to Bristol, where we really felt at home. Good old Virginia.

Carter was feeling great. He was tight, he'd had him a drink or two, and naturally I was driving. He was sitting there in the passenger seat, just taking a nip now and then, looking at the countryside going by. That was what I thought he was doing, anyhow.

What he was really doing was fixing for an ambush. He knew the Bolicks would be headed our way, and he wanted to run 'em down. We knew what kind of car they had. It was an old black Lincoln. So Carter got a notion to keep a lookout for 'em to come our way and then chase their Lincoln down so we could have a little visit: "Keep your eyes out for the Skies, everybody. I just want to stop 'em and properly talk to 'em before they head down South. Who knows when we'll see them boys again?"

We were going up a mountain road, and sure enough, here come the black Lincoln, barreling the other way, and it shot right by us. Carter like to have a fit. "There they are, Ralph! Turn around, Go catch 'em, Ralph! Let's chase down the Skies!"

You'd a-thought I was a hired hand instead of a blood brother, and I done just what he told me to. Habit, I guess, and to tell the truth, I was in the mood for a little fun myself. I take a lot of pride in my driving. I've only been in one bad wreck my whole life, and I wasn't behind the wheel for that one. I can handle most anything on four wheels pretty well, so I was just as game as Carter was.

I swung our big Buick around and pulled a pretty slick U-turn and we made chase. I gunned the engine, and we shot back down the mountain about a mile behind the black Lincoln. The road was a little two-laner, and I was fixing to overtake the Skies and wave 'em over like we was the state police. Just give the Bolicks a little scare and then have a laugh with 'em. But the scare was on us. Down at the bottom of the hill was a narrow one-way bridge that could just barely fit two cars taking it careful and slow. I took a chance and went for broke. I already had the Buick wide open on the slope, so there was no stopping us now.

Right before we hit the bridge, there was an old Model A Ford truck coming the other way, and it was too late to slow down or swerve to the side and run off the road to let it pass. I had to stay on course or we'd have flipped the car for sure. I had to take that bridge with maybe half a lane and no room for a mistake. Well, I going well past 70 mph, I mean I was really a-flying, and had only a few inches on each side, but somehow we made it through, just barely squeezed by without scraping the truck or the side of the bridge.

I was shaken up by how close we come to disaster. I hit the brakes to get ahold of myself, white-knuckling that steering wheel; I really thought we'd bought the farm. I looked over and Carter was as pale as a ghost. Nobody in the car said a word. For once even Carter was speechless.

"Boys," I said. "Ain't no need to get ourselves killed."

So we called off the chase and let the Lincoln go. I turned around and we headed back to Bristol, feeling lucky we were still in one piece.

We was real good friends, the Skies and us. The Bolick brothers were nice, polite fellows, they was what you call good people. And nice as they were, they had talent to burn. They never bragged on themselves, because they didn't need to. Everybody knew they were one of the best brother teams in country music.

Earl was older and he sang lead and played guitar. Bill sang tenor and picked a beautiful mandolin. They had what they call a close-harmony style, a sound that only brothers could get. You could hear a lot of church in their singing. And there was a quiet grace in the way they blended their instruments with their voices. Like they was borned to it. But any musician will tell you how hard it is to make it sound so easy.

The Bolicks weren't songwriters, but they knew the old ballads, like "Banks of the Ohio," and hymns, like "Come to the Savior." The way they had it figured, there was plenty good songs already, and their job was to sing 'em better than anybody, and they had about the most perfect harmonies around. What Carter and me liked the most was, you could understand every syllable of what they were singing. They never slurred their words; they had the best diction outside of a grammar class, and they always stayed true to the song and the story.

We worked a lot of early morning radio shows with Earl and Bill, at WCYB in Bristol and at a station in Raleigh, too. They were about ten years older than we were and they knew the business. They'd made records back in the 1930s for Bluebird, which was RCA's budget label, and they sold for thirty-five cents. Those records, by the Blue Sky Boys and the Monroe Brothers, were popular all over the South. Carter really loved the Bluebird 78s, and when we were in Bristol, Earl would have us over at his place and play those old Monroe Brothers 78s on Bluebird for Carter. One of his favorites was "Feast Here Tonight" that we later done our own way, as "Rabbit in a Log."

The Bolicks weren't hillbillies like we were; they from cotton-mill country in the Piedmont area of North Carolina, down in Hickory. Their parents worked the thread mills and worshipped at the Holiness Church. Earl and Bill took the singing they heard in the churches and put it on radio and records to stay out of the mills.

It wasn't too long after the time we tried to chase down the Skies, they retired from music. They figured they were out of style, and they were tired of the road. They worked day jobs for years. For a while there, Earl made false teeth for a living. In the sixties, they came out of retirement and played a lot of shows during the folk revival. They sounded just like they did when they stopped in '51. Maybe even better. They wouldn't change their style for nothing and I always respected them for that.

It was when we were working the Skies' old radio show in Raleigh, North Carolina, that we got a call that was our big break. It was 1948 and we were taking a breather from Bristol, playing regular on WPTF in Raleigh. One day we got a call from New York and it was Art Satherly, an A and R man for Columbia Records. We had never heard of him, but we knew all about Columbia and this could be our shot.

We'd always dreamed of recording for Columbia, the label Bill Monroe was on, but we reckoned that was impossible, and now the impossible was about to happen. We knew Columbia was the best label there was, same way Cadillac was the best car. We'd already got our Cadillac, and now it was time to get us on Columbia. Then we'd really be riding in high style.

Carter got off the phone, said this Mr. Satherly was flying down to meet us right away. Carter always had premonitions about things. He told us this was what we'd been waiting for. We didn't know Satherly was the one who first made Gene Autry into a national star back in the thirties, and that he discovered and promoted country legends like Bob Wills and Roy Acuff. He had a lot of weight and influence at Columbia, where he was head A & R man for the country music division. It's probably a good thing we didn't know all of that, because it may have been too much for us to handle.

Satherly got into Raleigh and rented a couple of rooms at a nice hotel downtown, and we went over to see him. He was an older British man with silver hair and a dove gray suit right out of the movies. Not like any suit we'd ever seen in person, anyhow. He had class money can't buy, and he was just as nice to us as he could be. He was that way from the first handshake, before we played our music for him. I believe he was impressed by our manners, and I know we were impressed by his.

We set up right there in the hotel room and played a few songs. It wasn't a real audition, though. Satherly had already made up his mind. "That'll do just fine," he said. Then he dug down into his leather briefcase and got a contract and we signed up right then. It was a multiyear deal for exclusive recording rights with Columbia Records.

What Satherly did next, I'll never forget. It was one of those times when you know you've gone up to a whole new level, way up above what you've been used to. He reached into his coat pocket and pulled out a $500 cash advance and handed it over. "I thought you boys might need a little money to tide you over," he said. "There's plenty more where this is coming from." That was more than we made in a few good nights playing shows in eastern Kentucky. It was strange, after never getting paid a cent by Hobe for all those Rich-R'-Tone records, and here was Columbia paying us even before we cut a record. Seemed like a better way of doing business, to our way of thinking. Course Satherly was making what he figured was a sound investment, and he knew exactly what songs he wanted. There were four he said he wanted real bad, the ones we'd been doing on the radio that people really had a hankering for: "Little Glass of Wine," "The White Dove," "Little Maggie" and "Pretty Polly." These were the ones filling the mailbags. When he said those last two, I got nervous right off. Those were my showcase songs. That meant I'd have to sing lead all by myself. I was wondering if I'd be able to pull it off. I didn't think I was ready for that yet.

We'd be recording at the Castle Studio at the old Tulane Hotel in Nashville. It was where all the *Grand Ole Opry* stars made their records. Nashville was a magic word to us. It was what we'd been working for and dreaming about since we were little boys listening to the *Opry* on our battery-powered Philco. It meant we had made it.

Our record deal was good news for us, but it made Bill Monroe go ballistic. He'd been with Columbia for a few years and he'd cut some of his greatest songs there with Lester Flatt and Earl Scruggs. So he considered the label his home turf. He wanted to be the only artist on the roster doing his type of music, and he wouldn't stand for any others. Around this time, Flatt and Scruggs left him and they started up the Foggy Mountain Boys, so Bill saw any bluegrass-style band out there as competition. He told the Columbia executives if they signed the Stanley Brothers, he was going to leave, and he was as good as his word. He went over to Decca, where he spent the next couple of decades.

Columbia was very keen on us; they gave us the best treatment we could ask for. They had also signed up Wilma Lee and Stoney Cooper, who had recorded for Rich-R'-Tone. For Hobe they had gone by the same name as us, the Clinch Mountain Boys. Columbia wasn't having any of that; there was only one outfit with that name, and that was the Stanley Brothers. So Wilma Lee and Stoney changed the name of their band to the Clinch Mountain Clan and that made everybody happy.

There was a hitch, though; we had to wait to record because of a workers' strike that affected the big labels. The wait worked to our advantage, I believe. During that time, we started to work out our own style. While Carter was coming up with his songs, we were coming up with a new way to sing his songs. It came out of a lot of rehearsing, and we knew right off we had something special that would set us apart. It became known as the "high trio." Usually with trio harmonies, you had a lead vocal and then you had a higher tenor part and a lower baritone. We worked out a new arrangement with Carter on lead, me on tenor and then Pee Wee singing a high baritone way up top of all the voices. You may have heard the term "high lonesome" to describe bluegrass singing; well, our high trio was the highest and lonesomest thing you ever heard. To my knowledge, it was the first time it was done in our type of music.

Our first trip to Nashville was all business, and we rehearsed all the way, working out our new vocal parts and making 'em all fit together.

Once we got there, we didn't have time to tour the town at all, or see much of anything except the inside of the studio. We just did the sessions and went right back home. At the time, Castle Studio was the place where all the companies recorded country musicians in Nashville. This was before the major labels had their own studios there, so they all used the facility the Castle Recording Company had built in the old ballroom at the Tulane Hotel. The hotel was a big six-story building that took up a whole corner block at Eighth and Church streets in downtown Nashville.

Like a lot of places you hear so much about, the studio was nothing like you thought it might be like. It was a dump, to tell you the truth. Just a smoky little room full of recording equipment. Back then it wasn't looks that mattered but the sound you got. The Tulane is long gone, but the records made there have stood the test of time.

Mr. Satherly made a special trip to Nashville for our first session. Flew in direct from Los Angeles, where he'd been overseeing sessions by Stuart Hamblen, the popular country singer who had a big hit with "This Ole House."

Mr. Satherly had really taken a personal interest in us and he wanted to be there to help put us at ease. Satherly was firm on letting us record in our natural style. He said there was already plenty of slick commercial country. He loved old-time music and he'd spent his career chasing it down, traveling fifty thousand miles a year all over the South to find bands and singers to record. He was responsible for a lot of those old 78s from the 1920s that we heard on our parents' Victrola.

When Mr. Satherly signed us, he wanted us to sound like the Stanley Brothers the people heard on the *Farm and Fun Time* show. He wanted to let us loose like he did with Roy Acuff, who'd become so popular during the war years, just a farm boy from East Tennessee. We were backwoods even compared with Acuff, and Mr. Satherly wanted to get as much of that on record as possible.

In those days, major labels did it not much different than Hobe and his portable disc cutter; we'd all sing and play around the microphone, and it was a live performance, and that made it more exciting.

What made Carter's songs different was that they went deeper than most country songs, even deeper than Monroe's songs. Carter was seeing things from a new perspective. The road set his imagination free, and he put his own feelings onto the countryside rolling by, and the land and everything in it was alive with that feeling.

And that's what you hear in "The White Dove" and "The Lonesome

River" and "The Fields Have Turned Brown," which were the highlights of the early Columbia sessions. And in his singing he could make you feel what he was feeling, and the river and the willows and the doves were part of that sadness, too. What really put the new songs across was the high trio singing, with Pee Wee grieving out over top the high harmonies of Carter and me: We'd found a sound as lonesome as Carter's words.

What Carter had done was to imagine the saddest things he could imagine, and then make a sort of hymn out of that sadness, where it's so sad it turns into something beautiful. A lot of his songs from the Columbia sessions have become standards, and at every bluegrass festival you can still hear them sung.

Course, at the time, we only knew that they weren't hits, they weren't selling as much as we'd hoped and Columbia had hoped they would. This was a big disappointment for Carter, especially after those Rich-R'-Tones had been so popular. His only consolation was the fact that sales were low for most everybody in country music just then, so it wasn't the Stanley Brothers that was the problem. We just kept on going.

For our second session for Columbia, we finally got around to doing the old ballads that featured me singing lead. First one we did was "Man of Constant Sorrow," and I was scared to death. It didn't matter that I'd done it a hundred or more times on the radio and on the road. This was the big time, and the studio light was blinking and there was no one but me to sing it. That's what had me worried: singing alone. Harmony singing didn't bother me a bit, but getting behind that mic on your own was different. You're it.

Our arrangement was different from any other way we'd heard that song. We changed the tempo and really made it move. I worried my lines like my dad used to out on the porch, but I set it to a new timing. It fit the words better, because it's about a man on the run. He can't sit still, can't be soothed, can't slow down. It's about trying to outrun your troubles and never finding rest. Even a train ain't moving fast enough. There's no way out, but he keeps moving anyhow.

What really made the song move was the fiddle playing Les Woodie done. Listen to his fiddle hug the melody line and you can hear the worries chasing that man. They won't leave him be no matter where he goes. Les once told me he was never happy with the breaks he done on that, but he should've been well satisfied. He set the standard for every fiddler who's played "Man of Constant Sorrow" since.

If anyone came up short on that record it was me. I've never been satisfied with the way I sang on that. I can tell from my voice I wasn't able to put all my feeling in it, because I was so scared. After you get seasoned and you get used to things, you can put everything you've got in there. I was holding back. When I listen to that record now, I hear how scared I was more than anything. Maybe the fear I hear in my voice fit the story of the song. I do know that the first recording I did on "Man of Constant Sorrow" helped save the song from dying out. The record on Columbia gave it a new life, and that song has followed me ever since, and I still sing it every show I do.

By the time I sang on "Pretty Polly," I wasn't nervous anymore, and I've always liked the record. That song calls for a banjo with some bite. Willie stabs her to death and then he digs her grave. The banjo needs to stab just like that knife and dig deep just like that shovel, and it needs to match the singing as close as can be. That's how I'm different from Earl. I sing along with my picking. If I put a slur in a word, I put it into my banjo the same way. They's both proper instruments, the voice and the banjo. I try to make my banjo sound as much like the sound of the words as I can.

Satherly was back for the second session, and we brought him a present to thank him for believing in us. It was a country ham from the old home place on Smith Ridge, and he was real grateful and pleased by our choice of gift. He had really taken a shine to us, and not just as musicians; he enjoyed our company and we enjoyed his. He had come up in the country, too, way out in the farmland of England. When he was a boy, he'd slept in sheepskin blankets under the open sky. He'd ask us what it was like growing up in the mountains, and we would swap stories about the old ways.

Here was a man who loved the country life as much as he loved the music, and he was running the show at Columbia. We felt like his chosen sons, and we figured everything would work out fine with Satherly behind us. It goes to show how much we had to learn about the music business. You can be on the top record label with the top man on your side, and it don't mean a thing. Like always, we had to find out the hard way.

CHAPTER NINE

Back to the Mountain

"I'm going back to the old home, back to the place I loved so well
Where the sweet waters flow and the wild flowers grow, back to the old home on the hill
I know my dear old mother's waiting, waiting alone on the hill
With silver in her hair and a twinkle in her eye in the old cabin home on the hill"

—"THE OLD HOME," THE STANLEY BROTHERS

Through the years I've often wondered just how the Stanley Brothers stayed together as long as we did. There were a lot of times in the early years when I felt like music was too tough a way to make a living. I'd think about being a veterinarian or a farmer. Something where you didn't have to always be traveling the hard road, wondering if you'd have enough money for gas to get back home.

That was how I felt after that third session for Columbia. The records were something we could be proud of, but they weren't much in the way of big sellers. It wasn't like I thought it would be, where we'd hit the big time and life was going to be like gangbusters. Instead of hitting the big time, here we were right back in Bristol, playing the same little schoolhouses and movie theaters and miners' union halls, same old faces in the crowd. The *Farm and Fun Time* show didn't seem so fun anymore.

In 1951, we lost our fiddler Les Woodie and a couple other Clinch Mountain Boys, when they were drafted into service for the Korean War. The show dates and personal appearances were coming few and far between. The band was barely a band anymore, and business was slowing down. For once I didn't mind, because I was all give out from the road. I was running on empty, same as that old Packard of ours. I told Carter I was heading back home to Smith Ridge. I said it was probably just for a while, just to get some rest and get my strength back up. Deep down inside, I wasn't so sure if I could hack it anymore.

I was only twenty-four years old, but I felt ready for permanent retirement. Carter was fine with my decision. He said anytime I wanted to start back back up, just give him a call. He figured I'd be raring to go again before too long, after sleeping late and fattening up on our mother's home cooking. "Get you some color back in you," he said. "And when you're ready to go again, I'll be ready, too."

Carter had another reason he didn't mind taking a break from the Stanley Brothers. It would give him a chance to live out a dream of his, which was playing with Bill Monroe. Jimmy Martin had just left Bill's band to join up with Bobby Osborne, and Bill asked Carter to join on as his lead singer.

You may be wondering how Bill would want to hire Carter after all that had happened between him and the Stanley Brothers. It's true he was sore at us for a good while after we done "Molly and Tenbrooks" before his record come out, and especially after we signed with Columbia. He really did believe we was trying to steal his music. But that was before we'd ever got to know each other. He was misinformed a lot and I reckon we were, too. It was just a lot of hearsay.

A lot can change real quick when you stand face-to-face with a person. Even someone who you think is your enemy. You get to talking, and you look a man in the eye, and that's when you decide what's what. That's how it was with Monroe, for me and Carter both. After we learned Bill and after Bill got to know us, all the hard feelings went by the wayside, and we were behind each other.

So Carter told Bill he was ready to be a Bluegrass Boy. He'd idolized Bill ever since the show at Ervinton High School when were just a couple of wide-eyed mountain boys. Carter spent a few months with Monroe, and he loved every minute. He cut some records with Bill in

Nashville, including "Sugar Coated Love" and a gospel quartet number, "Get Down on Your Knees and Pray." He fit right in with the Bluegrass Boys, and Monroe was tickled to have Carter singing for him. It was a good match for the music and for everything else, because they became real good friends. Bill was like an older brother to Carter.

Before he left with Bill, Carter built him a little house on the old home place, across the road from where we grew up. He needed a place for Mary and their children and he could still be close by our mother. I was still single and I lived with her. Pee Wee and his wife, Hazel, needed somewhere to stay that winter, and they came to live for a while on Smith Ridge, too. My parents used to have a little country store that once belonged to my uncle Morgan Stanley. It was near the home place and had gotten kind of run-down, so we fixed it up and built partitions in there for rooms to make a place for Pee Wee and Hazel.

It was good having Pee Wee and Hazel up on the mountain. Hazel was a local girl from Wise County, and her dad was a coal miner and they had some acres on a little farm close by Norton. Lee had once come over to look at the timber at their place, a few years before. Pee Wee and Hazel had met when we were playing at the radio station in Norton, down from the corner drugstore where she worked at the soda fountain. It was Carter who introduced them, and he was best man at their wedding. He always liked playing matchmaker.

Carter was waiting on Bill to give him the word to hit the road. In the meantime he got by lending a hand at my dad's sawmill and other work he could find. Carter and Pee Wee always stayed close, and they still had the old itch to go out and have a good time. One day they headed off the mountain and drove down the Coeburn side to visit at somebody's house. They stayed past dark and a big blizzard came blowing in, one of them early spring snowstorms that come out of nowhere in March. It snowed and snowed on into the evening and it got late and still no word from Carter and Pee Wee.

There were only three dirt roads you could take to get up and down the mountain, and they were all snowed under. It must have been two feet deep, and it still hadn't stopped snowing. Hazel called over, and she was worried. "Ralph, how in the world are they going to get back up the mountain through all that snow in that car?"

I told her we both knew that Carter and Pee Wee were crazy as a couple of fox squirrels. I told her not to worry about a thing and that I was sure they had enough sense to stay put, spend the night and head back in the morning. Hazel said she was close to sending out a search party, which would have meant me. I was in no mind to go out in that weather. It was still snowing hard and I told her to just go to bed.

Long about midnight, we heard a commotion. There was Carter and Pee Wee, whooping and hollering, riding a horse they'd borrowed to make the trip back up the mountain. They had both jumped on that horse and rode there together through the storm, laughing and carrying on the whole way. Carter put the horse in the barn, hitched her up like it was nothing. Pee Wee said he'd never had a better time playing in the snow.

When Carter finally left the home place and went on the road with Monroe, I went back to the land. I wanted to try to make a go at being a farmer. Well, I don't have to tell you it didn't work out too good. I had Pee Wee with me, and neither of us much knew what we were doing. So the first thing we done is take some agricultural classes, and we sort of enjoyed that. But going to farm school is one thing, and working a farm is another.

It started out like a lot of projects do, where you think it's going to be easy, until you start, and you realize it ain't going to be nothing like you thought. Well, me and Pee Wee hitched up a team of horses and plowed a field and that was about it. I saw right away there wasn't much of a future for me in farming. And I knew, as tired as I was of the road, I missed music too bad to give it up for good. So I just bided my time and waited to see what was in store.

By the summer, Monroe's banjo player Rudy Lyle was called into the service, and Bill needed a temporary replacement while he hunted down a new man. He asked me to help him out on a few show dates, and I was happy to fill in. At that time Pee Wee was also taking a break from music, and he traveled along with us, not to play—Bill obviously didn't need a mandolin player—but just to be on the road with his idol. He loved Bill more than anybody, even more than Carter did, and he wanted to tag along for the fun of it.

And it was a lot of fun playing with the Bluegrass Boys on a few shows. Bill made a fine boss to work with. I was surprised how well I fit into the band, and he was well satisfied with my banjo playing. Bill liked the new setup so much, with Carter singing lead and me playing banjo, that he offered to take us on full-time. I believe he thought the Stanley Brothers and him together would be a force to be reckoned with. Bill was figuring that together we'd make the best combination around, maybe draw crowds that even Flatt and Scruggs couldn't get. It'd be two name acts for the price of one. He was so sold on the idea, he said he'd give us equal billing. Told us he'd call the new group Bill Monroe and the Stanley Brothers. For Bill, this was a big deal, being such a proud man as he was, to share the name of a band he'd built up on his own. But he was willing to do that if we would stay with him.

Now, Carter, he was all for it. He was having a fine time, and he didn't see any reason to stop a good thing. But I wasn't so sure. I really didn't want to go with Bill regular like Carter did. I always told Carter it was going to be the Stanley Brothers or nothing. Just like when we first started out with the Roy Sykes band; I felt the same way about it then, and I hadn't changed my mind. I wasn't interested in working for another man, even if that man was Bill Monroe.

So I told Bill it was an honor to get such an offer from him, but I was so tired from the road that I wasn't sure I wanted to stay in music for a living. I knew that traveling with Bill for more than a week was more than I could take. We'd been up most of the time either playing shows or driving to the next town, and I don't think we'd checked into a hotel the whole trip, just catching some shut-eye in the car when we could. I was beat. I wasn't ready to go back full-time. My constitution couldn't take it.

But with someone like Bill, you give a lot of respect and you don't take anything for granted. He was serious about the offer and he deserved a serious answer. I didn't want to give him a lot of bellyaching. I said I'd give it some careful thought, and I'd let him know for sure after a few days.

This was in August of 1951. We finished up a show in Raleigh, North Carolina, and then me and Pee Wee headed back home to Smith Ridge. What happened on the way back was something that probably helped keep the Stanley Brothers alive, even though I almost got myself killed.

I drove a few hundred miles north, until about six o'clock that morning, and then Pee Wee took over for the last leg of the drive back to McClure. I got into the backseat and went to sleep, dreaming about the sausage breakfast my mother would have ready for us at the old home place. We was driving out of North Carolina, heading through east Tennessee, which was a part of country we knew real well from so many show dates in the area. Maybe an hour after that, outside Shouns, near Mountain City, was when it happened. Pee Wee drifted off behind the wheel and we hit a truck coming around a bend.

The head-on collision threw me out of the car. I was sleeping like a log in the backseat, and that's probably what saved me from getting killed. The crash knocked me out and I can remember waking up, just staggering along the road, seeing blood and not knowing where I was. Then I saw the accident scene with car parts and people laying on the ground. Pee Wee wasn't hurt to amount to much, but it scared him to death. He was shook up so bad, he couldn't even tell the officer his own name.

The truck we hit was full of day laborers, and they were all banged up, broken hips and everything else. It was six men total and a lot of injuries, and they all sued Pee Wee and me over the accident. That was one of the reasons me and Carter copyrighted some of our songs with our half sister Ruby Rakes's name, to keep the royalties safe. We ended up settling on the damages and it wasn't much.

I found out later the accident wasn't all Pee Wee's fault. Before the wreck happened, the truck had swerved around an old man known in the area as the Old Prospector. He lived over in Damascus, Virginia, and he drove an old World War II army surplus jeep up that road every morning. He believed there was gold buried on top of Long Hope Mountain there on the edge of North Carolina. He'd make the drive through Mountain City on the way to hunt for that gold. He drove like a maniac, swerving all over the road. He always shorted the curve, and that's what caused the collision. Thing was, the old man kept right on going. He didn't even know there was an accident.

Anyhow, I was banged up, but I wasn't hurt that bad, not as bad as I could have been. Pee Wee's car was totaled. It had flipped over and upended in a cornfield by the side of the road, and it was crushed like a tin can, so I knew we were lucky to be alive. I had some deep cuts and gashes on my face, there's still a scar above my eye. And I had an injured back and whatnot. It was enough to keep me in the hospital three or four days, and it took a few months to recover.

Being laid up for such a long time gave me some time to think about things. I knew for sure I didn't want to go with Monroe, so that was settled in my mind. As the days dragged on, though, setting in bed with nothing to do, I got that old familiar itch for music and I knew the only cure was to scratch it. That meant getting back with Carter and giving it another shot.

Like always, Carter was all for it. That was our deal. Stanley Brothers forever. Till death do us part. We really believed in each other, and that never changed, no matter what. By the time I got my health back, Carter was ready to leave Bill and start up with me again. He said it was a dream come true to play with Bill, but now that he done it, he didn't need to do any more of it. The real dream was getting our band back together.

We had our work cut out for us, though. We had to go on without our favorite Clinch Mountain Boy, the very first one we ever had. Pee Wee had decided that the money he made as a professional musician wasn't enough for him to raise a family on. He took an engineering job to work on road construction projects. He always kept a hand in music as a hobby, playing nights after punching the clock, and he helped us out at a few sessions later on. But that was the end of his run as a full-time Clinch Mountain Boy.

I can't tell you enough how important Pee Wee was in establishing the Stanley Brothers. He was there with us when we first struck out on our own, and he was there for our first radio show, our first record, our first everything. He set the standard for all the Clinch Mountain Boys, by the way he played and the way he held himself as a person. He was as good a friend as he was a musician, really more like a brother. He was solid and he was true. You have to have a foundation to start with, and Pee Wee helped lay the foundation for all the work we done after.

Without Pee Wee, our sound would never be the same again. He was a fine mandolin player, but it was his singing that we'd depended on most for so long. It was such a big part of our harmony, especially the high lonesome sound he had on his vocal part for the high trio arrangements. It was what fans loved most about our singing, and it helped set us apart. Jimmy Martin once said to me, "You'll never have another high trio as good as it was with you and Carter and Pee Wee." He was right.

But there was a positive that come out of the bad. With Pee Wee gone, we were forced to move even further away from Monroe, and that was good for us. Pee Wee played the mandolin and sang so high, he liked to emulate Bill and he did most of the tenor singing with Carter. So that gave us a lot of Monroe echoes in our music, even when we weren't trying. We were always looking for a style of our own, and that may have held us back a little and put us too much in Bill's footsteps. After Pee Wee left, that's when Carter and me started doing all the duet singing together, and that allowed us to develop our own sound.

First thing we done was get us a new mandolin player. Curly Seckler had been with Flatt and Scruggs. Curly was great on the harmony singing, and he didn't sound nothing like Monroe. He was a little older than us, and he knew people in the business, and he was in good standing.

Then we got hold of our old fiddle player Bobby Sumner again, and he stayed a short while, and then he disappeared on us again. So we got a good replacement with Charlie Cline from the Lonesome Pine Fiddlers, whose brother Curly Ray you'll be hearing more about later.

One more thing that gave us a big boost. We got George Shuffler, who would become one of the most important Clinch Mountain Boys ever. He'd been playing bass with Jin and Jesse, but he was ready to move on. We found George when we were playing a little schoolhouse, Salem

School, in Morgantown, North Carolina, about twenty miles from his hometown in Valdese. He came from a big musical family. Our old fiddler Les Woodie grew up just down the road, and he used to hang out there at the Shuffler house to play and sing. George could play just about anything with strings—anything except fiddle anyhow—but he was best at guitar and the big stand-up bass. We needed a bass man at the time, so that's what he played. He stayed off and on with the Stanley Brothers for the next seventeen years. In the later years when we couldn't afford a full band, George got so close to me and Carter, not just singing and playing together but living together, he became known as the third Stanley Brother.

Curly helped get us a job at a station, WVLK, in Kentucky, near Lexington and Versaille. We had passed through close by there for a brief spell at WLEX a year before that, but this was something different. This was the first radio program where we got a salary. Even after five years with WCYB, we never got a nickel for the *Farm and Fun Time* show. We still made all our money from show dates, songbooks, and whatever else we could sell on our own.

It went good from the start. We played a lot of territory in that part of Kentucky we hadn't covered before, and it was ripe and ready for us.

We worked a morning program every day for WVLK, and got us a sponsor, a tobacco warehouse out of Versailles. We'd play personal appearances five or six days a week, and on Saturdays we'd work the Kentucky Barn Dance, which was broadcast on WVLK. Curly had helped get the barn dance going with Flatt and Scruggs, and it was real popular. So we were getting two regular salaries. It wasn't much, but when you put that together with money from the show dates, it wasn't bad.

This part of Kentucky is very different from the eastern part of the state near where we came from, close by the Virginia line. The land is wide open with rolling fields and pastureland, not mountainous at all. It's in the heart of Bluegrass horse country. Now, we raised horses where we came from, but we had horses for work. We used 'em to plow the fields and help with chores around the farm. Around the Lexington area, especially down by Versailles, it's a whole different thing. There are well-to-do farms, with miles and miles of white fences, where they raise prize Thoroughbreds for the big races. They treat their horses like royalty.

So this was a big treat for horse lovers like me and Carter. We took advantage of the opportunity. When we got a little spare time from the radio program and the shows, we'd go out on those big fancy farms and watch the men train the racehorses. It was fun to see how much they pampered these big, beautiful Thoroughbreds that were worth millions of dollars. They'd brush 'em down and trot 'em around the track, take 'em high stepping, and run 'em the quarter mile. And you've never seen finer horses. Of course, they would breed the horses there, too.

One time, we were spending a lazy day at a private farm in Versailles. On this afternoon, they were breeding a pair, and the stud got up on the mare's back, you know, and weighted on her. We grew up on a farm, of course, so it wasn't nothing for us to see that. But what we saw next we could hardly believe. We happened to look down the way, and we saw a middle-aged woman, a tourist or sightseer like us, and she had wrapped herself around a pole and she was just a-grinding away right out in the open, just matching them horses. She didn't know anyone was looking or she just didn't care. She was getting well acquainted with that pole, and she knew every turn to make. The horses got her all excited, I reckon, and she just couldn't help herself from joining in the fun. Carter and me watched her and we couldn't hardly stop from laughing.

In the summer of 1952, we switched jobs again, something a little closer to our home base in Bristol. It was a good opportunity: an early morning show at WOAY in Oak Hill, West Virginia. Oak Hill got famous later that year when they found Hank Williams dead there in the back of his Cadillac. Hank had been driving all night to a New Year's Day show in Canton, Ohio. His chauffeur pulled into a gas station in Oak Hill and checked on him, and his heart had just give out on him. The drink and the pills finally caught up with him, and the hard traveling, too, the same grind we were going through.

Before the year was out, we got homesick again and we went back to our base in Bristol. We were always welcome back at WCYB, and the *Farm and Fun Time* show was something we could always count on. We missed being home, and we missed some of the regulars we had with us when we were working out of Bristol.

One of our favorites was Fiddlin' Cowan Powers, a real old-timer if there ever was, known all around these parts, a true pioneer of country music. He made a gang of records for Victor in the early 1920s, some of the first honest-to-God hillbilly songs ever to make it onto record. Cowan was cutting records in New York City years before the Carter Family got started. My parents used to have some of his old 78s for their windup Victrola. Fiddle reels and dance tunes like "Ida Red," "Sourwood Mountain," "Paddy on the Turnpike" and "Cripple Creek."

But times had passed him by. His music was out of fashion. Radio was in and the old Victrolas was out. People's tastes had changed. He was retired, living in Castlewood, not far from where we was from. He was well up in age then, in his seventies. But he had plenty of vigor; he'd married a redheaded gal thirty years younger, and they had a son.

Carter first met Cowan when he was playing with Roy Sykes. Carter said nobody in the group had any time for the old man. Too much of a generation gap. But Carter and Cowan hit it off and struck up a friendship. Carter always got along well with old folks and I did, too. We always showed them kindness and respect. Carter would pump the old-timers dry for talk of the old days. He always liked hearing the stories they told. For a songwriter, stories are what matter most. It's their inspiration.

Cowan had heard us on the *Farm and Fun Time* program, and we got reacquainted. Next thing you know, the old man was on the road with us, as a special guest. First for a day or two, then he got to traveling for weeks at a time. Most other young bands wouldn't have dreamed of taking an old-timer like Fiddlin' Powers. They reckoned it would slow 'em down and get in the way, maybe, and bring trouble they didn't need.

We didn't think so. We felt we owed it to Cowan for helping pave the way for country musicians. We believed he deserved another chance to do what he loved and to see new places he hadn't seen, too. I reckon it helped him; he seemed to get stronger with every trip he took with us. The road gave him a second wind.

Now that I'm past Cowan's age, I can tell you the road has given me many a second wind; it's what keeps me going today. I could never just sit and lay around the house all the time. I have to be playing music for the people.

On our way to a show, we'd pick up Cowan on the road outside his house in Castlewood, not too far down Highway 58 in Russell County. He'd be there at the mailbox waiting on us, fiddle under his arm, checking his gold watch that hung on a chain from his vest. It was an old Elgin pocket watch like the kind railroad conductors used to carry. He loved his watch; it was his most prized possession. He thought he had the best watch in the world and wouldn't take nothin' for it.

Carter loved to tease Cowan and used to play a joke on him and his watch. We used to travel a lot west across the state line into eastern Kentucky, an area where the time zone changes from eastern standard time to central standard time. We'd be rolling through some little town, one of those county seats with the little town square and a courthouse with great big clock on top.

At a stoplight, Carter would nudge the old man, who was usually dozing off or daydreaming in some reverie.

"Cam," he'd say. "Cam" was what Carter always called him. "What time is it?"

Cowan would pull out his watch and say, "Two o'clock."

"That's not right, Cam. What's wrong with that watch?"

"Ain't nothing wrong with my damn watch."

And Carter would point at the courthouse clock, which of course was an hour behind eastern standard time. "You look at the clock, Cam. It's one o'clock, not two o'clock."

Cowan would check his watch and then look over at that courthouse clock. He'd shake that watch, hold it to his ear, knock it on his knee.

Cowan never did figure out what was wrong. Nobody had told him a thing about time zones. We never let on about what we done to him. He couldn't understand how his Elgin had let him down. Course, when we got back home to Virginia, his watch would be back on the right time. It worried him about half to death.

We loved having Fiddlin' Powers ride along with us. He was like a grandpa to us, since we'd lost both ours early on. He felt the same about Carter and me; he called us "his boys." You could learn a lot listening to him—about music and all kinds of things.

He made the miles go by easier, telling us stories from the old days. He said he went to school long enough to learn to write his name and he never went back. As a young man, he farmed some and worked in the carpenter's trade, but he really made his reputation as a leather maker. He had a custom pattern he'd cut out of a whole cowhide he used to make leggings from. Leggings were in great demand back then. In the days of World War I, all the young men wanting to dress well and look smart had to have leggings. He made a lot of gun holsters, too. Back then, every man in these parts had to have his own underarm holster because he'd be packing heat for protection.

After his wife died of TB, Cowan decided to take his children on the road as a musical family. He'd won a lot of fiddle contests, and his kids took after him, Charlie on banjo, Orpha on mandolin, Carrie on guitar and Ada on ukele. He was awful proud of the fact they were the first family string band from Appalachia to make records. Up until then, the record companies didn't think hillbilly music would sell, but the Powers family proved that lots of folks wanted the old-time mountain songs, when they were done right.

Back in the 1920s, they were a big deal. You would see handbills and posters touting Fiddlin' Powers and Family as "The South's Greatest Old-Time String Band from Old Virginny." He told us a funny story about those handbills. They had a formal group photo of the family, everybody in their Sunday best, the girls in long dresses and white stockings, the men in black suits and bow ties, Cowan's gold watch and chain prominently displayed. The only problem was the look on Cowan's face. It was a mean, angry stare, more like an outlaw than an old-time fiddler. He told us there was a good reason for that ugly mug he gave the camera. The studio photographer was flirting with his eldest daughter, Orpha, and he didn't like it one bit, so he was in no mood to smile.

In their heyday, Fiddlin' Powers and Family took in $200 on a good night for a show. For a two-day recording session in New York City they could earn a check for $750. That was big money back then. Course, it couldn't last. Nothing does. The Depression hit, and the music business got hit hard, along with everything else. The daughters grew up, got married and started families of their own. Cowan's son, Charlie, who played a good clawhammer banjo, went into the army and later served overseas in World War II and died of starvation on the Bataan Death March. The Depression and war both broke up a lot of the old-time family bands.

Cowan kept at music as a pastime, mostly at fiddle contests and such, but he never could put down his fiddle for good. That's something I can understand. This music gets in your blood, and it never leaves you.

His music was real old-fashioned and frozen in time, but we loved having him as our special guest. The people loved him from the old days; they still remembered those Victor records by Fiddlin' Powers and Family He could still play, too, he hadn't lost it.

We always had some fun with Cowan on the road. When Leslie Keith was still fiddling for us, sometimes he really got along with the old man; they knew each other from fiddling contests in the old days. Leslie would joke on Cowan an awful lot, and Cowan would give it right back. Leslie gave Cowan the nickname "Val Cooney." And Cowan put the name "Gar" on Leslie, and they'd always be throwing them funny names at each other. To this day, I still don't know what they was laughing about.

All his time with us, Cowan never got a salary. He didn't want money, just the chance to play his music and hear the crowds again. We fed him and let him have his fun, and he had the time of his life right up until the end. Now comes the sad part, but it ain't all sad because Cowan went out probably the best way a musician could.

We were at a show date in Glade Spring, Virginia. It was the Summit Drive-in, and the parking lot was full of cars. Like I told you, we played a lot of drive-in movie theaters back then. They'd have a double feature and we'd play our music in between the movies. The stage was on top of the concession stand, with some steps or a ladder rigged up.

Well, Cowan climbed up the ladder to the stage and started in on his portion of the show, a couple of fiddle reels. He played "Cluck Old Hen" and was closing out in fine style with "Katy Hill," and he had the crowd with him all the way. Then, right in the middle of the tune, he just up and cut it off mid-bow. Said he was feeling bad.

We helped him down from the concession stand and he went to catch his breath and sit in the car, which was parked under a shade tree nearby. We closed the show early and checked on him. He looked poorly, real pale and drawn, and he said he had an awful pain in his chest. We knew it was serious. Course, we told him different, and we played it down. We told him not to worry and tried to cheer him up the best we could.

We packed up all the instruments and took him right away to the hospital in Abingdon; it was more than twenty-five miles and I drove as fast as the car could take us. Carter was rubbing the old man's chest, trying to comfort him, but he suffered something awful.

Once we got to Abingdon, we checked him into the hospital and hoped for the best. Not too long after, though, the doctors pulled us aside. They said call Cowan's family and tell them to come right away if they want to see him, because he wasn't going to make it. He hung on through the night, but the next day he died.

The doctors said it was a heart attack got him. He was seventy-six years old, and his ticker just gave out and he got it all at once right there, doing what he loved. That ain't a bad way to go. I know many a musician who'd want to go out just like he did.

Traveling with Cowan was some of the best times we ever had on the road. We kept pretty close to Bristol during those days, and I was happy to be back close by Smith Ridge. It was less than an hour's drive from the home place. Every chance I could, I'd go back and spend the days off with my mother.

Lucy was getting up in years, past sixty now, and she was all alone up in the old house. Carter would stay with Mary and his kids, and I would stay with Lucy, and just spend time with her and help her out as best I could.

Now, here I'd been a professional musician for years, and I'd seen some of the wild side of life, but at that time I wasn't much interested. I hadn't found any woman could compare with my mother. Even if I had, I wasn't ready to make a go of it. The main thing was that I didn't want to abandon my mother. I knew that I was all she had left, the son she could count on to be there for her.

Carter was married with kids, so he had his own family to worry about and support. And he'd never really been there for our mother like I had, in those years after our dad left. So I felt like she was still needing me. She still had me, at least, and I believed that was something. I was the same mama's boy, all grown up.

I remembered all the times, how she lived for us. It stayed on my mind, and I never forgot. How she sacrificed for us boys; how she wore holes in her stockings to buy Carter and me school clothes. How she'd stay up late sewing quilts for our beds. Always, she'd go without so we'd have what we needed.

Now, Carter felt the same way I did, he just showed it in a different way. He may not have been there with her like I always was, but she was always on his mind, and the feelings he had came out in his songs. In his music, he could always return to the scenes of childhood on Smith Ridge, with our mother. Course, in most of Carter's songs, she was already in heaven, looking down on her boys. In "Vision of Mother," he sang, *There's a place up yonder, where my loved ones wait for me/I saw Mother in a vision, kneeling there to pray for me.* My mother kept all our records there in the house, along with the news clippings on her Stanley boys.

I think she took a real pride and quiet satisfaction knowing she was the first to spot our talent, and all the records and newspaper stories were the proof that we'd made a success out of music. Now, she was like any mother, too, and she probably thought we deserved more. She saw how much we were struggling to make ends meet, working the radio show and playing show dates all around the mountains. She knew it was a hard road for us. She was worried for our health, much more than her own.

I would have liked to give her more than a stack of records. It didn't seem like Carter and me had much to show for what we'd done in the music business. The old home place still didn't have electricity, no indoor plumbing, nothing in the way of modern conveniences. My mother didn't mind at all, but I would have liked for her to have more.

Sometimes I'd think maybe the dream of making it in music was just a dream after all. Maybe this was all we'd ever have. Just our little show on WCYB and our little crop of fans in the coalfields and farms. Maybe fame and fortune just wasn't in the cards.

We drove back to Nashville for our last session for Columbia. It wasn't the same as before. Satherly wasn't there, and the good feelings we had about our chances for breaking big were gone. The wind was out of our sails, and we could tell the label had given up on us. We were old hat and they rushed us in and out of the studio. Our contract expired and it wasn't renewed. Columbia dropped us and we had no takers.

The shame of it was, we were sounding as good as we ever had. George Shuffler added a lot with his bass playing, and we still wanted to make records. We went back and did a final session for Rich-R'-Tone, and for that we had a fine mandolin player named Jim Williams, and he could sing, too. But it felt like we was going backwards, recording for Hobe Stanton again.

The records we did for Columbia sold pretty well, but not as much as we'd been hoping. The thing was, there was more to a record's success than hitting the country charts. The people who did buy 'em, well, they became our new fans, even if they were a thousand miles away. Those Columbia sides done their work by putting our name out there to fans we didn't even know about, well beyond the broadcast range of WCYB. That was the power of a major label like Columbia. The Rich-R'-Tones never was distributed outside the Appalachian area, but the Columbia records made it across the country, to places where our music was something new and different to people who'd never heard of the Clinch Mountains until they saw the name printed on the label.

They had a big effect on the people who heard them. Porter Wagoner was growing up in the Ozarks way out in West Plain, Missouri, and he said he wore out his copy of "The White Dove." He told me years later it was the first song he learned the words to, and he'd sing it with his brother, pretending they were the Stanley Brothers. Up in Chicago, a college student named Larry Erhlich got hold of a copy of "Man of Constant Sorrow" with "Pretty Polly" on the flip side. He was like a lot of young boys from the city who became Stanley Brothers fans, like Bob Dylan, who did a rendition of "Man of Constant Sorrow" on his first album. Later, they would help kick off the folk revival, and that would help us a lot during the lean years in the early sixties.

You just never knew where those records ended up. Bill Malone, the historian who wrote *Country Music, U.S.A.,* was just a boy growing up in East Texas, where there was no such a thing as our kind of mountain music: "When I heard Carter and Ralph singing, the sound was just so lonesome and crisp and clear," he later said. "Being on a farm in East Texas, it was really romantic to think about those Virginia mountains. I had images of isolated coves and people way off the beaten track."

Just like the old phonograph records of the Carter Family and Grayson and Whitter done for Carter and me, our Columbia records were working the same spell on people from all over. Course, we didn't know any of that at the time. We just figured we'd failed a little, you know, in our goal. Maybe came up short.

We knew we had fans in the Bristol area, and we were proud and grateful to have them, but we'd been playing the same territory for too long. You get tired of chocolate pie, even if it's your favorite dish. That's what happened to us in Bristol, for us and for our fans. The crowds started going down because people had already seen us again and again.

That's when we'd head out to new territory. We worked the WWVA Jamboree in Wheeling, West Virginia., which was probably the biggest outside of the *Opry*. We went to Winston-Salem, stayed a month or two at a station there. And we pulled some big crowds at the Carolina Barn Dance, MC-ed by Cal Calhoun, out of Spruce Pine, North Carolina, a little railroad town on the Clinchfield line high in the Blue Ridge Mountains not too far out of Asheville. They'd pack in more than six hundred people for a Saturday night show, and when you consider the entire population of Spruce Pine was only a few thousand, that was quite a crowd.

We even went down to Shreveport, Louisiana, stayed a few weeks there; had all our suits stole right out of our Packard, too, by a slicker who seen our unlocked car with out-of-state license plates.

Then we got something closer to home, up in Huntington, West Virginia. We played at a radio station there, WSAZ, and also did a show on a TV station there. To my knowledge, we were the first hillbilly band to do a regular broadcast on television. We were pretty bad excited to be playing in front of a TV camera. It was new to us and new to viewers, too. It didn't do so well, though; it was too early for television. Most people in the mountains couldn't afford TV sets, so they couldn't watch the program.

Well, we'd work the new areas, and we'd do all right and it was good to get some new fans. But we'd always get homesick and come back to Bristol.

As rough as it got, we enjoyed being on the road in the early days when we was still young and everything seemed new to us. We'd get to see things most folks had to take a vacation to travel to see, like Cudjo's Cave in Kentucky. And you can't ever trade in for the experience you get out in the world.

On them all-night drives when you'd get wore out and groggy, you'd see strange things, like something out of a vision or a dream. You'd have to pinch yourself to see if you were maybe seeing things that weren't really there.

Late one night, we were driving somewhere in Kentucky after a show. We came up on a big, long bridge that was stretched across the river. We had made it to the middle of the bridge, when right smack-dab in the headlights, there was a big white horse come out of nowhere. Somehow or other, he got to running on the bridge and he ended up in the center of the road where we was headed.

Well, the horse froze when the lights hit him, and I tried to steer the car around to the side, but it was too late to make a difference. He just reared up on his hind legs and jumped off the side of the bridge and disappeared into the dark. The headlights spooked him and he jumped for his life. I reckon he went into the river. Don't know if he drowned or not; we didn't have time to stop the car and find out.

We had more than runaway horses going by the wayside. Another night, we were on a back road way out in the country. It was real dark, no moon, no stars out, no nothing. I don't even remember what state it was. Just that we was hurrying to make a show somewhere far away. Carter wanted to get out of the car and stretch a bit and heed nature's call. I pulled over to the edge of the road as best as I could see. Carter got out and he just took one step and was gone, right over the embankment nobody could see. He went falling and rolled down the hill into a hog lot.

And he must have woke 'em up angry, because them hogs started running him down. Somehow he managed to get out of there. He didn't get hurt, but he was lucky he didn't break any bones or get ate up by them boar hogs. They will come after you; that's their territory and they defend it. Carter got back in the car and he had his traveling clothes all muddy and messed up. He told me next time he'd wait until we found a proper restroom; he said he'd never been scared like that in his life.

Lot of fun and foolishness on the road, and a lot of temptations, too, with women and especially with drinking, and drinking was Carter's weakness.

Now, we used to like pretty girls, I'll admit it, and there was plenty of pretty girls on the road; I don't care how far back in the mountains you'd go, there was always some. We'd meet so many girls at the shows, some just to talk to and meet with; and some for this, that and the other. Now, with these girls you'd see on the road, you could look at them and not get in trouble. But, sometimes, you know, you'd get with one and maybe go a little too far. I'm an old man now and a different man, too; when it comes to the women, don't bother me at all now and hasn't for many years.

Women was one thing, and that was your own private affair that was away from the public eye. Drinking was a whole different situation; it was public and out in the open. You have to understand when and where this all was happening, the time and place where we were coming up as musicians, which was the Southern Appalachians in the years after World War II, before there was such things as TV and other such diversions.

Back in them days, wherever, and I do mean wherever, there was music, there was liquor. Didn't matter if it was a barn dance, a corn shucking, a fiddler's contest or a Stanley Brothers show, there was bound to be drinking.

Music was an entertainment and a break from hard work, and it was there to help you forget your troubles. The drinking that come with the music was sociable and it was neighborly, and it was an insult if you turned down an offer to take a nip. To partake was just considered good manners back in the mountains.

Carter loved to talk with people who came to see our shows; he loved to drink with them, and they loved to drink with him even more. People were always buying him a drink, bringing him a drink, wherever we went. Everybody wanted to drink with Carter. After the show, before the show, anytime. And that was hard for him to turn down. He just had a weakness, you know, and he just got too far gone.

At the shows it was always the same setup. Some local fellows there would get to drinking and they'd offer me and Carter a drink, and if you drank with them, they thought they was doing big-time stuff. It was something they could go back home and tell their friends: "Well, we got drunk together last night with Carter Stanley and we had a big time." And they thought because of that, they were up in the world, see, they felt that boosted them in the eyes of their friends.

And this happened just about every show we played in every little town we traveled to. Carter, being of such a sociable nature, he couldn't say no. And he got to depend on it, and it got to be a habit. A lot of people like Carter, they love whiskey and moonshine and beer and everything else. I never got the habit, because I never did enjoy the taste of whiskey in the first place, and I never could stand beer, neither. I've had people come up to me and say, "Boy, we used to have a big time and get drunk together, didn't we?" And I never even drank a drop with them.

Now, I'm not perfect in that; I took a drink now and then, and I've made my mistakes and I've done wrong, too. I had my problems. I used to take a drink of whiskey or two; it would help me if I was nervous sometimes, or feeling like I needed it. I'd take me some drinks for the little boost it would give me, and to build my nerve up a little, just a few swallows to get up on the stage before a show.

What whiskey did for me was made me feel more jolly and more talkative, which was good for me, being so shy. It helped me talk with people. It never did make me want to be mean or make me crazy or anything like that.

Drinking is different for everybody, and I just never got that far into it like Carter. Don't make me better; I was fortunate to be that way. I never did let it get ahold of me. I could take it or leave it, but I guess after you get so far along like with Carter, it's habit-forming. When you get to where you crave it and have to have it, that's when it takes ahold of you and that's what happened to Carter.

Of course, early on, he could handle it mostly. It didn't change him, just made him more like Carter was anyhow, talking and laughing and having a good time. He never let it affect his playing and singing in the shows early on. Maybe it helped him in some way, writing his songs and getting his ideas. I can't rightly say when it went from a good thing to a bad thing. All I can tell you is, over the years, it just kept tightening the grip on him, and there wasn't nothing I could do to unloose that grip. He wasn't going to let nobody tell him how to live or what to do. And I had to live with it just like he did. I would never quit him; no matter what, he was still my brother.

CHAPTER TEN

Mercury Rising

"Listen to the spirit and sincerity of the Stanley Brothers as they sing such beautiful hymns. They really live and feel their music to the point where they do much more than just play it. We, at Mercury, are extremely proud of the Stanleys, these hardy men of the hills, who are so true to their heritage."

—FROM THE LINER NOTES TO *THE STANLEY BROTHERS: COUNTRY PICKIN' AND SINGIN'*

You've probably heard about the Wilderness Trail, the one Daniel Boone blazed back in the late 1700s. He came right through our neck of the woods, crossed over the Clinch River and pushed on to the Cumberland Gap, opening the way for the pioneers in their Conestoga wagons to settle the new Western frontier. The promised land.

By the time I was coming up in Dickenson County, near the place by the river where they say Boone stopped to pray, we had our own Wilderness Trail, our own road to a better life. It didn't go west, though. It went north, from Weber City and Norton and Pound across the Kentucky border through Pikeville and Paintsville and Ashland, across the Ohio River through Portsmouth and Columbus and points north, all the way to Michigan. On the maps it was Route 23, but it became known as the Hillbilly Highway.

After the coal boom years, and after they'd cut down the virgin timber, the people around here who worked the mines and the sawmills were plumb out of luck. There weren't many jobs to be had in our particular place in the world. It's still like that today. So they packed up and headed up Route 23, to find a better life in the North, where the factories where bigger than a whole town you'd find back in the Appalachians.

Dwight Yoakam was from Pikeville. He wrote a song that tells the story of so many mountain migrants who rode on the Hillbilly Highway: *They thought reading, writing and Route 23 would take them to the good life they'd never seen/They didn't know that old highway could lead them to a world of misery.*

They found out fast that the Promised Land wasn't all they'd hoped for. Pay was low, the city was big and strange, friends were few and far between. But that didn't stop them from leaving their homes and everything they had. Thousands and thousands kept right on a-coming north. This was the era before the interstate highway system was built, and Route 23 was the only way to go. It was six hundred miles of rough road, and it took more than sixteen hours, and that's if you was lucky and didn't have an engine breakdown or get a flat tire. I'm speaking from personal experience, because I was once one of the pilgrims on the Hillbilly Highway.

It was the winter of 1953 and Carter and me had decided to lay off the music again. It was the off-season, so we didn't have many show dates lined up. It seemed like a good time to take a break and try to earn some money until spring, when we could go back on the road again. Carter had a growing family, with hungry mouths to feed, and we couldn't afford to take time off without any income.

So Carter and I traveled up Route 23, same as the other migrants, and we went all the way to Michigan. I think it may have been the longest road trip I can ever remember. On our long drives to shows, we knew people were waiting to hear us and maybe cheer a little for us. A road trip to play some shows may tire you out and wear you down, but it gives you something to look forward to. This trip north on Route 23 was different; it just made you dread what was at the end of the line.

At the time, I didn't have much cause to complain. We were better off than most because we already had our jobs lined up at the Ford Motor

Company outside Detroit. And we knew were just going for temporary work. It was just for a while, to get some regular paychecks to tide us over. It may have only been for a few months, but it felt like a life sentence to me. It's a well-known fact that a lot of musicians don't much care for real jobs. Well, that was me. I wasn't cut out for the factory.

It was at the Ford manufacturing plant in Dearborn. I hated it so bad I just couldn't stand the thought of it. Somehow or other, I got assigned to the job of spot welder. Now, I can't even replace a spark plug, and here I was, supposed to be welding floorboard pans for trucks on the assembly line. I kept thinking: "This whole setup is a big mistake. They got the wrong man. I ain't no spot welder. I'm a musician."

I worked the night shift, three in the afternoon until midnight. Every time I'd step inside the building, I'd get so sick nearly to where I had to upchuck. Just the look of the place was enough to throw me down. The thing was, I had it easy because I was the relief man. Each man had ten minutes every hour to take a break, and I'd take that man's place until he went back on the line. For most of the shift, I'd go hide so the bosses couldn't see me. I spent a lot of time in the bathroom, reading the newspaper and getting sick. I worked about eleven weeks and I hated every minute. It was the only real wage-paying job I ever had.

Carter worked at the plant, too, for about three weeks longer than I did. He didn't like it any better than me. Our mandolin player, Big Jim Williams, had come up for work, too, and he dragged us to see a show Jimmy Martin put on. After leaving Bill Monroe's Bluegrass Boys, Jimmy was fronting his own band, the Sunny Mountain Boys, and they tore the place up. The show gave us the music bug something fierce.

Afterwards, Big Jim got me and Carter aside and gave us a serious talking-to.

"You boys are too good to be working in this factory," he said. "Let's get back to the business we were born for."

We never had figured to quit the music business altogether, just a temporary job to tide us over till the weather broke, so it wasn't like Big Jim was saying anything we didn't already know. But sometimes you need somebody else to spell out what you've already been thinking.

Next day, Carter got on a pay phone and called Dee Kilpatrick, the A & R man for Mercury Records in Nashville. He told Dee we had the best band we ever had and he had some new songs and we wanted to get it all on record for posterity. We knew Mercury wanted to beef up its hillbilly roster; Flatt and Scruggs had just left for Columbia, so it was like a trade, I reckon, and the idea was that everybody would come out ahead. There was plenty of room for our kind of music in Nashville, we figured, and Dee felt the same way. He told Carter he was ready when we were. We put in our notice at the factory, and I said good-bye to welding floor pans forever. By August, we had signed a contract with Mercury and we were headed to Nashville.

On the way, we rehearsed the songs we were fixing to do. Big Jim Williams would take out his mandolin and get a key and we'd go from there. Course, I was driving so I couldn't play my banjo. The old Packard was full of music the whole trip to Nashville.

Carter and me, now, we were perfectionists. We expected all our sidemen to do just like us. Of course, for us it came easy, and that's why nothing beats a brother team. We were real natural, Carter and me, because we'd grown up together and done everything together since we was little boys. We spoke our words alike and we liked the same things, and so it all fell into place for us. Like Carter once said, with brothers, you even burp the same way. Well, we took it for granted, and we figured all the Clinch Mountain Boys would just follow right along with us like they'd been raised up on Smith Ridge, too. Looking back now, I think we asked too much sometimes, expecting our sidemen to fall in behind us.

One of our best fiddlers, Art Stamper, came to us so green that we had to send him home. He was sixteen years old, a skinny little feller from a little farm in Knott County, Kentucky. That's tucked back in the mountains between Hazard County and Pike County. We had met him in a little coal-mining town called Hindman, where we played a show. We needed a fiddler and he joined up with us.

Art was already winning contests all around there. He'd learned from his dad, Hiram, one of the best old-time fiddlers in eastern Kentucky. Somebody ought to do a study on why so many great fiddlers come from down in that corner of the state. They have a wildness to their playing, and at the same time there's a sweetness, like a fox grape you find early spring.

But it turned out that, good as Art was, he didn't fit with our style. At that time, he was too old-timey for the hard-driving music we were working out. We had a different timing, and it was hard to pick up on. He was playing hoedowns like "Possum Up a Simmon Tree" like his daddy taught him. That's more for dances than it is shows like we did. We needed him to follow the melody, more in the bluegrass style. Art was hungry and full of fire and we saw potential in him, but he wasn't ready.

Carter just told Art as kindly as he could that he'd have to work at it before he could join up with us. "We like what you got, but we need more of the Stanley Brothers way of fiddling, and we know you can do it," Carter said. "Now you go home and practice hard and learn how to play this style and we'll have a place for you."

Well, a lot of young musicians might take that as an insult. They might not listen to any advice and decide to keep playing however they want to. Stubborn. But Art wasn't like that. He done exactly what Carter told him to. He listened to Stanley Brothers records and he rehearsed. About three weeks later, Art came back and he was a different fiddler. He had it.

Art later said he hadn't done much except tone down his playing. Before he joined us, he'd been with the Sauceman Brothers and Buster Pack down at WCYB. "These bands had a certain sound, and they played real loud," Art later said. "The Stanley Brothers had a whole different approach. They was more mountain than the other bands. The Stanley Sound was simple mountain music, so simple it was a lot harder to play. So I had to learn to quiet my fiddle down a little bit."

What Art had learned was the way you fit into a song. He turned out to be one of our finest fiddlers in the history of the Clinch Mountain Boys. I know that even today there are people who still talk about his playing on our records.

We'd been down this road before, Carter and me had, but some of the boys in the band were living out their dreams for the first time. We rolled into Nashville to record and everybody piled out of the Packard. Big Jim Williams stretched out his long legs and got to carrying on like he'd hit the jackpot.

"Good ole Nashville, Tennessee!" he hollered. "Finally made it!"

Then Big Jim threw his mandolin up in the air. He was so excited he'd chucked it out into the street and broke it. His F-4 Gibson was cracked pretty bad, so we called Bill Monroe to try to borrow another mandolin for the session, but Bill was out of pocket. Big Jim stuck a piece of cardboard down in the crack to kill the rattling noise and that did the trick. Back then, you just had to make do.

Our first session for Mercury was one of those times when everything goes right, and you go right along with it. You don't rightly know where it comes from, and you don't ask. We had the songs, we had the musicians, and we had the sound. I believe it was the beginning of the Stanley Sound we became known for. I can't explain it too well, but there was drive in our playing we'd never had before.

We had a pride in what we were doing that only comes once or twice in your life. Part of it was our youth. We were young and we had something to prove. We didn't know if this was our last shot at the big time, and we weren't going to blow it. We were feeling confident and we put on the dog.

It was a one-day session at the Owen Bradley Studios, where all the big country hits were made. This was a modern facility, the best Nashville had to offer, and they didn't spare any expense. They wanted performers to feel like they was special. They laid out all sorts of nice, expensive things to remind you: "Hey, country boy, you've made it to the big time."

There were the best suits right off the rack. You could just pick 'em out and try 'em on. Shoes, too. Over in the corner, there was a table with bottles of whiskey where you could get refreshed and get you a shot of courage. A lot of performers would step into the studio and they'd get nervous with the whole gang of engineers glaring down through the window of the glass booth. It might take a whole afternoon to get one song done right, and that was valuable studio time ticking away.

But the fancy setup didn't rattle us a bit. We felt like we deserved it, to tell you the truth. We'd already recorded for Columbia; we were veterans. What it did was make us feel like turning it up a notch. We were all of us hopped up, with energy to burn. It made us reach higher, in the singing and the playing, too. Some of the tunes, we might have gone from G to B, which is three or four frets higher. We realized we had to have our own sound, and that's what we were gunning for.

We were raring to go, and we didn't make mistakes like some other bands. We'd go from one song to the next, just like we was on the radio back in Bristol. The whole session went like clockwork and Dee Kilpatrick was praising us up and down. He was used to musicians flubbing their solos and singers who couldn't get it right the first take. But we rolled along and nailed it almost every time. At the end of the session, we opened a fifth of good old Kentucky bourbon and he gave us a toast.

"You're about the best outfit I've ever cut, and I've had a lot come through here," he said. "You Virginia boys don't mess around, and you don't cause me no trouble at all. It's a real pleasure to be working with professionals who know their business."

Carter wanted to do nothing but original songs, and they were some of the best he'd ever done. He had his own style now, and the themes were more about man and woman and the ways of love, instead of always missing Mother and Daddy and the old home place. He'd grown up, and his songs reflected how much he'd matured as a man and as a songwriter. Romance for him wasn't about just spooning; it was about grown-ups trying to work things out when the going gets rocky. It was about real-life love like it really was, with all the trials and tribulations.

In that one session, we cut "(Say) Won't You Be Mine," "The Last Goodbye," "This Weary Heart You Stole Away (Wake Up Sweetheart)" and "I'm Lonesome Without You." You can go to any music festival around the world and you will hear bluegrass bands playing and singing these songs.

Carter knew right off there was something special about those first Mercury records. On the drive back from Nashville, he did something he very seldom did, which was to brag on himself and on us. Carter didn't often hand out compliments to the boys in the band, or to me, either. Praise can do as much harm as it can good.

It's like the old saying from down on the farm, "When a horse is running, you don't stop to give him sugar." I still follow that in my dealings with my band even today. You get too easy with compliments and pats on the back and it can get in the way of good work instead of encouraging it.

Being such a perfectionist, Carter was just as hard on himself as he was on any of the other Clinch Mountain Boys. He'd always find something we could improve on, something to work on. Never satisfied. That's why what he said in the car on the ride back from Nashville was so surprising. We were way out on the back roads somewhere and it was real late, when everyone was drifting off to sleep or lost in their thoughts.

"I just want to tell you boys," said Carter. "I feel like this is the best stuff the Stanley Brothers ever recorded."

I don't want to brag on myself either, but part of the reason we sounded different was that I had stepped up on my singing. I think I was in better form than I had been on the Columbia sessions. With Pee Wee gone, I had to sing like I never had to before. It was just the Stanley Brothers on the duet singing now; I started to lead Carter with my tenor, and that styled it from then on. That microphone didn't spook me like it used to. I just figured it was time to show what I could do.

A lot of people say the first Mercurys were the best records we ever cut. At the time, I knew we'd done good, but I didn't know they would become classics. Now I listen to these recordings and I like them very much, which is rare, because usually you can always hear something you feel like you could have done better. But with the Mercury records, there was a kind of magic that you only get once or twice in your whole career. I think every band has a highlight in their life, when you're really on the ball and the songs are coming to you fast. All you do is play your music natural and it seems to come right easy. There's a certain time when things come to you. And that was the time for us: "To say the first Mercury session was hot would be a woeful understatement," writes Bob Artis in his history book, *Bluegrass*. "Carter's lead singing was strong and self-assured, and Ralph was sending his hard mountain tenor right up through the rafters. The younger Stanley was playing his banjo hard and loud, establishing once and for all the Stanley style of bluegrass banjo."

The Mercury contract was just what we needed. We were on a major label again and we'd made what we felt were the best records of our career. They were played on radio and on the jukeboxes. Everywhere we went, we heard Stanley Brothers records.

There would be no more breaks for resting up. No more furloughs in the factories, welding floor pans. From that time on, we were a full-time working band. And we decided to keep Bristol as our base and keep everything close to home. With a record deal, we didn't need to be running ragged all over the South, hopping from station to station.

We found a way to play new towns in the WCYB broadcast area, ones we hadn't hit on the first few go-rounds. That way we wouldn't play out the territory like we'd done before. It helped that we got some regular work outside the Tri-Cities that was easy driving distance. We'd travel to Richmond and play the Old Dominion Barn Dance, a very popular broadcast out of WRVA, which had a strong fifty-thousand-watt signal that reached well outside Virginia. It wasn't the *Grand Ole Opry,* but it suited us fine. They had Sunshine Sue and all kind of talent, and that was as far as we needed to go at that time. We could play Saturday night and be home to get some sleep.

So here we were, all of us under thirty years old. We were "Exclusive Mercury Recording Artists." And making the best music we'd ever made. It's the same old story: You're young and you're on fire and you think nothing can stop you. Course, something always does. For us it was Elvis and rock 'n' roll.

We didn't see it coming, leastways me and Carter and most others didn't. Bill Monroe was probably one of the first who realized that what Elvis was doing wasn't no fad. He knew it was something new, something real.

In August of 1954, we were back in Nashville to do another session for Mercury. The night before we were set to record, Carter met up with Bill Monroe for dinner after the *Opry,* and then they went over to the WSM studios. Bill said there was something he wanted Carter to hear. He put on a record of "Blue Moon of Kentucky" that Elvis had cut for Sun. This was one of Bill's signature songs, one he'd wrote himself and recorded in 1946. Bill played it in waltz time. Real pretty and sad and lonesome.

Elvis changed the tempo and made it fast and put a new beat on the song. He done it rockabilly-style, which was totally new at the time. As the record played, Carter and some others in the studio were cutting up, because they thought it was funny. Everybody was laughing except Bill. He let the record play again, and he was dead serious. He looked real sternly at Carter, like a father giving his son a good talking-to. "You better do that number tomorrow if you want to sell some records," he said. "I'm gonna do it myself next Sunday."

The next day, Carter decided to take Bill's advice and try "Blue Moon" in the Elvis style. It was Bill and Carter's idea and I just went along with it. I didn't care for it myself. They thought maybe it would work for us. Carter was always saying, "Let's try something new." I've always been more conservative in my taste. For me, the old-time way is the best way.

Bill came by the studio to sit in on the session and root us on. I know Bill meant well, but it didn't feel right to me. It was too upbeat and it didn't fit the Stanley Brothers style. And I was right, because it didn't sell well at all. Bill recorded a new version the next week at the fast tempo and his was a flop, too. Now, Bill was trying to help us, but he wanted to help himself, too. He wrote the song, so he would collect on royalties no matter who recorded it. He figured Elvis and the rock 'n' rollers were good for business, and that'd be good for everybody. He was wrong.

I didn't have anything against Elvis. He was just doing what came natural to him, same as we were doing. I always liked his gospel songs. You could tell, when he was singing hymns, he meant it. Deep down, though, I never cared for rock 'n' roll. It didn't do anything for me at all.

It sure didn't help us any. For the teenagers and a lot of their parents, we sounded as old-fashioned as Fiddlin' Powers. That's when the word "hillbilly" started to hurt business.

The rock 'n' roll trend, with Elvis Presley and all the rest, changed everything around for our kind of country music. It just about turned Nashville upside down. Things got really tough. Record sales, personal appearances—everything dropped off. A lot of entertainers just couldn't make it anymore. They had to quit the music business.

As far as hillbilly music, there weren't many of us that was able to survive. Bill Monroe, Flatt and Scruggs, Reno and Smiley, and the Stanley Brothers. We just fought to survive the best we could. It wasn't about making it big anymore; we'd already done made it big back in the forties. All we wanted to do was keep making music, and the way we made it was staying on the road. Only now we weren't so young and carefree. We were getting tired, feeling whipped. But we just kept on.

Rock 'n' roll was pushing everything else off the radio, but we still listened to the local stations like WCYB playing hillbilly. We were driving to a show and everybody was cutting up when a song came over the car radio that made everybody hush up. *O come, Angel Band, come and around me stand/O bear me away on your snow-white wings to my immortal home.* Carter always was looking for them mossy old hymns, and this one hit him like a lightning bolt. "Ralph," he said. "Pull over and find a pay phone as quick as you can. I want to find out who's doing that song."

Carter called the station and found out it was the Webster Brothers. They had got it from an old hymnbook, same way we got a lot of gospel songs. It went back before the Civil War. People always used to ask us how we found so many songs from the olden days. They're all around if you just listen, on the airwaves, tucked away in old forgotten hymnals. All it takes is someone to dust 'em off and shine 'em up and make 'em new.

Songs are like birds sowing wild seeds, carried by the wind to places unknown. That was how we stumbled on "Angel Band," and it's been a Stanley Brothers favorite ever since.

For a lot of people, "Angel Band" is the first Stanley Brothers song they ever heard, from the soundtrack to *O Brother, Where Art Thou?* They used it on the end credits and it's the only song in the movie where you hear the whole thing all the way through. I hear many a time nowadays, people want it sung at their funerals.

Let me tell you, some songs have that effect on people. They hear something deep and it pulls them in. Back then, we'd usually air out a new song on our radio show to see how it would fly. Well, we started playing "Angel Band" on *Farm and Fun Time* and people took to it right off. So you can see how a song like "Angel Band" made a mark with people over the span of a long fifty years: different time and different place and different audience. Same song.

Chapter Eleven

Hard Times

"The boy back here with the five-string banjo, he's been kicked all over the country and he's still able to take it, I believe, and he's still got the banjo in tune! He's from Dickenson County, Virginia, around Clintwood. You've heard him on Columbia and Mercury records. That's the youngest one of the Stanley Brothers, friends, Ralph Stanley!"

—Carter Stanley, onstage at New River Ranch, Rising Sun, Maryland, 1956

Elvis just about starved us out.

We had some hard times, some rough years in the mid 1950s. I still had my little farm, and I'd always raised a small herd of cattle on the side. Nothing much, but it was something. I remember one winter things got so bad I had to sell thirteen head of cattle to pay wages for the band.

Times like that, I'd get down. I'd want to quit and maybe try something else besides music. Carter wouldn't hear of it. I'd have probably quit several times if it hadn't been for him. I thought there was other ways to make a decent living. Carter wouldn't let me, though. He'd hold me right to it.

"Well, maybe next week will be different," he'd say. "We've got a good show coming up next Saturday night. It's coming. Just hang in there. It's coming."

Carter had a way to make me not give up and to give me hope that something better was just around the corner. He was so determined to make it a career, ever since we first started. He always found a way to look on the bright side.

He knew that we couldn't let things get us down. We had to put on shows for the people and to do it right and proper; we had to give our very best, no matter what we were feeling inside. We went places where we'd have to play the show before we could afford to eat supper or buy gas to get home with. It was either draw a crowd or go without.

We couldn't let on how hungry or how tired or how worried we might be, because that would ruin the show. You couldn't tell a bit of difference in us than if we had a million dollars in our pockets. We may have been near broke, but we never let that break our spirit. We were showmen, and we were professionals, and that's the way we looked at it.

And let me tell you. We *were* hungry. We got used to eating a lot of Vienna sausages. We'd get us a big hunk of bologna and a loaf of bread, and the whole band would live off that for a while. We'd eat hamburgers, and when we got tired of hamburgers, we'd go into a restaurant and sit down and I'd say to the waitress, "Give me a bowl of beans and a big onion." And that would do us.

Anyhow, we still found a way to stay busy. We started booking shows up North, and that really helped us. The Washington and Baltimore areas had a lot of fans who had moved from the mountains for jobs after World War II. They worked for the government in Washington and for the big factories in Baltimore. They loved hillbilly music, and they really loved the Stanley Brothers.

One of our favorite places was an hour north of Baltimore, a country music park called New River Ranch. It was run by Ola Belle Reed and Alex Campbell, and they had weekend shows that would draw a thousand people at a $1 per car. It was a little wooden stage under the trees, next to a creek there by the U.S. highway, and they had to string electric lines back in there for the lights and PA system. We didn't mind the conditions a bit. We were just glad to get some fans to come see us.

Carter was always thinking about the people listening who were sick or feeling poorly. The aged and the lonely and the scorned. On our radio programs, he'd talk to them and comfort them and the radio was the way he could do that: "We'd like to say a special hello to all of our sick and shut-in listeners, wherever you might be," he'd say. "Bless your heart for tuning in. We appreciate it so much and we're pulling for you."

Carter cared for the outcasts and unfortunates, anyone down on their luck or up in years and especially children; his heart really went out to 'em. He just couldn't stand watching anyone go without. One time, we stopped at a restaurant after a show. This was back in West Virginia, with half-dead mining towns where people were really hurting. We hadn't made more than three or four dollars apiece for playing, about enough for a meal, so we sat at a booth and got our orders and started to eat.

Nearby, there was a little boy sitting by himself, watching us chow down, eyes wide and not saying a word.

Carter looked over and said, "Are you hungry? Would you like to have something to eat?"

"Yes, sir," said the boy. "I would."

He didn't have a penny on him, and he hadn't eaten for days.

So Carter invited him over and he bought him a big plate with pie for dessert and everything. And the little boy sat with us at the table and ate every crumb laid in front of him. And Carter ordered some more and kept pouring food into him and the boy just ate and ate, he was so hungry.

There was another time, another little boy. It was on a back road, Lord knows where we were but it was way out in the sticks, and this boy is walking along the road barefoot. Carter told me to pull over and so I did. He got out and talked with the boy. And we drove to the nearest town and bought the boy a new pair of shoes.

Carter was more open about it, but I felt the same way. Our parents taught us everyone was born with a gift. Some find it, and others don't ever find it. One fellow we met in those days had a gift that was out of this world and we gave him a chance to show it. His name was Lindy Clear. He was from near Lebanon, in a little town called Hansonville, not too far from Bristol, way out in the sticks on the edge of Russell County.

From what I heard, Lindy's parents had named him after Charles Lindbergh. He had some birth defects that made him different in his looks and in the way he was. His head was too big for his frame. Back then, people'd say he was "touched"; nowadays they'd probably call him disabled, but all we saw was his talent. Loads and loads of talent. He was a natural-born musician; he could play the bass and accordion and piano and even the pump organ, but his real talent was making sounds. Without any instrument except his own self. I guess you could say he was an imitator. But it don't get across half of what he could do.

He had his own ways, Lindy did, in just about everything he did. He slept under the stars and he could make any sound on God's green earth.

The way I remember it, Lindy came up to us one day at the station and said he had something he wanted us to hear. He already had a fifteen-minute spot on WCYB playing accordion and a ragtime-style piano, but we didn't have no use for that. Nothing wrong with pianos or accordions—people forget that Monroe used an accordion early on—but they don't fit into the Stanley style of music. So we were on a break from the *Farm and Fun Time* show, and we had some time to kill.

Carter had seen Lindy around the station and he took a liking to him. "Son, what all is it that you can do?" I don't think Carter was expecting much, just being neighborly.

Lindy said he was going to do an old farmer driving his Model T Ford over a mountain. Lindy stood there and made the sounds of a Model T engine firing up and then backfiring and then sputtering up a mountain road and then blowing out a tire on the way down. Carter looked at me with a big grin on his face, and we hired Lindy right on the spot.

Carter gave him the stage name "Tennessee Mort," or sometimes just "Cousin Mort," and he became one of the most popular Clinch Mountain Boys ever. We took him on the road, and he was a big hit wherever we went. He played the bass fiddle for us, too, but it was the imitations what made his name. There was nobody else like him.

Mort was the oldest of his brothers and sisters and he didn't have friends to pick and sing with. He didn't have any banjos or guitars or anything like that around the house. He taught himself to bang out some tunes on the family piano, and when he got tired of that, he learned to make music with his mouth and his hands and his feet. He started out around the family farm doing animal sounds and worked his way up towards cars, trains and planes.

Mort used to perform at livestock auctions around the area, and that's how he first got known. He could render the sounds of any barnyard animal you can name, from a rooster and a turkey to a cow and a hog.

He was a storyteller, really, and he put you right in the thick of it, the way life on the farm really was. It was real down-home stuff. He'd give you a braying mule calling for hay and he'd split your ears just like the mule would. When he did a hog eating slop, he'd holler, "There goes the tomato!" and he'd give you the whole tomato going down the hog's gullet. The crowd ate it up just like that hog.

One of his best skits was "Ringing the Pig." Back then, farm people used to put an upholstery ring on the snout to keep the pig from rooting under the fence of the hog pen. Mort would act out the whole scene. It always started out nice and easy, with someone out in the hog pen, stepping light to sneak up on the pig and try to get the ring on him. Course, the pig would get to squealing and make a run for it, and Mort would follow the family chasing down the runaway sow: "Sooooooey!! Hold him, Grandma!"

And you never heard a dogfight until you heard Tennessee Mort. He called it "Dog Meets Dog," and two dogs wasn't enough for Mort; he liked to have three going at it. There was a baying old hound named

Bowser and a big, growling German shepherd named Fido, and a little feister named Trixie, who always ended up a-whimpering and running off.

Mort worked the microphone rough as an old chewed-up bone, and with all the growling and snarling and yapping, you'd get to looking around to see them mutts going at each other's throats. But it was all Mort. There was no tricks to it.

He'd give you everything from a timber rattlesnake to a crying baby. He'd do a fat ugly toad: "A great big ole green fella as big around as a plate," he'd tell the crowd. "He tastes good in a frying pan after he gets through hoppin'!"

The country people loved Mort because he knew how wild it'd get on those farms way back in the sticks. Noisy, messy and more action than a cowboy movie. Anybody thinking the country's all peace and quiet knew different after hearing Mort.

Then he'd render a freight train a-chugging down the tracks. There's many a harmonica player can imitate a train, but Mort could do it just with his mouth and a microphone.

Mort's most popular routine was probably the old Model T Ford. Like always, he went straight to the details, hollering like some auctioneer he'd probably seen: "Nineteen thirty-eight Model T, V-8 motor, bald-headed lugs and air-cooled head, cut pistons, four-barrel carburetor, a double-super-charged hot-rod car . . . AND A MAN A-DRIVIN' IT!" Then he'd start with a sputter, with Carter playing an old farmer winding the crank engine, and finally take that ole car chugging up a steep hill. When Carter finally got the Model T going smooth, Mort would blow out the tire and Carter would stop and shake his head and get out and walk around to check the flat tire.

The only thing more fun than watching Mort do his thing onstage was watching Carter's expressions while he did it. He enjoyed it more than anybody. He used to introduce Mort all kinds of ways. "You folks have heard of Frank Sinatra, haven't you?" Carter'd say. "Well, this here's his brother, Not-So-Hot-Ra."

Sometimes, Carter would maybe go too far poking fun and Mort would give it right back. Once Carter told the crowd it smelled bad up on stage because Mort never took a bath, which a lot of the time was true. Well, that was getting too personal. So Mort waited until later in the show when Carter started into a really sad love song, and Mort got to making googly eyes and the most god-awful faces while Carter was trying to sing. And he stole the show from Carter, just to get him a little revenge.

And Mort was a help with the music, too. He was fair on the bass fiddle and he could keep time all right, whatever we needed. But he'd be pulling wild stunts all the while. He'd take the frog off the fiddle bow—that's the hair hanging off the end of that bow—and he'd pull it across underneath, playing all four strings at once, and he'd make the fiddle sound just like a church organ.

Mort never did have a regular job that I knew of. He stayed with us a long time, most of the late 1950s on and off. He was with us for the 1959 Newport Folk Festival and at our first college show, at Antioch College in Yellow Springs, Ohio. The crowds loved him wherever we played, but it was the country people who loved him the most.

We'd always pick him up where he lived with his parents on a country road outside Hansonville near Lebanon. Mort never made us wait. He was always standing there waiting out front of the little white house below where Little Moccasin Gap cuts into the Clinch Mountains. His dad, Homer, ran a general store on the bend of the road, and sometimes you'd see his mother, Winnie. They was good country people and I think they were grateful we'd found a way Mort could make a living.

We helped him but he helped us a lot, too, because he made our shows more entertaining, and that's worth many a hot picker. Now, I won't lie to you. Mort was an odd character and he could be a handful to travel with, if he wasn't in the proper mood. Most of the time, he was just happy to go with us, it didn't matter where. But sometimes he had a problem with the other Clinch Mountain Boys. He was very particular about who he liked and who he didn't like, and there wasn't much room in the car a lot of times—especially with some of the heavier fiddlers we'd have along—and he was more particular than most about who and what was next to him. For a while there, we had Chubby Anthony playing fiddle with us.

Chubby was from Cherryville, North Carolina, and he was was one of the best and it's a shame he ain't better remembered. His "Black Mountain Blues" was every bit as good as Leslie Keith's, and some will tell you it's better. For a while there, we paid Chubby twenty-five dollars a week plus all the hot dogs he could eat, and you'd be surprised how much that arrangement cost us in the long run. Chubby weighed every bit of three hundred pounds and took up a lot of space in the car, and that didn't set well with Mort. And even worse, he liked to cut up with Mort and poke fun at him. Chubby wasn't a bit shy about his joking and he made him the butt of some jokes and Mort didn't like that.

One time we started down the road to play some shows in Florida. Mort was in the backseat, working on some of his personalized renditions of fiddle tunes. He was the only man I ever heard of who could do "Turkey in the Straw" by popping on his cheeks. We crossed the North Carolina state line, and I mentioned that we had to stop by Chubby's place and pick him up.

Mort sucked his cheeks in and got a real sour look on his face.

"Uhhhhh, you mean Chub's going, too?"

"Yeah," I said. "He's coming with us on this trip. Chubby's going to play on our Florida shows. What's the matter?"

"Well, I believe you can just let me out and I'll go on back home," said Mort. "I ain't a-traveling nowheres no more with Chub."

I didn't want to let Mort out on the road with no ride back, but he was used to hitchhiking. It was how he got around most of the time. And besides, I knew he'd made up his mind. He could be as stubborn as a mule when he wanted, and there was no arguing with him about it. He'd just clam up. That was the only time you couldn't get any sound out of Mort. And that weren't no fun, least of all for him. He was born to spout off, and when he went silent the world didn't seem right somehow.

Nobody said a thing for a few miles and then Mort pointed to a spot along the road and he said, "That's the spot, right there." So we dropped him off, without so much as a "so long," and he made his way back to Hansonville somehow.

The only problem I ever had with Mort was when he'd complain about my driving. That's one thing I can't abide. I take my driving as serious as I do my singing. And I especially did back in the early days, when the country roads like to kill you. Driving the way I did was the only way to keep us alive so we could keep singing.

Now, I'll be straight with you. A lot of the time, driving to a show meant what the police called speeding. When you've got to make eight hundred miles all night from east Tennessee to Pennyslvania for a 2 P.M. show, you've got to move or you're going to be late and you ain't gonna get paid. So you learn how to do 80 mph when you need to. And when you get stopped, you learn to talk like a lawyer to get yourself out of a ticket. So I got to be a good driver, and good talker when I needed to be. You don't need to mouth off to talk your way out of a ticket. You just state your case and hope for the best.

Mort didn't like speeding at all. He was a 55-mph man, and he watched the speedometer like a hawk. He'd get on me when he saw that needle move to the right, and it would drive me crazy. I'd just keep hauling down the highway and pay him no mind.

One time, I was speeding through a little town in Alabama, real late at night. There wasn't nobody out, the road was clear, and I had to make time. But Mort was jumping out of his seat. He was really laying it on me to slow down, and I just wasn't listening. And the rest of the boys was on my side, and they were telling him to hush up and go to sleep. Finally, Mort hollered out, "Stop this car, right here. I'm the justice of the peace and I'm arresting everybody in the vehicle!" We told him that meant he was under arrest, too, and that finally made him shut up.

Carter was real protective, because there was a lot of people like Chubby that made fun of a man like Mort. It's natural when people see somebody different, and Carter made sure people knew Mort was worth something. He'd introduce him as the mayor onstage, and a lot of people believed Mort really was a mayor of a town because of how serious Carter was when he said it. Carter also liked Mort for selfish reasons. Mort's talent made him a good partner for the practical jokes Carter liked to pull.

One time we came through Baltimore on the way back from a show. We stopped at a nightclub downtown to say hello to some people we knew. Outside was a full moon and inside was a full bar, and those two things gave Carter one of his ideas. He told Mort to stand outside on the sidewalk and howl at the moon and see how fast he could clear out the bar. So we went inside and left him out in the cold. Mort didn't mind because he liked pulling pranks as much as Carter did.

We sat in there for a few minutes, and Mort started into his Bowser-the-hound routine. He was in fine voice, and he sounded so real that the bar emptied right quick to see what all was going on. When the crowd spilled out on the sidewalk, Mort didn't let up; he just kept on howling at the moon. He wasn't going to stop until Carter told him to, no matter what. Everybody in the crowd thought Mort was crazy, and that tickled Carter to death. He never let on that Mort was traveling with us, right until the very end, when we all piled into the car and drove off, with Mort still howling from the backseat.

Later on, Lindy left us, and that was the last anyone heard of the character called "Tennessee Mort." The fans missed him for years after and they'd ask about him like you would about family.

After Lindy left the Stanley Brothers, he worked for a short while with Charlie Moore out of Spartanburg, South Carolina. Then he finally up and quit the music business altogether. In the 1960s, he took to the road evangelizing. He'd play organ and preach at little Baptist churches around southwestern Virginia and beyond. He'd preach and play for whatever the people would care to give him. Living out of his car and taking his message to the people.

All his life, the place Lindy loved best was the South Holston River. It runs near where he lived in Hansonville. A lot of the time he'd spend the night by the riverside. In the summer of 1971, Lindy was down by the river there out near Abingdon and he got caught in a rainstorm. He pulled off the road and locked his doors to wait out the downpour. Somehow he fell asleep with the air-conditioning on, and police found him dead inside the locked car with the motor running and the AC going full blast. They said it was accidental carbon monoxide poisoning that killed him. He just suffocated to death. He was forty-one years old.

Lindy sure brought some fun to the Stanley Brothers shows, but it wasn't the kind of excitement a lot of people expected after Elvis hit. The rock 'n' roll made the teenagers go wild, but I ain't sure it helped the country any. I know for sure it wasn't good for country music, not the kind of traditional country we played.

It was some tough times. Mercury records weren't selling; after almost ten years we were still playing Bristol. It seemed like people were tired of us.

The pity was, we had one of our best bands with us at the time. We had a mandolin player named Curley Lambert we found in the Lynchburg area. Before you get too confused, Curley's real name was Richard but we nicknamed him "Goat," which I'll tell you more about later, and he was no relation to either Pee Wee Lambert or Ray Lambert. Curley could really nail it on the harmony singing. Then we'd also got us a fiddle player, Ralph "Old Maid" Mayo, who was from Kingsport in east Tennessee, not far from G. B. Grayson's stomping grounds, and he was raised on the same Grayson and Whitter records we were; he could get that old-time lonesome tone from a fiddle like Grayson could. Carter hung the nickname "Old Maid" on him and I can't for the life of me recall exactly why, other than he just liked the sound of it and thought it was funny.

They had a wagonload of talent for two men, and later on they played with us on "Rank Stranger," with Curley on mandolin and Old Maid on guitar, that a lot of our fans say is our best record. Just this past summer the Library of Congress added "Rank Stranger" to its National Recording Registry for preservation; there are only two hundred fifty "culturally significant audio recordings" on the registry, so it's quite an honor, especially when you consider the Stanley Brothers still ain't in the Country Music Hall of Fame. What I'm really trying to tell you is, this pair of Clinch Mountain Boys brought some wonderful playing and singing to our sound.

Around that time, a young man named Larry Ehrlich came by the studio at WCYB. He was a fan from Chicago. It meant a lot to us that we had fans; even if we weren't making the country charts, at least we had people who believed in us. Our music was reaching people from way beyond the Clinch Mountains. Erhlich was a college student who'd first bought the record of "Pretty Polly" we did for Columbia.

He had made the long car trip by himself to see us, and he wanted to record us on his reel-to-reel machine he'd brought with him. Just told us to sing some old-time songs that we liked from the early days but didn't get the chance to feature much onstage anymore. We were happy to do it, and we had a good time, too.

When the tapes came out almost fifty years later, Larry wrote some notes for the release. I think his words will give you a good idea of what it was like for an outsider to come down and meet us and later to reminisce about it. Like a snapshot in time. And it also helps me remember, too, and be grateful that fans like Larry stayed loyal to us through the years. I don't know if we would have been able to keep going without their support. The album was called *The Stanley Brothers: An Evening Long Ago,* and here's what Larry wrote:

> I first met Carter and Ralph Stanley when I was about twenty years old and they were not much older. They were, in personality and temperament, seemingly quite different from each other. Carter was engaging, outgoing and conversational.

Ralph, while friendly, was reserved, deferential and rarely said much.

I probably have never seen two men as close to one another as were the Stanley Brothers. When they sang together, the perfection of that closeness was there for the world to hear. And yet their voices were very different, one from the other. Carter sang with the greatest ease of any singer I have ever watched. His unique, impeccable phrasing and timing were the result. He had the most tender voice I have ever heard. I have never heard a lead singer I would consider his equal.

Of Ralph Stanley's voice, what can be said? It is a voice like no other voice. I have heard people say that Ralph's voice sounded old when he was young and that he has grown into his voice. I don't think so. I think Ralph's voice has always reflected a mysterious blend of the cerebral and the instinctual that reflected his life experience at the time.

This recording was made one spring night in 1956, in Bristol, Virginia. After a long day of radio shows, barn dances, hog auctions and the like, Carter, Ralph, Curley Lambert, Ralph Mayo and I went to the WCYB studios around midnight where I set up the mike, asked the Stanleys to sing some of the old traditional songs and turned on the tape recorder.

I was born and raised in the red brick tenements of Chicago's South Side. Socially and culturally and attitudinally light years from the ridges and low ground of western Virginia.

How then did two boys from those ancient mountains reach across time, space, geography and background to touch the very hearts and souls of tens of thousands of seeming strangers as me? It was simple, really. What they said, and especially the way they said it, held up a mirror so that we knew our own fear of lost loves, capricious turns of fate, unfulfilled lives and the hope of something better were not singular.

Above all, the Stanley Brothers sang of death—before and after.

In other words, they told us of things we already knew, and they told it in ways thrilling, beguiling and comforting.

So you see, here we were, thinking we'd somehow failed because we couldn't make it as a commercial success, and here was youngsters like Larry who held our music in high reverence. You couldn't fill the gas tank with it, but it did make you feel like you were doing something worthwhile. It wasn't just Larry Ehrlich coming from miles and miles to see the Stanley Brothers. Though I reckon he did probably travel the farthest. We'd started to notice others showing up to record our shows, especially at the country music parks around the Baltimore and Washington area. Always young fans, and a lot of musicians, or fans wanting to be musicians. John Duffey and others, some of what they called folkies, mostly Northern boys who didn't like Elvis any more than we did.

I liked to have a little fun with 'em. I'd look down from the stage while they'd set their tape recorders and their fancy microphones next to our little mic stand: "I see we got the recording industry again here today," I'd say. And they'd get sort of nervous, because of course, I wasn't smiling when I said it.

We didn't mind they was making tapes of our shows; back then, that sort of attention was about all we had to keep us going on some days. I'd tell them to sit tight and get the equipment just right, because I wanted to try out a new banjo tune; I'd tell 'em to make sure and get a good recording so I could listen to the playback tape and see if the new tune was a keeper or not.

The thing was, all during the fifties, when times got the hardest, I had banjo tunes coming out of me like I'd never had before. I was playing the best banjo of my life. I mean not only the way I was playing but the banjo itself. It was my favorite banjo of all, and to this day I still regret the day I swapped it for a pile of money and guns. Worst trade I ever made.

Here's the whole sad story, and I hope it helps somebody out there who's as bad for swapping as me. There may be a lesson in here somewhere. You remember the old yellow banjo I'd got at Tom's Creek commissary? Well I wasn't getting the tone out of it I wanted. I had been a-wanting to buy an old Gibson Mastertone arch-top, and I heard about this fellow named Mac Crowe who played banjos and traded in banjos. I heard he had some real nice ones, including a 1923 Gibson he'd bought brand-new in 1923. He lived in Maiden, North Carolina, a little town below Hickory, and I drove down to see him. It was a beauty, a silver arch-top with cloverleaf inlay, and it sounded as good as it looked. I played it and I liked it and I asked him what he wanted for it, and he said $275. I pulled out the money and paid him and brought it back home.

Now, this banjo was the one I used on the Mercury recordings and my first instrumentals, like "Hard Times" and "Dickenson County Breakdown" and "Big Tildy," and it just had the tone I'd always been looking for.

Then like a fool I threw it away in a trade. I've always been crazy to trade, and a man tried for two years to trade me for it, and he wouldn't let up and he kept adding to the pile of what he'd give me for it. One day, I finally just gave in, I don't rightly know why. He was offering some good money and a Ford truck and two or three expensive guns; I don't remember what all it was, just a whole pile of stuff, and I took him up on the offer. And then I spent the next forty-odd years trying to get it back and I never could.

This fellow lives in Marion, North Carolina, and I've been back several times and never had any luck. I tried everything. We got to talking a long time and he said he was wanting the fiftieth anniversary Stanleytone banjo, which was custom-made and collectible and whatnot. So I drove down there with a Stanleytone and he was going to do a straight trade with me; he had the notion and I really thought I was going to get the Gibson back. He was ready, but he never could give the final word. I think his wife talked him out of it; she said, "Well, you've had it so long, you better not let it go."

I reckon it'd be worth $45,000 or $50,000 now, but the price don't matter to me. It's still my favorite banjo, and I still wish I'd never let it go. So all you traders be careful, because you might lose what you love most trying to get a good trade.

Things couldn't have been better banjowise, but moneywise and everything else, it was was just about the worst. Then, when you'd think things couldn't get any worse, we had a flood nearly washed away our little part of the world, and us right along with it.

We were heading home from a show in Grundy, only an hour or so north of the old home place, when it hit, the biggest storm in years and years. Floodwaters surged into the Cumberland Valley over four states, and our area got hit the hardest. We got as far as Haysi, where the Clinch River washed away buildings and cars like they was toys, and water stood fifteen feet high in the streets even after the flood receded.

We was driving like gangbusters on a dirt road headed for Smith Ridge, when the road got washed out; we were lucky we'd just made it to high ground, so we parked the car and waited it out. Everywhere below us was the most terrible disasters; there were little towns swept away by the rushing water, and some people were drowned and never seen again. One old woman was out there stranded and had to be rescued from the top of her outhouse way downriver; she'd done tied it up to a tree trying to save it, and it broke loose and she was a-hanging on for dear life.

We stood up on that hill and watched the whole country there underwater, and it was about the sorriest sight we'd ever seen. Carter wrote a song about it right then and there; we stayed over at a friend's house close by, and next day Carter sang it over the phone to a record producer in Nashville. It was called "The Flood," and we cut it a week later at the WCYB studio in Bristol. Our last session for Mercury came that winter, and we cut another song about a local tragedy, when a school bus in Kentucky crashed and most of the children died. So we had two what they used to call tragic songs, "No School Bus in Heaven" and "The Flood," out at the same time, and Carter really thought they'd do gangbusters. But they didn't sell.

Times had changed and people wanted country hits like "Candy

Kisses" and "Send Me the Pillow You Dream On," not songs about people getting swept away in floods and schoolchildren dying in the mountain ravines.

Our Mercury contract expired and they didn't renew.

We were right back where we started again, playing a radio program that didn't pay. The good ole *Farm and Fun Time* show wasn't a bit fun no more.

CHAPTER TWELVE

Makin' Some Hay

"Hello there, stranger, could you tell me how far it is to Little Rock?" "Well, no sir, I couldn't, but there's a devil of a big 'un down here in Pap's old field."

—"HOW FAR TO LITTLE ROCK," THE STANLEY BROTHERS

I ain't a big believer in luck, good or bad or blind, because I ain't had all that much in my career except for *O Brother,* the blindest best luck of all, which came awful late for me. I'm more of a believer in hard work than anything else. But I do believe a lot in getting a break, and when you do get a break, I believe in making hay while the sun shines. And that's what happened in 1958.

It was really two big breaks and they came from where you'd least expect it. The first was a TV show in Florida, sponsored by a company that made mobile homes. For the next few years, the show paid the bills and gave us more financial security than we'd ever known or would ever know. The second came from a Cincinnati label called King Records, run by Syd Nathan, who gave us the freedom to make our music at a time when Nashville had shut the door on us; and the crazy thing was, during our run at King we recorded the only hit song of our career.

The first break came when we heard from a fellow named Aubrey

Fowler, who had started a popular Saturday night program in Florida called *The Suwannee River Jamboree,* billed as the "Deep South's Country Music Show." Jim and Jesse had built up a good following on the jamboree and made it quite a hit in the northern part of the state. When they left, Fowler figured another brother team from Virginia would keep it going strong, and he called us.

It was just an instinct, really, and a spur-of-the-moment decision. We figured we'd wore out our welcome in Bristol, and so we just up and moved south to see what we could do in the Sunshine State. It helped a lot that Jim and Jesse had already found a new market for our brand of hillbilly music, so we headed for Live Oak and started headlining the jamboree, and it was doing well. After we'd been there a few months, we got a sponsorship from the Jim Walter Corporation, which manufactured shell homes all over the South. We signed on and helped kick off a TV show, on WJXT out of Jacksonville, plugging the shell homes and playing our music. The work was good and we had a steady salary paid by the sponsors, more than we'd ever earned; and the best thing was, we didn't have to make those long drives crisscrossing all over the country playing shows for percentage.

For the next few years we had a circuit we played five nights a week. We had a weekly tour on three or four TV stations—Jacksonville, Orlando, Tampa and Fort Myers—and we'd make that circuit every week.

Sometimes we'd play an open house at one of the towns where Jim Walter had a headquarters, and we'd work these events about every Sunday and they'd pay us for those, too. We played open houses all over Florida and Georgia and some in Alabama and Mississippi. It was a regular road schedule we could handle, no zigzagging back and forth to the one-nighters, and it didn't tire us out.

The Walter people liked us because our show helped boost sales for their shell homes; we liked the sponsorship because we finally had some financial security. And the people down there, they fell for our music, they went right for it. We got so popular they booked us to make a syndicated radio program called *The Jim Walter Jamboree,* a fifteen-minute show we taped in Atlanta; we had a lot of fun with those radio spots, and

Carter reworked our old theme song from the *Farm and Fun Time* show and came up with a jingle for Jim, our new employer:

Hello everybody everywhere
Your Jim Walter show is on the air
For a home of your own, no more rent to pay
See Jim Walter right away
Oldest, largest, builders of the best
They've had more experience than all of the rest
So for a home of your own, no more rent to pay
See Jim Walter right away

We got our own homes in Florida, and they weren't no shell homes, neither. I bought a thirty-acre farm just outside Live Oak, about four miles out from Route 129. I had a few head of Black Limousine cattle and I stocked a little pond with bream and bass. I did some fishing and let Carter do his coon hunting.

He hunted a lot in the fall and winter with our friend Howard Pepper; they had access to a couple of big farms in Suwanee Country, and they'd drive down those dirt roads in a pickup and turn the dogs loose and have a time. They'd roam those pecan groves at night in the pitch black and follow the barking and point the flashlight up in the tree and sometimes there'd be an ole sow coon and two or three young'uns up there. Ol' Man Pepper would shine the light up there and it would light up like a Christmas tree, all them coon eyes shining right back. They'd take a shotgun and bring 'em down and cut 'em and quarter 'em.

Carter had some fine coon dogs. George Shuffler's brother gave Carter a young pup, and Carter namerd him Ol' Dude and he made a powerful coon-hunting dog. He was black and tan and he finally got heartworms and died. Carter said he was the best dog he ever had.

Carter liked to squirrel hunt, too. He'd take his sons, Carter and Bill, with him, and he'd take off his shoes and leave his socks on so he could slip up quiet on those squirrels and shoot 'em out of the tree.

Now some people think Carter got his nickname "Chase" because he loved hunting coons and squirrels and such, and it did make a nice fit and all, but the truth is I hung that name on him and it didn't have nothing to do with that. Back when we was boys, there was a man named Mr. Chase who was a big wheel in Clintwood and he had the finest mansion in town, and we'd pass by it all the time. Everybody looked up to him, so I started calling Carter "Chase" and it stuck.

I didn't fool much with hunting in Florida except for a time or two; I was scared to death of snakes, and the whole territory was crawling with snakes, so I stuck to my fishing and my cattle.

Carter got him a nice brick house with a white picket fence on Ruby Street, right in the town, where he lived with Mary and their four kids. He was glad he finally had money coming in steady to support his growing family; now he could be with them a lot more than he could when we were playing all those one-nighters back around Bristol. He was a good daddy and he always missed his children.

The change of scenery down south was good for us. When you have new surroundings it tends to inspire you a little. I woke up one morning just before dawn with some songs on my mind. I knew if I didn't get up and write them down, I'd forget 'em right off. So I got up out of bed and wrote four songs before I went back to bed. One was a recitation called "Prayer of a Truck Driver's Son" and one was a gospel song that I actually woke up singing. I will tell you more about that in a chapter about gospel music, but just now the main thing I'm saying is, you've got to get it down as best you can when the inspiration hits you.

Now, with a professional songwriter, I guess he'll sit down and write a song anytime he wants to get to work and do it. But with somebody like me, I think you have to let the songs come to you and grab 'em while you can. If I'd a-waited till the next day, I couldn't have wrote three words. There's been other times where I've thought up parts of songs but I didn't get 'em down on paper and they just disappeared and I never could remember them again. Nowadays, old as I am, I can't hardly remember the words to songs I'm singing, and I have a paper to read the words onstage. That's the age creeping up on me, I reckon.

Florida had the same pull on Carter as it did me. He started writing lots of new material, some of his happiest songs like "How Mountain Girls Can Love," and the good mood carried over into a lot of pranking he pulled with George Shuffler. Down in those parts, there were a lot of little citrus groves and roadside stands with people selling souvenirs and local produce like oranges and such. One of these stands had a black bear in a big cage there for the people to look at while they stopped on the road. George got the idea for him and Carter to give the bear a couple boxes of chocolate Ex-Lax, and check on things when we come back that way after a show. Well, when we drove back through the next day, the bear was a-laying in his cage in about three inches of his own mess, all over the bars of the cage. They pulled the same trick on our uncle Dewey's dogs when he came through one winter, a couple of big lazy ugly old hounds a hundred pound each that Dewey called his "bear dogs," and when Dewey tied 'em up in the pines, they messed up the whole yard and all over Dewey's winter rations and whatnot.

During our time in Florida, we got to know George Jones real well and became good friends. He was always our favorite country singer, me and Carter's both. George was from East Texas and we met him through Starday Records, run by Don Pierce who managed George then. We were on some package tours with George, and one time we went to see him play a show in Orlando, and he sung a new one he'd wrote, "The Window Up Above." We told him how much we liked it and he let us cut a record of it even before he did. That's the way George is, just as generous as they come. He and Carter would stay up all night playing poker at the motel. I know for sure they did because when I got up in the morning, they'd still be at the table, drawing hands and talking and laughing.

So you can see we was having a little fun in the Sunshiny State, and enjoying ourselves as best we could; and then things got even better with the second big break. And I'll tell you, we mostly made this break for ourselves. We called Syd Nathan of King Records in Cincinnati, out of the blue, and he was ready to sign us. No audition, no conversation really, just a "Hell, yes!" from Syd booming over the phone line. We decided to try King, which had the slogan "If It's a King It's a Hillbilly," because Reno and Smiley was doing good on that label and we played a lot in

Cincinnati and Dayton, so we had a big fan base in that area of Ohio. As for ole Syd, well, we had a hunch Syd was our type of boss somehow. We just went with our gut, and it turned out to be the right thing to do.

It was good timing, really. Syd had just struck it rich with James Brown, and he was looking to beef up his hillbilly roster. King was an independent label, but it was big enough for what we needed and it had national distribution and years and years of hit records on jukeboxes from coast to coast. It was one of the few labels that didn't have segregation in the performers or in the front or back office neither: R&B performers like James Brown and Hank Ballard recorded there in the same room as Cowboy Copas and Reno and Smiley and Grandpa Jones.

Syd didn't see things in black-and-white; he only saw green. Selling records was all he cared about, with every waking hour, and I believe it was what he dreamed about when he went to sleep at night, too.

Syd was one of the last of the old-time, cigar-chomping, hollering and cussing record men; he said he had "shellac" in his blood. He was short and fat and bald and he had thick glasses with the Coke-bottle lenses; he could barely see a thing, but he had some ears that could hear a hit record. He always had a big cheap cigar stuck in his mouth and he cursed with every breath.

He'd started King back in 1946, after he saw how used records sold like hotcakes in the pawnshop he was running at the time. His big seller early on was the Delmore Brothers, and that's the sound he always liked the best: singing and guitars, maybe a harmonica, too. He didn't like fiddle and he didn't like banjo either; he thought it was too much for the public to take. And he hated mandolin because so many bluegrass bands used a mandolin. He wanted something different to set his bands apart from the crowd; he was looking for the guitars like the Delmores used. They had a lot of popular records, like "Freight Train Boogie," back in the late forties, and he wanted us to replace them as King's premier hillbilly act.

So that's why we started using a lot of lead guitar, and that became a hallmark of the records we made for King. And I give Syd a lot of credit, because neither me nor Carter much liked the idea at first, but it ended up working fine, and we really set ourselves apart with the sound we got. Nobody else had it then or since.

The thing about Syd was, he really ran the whole show top to bottom; he was the king of King, and he lorded over his little empire in an ugly old factory building in Cincinnati. Syd had it all right there under one roof: recording studio, pressing plant, distribution and art departments, business and A & R divisions, and manufacturing. Syd even made the cardboard for the album covers.

Now, when we went into the studio for our first session, Syd was right there in the control booth, waiting for us like a hawk. He done everything his way, and that meant he sat in on any session he felt like. Well, he watched us for a while, sweating behind those thick glasses and a-swearing at his engineers, and we played a few numbers, and as usual there wasn't a hitch or a mistake or nothing. After maybe three songs or so, Syd stood up and shouted, "Hell, you boys know more about it than I do. You sure as hell don't need me to be here." And he hotfooted right out of there and he never sat in on another session.

One thing I want to say right off. I've heard so many tales about Syd Nathan yelling and screaming and carrying on, and most of it is probably true, but he always treated us excellent and extra good, just as nice as could be. In fact, he never did say a loud word to us that I can recall. Maybe because he didn't need to fool with us in the studio and it saved him time and money, I don't rightly know. I think it was because he respected us as professionals, and it was the same after Carter died when I went solo. Whatever the reason, I've never been treated better by any man in the business than Syd Nathan.

Now, don't get me wrong, Syd was no Boy Scout; this was a man who'd got his start as a drummer in a speakeasy. I did see him enough around his office to hear him cuss and see him get salty with just about everybody else in the building. He'd come out with them big, foul curses and he'd sit there and fart as loud as he pleased, his secretary right there by him; he didn't care, he'd just rare up and let 'em fly. There wasn't no one like Syd; we need more like him, I'd say. He said what he meant and he meant what he said and he didn't care who it hurt. I don't think he cared about nothing except music and money, and I guess he liked money the best. He was a good businessman, always wore a suit and tie, and he ran a good business. I know one thing: Whenever we needed a cash advance on the royalties, he always sent us a check, whatever we needed.

We cut our first album for King in two days, and that's pretty much how it went for the fifteen albums we done for Syd over the years. The first session, Carter had a couple originals, "How Mountain Girls Can Love" and "Think of What You Done," and we did a train song we always wanted to do, a reworking of the old Grayson and Whitter tune "Train 45." Carter played the conductor and he hollered, "Leaving Union Station, Cincinnati, Ohio: all aboard for points south!"

Now, if you hear the first album, you know it was full of banjo and fiddle, too, with Ralph "Old Maid" Mayo doing some of his best playing. Syd did try to keep the fiddle out and not much banjo, either, but we didn't listen to him on that; we used both as much as we pleased, and we mostly did what we wanted to. One time later on, though, Mayo got sidelined. Syd was boss and he told Mayo to sit out a whole session, and Mayo wasn't a bit happy; he did what he was told because Syd was paying for it. So the Old Maid ended up getting drunk waiting on us while we finished recording. But not long after that happened, Mayo was right back in the King Studio on fiddle when we did a whole album of gospel quartet numbers, *Good Old Camp Meeting Songs*, and you can hear Old Maid play one of the prettiest solos he ever did on Carter's "Harbor of Love."

Syd let us do our music our way, most of the time anyhow. What Syd was most interested in was giving us songs to do; he'd bring us songs, and usually they were good songs, like "Stone Walls and Steel Bars." He'd even try to tell us what he wanted by singing a song he thought would be a hit—and he couldn't sing worth a lick. Now, sometimes, he'd want us to do one we didn't like. He wanted us to record a song Hank Ballard made a hit with on the R&B charts, "Finger-Popping Time." It worked fine for Hank but I didn't want to do it. It was Syd's idea, and Carter went along with it a little better than I did. It wasn't my will to do it, but it was an interesting session, because some of Hank's band, the Midnighters, and some of James's band, too, and even some fellows from the shipping department—they all came by the studio and helped us out with the finger snapping on that song. Syd was wrong on that; he thought it'd be a hit with the hillbilly audience, but the record didn't sell any good, it didn't fit our style.

Now, about the guitar sound Syd wanted so bad, well, we didn't want to copy some old Delmore Brothers records. We had George Shuffler with us then, and he worked out his own style on his old Gibson guitar, which came to be known as "cross-picking," and it suited us perfect. George said all he was trying to do was fill in where he felt it was needing it, when we was catching our breath. Well, he done a lot more, because our King records are known for his picking as much as for our singing. In all my years, I never heard any guitar player that could pick it out as clear and true as George, just as clear as a bell. He played the same notes on guitar as Carter and me sung 'em. One gospel album we did for Syd, *Hymns from the Cross,* was really just a trio of Carter and me and George, but we blended together so well you didn't even miss the baritone. So George really did earn his name as the "third Stanley Brother."

We recorded so many albums for Syd and most of 'em we knocked out in sessions that only lasted a few hours. We'd travel to Cincinnati and play some shows in the area; we'd do the shows at night and record at King during the day. Then we'd drive around town and find us a church or a historical site and make pictures for the album covers, and Syd would have those records out almost as quick we could get home.

Sometimes we'd be driving to Cincinnati and we'd be ninety miles outside of town and start trying to come up with material. Carter would turn around to George Shuffler in the backseat and say, "Aunt, what are we going to do?" And Shuffler would say, "Lord, I don't know!" So we'd walk into the studio many a time not knowing a thing we was going to do, and Carter would come up with a few new ones right on the spot and we'd learn a few more songs Syd had ready for us and we'd cut 'em right then and there. We'd been at it so long, each man in the band knew what the others could do, and that means a lot in this business.

One thing I need to tell you real quick is how George got the nickname "Aunt." George had sound that just blended in with us on the trio or the quartet both; he could play lead guitar or bass, either one, and he could ding a bass or a baritone part, either one. He traveled and played with us so much through the years, when it was just the three of us on the road, they called him the third Stanley Brother. Well, one time we played a show with the Carter Family when it was Mother Maybelle and the girls. One of the girls, Anita, was sick and wasn't there and so George filled in on bass fiddle and they named him Aunt George, so we started calling him that too, sometimes, when we wasn't busy calling him Uncle George.

Anyhow, the way we ended up with our only country hit shows you how loose things could get at King. We had done a whole album in one day, seventeen songs, and we needed one more to complete the session. And we couldn't think of nothing else to do. Somebody spoke up and said, "What about 'How Far to Little Rock'?" I said, "Oh yeah, it won't hurt to put one bad one on the album." And that turned out to be the biggest hit seller of our career.

"How Far to Little Rock" was a comedy song we had worked up through the years; we had first learned it when we was boys, from a carpenter named Fletcher Moss, who built a house for one of our half brothers. He was from Pike County over the Kentucky line, and some weekends he'd come over and stay with us, when we was first starting to play music. He had a custom banjo with a guitar neck and he'd help us with songs, and he'd take his fiddle and play "Arkansas Traveler," which is what he called it, only he would ask the questions and answer them, too, like a little one-man show on that tune. We just took Fletcher's old "Arkansas Traveler" and added our own jokes to it through the years, me and Carter trading one-liners over my banjo picking. We worked that song for years on the stage, and the crowds always liked it. Well, it was a funny song and record buyers liked it, too. "How Far to Little Rock" made it to number seventeen on the country *Billboard* charts in 1960. Then we thought it was really funny, because we'd just cut the joke song as a joke, which it was, and then the joke got us our only hit. Makes you wonder about the music business.

King was good for us, and we were good for King. We didn't make Syd as much money as James Brown, but we stayed with Syd for longer, and I believe we helped King survive as long as it did. Last year, I went back to Cincinnati for a big celebration they had there in honor of Syd and his legendary King Records. They unveiled a historical marker down at the abandoned, run-down King building on Brewster Avenue, where so many of us cut some of the best records of our careers; it said: "The King of Them All: From 1943–1971 King Records forever changed American music. Owner Syd Nathan gave the world bluegrass, R&B, rock and roll, doo wop, country, and soul. With stars from James Brown to the Stanley Brothers, and its innovated, integrated business model, Cincinnati's King Records revolutionized the music industry."

After the ceremonies and such, there was a concert at the historic Emery Theatre downtown, and it was really something. Of course, James Brown and Syd Nathan have both passed on, so there wasn't many old-timers besides me. I don't reckon Syd would have tolerated too many of the musicians performing, outside of my band. It was mostly youngsters in the audience, and I was headlining the show with James's former bass player Bootsy Collins. By the time I went on stage, I'd got so choked up on all the smoke in the theater I could hardly sing. It was the funny-smelling kind, too. Well, to tell you the truth, the room was so full of pot smoke you couldn't hardly see and it choked me down. I never thought I'd miss the smell of Syd's cheap cigar, but that night I really did. There was a lot of rock 'n' roll on that show and I'd a-loved to hear what curse words Syd would have used to describe some of the music that evening.

The setup we had in Florida seemed too good to be true, and it wasn't too long before it fell through. Sales for the mobile shell homes were down and Jim Walters dropped us; we tried to sign up with a rival home builder called Bevis, but it was a bust and it about broke us.

Just like that, we'd lost our sweetest deal; we still kept on making records for King, but now we had to go back on the road to make the paycheck. The long, hard road, the one we thought we'd left behind for good.

Chapter Thirteen

The Road

"Lost all my money but a two-dollar bill
Homesick and lonesome and feeling kind of blue
I'm on my long journey home"

— "Long Journey Home," the Stanley Brothers

They say comedy ain't pretty, and Chick Stripling was living proof. He was a big, red-faced fellow with a big, thick neck on him and jowls like a bulldog. Every hat he wore always seemed too small for his head. He had the type of head you bust down a door with. Chick was our comedian and bass player and one of the best entertainers in the business. But just now he was playing the bully and he'd had too much to drink. I was standing close enough to smell his breath and I could see the wild look in his eyes. I had a chair in my hands and I was fixing to kill him.

We were in a little roadside motel outside of Baltimore and times were tough. This was the early sixties, not long after the Jim Walters Corporation dropped us and we hit the road again. Things were almost as bad as the days when Elvis first came on the scene. After more than half of our lives on the road, we reckoned we deserved more than an Oldsmobile with no air-conditioning that was always running low on gas.

We couldn't even afford to carry along a fiddle player. I've always believed that my kind of old-time mountain music, to be done proper and right and the way it ought be done, demands a fiddle. And we couldn't bring one along.

In those years, a lot of country acts slicked up their sound to try to follow the crowd. They let producers saddle them with fancy strings and background singers. They plugged in their instruments. They went uptown. They called it the Nashville Sound.

Me and Carter, we didn't go for that. We wanted the Stanley Sound and nothing else. We knew we weren't kids anymore, and we weren't going to try to play for kids, either. We didn't try to go uptown or change our sound, because then we wouldn't have been the Stanley Brothers. Hit or miss, we wanted to keep our style of music and be natural. But that stubbornness cost us a lot; you always sacrifice a lot to follow your dreams.

Bad as things were, though, we could always find plenty of work in Baltimore. Like I told you, lots of country people came there for factory jobs during World War II, and they stayed on in the years after, working for Western Electric and Bethlehem Steel. Mountain people, most of 'em, homesick for the music from where they came from. So there were plenty of places like the Blue Jay, the Cozy Inn, the KY Bar, the Garden of Eden; there were so many I can't hardly remember just a few, the kind of taverns where you were lucky to get out with your life.

I don't much like to play in a bar. Never have. People ain't themselves when they're in a bar, and they don't pay attention to what you're trying to do. After they get a few drinks in them, they're not the same as when they came in the door. Most drunks don't make good listeners, and that makes it hard for a musician to do his job. You might sing 'em "Pretty Polly" and then five minutes later, the drunks will holler, "How 'bout playing 'Pretty Polly'?"

We didn't have to play too many of the real rough beer joints, because we had local promoters who were Stanley Brothers fans and they kept us in the better venues, and there was plenty of those, too. We'd book a four- or five-night run in the area, maybe the Hi-Fi Club and the Shangri-La, and big auditoriums like Overly Hall, and make enough for a nice haul. We called it hamburger money. It was just survival.

We'd base ourselves at a motel on U.S. Highway 1, a few miles north of town, close by Bel Air, where John Wilkes Booth was from. Across from the motel was a tavern with a barbershop in the basement. This suited us fine, get us a haircut and hot meal, not as good as our mother's home cooking back on Smith Ridge, but good enough.

I was on the phone making arrangements so the promoters were ready for us. There were all sorts of details to hash out, and I had to listen up real good. This was a business call. Well, Chick had been drinking again, and he was in the corner making noise so I couldn't hear on the phone. The liquor always put Chick in a volatile mood. If he didn't have too much, it worked just fine, because it was part of his job to wake up the crowd. But sometimes the bottle just made him a bully. Long about then, he wouldn't go by the name Chick anymore, or even his given name of James. He'd start calling himself by his initials, "JW," and that's when you knew trouble was brewing.

A lot of people think Stanley Brothers music is all about sadness and tragedy and mothers dying, and that's why some have called our music the "graveyard sound." But like you've found out from Wine-Sap on down to "Little Rock," comedy and entertainment was as important to our show as Hymn Time. And Chick was worth his weight in gold when it come to that.

With Chick, we had not only a solid bass-fiddle man but a showman who could really light up a stage with his jokes and his dance routine. He had the music, he had the comedy, and he had his dance: Three for the price of one was how we figured it, and his drinking came with the whole deal. It was something we could stand. And, bad as our finances were, we needed a laugh just as much as anybody in the audience did.

Chick had worked with all the big acts in Nashville, and most weren't as lenient as we were. I heard he rode with Bill Monroe for a short spell. Now, Bill didn't allow drinking whatsoever, but that didn't stop Chick. He just rigged him a hose in the back of the bus, some sort of contraption that snaked up from under his seat to feed him liquor so Bill wouldn't catch him.

When Chick made some good money, he'd get a good drunk going and he'd just disappear and they'd have to fire him. So he'd bounced around for years by the time he joined up with us. We figured we'd take him on. We weren't making enough for him to get too far gone anyhow. As far as trying to rein him in, we knew that was a lost cause. You'd no more put rules on Chick than you would on a wild boar.

Chick had come up the hard way, same as we did. And we respected that, because it's not easy to start with nothing and make something out of that. And Chick done even more, he created something the world had never seen before. It was called the Butter Paddle Buck 'n' Wing.

Here is what happened, as I understand it. Chick grew up on a hog farm down in south Georgia, which is the heart of peanut country, out near Valdosta. His little town had a train depot, a whistle-stop where passengers got out and stretched their legs. Chick decided to make some money selling boiled peanuts down at the depot. There was some competition on the platform from other kids, so Chick got a notion to make up a little ole dance, something to set him apart. Once he started dancing, business started booming.

He called it the Butter Paddle Buck 'n' Wing.

Lord, there was nothing else like it. It was out of this world. It was a tap dance, partly, the old soft-shoe, with daredevil moves that were Chick's alone. What made it unique was that at the top end of all this fancy footwork was big ole Chick. Big as a bouncer in his baggy suit, and his limbs so loose you'd have swore he was floating above the floor. Talk about your amazing grace, Chick had it.

Chick was what you they call "natural-born." It was a gift he had. He could hear a song like "The Chicken Reel" and make it come alive in his feet. He'd pop the floor right on time and never miss a beat, keeping that rhythm no matter what. Now, he was a fine comedian and musician, too—he could even play a real pretty old-timey fiddle. But it was the Butter Paddle Buck 'n' Wing that put him over with the crowd.

When we traveled on package tours with the top country-music stars, it was Chick who got their attention. They'd sidle to the edge of the stage to get a close-up look. Carl Smith, Faron Young, Tex Ritter—they'd be following every move he made. They'd be wide-eyed and grinning like kids on Christmas morning.

So you can see how Carter and I could look past the drinking. If Chick had a-treated himself right, there would have been no stopping place for him—he could have gone to Hollywood. But he didn't have the right personality; that's the way it is for a lot of people. Success scares them. So he'd go on the bottle and go out of control.

One time I was down at the barbershop across from the motel. I slid into that chair ready to get me a relaxing haircut and a close shave. Then I heard the tapping sound in the tavern up above, and I knew who it was. I could hear Chick dance for a little bit, and then he'd stop and it'd get real quiet. You could hear him tell one of his jokes he was famous for and then you'd hear the outburst when the people just bust out laughing. He'd pass his hat to get him some more money for drinks and then he'd start dancing again.

When I left the barbershop, there was Chick ahead of me. I don't know whether they threw him out or if he left the bar on his own, but he was trying to get across that six-lane highway. He didn't bother looking either way, he just barreled ahead. The traffic was a-flying and he just weaved through there like it was nothing. He made it back across; I don't know how, but he did. For Chick, that was probably nothing compared to getting across his bedroom floor back home. He had to be light on his feet when he was coming in late at night and didn't want to wake up his wife.

I tell you all this by way of preamble, so you can understand what I was facing in the motel room. Chick had been dancing for drinks and he'd had more than his fill. That's when the bulldog turned into the bully.

I was wrapped up in my phone call, so I made an easy target. Chick knew I couldn't leave the room. I kept telling him to hush and let me conduct my business. He wanted my undivided attention and nothing else would do. His eyes narrowed to slits in that pudgy, pasty face of his.

"Listen here, cat shit," he said. "You don't tell me what to do."

That's when I put down the phone, picked up a chair and decided I was going to kill him. I'm not a fighting man by nature, never have been; I'm not even what you call hot-tempered. But when you push me too far I push back, and Chick had pushed past my limit. I held the chair over my head and told him my patience had run out. He kept on badgering me, and he made a move.

Then, from the other side of the room, like the cavalry in some old western movie, here came Carter, like he done so many times, to help out his kid brother. He put his hands on the chair.

"Step back," he said. "Little Man, you don't need that."

Little Man was one of the nicknames Carter had hung on me. It was a name he threw around when we got to arguing. Like I already told you before, we had our disagreements like any other brothers, but never too bad that we couldn't patch things up. One thing Carter wouldn't abide was someone picking on his little brother. I knew that, and I wanted him to teach this bully a lesson. So this was one time I didn't mind him calling me that.

"Kill him, Carter!" I said, and I meant it.

Carter set down the chair real gentle, like he was tidying up the room for guests. Then he started in on Chick, just ripped him up with his fists flying, until poor Chick had blood running off him. It happened fast, but it was something fierce, and when Carter got done with him, he had beaten Chick nearly to death.

It was a pitiful sight. Carter stood over him, sorry for what he'd had to do. Chick was bleeding all over the carpet, as bad as a stuck hog. Carter said, "You had enough, Chick?" and reached out his hand to help him up. Chick was hunched over, heaving so much he could barely get out a word, but one was enough: "Yeah."

Well, Chick was bleeding from his nose and who knows where else. He was a real mess. Carter helped steer him into the bathroom and cleaned him up, washed that blood off him. Then they came back into the room and sat down and nobody said nothing for a while, Chick breathing heavy. He got that slit-eyed look he had before, and he said, "I want some more." Even though he was whipped, he was still game. If you've ever seen a chicken fight, you've probably seen how awful it gets near the end when the losing rooster is all tore up but it don't have sense enough to give up. Chick was that rooster.

So they went at it again. And Carter done the same thing to him. Strange thing was, as painful as it was to watch, I knew Carter was right to hand it to him twice like that. Chick had it coming to him. He had always been used to bullying people. But this one time, he got set down and put in his place, thanks to Carter.

But I have to say that I wasn't sorry Carter stepped in like he did. I don't think I could have taken on Chick by myself, even with a chair.

Chick was a sight. Both of those eye slits had shut for all the swelling. He was one big bruise. Kept asking where his hat went to. He finally surrendered for good, and went into the bathroom and cleaned himself up.

For that night's show, Chick was his old self, battered as he was. He did everything he was supposed to do. He played his bass and told his jokes and danced his dance and went over like gangbusters. He knew how bad he looked onstage—worse than your average assault and battery—so he made a good joke about it. That's what a real professional showman will do. He takes any situation handed to him, no matter how bad, and he makes it part of the act. So Chick just grinned and says to the audience that yes, he had a good whipping and deserved it, too. He told the old joke about the man who got caught in bed with another man's wife and had to pay the price.

"If you want to know what's wrong with me, well, I was living the life of Riley." Then he squeezed a wink out of them swollen black eyes that must have hurt like the dickens. "And what happened was Riley come home."

I felt bad for Chick, to be honest, but I felt more sorry for Carter. Sorry he had to waste the energy he had—and Lord, he was running close to empty on that. He already had enough to worry about besides protecting his kid brother from a homicide charge.

Carter was the one who kept us going when we felt like giving in.

Many's the time you felt you'd had enough. "Something better's coming round the corner," he'd say, and you could tell he wasn't whipped, and his face would light up. And no matter how tired or fed up you were, you'd all of the sudden feel everything was going to be all right.

But all that was going to change, and I'd have to be the one who carried the show and kept the brother team alive. Carter's time was running out.

CHAPTER FOURTEEN

Brother's Keeper

"I left my old home to ramble this country
My mother and Dad said, 'Son don't go wrong.
Remember that God will always watch o'er you
And we will be waiting for you here at home.'
'Son don't go astray,' was what they both told me,
'Remember that love for God can be found.'
But now they're both gone, this letter just told me
For years they've been dead, the fields have turned brown"

—"THE FIELDS HAVE TURNED BROWN," THE STANLEY BROTHERS

Nothing hurts a man more than when he gives it his best and it ain't enough. He keeps reaching down inside for more, and he keeps trying. But somehow it doesn't work out. By the early sixties, Flatt and Scruggs and the Foggy Mountain Boys were making hundreds of thousands of dollars a year. They were stars on the *Opry* and they were playing Carnegie Hall. They had a national sponsor, Martha White Flour, and a number one hit record, "The Ballad of Jed Clampett." They were hot.

The Stanley Brothers, well, we were playing for wages, still waiting for a decent payday. Just surviving. We weren't making enough to carry a full band. Carter knew we were as good as Flatt and Scruggs. Maybe we were better. It didn't matter one way or the other. They were dining on steaks and we were living on Vienna sausages. They were riding high in a big fancy bus and making the big money. We were crowded into a car and staying with friends to save on motels.

You'd see Flatt Scruggs on the *Beverly Hillbillies* TV show and getting their name in places none of us others could. I know it rankled Monroe a lot; it really hurt Bill's pride, and it did Carter's, too. He would try to shrug it off, like he always done. He'd always try to look on the bright side. He had so much pride, and he always kept his sense of humor. "You know, boys," he'd say. "The sun don't shine on the same dog's ass every day." He'd throw back his head and laugh and you could see his gold tooth. But I could tell it was bothering him. I could tell it was gnawing at his insides something fierce.

Somebody later on told me a story that I wish Carter had heard. We were playing an outdoor festival. Lester Flatt was sitting in the stands with his bass man, Jake Tolluck, and a fellow who was friends with both Flatt and Scruggs and the Stanley Brothers. Carter was leading us in a real pretty hymn, and the crowd was just as quiet as could be.

Jake leaned over to Lester—remember, this is his boss he's talking to—and he said, "Lester, wouldn't you just give your soul if you could sound like that?"

The fellow who heard this said Lester gave Jake a look like he wanted to kill him.

Another time, Lester himself said to George Shuffler, our sideman, something he didn't ever tell to us. "We got the Stanleys beat when it comes to picking, but no one can hold a candle to the Stanley Brothers and George Shuffler when it comes to singing hymns." And if you ever heard Flatt and Scruggs do a number like "God Loves His Children," you know they could do their gospel up right.

I don't tell you all this to put down Lester or to brag on Carter or George or me. I just think you ought to know how highly Carter's own rivals felt about him as a singer. He and Lester weren't on speaking terms for years, but each respected the other man's talent.

It came down to recognition. Lester was rewarded for his talent and Carter never was, at least not in money and popularity. And it really ate at him. I believe Carter couldn't accept that we never found the success he felt we deserved.

It was tough playing for wages not much more than we had first started out making in the forties. There was some times when we didn't hardly make enough for gas money to get back home. And there was others when we had to fight to get the money we were due.

Carter wasn't as good a businessman as he was an entertainer, so I handled the business side of things, booking shows and collecting the money and paying the band members and whatnot. Whenever we had problems with promoters, though, Carter would step in to set things right.

We had a show at a place called Crossroads in Northern Virginia, and we were late getting there. We didn't have good directions, and we drove all the way to Winchester, getting lost this way and that. We finally got to the club at 11 P.M., two hours after we were supposed to. But the people were still ready for us. We went ahead and played until 1 A.M. closing time and put on the best show we could.

After all that, the owner of the place wouldn't pay us. He said we broke the contract by coming late. Carter had some words for him, but it didn't do much good. "If he was any kind of man at all," he said. "He wouldn't have let us play if he had no intention of paying us." That was the kind of promoter who gives a bad name to the music business.

There was another time like that comes to mind, when we had a personal appearance at a school in Newland, North Carolina. It was a Saturday night and we were late but we played the whole show anyhow. The principal of the school didn't want to pay. He wanted to send a check on Monday to the radio station in Bristol. We were used to getting paid after the show in cash. That was the way we did business.

Carter told him the deal was cash on the barrelhead, and he pressed the principal but good. "Look, mister," he said. "You don't have to pay us for our sake. You need to pay us for the people that we owe." The principal went into his office and came back and said he was really sorry for behaving like he did. We collected, but only because Carter wouldn't back down.

Haggling for what you're owed, playing the same little schoolhouses where you started out. That would get any man down. Carter handled it by hitting the bottle harder. He didn't get mean the way some did, like

Ira Louvin smashing his mandolin and cussing out anyone within earshot. But it started to wear on him.

As always, Carter blew off steam by pranking. He and George Shuffler were some of the busiest pranksters in the business. They liked to work together, same as they done onstage, and like I told you about when we were down in Florida, their favorite weapon was with a little laxative they doled out when they got the notion.

There used to be a chewing gum called Beech's that came in a little box. Well, there was a laxative called Feen-A-Mint. It came in a little box, too, and it was just like chewing gum. They'd buy a few boxes of Beech's and a few boxes of Feen-a-mint and they'd switch 'em, put some of the Feen-A-Mints in the Beech's. They'd just give it to anybody as a prank.

They also had a lot of fun with the old Ex-Lax, which tasted just like chocolate candy. You'd have thought those were magic beans, with as much fun as Carter and George had with those chocolate Ex-Lax candies.

We were down in Florida, and they gave somebody the chocolate Ex-Lax as a prank. About two weeks later, we had a box mailed to us at the radio station in Jacksonville and it was filled with chocolate candy. Well, Carter and George ate that candy, and of course somebody had reversed the prank on them. We had a show in Live Oak about ninety miles from Jacksonville, and I forget how many times we had to stop at restrooms along the way. With some of them, they were a little bit too late to get to the toilet.

There were games we'd play to help make the miles go by. The roads we traveled were two-lane country roads, and there'd be nothing but farms and fields sometimes the whole way. It was pretty countryside, but that gets old after a while.

So we'd play a game called Horse. How you'd play was, one man took one side of the road and one man took the other. If you saw a horse, you'd get a point. A horse counted one point, a spotted horse counted three points, and a gray horse counted three points. And the man that got to twenty-one points would be the winner, and then we'd start all over again. A white horse counted five points, and we used to count a white mule as a game winner, until we got to arguing so much that if there was one little black hair on that white mule it wouldn't count. Carter'd holler out, "Nah, that's not a white mule nohow!" We'd have to stop the car and go out in the field and see if we could find the black hair on the mule.

Horse was the cause of some of the worst arguments I ever had with Carter. One time, Carter hollered out, "Horse with a spot, that's two points for me!" Well, I didn't see no spot on that horse. We must have argued for five miles or more, and we finally turned the car back around, but by then the horse had run off into another pasture away from the road. Carter didn't let that stop him. He walked a long ways, crawled under some fences and jumped a creek, until he finally found his horse and checked every inch but couldn't find a spot. Course, when he came back to the car, he swore to us that there was a tiny spot underneath. I only found out later he was lying to get his two points.

Another game was called Car. There was mostly Chevrolets and Fords back then, and one man would take Ford and the other would take Chevy and you'd get you a point every time you'd see one. And first man to get to eleven points was the winner. You can see how awful bored you can get when you're down to counting cars on the road.

Carter and me had a lot of falling-outs, but they never did amount to nothing. Traveling hard, you're gonna have discord now and then, and you find a way to reconcile. Sometimes we'd go down by the river and get us a big watermelon and split that thing open and salt it down real good and eat us some and we'd be ready to go again. I guess it was just more survival than anything else. We knew we needed each other. The Stanley Brothers was a team to us, like a team of plow horses. When one don't help and do his part, the big plow don't move and you can't get no work done.

Naturally we had our little differences now and then, but it's between brothers, you know, and any difference we had, why, we worked it out. We had a word or two many a time, but we always smoothed it out. It goes back to how we was raised up on the ridge: We played together, slept together, we was so close for so many years.

Money was something we never argued about. With me and Carter, everything was fifty-fifty. That was the way we dealt with it from the start, and that's how we done it right up until he died. Sometimes he'd put my name on a song he wrote and maybe sometimes I'd have his name on one of my songs. We'd pay off the band and the rest that was left for us, we split the money right down the middle.

Like I told you, I usually handled the money, and he was the one handling the stage show and MC work. We'd go out and play a percentage show, and back then it was usually cash, and he'd never question me on any of the money figures. He trusted me and I trusted him. That's why we made it as long as we did without breaking up.

It was respect for each other that kept us together. He respected me a lot, and I did him. If I thought of something, why, ninety-nine times out of a hundred, he'd agree with it. And that was same way I was with him.

When it come to the music, we respected each other the most. About the only thing we ever disagreed on with our music was the Dobro. In the fifties, the Dobro got real popular again, especially after Josh Graves joined up with Flatt and Scruggs. Josh was one of the best Dobro men in country music. Earlier on, he had played with Wilma Lee and Stoney Cooper. That's his Dobro driving the sound on "Walking My Lord Up Calvary Hill" and a lot of their Columbia records from that time.

When Josh started with the Foggy Mountain Boys in 1955, he really gave their music a big boost, and his Dobro guitar fit in good with Earl Scruggs's banjo. Josh could play fast and loud, and he could play slow and pretty. That Dobro of his really helped set them apart from Monroe and all the rest. Well, after a while with Lester and Earl, Josh offered to work with the Stanley Brothers, and Carter was willing to take him up on that offer. Carter was more ready to experiment than I was, and I think he figured the Dobro would bring us more fans the way it did with Flatt and Scruggs.

I liked Josh as a man and I liked his playing just fine, but I didn't want it in the Stanley Brothers. I didn't think the Dobro fit in with the old-time sound. It was too modern for me, and it seemed like so many groups were adding Dobro to copy Flatt and Scruggs. We had our own sound, and the Dobro would have messed it up.

Carter wanted to hire Josh real bad. He was really pushing for him, but I finally told him it was the Dobro or me. There wasn't room for both in our band. Carter saw how serious I was, and he gave in. I won out on that, and I'm glad I did. I never have changed my view on that. The Dobro is still very popular. Some will tell you they'd rather hear Dobro than banjo any day, and the Dobro's become a regular part of a lot of bluegrass bands. But not in the Clinch Mountain Boys, and not on any song by Ralph Stanley. I've never had a Dobro on my records, and I won't even discuss the Dobro no more.

Speaking of the Dobro reminds me of another thing I almost forgot to tell you. It's something a lot of people don't know, and I'm a little bit ashamed to have to tell you this. Once the Stanley Brothers used a steel guitar. It was in a session for Mercury Records in '57, and we got Little Roy Wiggins, one of the best steel players in Nashville, to help us out. Now, Roy had played for years with Eddy Arnold, which is about as far from our sound as anybody in country music. Usually the steel guitar was more honky-tonk than we were known for, but Carter wanted to try something new.

So we had Little Roy play some steel brushstrokes on a few songs: "If That's the Way You Feel," "A Life of Sorrow," and "I'd Rather Be Forgotten." This was Carter's idea, and I went ahead with it. The steel didn't bother me as much as the Dobro, and I don't think it hurt anything on these songs. The way they used it was in the background, just to add a touch. Even so, there were a few of the fans that didn't like hearing the steel, and they let us know it.

These records are now some of the all-time favorite Stanley Brothers songs for a lot of people. Ricky Skaggs did a cover of "If That's the Way You Feel," which brought that song to a whole new audience in the 1980s. Good as those songs were, they were some of the last we ever did for Mercury. The rock music had knocked nearly everybody down, and there was hardly any of the old bands still standing. Mercury finally dropped us. It'd be fifty years before I was on a major label again.

Carter and me still went back to Smith Ridge whenever we could, to stay with our mother. She'd always have a kettle warming up a big meal, the good home cooking we couldn't get at the diners and truck stops. She still had her big garden where she raised her own vegetables. Green beans, what they called Hanovers, sweet potatoes, peas and all kind of squash. Lots of the time George Shuffler would stay up at Smith Ridge, and he'd lay over for a few days with us on our breaks from show dates.

My mother and George became real close. He was like part of the family; he just about become one of us. My mother loved him just like a son, and he said she was one of the best friends he ever had. He called her Ma Stanley and he doted on her almost as bad as I did. He really loved her home cooking, too, the big cathead biscuits she made from scratch and sausage gravy she'd always have ready for us when we came in the wee hours after a show.

She knew we'd be hungry and beat when we'd come in from the road. Anytime we came in, morning or night, she was ready to get up and cook. It didn't matter how late it was, she'd always have her apron on and fixing us a meal. Tired as she was, she'd be over the stove and busy in the kitchen. Didn't matter what we said, she always insisted. She wouldn't let us talk her out of it. She was always looking out for her boys, and George was one of her boys, too. That was her way, and she never changed.

We'd eat and go straight to sleep. Then she'd be the first one up in the morning, and she'd rouse us up, even though she knew how worn out we were. "I'm sorry to have to do it," she'd say. "It's hard but it's fair!"

George spent a lot of time in my mother's garden, which was still her pride and joy. He got right down in the dirt with her. She'd have her homemade bonnet wrapped on tight to keep the hot sun off her face, and George would be right beside her, his shirtsleeves rolled up and sweat pouring down. He'd plow the garden for her and get in there busy with the hoe. He'd break the earth and set it out and plant it, getting all the crops ready. All the corn and green beans and tomatoes and cucumbers and Irish potatoes and mustard greens and squash. She got to calling it "George and my" garden, and they just enjoyed being together so much you'd hardly notice how hard they was working. Me and Carter got to joking that if you wanted something, you had to go through George to get it from my mother. They was that close.

Then, in the evening they'd set on the porch and play music together, George on guitar and my mother on her clawhammer banjo like she did when she was a young woman. It was good to see her smile and goof around and laugh. Music helped her forget her troubles and cares, and I'd watch her there, with her old bonnet flung off her hair bun and her feet a-tapping to the beat, and her mind fixed on the old songs she played in her childhood. She'd play "Shout Little Lulie," and her face would shine and her eyes would dance and I could see the young Lucy Smith again, the girl from Smith Ridge who could outpick any man for miles around.

My mother still doted on her boys; she knew we were living lean on the road, and she was always worried about Carter's health. But it was her we were more worried about, living alone on Smith Ridge and getting up in years.

We had a big scare when a fire hit the old home place with our mother inside. She was all the time canning, putting up something to eat for the winter; one morning she was in the kitchen canning apples when a dishrag caught fire from the old woodstove. She threw the dishrag down and it caught her on fire and the house went up in flames. It almost burnt her up, but she ran out of there just in time.

The fire demolished everything we had. All through the years, she'd kept all the Stanley Brothers records and souvenirs and pictures. Things that could never be replaced, all sorts of important papers. The thing I hated to lose most was my honorable discharge from the army. But we couldn't be too worried about such things, because we knew were lucky she had made it out alive.

The hardest thing for my mother was losing the house she was raised in, the house where she had raised Carter and me. She stayed with friends for a while, and I told her she'd be back on the ridgetop in no time. I wanted her in a brand-new house on the same spot and to have it furnished so it would be like the fire never happened.

I paid for the new house; I wasn't married at the time and I didn't have as many responsibilities and obligations as Carter, with his big family to support. I didn't have much money but I had good credit. So I paid for it by the month in installments. I was glad to do it; I was dedicated to my mother and I paid every dime.

I contracted out for the builders and had her in a new house in thirty days. The old house hadn't had indoor plumbing, so I put a bathroom in the new one for her and a lot of other modern conveniences, like central heating and air-conditioning. All the nice things the old house didn't have. And new furnishings, too. She got a better house, a better bed, a better everything. She enjoyed the conveniences I got her, but it wasn't the same to her. Even with all this and that and the other, she missed the home place just like it was when she had raised us. That's the way old people are.

Round about the same time, in 1961, we were playing a show in Ohio and we got word that our dad, Lee, had died from heart failure. We went ahead and played out the show and headed home to Virginia for the funeral. Lee had been doing poorly, and we'd known that the day was going to come sooner rather than later, but Carter really took that hard. He was closer to Lee than I was, and I think it weighed on him heavy, and he wasn't as strong as he once was.

Of course, he handled it, he had to, but he hated it to happen. Same thing with the fire at the house on Smith Ridge. His songs were all about that, losing your parents and finding the home place in ruins, and now it was coming true. His drinking got worse.

So many brother acts didn't last. Probably the most famous is Bill and Charlie Monroe. They only made it for five years. I don't know much about the breakup, other than that Bill wasn't satisfied and that they never made up. Brothers are like that.

Carter and me were lucky because we never got jealous of each other. We were too different in everything—looks and personality and singing—so we didn't feel in competition with each other.

And it was a matter of survival, too. It was tough enough making it as a brother team, and going it alone would just be even harder. We knew we had to stick together, no matter what.

There's one thing in that play they did on us that's false, the stage play about our lives I was telling you about at the start of the book. Carter never figured on going solo, and me neither. Neither one of us would have ever gone solo. He never wanted to break up the Stanley Brothers.

The biggest troubles we had were always about his drinking. It started to hurt him instead of perk him up. On the road, he'd carry his bottle with him to bed at night.

It became an everyday thing. He had his worries and he thought the drinking helped him with the worries. But he just got to where he had to have it. You can get hooked on dope or anything. He got hooked on liquor. I'd get on him about his drinking, but it didn't help. He'd promise you the moon, and just as quick as he got around to it, he'd chuggle again. Then he'd get on me for nagging on him. He'd swear at me and call me Little Jesus. I hated to be called that name the worst, and he knew it. He didn't want to be preached to; his pride couldn't stand it. It was how our worst arguments always got going.

No matter how we were feeling about each other, whatever differences we were having, we did our best to keep our squabbling private. We didn't want to let any arguments spill out on the stage. We were professional entertainers and we both believed that sort of thing had no place in the show. Our parents had always said you need to be at your best onstage. We tried to always take the high road.

Sometimes, it just couldn't be helped, and the stage became a battleground. It was mostly the petty type of thing the audience didn't even pick up on. You might be surprised at the little dramas that go on when a band is putting on a show. It was almost like an inside joke just between us brothers. But there wasn't nothing funny about it.

I remember a show we played at the Ash Grove in Los Angeles in 1962. This was the premier folk club on the West Coast, and these were big shows for us. We were getting our name out there to a new audience, college students and young people. It was the crowd Flatt and Scruggs had tapped into, and we were getting a piece of the pie.

On this tour, we had Vernon Derrick along with us on fiddle. He was from a little town in northern Alabama called Arab, out near Huntsville. He'd played with Jimmy Martin, and later on in his career he pulled a hitch with Hank Williams Jr. He's the one playing fiddle on "A Country Boy Can Survive," Hank Jr.'s big hit in the 1970s.

Vernon tore it up at the Ash Grove when he lit into "Turkey in the

Straw." It was early in the show, and I was still getting warmed up. Vernon was on fire, changing tempos at lightning speed. I messed up on my banjo break, but I recovered quick and I didn't think it stood out too bad. Vernon done so good he carried the day anyhow.

After the song ended, the crowd was going wild. This was the kind of country music they came to hear, done up the old-time way. But Carter was such a perfectionist, and he was bothered by my flub. He just couldn't let it pass without making a comment. He smiled over at Vern, and he waited for the applause to die down so everybody in the place could hear him: "Vern, you know what?" said Carter. "There ain't but one thing to say. Your banjo man let you down there. You're gonna have to rehearse him a little bit."

Now, that really burned me up. There was no call for Carter to do that. I knew I made a mistake, and if he wanted to say something, he should have said something to me backstage after the show. Here he was dressing me down in public. And this was the Ash Grove, where some of the people in the audience were Hollywood stars. I looked out in the crowd and there was the actor Dan Blocker who played Hoss Cartwright on *Bonanza,* the most popular show on television. Carter had me feel like a doggone fool in front of Hoss.

At the evening show, I decided to get back at him. There were a lot of Bill Monroe fans and Flatt and Scruggs fans, too, so we got a lot of requests to do their songs and we'd play some. By then we'd got to where we could play anything from "Salty Dog" to "Uncle Pen" and it would sound like the Stanley Brothers. So we would play those requests to satisfy the fans, and we were glad to do it.

We done a few Monroe numbers and the audience was eating it up. Carter was never one to dampen the mood, and he always loved to play Monroe. He was trying to remember some other songs of Bill's we could do, but he got stumped. So he turned back to me and he said, "Ralph, can you think of one?"

Well, I could have thought of a million Monroe songs, but I was still sore about Carter making such a fuss about my banjo flub. I wasn't in the mood to help him out of this jam. "You think of one!" I shouted so the crowd could hear. I figured he deserved it.

Carter took the high road. He let it go and he didn't say a word in response. He sort of paused and got lost in thought. Maybe he was realizing he shouldn't have called me out at the afternoon show. Somehow it triggered him to think of brothers that hadn't stayed together like we done.

He got the notion to tell the audience a little about the forgotten Monroe Brother, the one who got left behind while his younger brother Bill blazed the bluegrass trail. Carter had a love for the musicians who'd been down the same hard road as him, and he loved the music more than anything in the world.

"Charlie Monroe was never real well known out this way," Carter told the crowd. "Bill and Charlie split up before Bill really broke out all over the country. Charlie Monroe himself is a wonderful singer. I don't know how many of you have heard him, but he's one of the best. Bill is a good singer, but his brother Charlie is one of the unsung heroes, in my opinion."

I was standing there listening to Carter and I wasn't even mad at him no more. As only Carter could, he'd played the part of a peacemaker and turned the stage into a time machine. He'd bring the brothers back together by playing one of their songs. That way he honored the music he first heard as a boy when the voices of Bill and Charlie sang out of a battery-powered Philco radio back in the mountains, two brothers in harmony.

"I know a lot of you never really heard where the Monroe sound comes from and have never been there," said Carter. "Well, I have. The Monroe Brothers were born and raised in a little cabin down in Rosine, Kentucky, near Beaver Dam. I've spent time there. I'd like to do a number that Charlie and Bill done years ago for Bluebird Records, back in the thirties, when they first started singing in Hammond, Indiana, and then moved into the Carolinas and made a terrific hit. The houses wouldn't hold the people that come to hear them boys play. This song is called 'Drifting Too Far from the Shore.' I hope we can do it as well as they did back then."

It takes a big man to pay his respects in public, to humble himself before his heroes. It means you're confident with your own talent. I was there onstage listening to Carter tell the story along with the crowd. I wasn't sore anymore. Course, when we played the song, we did it Stanley Brothers' style, same as when we did our recording of it.

His way of setting up a song made you want to go out and learn more. "Here's an old folk song," he'd say. "It was recorded thirty-five years ago by a blind fiddler from down in Shouns, Tennessee, and a fella from Galax, Virginia. They went by the name of Grayson and Whitter. It's called 'Don't Go Out Tonight, Little Darlin'."

Carter and I were in it for the long run. We had a deal. We were going to keep going as long as we could. We never had any intention of breaking up. Anyhow, for a long while, the drinking didn't affect the shows, he was mostly just hurting himself.

When he was younger, he could handle the booze. It used to be no matter how bad things were going on the road, moneywise or what have you, or how tired and sick Carter may have felt, he always found strength in the music. Once he hit the stage, he came back to life. Everything changed in him, and he just glowed full of joy, peace and happiness. The music made the pain and suffering worth it.

That wasn't happening no more. He'd be singing and you could see the glow was gone and you could hear his strength leaving him. He looked haggard and pale. He was losing his greatest gift besides his singing, that way he had of talking natural and ad-libbing, the way he introduced songs and related to the audience.

In his last years, Carter was unhappy because he knew he was sick, but he was the kind of man who wouldn't give up. Even when he was feeling poorly, he could still put on a show like nobody else. He was a good talker even when he had laryngitis, and he took care of the MC-ing. He had an important job and he done it well.

Carter was such a wonderful and talented MC, he could please any kind of crowd, from Grundy, Virginia, to Ash Grove in Los Angeles. He was so used to speaking off the cuff. He never planned what he was going to say, just like we never planned our sets. We just sung whatever we felt at the moment and whatever requests we got from the audience.

But Carter got to where he'd forget the words to a song, or he'd freeze up when he was thinking of a little story to tell. He'd make slipups and jumble his jokes, and scramble what he wanted to say. His timing was off. He was losing his gift, and he knew it, and it hurt his pride.

In our last year together, Carter pushed me to do more talking onstage. I think he knew maybe he wasn't going to be around, and he wanted me to be ready for that day. I was always backwards about MC-ing. I wouldn't know what to say. I didn't want to be in the spotlight. I didn't think I was cut out to be the front man.

So Carter started to put me on the spot and tell me to introduce a song or try to peddle some records. He'd go off the stage after a few songs and just leave me and the band standing there. Sometimes I'd just tell him, "No, I ain't doing it." It didn't matter to him, he'd just walk off the stage. I'd either step up to the microphone and talk to the crowd or I'd go blank, just nothing but silence. You can't have that in a show, so I done a little MC-ing, because Carter forced me into it. I believe he did that for a purpose, figuring that I'd need that experience in the years ahead. The way it turned out, it was good for me, and it was something I'll always be thankful for.

In the meantime, George and me started carrying Carter in the music as well. I started to sing lead a lot more; a lot of times I could tell he just didn't feel up to it. For weeks at a stretch, at outdoor shows, especially where the weather could be a factor, and also at some radio stations where we played after a long night of driving, we had to make up for him. Carter'd lose his voice and we'd just have to shore everything up ourselves. We had to cover for him and not let it show. But people could see and hear for themselves. He was fading fast.

For a good long while, all Carter worried about was his Scotch, and he let me worry about everything else. He might call up the promoters and do some of that; anytime there was some talking to do, he enjoyed that. But not on the business side; that wasn't his thing. By now, Carter always had a little Scotch by his side so he didn't much care about nothing. In the early days, it was Carter who kept us going. Now it was me.

It wasn't an overnight change. It was years and hundreds of shows. It crept up on him, and it did us, too, dogging him on those one-nighters. And he never got wild with his drinking like some do. Most times, nobody would have noticed, but I always could tell, because with just one drink his voice would get weaker. He'd lose that sweet mellow tone he had, and his voice would get rough and cracky.

He was what they used to call a dram drinker; he just kept tight all the time. And he had a lot of help, too. Like I told you before, there were always fans buying him a drink, bringing him a drink, all the time, wherever we went. Everybody wanted to drink with Carter, before the show, after the show, anytime. And that was hard for him to turn down. He liked to have a drink with the people, he liked to socialize, have a good time, laugh and tell some jokes. Set the dark feelings and worries aside. He just had a weakness and he just got too far gone.

You might ask why I put up with Carter's drinking, and why I stood by as he went down the road to ruin. When he's your brother, you accept him for what he is, weaknesses and all. He had his burden to bear and I did, too. He was my brother and I loved him.

With some brother teams, brotherly love wasn't enough to keep it going. Bill and Charlie Monroe only made it four years together before they split because they couldn't stand each other when they were off stage, and they never reconciled. Charlie and Ira Louvin made it longer, but Charlie finally called it quits when Ira's drinking and bad temper made it too much for him to bear. Every man has his limits. But with me and Carter, it was different. We were sticking together no matter what.

One thing I noticed and it sort of bothered me and got me worried: Carter started featuring a lot of Carter Family songs in our shows. He done a beautiful slow rendition of "Single Girl, Married Girl" to showcase George Shuffler on lead guitar. And now he was all the time wanting to sing the Carters' "Will You Miss Me When I'm Gone?" But he wasn't just paying tribute, and I could tell there was a bitter taste when he sang the words out, like the way old A.P. sang "It'll Aggravate Your Soul." He was making it his song, like A.P.'s story had become his story, and it was like he already knew the ending:

Perhaps you'll plant a flower on my poor unworthy grave
And come sit alone beside me when the roses nod and wave

It was hard to watch Carter singing his own epitaphs right there onstage. It was hard to watch him hurting himself and not be able to help him. But the hardest thing of all was to watch him find the will to keep on going when most men would have lain down and given up. Carter played many a show when he wasn't up to it. He'd still go on the stage and sing his heart out no matter what because he believed he owed it to the people who'd come to see him. Night after night I watched him fight his fight, and he kept fighting all the way to the end.

CHAPTER FIFTEEN

Death Is Only a Dream

"My latest sun is sinking fast, my race is nearly run
My strongest trials now are past, my triumph has begun
O come, Angel Band, come and around me stand
Bear me away on your snow-white wings to my immortal home"

—"Angel Band," the Stanley Brothers

Carter was suffering in health for a long time, but he had a way of fooling himself and everybody else, too. He thought he was smarter than any doctor when it come to how he should live. He carried his leather bag like the kind that doctors had, and that's where he kept his bottle of Scotch or vodka or whatever did the trick. He called it his "medicine for the miles."

The bottle was the way he handled life on the road. He believed that it kept him going. That may have been so in earlier days, with a nip here to pep him up before the show and a nip there to ease his mind riding to the next. That was when he was young and strong. Now the medicine wasn't the good kind no more. It was a poison.

One of Carter's biggest fans and oldest friends was our doctor, Bruce Mongle. He was a very respected physician and surgeon. He had a practice in Bristol and he was our family doctor for years. When he wasn't sawing people open, he played a pretty good old-time banjo as a pastime.

He loved the Stanley Brothers and he loved Carter like he was his own son, and he wanted to help keep him alive.

Around Christmastime in 1965, Dr. Mongle came down to Florida to visit us for the holidays. Carter wasn't feeling well and he asked Dr. Mongle to stop by the house and give him a full checkup. So Dr. Mongle examined him and it didn't take long before he'd seen enough. "Carter," he said, "if you don't lay that bottle down, you won't see another Christmas."

Now, most people might be scared hearing that. It'd maybe make you think long and hard about what you're doing and maybe you'd change your ways. Carter wasn't like most people. He didn't even flinch, and he wouldn't hear of any such talk, even from a man he respected and loved so much as Dr. Mongle. He just sort of chuckled.

"Doc, you'll cross the river long before I do," said Carter, smiling. "I'll be around long after you're gone."

Dr. Mongle was right. Carter never did get to see another Christmas.

There had been some health scares, but Carter always pulled through, so I can see why he didn't take the doctor's advice. In his mind, he could always get his strength back. He felt like nothing could conquer him or keep him down long. "I'm gonna make it," I can still hear him say. "Don't you worry about me." And he always seemed to find a way to recover.

Of course, we did worry about him, especially in that last year. I'd tell him he needed to quit the bottle, and when I did, he'd lash out and call me Little Jesus. It hurt his pride, and he was a proud man in the worst way.

The other thing that hurt him was spending so much time away from his family and his young children, who missed him something awful. Every town we'd hit, Carter'd be sending money back home. So there he was out on the road to make money to send back to support the family, but then he can't be with them because he needs to be on the road to make a living. And sometimes it wasn't enough. For a while there, his wife, Mary, had to get a job as a waitress to help out, and it tore him up that she had to do that.

In the spring of 1966, we did our first overseas tour in Europe. There had been some acts over there, but most were on the USO circuit playing for the American troops. This was one of the first times, a bunch of hillbillies like us were playing for the people in a foreign land; it was something historic and we were proud to do it. They called it the American Folk and Country Music show, and they billed it as "another side of America which is seldom heard outside the country, the rural music from the Southern Mountains" and we were the headlining act, along with Cousin Emmy, the New Lost City Ramblers, Roscoe Holcomb and Cyp Landreneau's Cajun Band.

It was a three-week pull through Sweden, Denmark, Holland, Switzerland, Germany and England.

Onstage everything went well, and the people there really took to us. But behind the scenes, it was a mess. Chick Stripling was playing bass and doing his Butter Paddle Buck 'n' Wing for us. We figured he'd be a good draw, but it started real bad and just got worse. He got to drinking right before take-off and didn't stop for a week; he went crazy on the plane ride over; he was hassling all the passengers and he stumbled into the seat of one of the Lost City Ramblers who had his little baby onboard and Chick fell over and nearly killed the baby. He was hitting the hard stuff. We flew just about every day to a new city in a different country, and every time we'd leave a country, Chick would hit the customs store at the airport, where you could buy a quart of liquor for two dollars.

He'd start a scene nearly everywhere we went. At a restaurant in Sweden, Chick tried to order some scrambled eggs. The waiter didn't understand what he wanted. Chick kept saying, "I want some eggs now," and getting really irate and he finally started hollering *"BAWK-BAWK-BAWK,"* and he commenced to run around the place flapping his arms like some crazy old clucking hen, and all the diners there were looking over at us, sort of startled by all the commotion, and the waiter, who was really scared seeing Chick running drunk and wild, finally figured out what Chick was wanting and he said, "Ya Ya Ya Ya Ya," and hightailed it into the kitchen to get the eggs scrambled before Chick hurt somebody.

We put up with Chick for about a week, and we finally had to send him home before the tour was finished. Bought him a ticket, put him on a plane, and by then he was sobering up and he was real sorry for what he'd done but it was too late. We got Tracy Schwartz of the New Lost City Ramblers to fill in on bass for us and he done fine, but he couldn't dance like Chick.

On the German leg of the tour, we did a special live TV show in Baden Baden, which is a resort town in the mountains where they put us up in a fancy hotel with a spa. They had some American square dancers they brought in from a nearby army base, but they had some trouble do-si-do-ing to our music, which was kind of comical for us to watch from the stage; they was used to a stiffer beat, not my old banjo breakdowns like the "Clinch Mountain Backstep." I reckon we were too country, a little too mountain anyhow, for their slick routines, and to tell the truth I never did care much for square dancing at all except the kind you see in a John Ford western with the pretty gals twirling in the gingham skirts.

The Germans appreciated our music better than those dancers did; we were one of the first American groups had seen since the war and we played several other shows there. I hadn't been there since right after the war when I was stationed there with the army, and it was a whole different country. Back in '45, everywhere from the cities to the little towns was all tore to pieces, and now it was the cleanest place I ever saw; even the woods were tidy, no underbrush or leaves at all. It was like you took a broom and swept it clean, spic-and-span. They had built it right back up all nice and modern, like the war had never happened.

The same twenty years Germany was busy straightening itself out, Carter was busy wearing himself down and it really showed. He was doing poorly, in body and in spirit both. He was a shadow of the hardy young fellow that came to greet me at the Bristol train station back in '46, when our future seemed as bright as the neon sign of the WCYB radio station. Now he was tired most of the time; the jet lag wore him out. But it wasn't just the trip; it was all them years of hard road catching up with him. It was the first time I ever saw him really, really down. He was in a place where you couldn't reach him. He could still manage the job onstage, but it wasn't the same. His strength was gone and his old spark was fading, right in front of my eyes.

Strange thing was, after a long dry spell, he came up with a new tune on the flight overseas, he called "Wonderful World Outside," which he introduced onstage as "the first song I ever wrote on an airplane." It's about a prisoner, a lonesome man cut off from all the everyday pleasures outside the prison bars, and I believe that's how Carter felt. It was the last song he ever wrote.

In October, we attended the disc jockeys' convention in Nashville and his condition got worse. I'd seen it coming, and there was nothing I could do. He was getting sicker all the time. He would get tired and be sleeping in the car, and onstage his voice was failing him. This bothered him more than anything, that he couldn't sing like he used to. He was always such a perfectionist, and especially hard on himself. He knew it was coming, he just couldn't face it. And we had got so used to him bouncing back that we came to believe he would always make it somehow. Even me, I didn't think it was that bad until about six weeks before he died.

One of the last times Carter was able to play was a big weekend at the Wheeling Jamboree and Bean Blossom. On the way up, we stayed over at Melvin Goins's house. That morning, before the drive, we had a big country breakfast. Seems like it was one of the last regular meals Carter could take down. He had gotten so gaunt-looking. Food wasn't agreeing with him, but this was a favorite. He called it his "special dish," fried salmon cakes with thick good gravy and cathead biscuits. You eat that to start off your day and you feel like you can do just about anything. But as we were heading to the next show, Carter started hemorrhaging, spitting up blood in the back of the car.

Then, in November 1966, we were playing a show in Hazel Green, Kentucky. Carter done about three songs that night and he started bleeding at the nose. We kept playing as he walked off and went backstage to put a towel on that and clean himself up. We went ahead and finished out the show without him, but we had done that before. Only this time was different. We didn't know it at the time, but that show was the last performance Carter would ever give.

That night we had to drive up to Cincinnati and stop by King Records to get some boxes of records from Syd Nathan we could sell at our shows.

We were riding on the Mountain Parkway, headed to Lexington to catch Interstate 75 north into Ohio. I was driving and making good time, too, when I heard Carter from the back of the car, real weak-like, telling me to pull over because he was feeling sick. I stopped the car just in time for him to open the back door and pitch his head out. When we turned on the dome light, we saw he was upchucking blood everywhere. It was bad this time, real bad. I gunned that engine to get him to the hospital in Lexington, but after a while he said he was feeling better and he didn't want to go to the hospital. I think even then he knew it was just a matter of time, and he wanted to be home for the last go-round.

"Ralph," he said. "Just turn this thing around and take me home to Ma's."

So that's what we did, just headed straight for Smith Ridge as fast we could.

My mother was ready for us like she always was. I never seen her look as worried as when we helped Carter into the house. She knew something was different about these bleeding attacks. We all stayed the night, and then we left Carter at Smith Ridge and headed back to Kentucky to do a show. Even as bad as Carter was, we couldn't afford to miss any show dates, not even one.

We played at a courthouse in a little town called Frenchburg. It was a decent-sized crowd there, and we done our level best not to disappoint them, and then we headed back, with George at the wheel. One thing about Shuffler, he was as good a driver as he was a picker and singer, one of the best drivers we ever had, next to me. So it was a real surprise to hear the siren screaming and a patrol car come speeding up behind us. The officer shined his bright light on us and walked up to the car. We didn't know what we could have done wrong.

He tapped on the window and said, "Are one of you boys Ralph Stanley?"

"Yes, sir," I told him. "That's me. Is there a problem?"

"You better get down to Bristol just as quick as you can get there," he said. "You got a brother just at the point of death."

And he led us on an escort part of the way down, until we crossed the state line back into Virginia.

We got into Bristol, past the radio station where it had all started for us, and headed for the hospital. Carter was in the intensive care unit. He'd had another hemorrhage back home and they'd brought him here. Dr. Mongle was there and I reckon he saved his life. Carter had been bleeding at both ends. There was no way to stop the blood. So Dr. Mongle ended up giving Carter more than 120 pints of blood to stop his veins from collapsing. Any other doctor wouldn't have done that, he wasn't supposed to give him that much blood, but he went overboard to save Carter.

They still hadn't stopped all the bleeding, so Dr. Mongle finally sent Carter up to a specialist at the University of Virginia hospital in Charlottesville. Said they had no choice but to operate, and even then it was only a fifty-fifty chance of survival. Those was some hard words for Carter to hear, but he was game to try. The surgery went fine and the bleeding stopped, and doctors told him he needed to rest there for a few weeks.

We knew Carter was in good hands at the U.Va. hospital, and what he needed most was to get a lot of rest and not worry about trying to get back on the road like he always done. Carter seemed well pleased with his condition, like he'd whipped it once again. He sat up on his bed, cracking jokes. He seemed almost like his old self. I was feeling some relief about everything, and I went back down to Florida for Thanksgiving.

What I didn't know was that two of our half brothers came to visit Carter at the hospital over the holiday. He was back to his old tricks again, and he somehow talked them into getting him discharged early so he could finish his rehabilitation back home at Smith Ridge. He wasn't ready and doctors had told him that, but he said he couldn't stand being cooped up in that hospital room.

When I found out about Carter's escape, I drove back up from Florida, stopped by North Carolina to pick up George, and he drove us the rest of the way to Smith Ridge. We finally made it there on the last day of November not long before midnight, dog tired and worried as could be. Carter was laying on the couch in the living room and he didn't look good at all, even though he was saying he was all right. We had to go to another show the next night, and wanted to go to bed and get some sleep. Carter was wanting us to stay up with him, keep him company.

"You don't know how good it is to see you fellows," he said. "Up here it's just me and Ma. I'm lonesome and I want to talk to you boys, so let's set up for a while."

We kept him company as best we could, and being Carter, he was almost cheerful, as if by talking and carrying on he could make the awful suffering somehow go away like it was a bad dream. Long about 2 A.M. he started upchucking blood. We tried to get a wastebasket to hold it; he was just spewing out, couldn't stop. We knew we had to get him to the hospital in Bristol. When the ambulance pulled up on Smith Ridge, he was still trying to believe everything was going to be all right. He called out for me to bring along his shaving kit. George got into the back of the ambulance to keep him company on the ride over, and I followed in a little red pickup truck we had. Poor Carter, I was thinking, even the ambulance ride was as rough as could be, on those icy roads winding down the mountain, and then it was another hour's drive to Bristol.

George said that in the ambulance Carter was bleeding bad and they kept trying to squeeze it off and make it stop. Carter was still talking, but he was getting weaker by the mile. "Light me a cigarette," he said. "Would you, Aunt George?" He'd been trying to quit smoking but now he wanted one real bad. "I reckon it don't matter now," he said.

By the time we made it to the hospital in Bristol, Carter had lost so much blood that when they opened the back door of the ambulance, there was blood running out onto the ground. George had it splattered all over him. Carter only had a pint or so left when they wheeled him in, but the emergency room workers finally found a vein on top of his foot so they could get some blood into him and get him stabilized.

Dr. Mongle came in to check on him when he'd got some of his color back, and Carter was talking like it was just another scare.

"Doc," he said. "How far is this going to set me back? As much as that last one done?" I think part of him still wanted to believe that he was going to get better again. But I think he knew this time was different.

We knew it was bad right away after Dr. Mongle looked him over and told us it was as serious as it could be. The main artery to Carter's liver had ruptured.

Carter never talked about dying at all. Right on to the last, he stayed optimistic. He was talking about getting a new bus he'd always wanted, when he was well enough and we got back on the road. He seemed to be getting better, or at least not getting any worse. We were with him since he got there at three in the morning all the way past dawn. Along about 9 A.M., we got hungry and decided we'd go to a diner around the corner and get some breakfast and let Carter get some rest. He had leveled off and seemed to taking blood in and doing all right.

We had breakfast and got back to the hospital about a half hour later, and George stopped down the hall to have a cigarette. I told him to go ahead and finish his smoke and I'd go in and see how Carter was doing. I walked into the room and I saw death on him. He was dying right then and there. It's something you just know when you see it. So I called the nurse and she came running and told me to please step out of the room. I saw George coming down the hall and I told him right out Carter was a-dying. And it wasn't maybe ten minutes more and Carter was gone.

My mother was back home, praying and waiting on any word. She was doing poorly herself with Carter being so sick and all, so she hadn't been able to make it to the hospital.

I wish I could tell you I was the one that carried the news to her, but I can't. I'm ashamed to say I just didn't have the nerve. I couldn't face seeing her grief and sorrow, not right then. I knew how hard it would be on her. Even over the phone, I didn't figure I could handle that, either. It's something I'll always be sorry for.

So I just done the best I could under the circumstances. Before we left the hospital, I called a neighbor who lived right across the road and told her to kindly break the news to my mother, and to tell her we were on our way back home. Well, that was some long ride back to Smith Ridge. We pulled up to the house and my mother met us at the door. I could tell she'd been crying. Nobody had to say nothing.

There was no time to mourn because there was too much to do. We had to call all the family, like our half sister Ruby Rakes, to come from where she lived in Michigan. Then we had to make the funeral arrangements. George remembered that Carter had bought a suit in Norton that he'd wore at the DJ convention in Nashville. Carter had paid a lot for it and said it was the finest suit he ever owned. So we got it cleaned and pressed and had the undertaker put that suit on Carter.

The memorial service for Carter was the biggest ever seen in these parts, before or since. It shows how much the people loved him. There wasn't enough room at the funeral home in Clintwood to hold all the people, so they moved it down to the auditorium at the old Ervinton High School in Nora, the school where me and Carter had been students, where we'd first played on a stage as the Stanley Brothers. More than three thousand people passed by his coffin, and there were lines for a ways down the road. All those people waiting in the cold to pay their respects.

Bill Monroe was on tour down in New Orleans when he got the news. He had to break off his engagements so he could come to sing at the service. First he had to fly into the Bristol airport, then he made the drive through the ice and snow to the school. When he got there, Bill was worn out from traveling, and he put his arm on my shoulder and told me how sorry he was. I know Bill loved Carter like a brother and he was hurting real bad. But I still needed him to sing a hymn for Carter, because me and George were in no shape to do anything like that.

"I don't know if I rightly can, Ralph," said Bill. "I'm not sure if I'm up to it or not."

But George piped up right then, and I'm glad he did.

"Oh yes you can, Bill!" he said, and that was enough.

A couple of preachers from our church, Landon Colley and Stewart Owens, officiated the funeral. The coffin was laid out in the middle of the gym floor. It was dead silent when Bill walked out by himself, his footsteps echoing up to the rafters. He held his hat in his hand and sang the old hymn "Swing Low, Sweet Chariot" a cappella like we do it in the Primitive Baptist Church. Then he put his hand on the coffin and he said, "We'll meet again."

George and I were in the front row, just a few feet away. I don't know how Bill made it through the song without breaking down, but he did. And it meant the world to me.

I really don't remember much more about the memorial service, because I was so tore up. I reckon I was still in shock. There was a reporter from *The Dickensonian,* the local newspaper, and he tells how it was a whole lot better than I can:

"The large auditorium was packed, and many could not get in hearing distance at the funeral. This was, no doubt, the largest gathering at any funeral ever held in Dickenson County. Ralph's special friend in the music world, Bill Monroe, sang 'Swing Low, Sweet Chariot' in a most effective manner which lent solemnity due to such an occasion. People from every walk of life in this county were there to pay their respects to a country boy who had made good, and had endeared himself not only to the people of Dickenson County, but nationally and in many foreign countries."

There was another fine tribute at Carter's passing that I want to mention. It came from Roxie Rasnick from the little paper in Nora, and her words have come true in ways that we could have never foreseen: "His song is silent, his music is stilled, but the memories of him, to many, will live on and on."

On the way to Smith Ridge for the burial, Bill did his best to give us some comfort.

"Carter was put on this earth for a purpose," he said. "He was the finest natural lead singer there ever was, and I believe the good Lord needed a good lead singer and he wanted the best, so he called him home."

Bill was always a man of few words, but they were usually the right words.

During the night, it snowed again and it covered Smith Ridge with a blanket of white. Carter's coffin was in the sitting room and we had some breakfast. My mother was grieving something fierce. She kept saying she wished it had been her instead of Carter. She couldn't set still, she just didn't know what to do with herself. Nothing could help her with her loss. No matter how we tried, she could not be consoled.

It wasn't only my mother. There was a restlessness all over the ridge. Outside, we could hear Carter's coon dogs get to howling and they wouldn't let up, just kept moaning and baying. It was as mournful a sound as you ever heard. And Carter's favorite black mare, the one he always rode when he was home on the ridge, she was bucking and pacing up and down the fence, whining and snorting like she was in real torment. It was like they knew he was gone, too.

It was late in the day when we were taking Carter up to the graveyard. By the time we carried the coffin up the hill to lay him in the ground, there was a cold wind whipping off the ridgetop, and the pallbearers had a hard time carrying the coffin because of the snow and ice. Everybody was freezing out there, and the sun was going down behind the mountains. It was the prettiest, biggest sun ball I ever saw, just as big and red as could be. Burning. It sat there on the edge of the horizon for a good while, like it was hanging on to those ridgetops long enough so we could finish burying Carter before it got dark. By the time we made it back to the house, it was pitch black outside.

Chapter Sixteen

Goin' Solo

"Carter, you're at rest now in the hills you so often wrote about
I never dreamed, I never thought so soon you'd be called to rest
But the Man who calls our number, somehow you fit into his plans
I never questioned His decision, for I'm only human, just another man"

—"Hills of Home," a recitation by Ralph Stanley

After Carter died, I didn't know if I could take it, to tell you the truth. I always thought I was tough enough to take anything. But this seemed like too much. I wasn't sure if I could stand it emotionally.

Not long after he passed away, a week or so, I went off by myself and played some of our records and cried it out. It took a few hours. I just sat there in the car, just me and those old Stanley Brothers records, and I listened to our songs and cried and cried until I could finally quit crying. That was the only way I could get by. I got it out of my system.

Course, you never really get over it, but you find a way to go on. I can't question the Almighty. It was His will for Carter to pass on and for me to go on. All I could do was to try to make the best of it. But I didn't really know what to do, as far as the music. I was scared to go it alone. I was worried, because I didn't know if I could do it by myself.

We were more than brothers. We were a team that had been together for twenty years. Always together, onstage and off. I didn't know how the people would take to it without Carter. He was the one everybody loved so much. He was the MC and lead singer and the front man. I didn't know if I had it in me, if I could handle that stage on my own.

But some things happened that gave me the strength. First was my mother. She was grieving worse than I was. Crying didn't give her no relief and talking didn't help much, either. I would try to tell her it wasn't for us to question God's will; I'd tell her the day Carter was borned, the Lord knew the day he'd die. She was a believer, and she knew in her heart it was His will, but that didn't give any comfort. But she still had her other son and she gathered enough strength and she had enough vision to help set me straight on the path back to that stage.

"I think Carter would have wanted you to keep going and not give up," she said. "And I don't want you to quit, either." It was something only my mother could have told me, because she knew me better than anybody alive. She knew I could never do something that would hurt Carter, especially now that he was gone.

What she said hit me hard, because I knew she was right. I could hear Carter saying, "Little brother, don't let me down." I had to go back out and do my best, the way he had done for all those years.

Then the mail started coming in. I believe we got close to three thousand letters and cards from Stanley Brothers fans all over the world. They were supportive, telling me not to give up. "Don't let us down" and "If you quit, you've let Carter down and you've let us down, too." Then the phone calls, too, people telling me, "We were behind Carter and you, and now we'll be behind you even more. We've always been Stanley Brothers fans through the years, now we'll be yours." The support really helped me up. And it helped me stop feeling sorry for myself.

I needed to make a living, and music was the only job I knew. There wasn't much else I was qualified to do. I had done the factory work and the farming, and I was no good at that. Nothing else but hard labor, and I never did like that. You couldn't get me near a coal mine or a sawmill. It was going to have to be music.

All these things came together and helped me out of the hole I was in. I pulled myself up, and I made up my mind that music was all I could do, all I was ever meant to do, and I was going to do it.

We had some shows booked up North. I wasn't sure how the promoters would feel about me showing up without Carter, but they were fine with it. I called up Shuffler.

"George, this is misery," I said. "We might as well face it. We're going to have to do it sooner or later. We got the show dates coming up. Are you ready to go?"

George didn't hesitate even one second. He said he was ready when I was.

"Well, I can't stand sitting around anymore," I said. "It's driving me crazy. Why don't we hit the road and see what happens."

Our first show was in Buffalo. We drove up there, the four of us, in Carter's Mercury Monterey. It was me, George, Melvin Goins, and fiddle player Curly Ray Cline. Melvin's bass fiddle was strapped to the top, and there was snow coming down. We were running late, and I missed the exit off the interstate, so I made an illegal U-turn.

A New York state trooper saw what I done and he pulled us over. By the way he was looking us over, I could tell he was suspicious from the get-go. Not too many cars up that way with bass fiddles on top. I told him we were musicians and we were lost and we were late for a show. He didn't say a word, just looked right past me into the car, and that's when I realized he'd seen my pistol there on the dashboard.

We always carried handguns on the road; I'd kept a .38 Special in the glove compartment since the WCYB days. We played a lot of rough places back in the country, remote rural areas miles from any towns. We'd never had to use the guns, but we had them just in case. You didn't want to get stopped out there on a rural dirt road late at night with no protection, loaded down with cash receipts.

Those were tough years if you were a country musician traveling, especially in the North and places outside your own area, where the authorities didn't know who you were and didn't care. Johnny Cash had just been caught bringing dope coming out of Mexico. A lot of the public, and the police, too, thought country musicians were criminals and outlaws. They had a bad reputation.

I remember when we were trying to book a room at a motel in Warrenton, Virginia. This was in the early 1960s, and it wasn't too far in the sticks. Warrenton is horse country about two hours outside Washington, D.C., and we passed through the area a lot. We were signing in and the man behind the desk looked out to the parking lot and saw the bass fiddle tied to the top of the car. He set down his pen and gave us a real going-over.

"Y'all play music?" he said.

"Yeah," I said. "We're the Clinch Mountain Boys. Ain't you heard of us? We play shows around here all the time."

"Get outta here," he said. "We don't rent rooms to musicians."

It turned out George Jones had just stayed at the motel a week before and he'd thrown a television set through the window. George got drunk and started shooting up the room and tore up the walls and everything with it. I don't need to tell you we didn't get a room that night.

Around about that time, we had our own run-in with Johnny Cash. We were up in the Northeast and we got into a place to play a show on a Saturday night and Johnny came running in the building with his guitar and the promoters told him, "You were supposed to have been here last night—Your band's done played and gone!" Johnny was young and real skinny and he looked like he hadn't slept for a week, but at least he was honest and he was still trying to make his show date, even if he was a day late. But see, we weren't as famous as a big-time country star like him; we couldn't afford to do something like that and not make a show.

Anyhow, with country musicians raising a ruckus everywhere they went, we could tell the New York state trooper didn't like us. He had a carful of hillbilly musicians with a loaded gun on the dashboard and it was probably the first time he had ever pulled over any vehicle with a bass fiddle on top. He was giving us the evil eye, and he wanted to know whose gun it was.

At first, Curly Ray decided the gun was his. He was going to take the fall. He started to explain everything, but then he panicked and backed down, and he said, "No, that pistol's not mine." The situation was too sticky for him, and he backed out like a crawfish. I was just as yellow-bellied as Curly was; I didn't say nothing. And Melvin was scared stiff, too. Didn't say a word.

George stepped up to save us. "That's mine, Officer," he says.

Then the trooper checked inside the glove compartment and found another gun.

"Well, who's is this, then?

"That's mine, too."

George knew they could only get him for one gun anyhow. There were other guns in the back trunck, but the trooper didn't look in there.

I owe George a lot for stepping up like that, taking responsibility for both guns. It could have been a real mess. They could have arrested everybody for carrying a concealed weapon. In New York, it was a felony charge. But George took it on himself to keep the monkey off my back at least. He really stepped up to bat for me.

They took George downtown to the jail and booked him, while we went on to the show. George later posted bail and played the last set with us. Taking the rap for the guns took a lot of courage.

George and me got a lawyer and we went back up to New York for the trial. We didn't know what we were up against, but we both were expecting the worst. In Virginia, this would have never even gone to court. In New York, carrying a concealed weapon was a serious offense. He was facing a year or two in prison, maybe more. The judge looked us over, and we told him what happened, how we were musicians late for a show and had overrun the turn for the exit. We tried to explain how we carried guns for self-defense, when were playing shows real late at night in coal-mining towns deep in the mountains. In our line of work, we said, we needed the pistols to protect what we earned and had never had to use 'em yet. We wasn't robbing nobody. Of course, the officer made a pretty big show of his big bust, telling about how the guns were spilling out of the car, like we was armed and dangerous.

Well, the judge saw through it. He was on our side all the way. "You boys don't look like outlaws to me," he said. "I'd be carrying a gun, too, if I was you."

The judge fined George a hundred dollars and said he was sorry for the whole thing. He wished us luck with our music.

It wasn't long after that George left the band. It just wasn't the same for him without Carter around, not only for the singing and playing but the pranking, too. The new setup wasn't right for him and we both knew it. Naturally, it wasn't easy to part ways after so many years together. We'd get sore at each other because we knew everything had changed and wasn't a damn thing we could do to turn back the clock; it finally did come to a boil, when we was coming back from a show in Pikeville, Kentucky, home to Coeburn.

George was driving the old Air Coach bus we were using, and he was messing with the brakes while we was hauling down Route 23, the old two-lane Hillbilly Highway I was telling you about. See, George was one of the best drivers, and he was doing it on purpose, putting on the brakes hard on every curve. I was lying on the bed trying to sleep and every time he'd hit those brakes, I'd roll out of the bed onto the floor and then crawl back up in bed and then he'd throw me out again, must have been thirty-six times from Pikeville to Jenkins. I knew he was doing it just to get me mad and it worked.

When we finally made it to Coeburn, I was banged up and wide awake and hot as the brake pads, and I just told George, "You can show up if you want to next week, but if you do, there's just one of us getting on this bus." He was already ready to quit anyhow, so that's how it was. It didn't amount to much in the long run; he joined up with Don Reno and did fine with him and others after that, and there was no hard feelings.

George and me are still real close to this day, and he always makes the drive from Valdese, North Carolina, to play our big bluegrass festival at the old home place every Memorial Day weekend, along with the other former Clinch Mountain Boys. He was one of the best we ever had, not just the Shuffler-style guitar cross-picking but his bass playing, too. With his singing, he had a sound that blended with me and Carter on the quartet or the trio, and he could sing a bass or baritone part, either one, and he sung lead for me, too. George is one of the few who earned the right to say, "I didn't work *for* the Stanley Brothers, I worked *with* them."

First the Buffalo gun bust, and then George was gone—it seemed like it was a bad way to start things off without Carter. I reckon he would have just laughed the whole thing off, gone back and found a way to make it work with George and then probably start pulling gun pranks on Curly Ray. But it seemed like a bad omen to me. Instead, I got a real break because I found a new lead singer.

Like you might figure, I found him in Ohio. I found my wife, Jimmi, in Ohio, and I found two of my lead singers who replaced Carter in Ohio, too. In them days, we played so many shows around Cincinnati and Dayton and Columbus and Middleton, we used to just about live in those places. We always had friends and supporters. People like Jack Lynch, who would help us out on bass and later helped carry Carter's coffin up to the cemetery on Smith Ridge.

In February, we were playing in Dayton, it was just me and Curly. Jack Lynch was backing us up. He was in the house band at the bar there, the Lee Brothers, which was fronted by a singer and banjo man named Roy Lee Centers. Kentucky-born and Dayton-raised, like some of the best bluegrassers. So I'd known about Roy Lee for a long time from the club scene in Dayton. He used to come to our shows; he was a big fan of Carter's.

Roy Lee could really sing, he had the gift. I'd see the Lee Brothers open up for us, and I studied about Roy Lee. I had thought maybe he might be the man to take Carter's place. But I was afraid that with him playing in them rough bars all the time, he might be a drunk or tough or what have you, and I was afraid to take a chance on him. And to tell the truth, there was another boy, Larry Sparks, who wanted the job more than he did. Lot of times, it's who wants it most gets it.

Jack Lynch had told Larry to come by the bar that night because he'd heard I was looking for somebody. Larry was barely eighteen and he'd worked a few times for the Stanley Brothers during Carter's last year. The work was a few shows dates around Ohio and Michigan, but he was hired for his lead guitar and that's all he done was pick the guitar. So I didn't know he could sing and he was too shy to tell us otherwise.

That night in Dayton, Larry got up and sang a few with Lynch and the Lee Brothers. What he was doing was auditioning in this little beer joint, and he done good. He had what I was looking for, the voice and the guitar both. And he was young, so I figured he hadn't picked up too many bad habits from those bars. Larry saw it as a job—I liked that he was serious and didn't say much. I didn't need a funny man; I already had Curly Ray Cline if I wanted to laugh.

After the show, I went over and talked with Larry, and I asked if he wanted to join up. He said yeah, and I hired him on the spot. The next day he was with us.

Not long after that, we played a benefit show for Carter in Maryland.

Dr. Mongle had waived all the medical expenses. He said we didn't owe him a penny for all he done trying to save Carter's life. That was a big relief, and I've always been grateful for him doing that. But Carter's widow, Mary, had five children and a lot of bills to pay. She was working as a waitress to try to make ends meet. Anything would help, and we wanted to raise some money for them.

The benefit concert was a big success. We held it in College Park, Maryland, and all the big-name bluegrass performers came to help out. It was more like a reunion than a show. For some it was a tough pill to swallow, seeing old enemies face-to-face. Bill Monroe was sharing the stage for the first time with musicians he hadn't spoke to for years. He was willing to set aside his old feuds for Carter's sake.

Now I had some real business to take care of. With Carter gone, I went to see Syd Nathan at King Records in Cincinnati. Carter and me were supposed to record an album for Syd at a session back in the winter sometime after New Year's. After Carter died, it was put on hold. I was worried that with Carter gone, maybe the deal was off. Maybe what Syd wanted was another Stanley Brothers record or nothing. Maybe he wasn't interested in a record by Ralph Stanley by himself.

After twenty years in the business, I didn't know where I stood.

Seemed like I was back to square one. So I just got up the courage to tell Syd I was ready to make a record. I asked him if he wanted to me to stay on with him.

Syd's eyes bulged out from behind those thick glasses, and he looked like he was going to have a heart attack. He stood up from behind his desk and leaned toward me like he was fixing to keel over. Then he reared back and puffed out his chest like some haughty old judge. He was waving his cigar, blowing smoke out his nostrils and swearing with every breath, same old Syd, only his asthma had gotten worse, his eyesight down to nil. But he still had records on his mind.

"Hell yes!" he said. "The Stanley Brothers have done real well for us. Who knows, you might even do better."

To hear Syd hollering was just like old times. To have him behind me, well, that was a big boost. Syd wasn't going to let Carter's passing stop him or me from making music. It only made him more determined. He was a businessman, and he believed in sticking by what done you good in the past. He had faith in me, and that gave me faith in myself. I couldn't have asked for a better arrangement. All Syd wanted to know was when could I come up and cut some records.

I wanted to get the band ready, and we'd only been together a few months. I had bought a reel-to-reel tape recorder so we could rehearse some new songs. We stayed at the old 5th Avenue Hotel in Cincinnati, getting our material ready for the session. We had already worked on some of the songs before Carter died, but with him gone, it was like starting all over again. He had always done the lead singing, and now Larry Sparks had to fill that role.

Well, it worked out just fine. I knew I could never replace Carter, but I've always been able to find a singer that would work out, and Larry was the first in a long line of singers who got the job done.

When we got to the studio, we realized it wasn't Larry's voice that needed help, it was his guitar. Not his playing, but the guitar itself. It was just a piece of junk really, barely stageworthy and by no means good enough for a recording session.

I took him aside, and I handed him Carter's D-45 Martin, the one with the herringbone inlay. "Just go ahead and use this," I said. "I know he would have wanted you to play it."

It took him a while to get used to it, because Carter had tuned it up higher than usual for the way he played rhythm guitar, but Larry got comfortable with that Martin. So he played Carter's guitar for about a year.

Then, when we were taking the picture for the album cover, we wanted to make sure everybody dressed alike. And so I figured Larry ought to have the same boots we had, which were the little black leather slip-on boots we had back then. So I took Carter's boots and handed them to Larry just like I did the guitar. "While you're at it, you can just go ahead and wear his boots, too."

I recorded three albums for Syd, and right from the start I was aiming to establish my own sound, which was more old-time mountain-style than Carter was really comfortable with. I decided to feature Curly Ray's fiddle as much as I could. For the first record, *Brand New Country Songs*, I wanted put my own stamp on some songs that bluegrass and country fans hadn't heard before. I found some material that fit my voice like "Hemlocks and Primroses," which was a fairly recent song but sounded a few hundred years old and was adapted from some mossy old British ballad by a songwriter from West Virginia.

The first album got a real nice welcome, like this one from *Bluegrass Unlimited*:

> Ralph Stanley's efforts at keeping alive the kind of great old time music he so strongly believes in have been frequently chronicled in these pages. This album is the first fruit of the post-Carter band, and if the Stanley sound isn't quite intact it's because this music is closer than ever to its mountain roots. Ralph is in company with some first-rate musicians: fiddler Curly Ray Cline, guitarist Larry Sparks, and Earl Taylor, who doubles on mandolin and harmonica. They play in sympathy with Ralph as Monroe's best sidemen have always done with him. Sparks's lead singing tends to be weak because of the youthful quality of his voice, though it sounds fine in harmony with Ralph.

I was proud of the positive reviews, but what I was worried about was how the fans would take to my first long-playing album without Carter. They took to it just fine, and I did my best to make sure of the fact by selling them myself on the road. I knew Syd was doing his best, but I wanted to make sure I had plenty for the record table after the shows.

I had a carpenter make me a custom cedarwood box about four feet long. It was like a hollow trunk, really, and we could lay everything in there and I had some extra space to store my King albums and singles and some of our equipment. I got him to stencil on the sides OLD-TIME COUNTRY MUSIC and strapped the box on the roof rack of my new green Bonneville station wagon, and that's what I took to all the show dates and bluegrass festivals. I wanted people to know I was different from the crowd; I had my own music that was built from the past just like that wooden box, and I was proud to carry on the tradition, even if it meant hauling it around on top of the car. I wanted to make it clear that when it comes to sticking to my roots, I wasn't one to fiddle-faddle around.

I wouldn't have changed for nothing. I just felt like I might still be around when a lot of the new young bluegrass bands wouldn't be. I figured maybe when the dust settled, I'd be the last man standing.

CHAPTER SEVENTEEN

Visions and Dreams

"As I walked into the Wayside Tavern, the smell of drink was in the air
I threw my money on the counter, this pretty maid was standing there
My thoughts they drifted so far from me as I looked upon her lovely face
I knew she was my kind of woman, no one could ever take her place"

—"GIRL BEHIND THE BAR," THE STANLEY BROTHERS

Visions are like dreams, only you can be awake when you have a vision. You don't make visions happen. They happen to you. They come from somewhere outside, most often from above, I believe. Some people have 'em setting in church and some have 'em when they're in prison. Carter got 'em in the backseat of a '46 Packard hauling down a mountain road at three o'clock in the morning.

You don't make a vision happen. They happen to you. They come from somewhere outside, most times from above, I believe. Some people have a vision when they're in church, and some have a vision when they're in prison.

The most beautiful vision I ever had was in a bar in Cincinnati, Ohio. It was one of those visions that turn out to be real. The vision was named Jimmi, and I was lucky enough to marry her.

I can tell you right now the date: December 13, 1961. It was a bluegrass club called the Ken-Mill. Some of the boys gave it the nickname the Gin Mill, but it wasn't a rough or rowdy place, just an old brick building with a neon sign on a run-down street. The man who owned the Ken-Mill was Stu Salmons. He was an honest, no-nonsense fellow and a big bluegrass fan, and you can't ask for any better. His wife, Ann, helped him behind the bar, and together they ran a class operation. They were fine folks and they both loved the Stanley Brothers, and we always knew we had a place to play in Cincinnati.

The Ken-Mill wasn't too big, but it was always packed with people, one of the best clubs in Cincinnati for hillbilly music. Most nights there were fans from the Cincinnati area and from across the Ohio River in Covington and Newport, Kentucky. And it was a mixed crowd, with a lot of college students. There weren't many fights or much carrying on, because everybody was there to hear the music. There were faces we saw every time we came. A few nights booked at the Ken-Mill felt like playing for friends and family.

But on this cold December night, a new face caught my eye. At a table right next to the stage was a woman I'd never seen here before. She seemed out of place. I could tell she wasn't a regular. She was sitting real quiet and proper, like she just happened to be caught in there. I found out later her brother-in-law and sister had talked her into going. I'm glad they dragged her down to the Ken-Mill that night, and after she got to know me, Lord, she was glad they did, too.

Carter and me had already started singing when I saw her not more than ten feet away, and the sight of her just about stopped me dead in my tracks. It was all I could do to finish out the song. She had long, dark brown hair and big brown eyes. And the rest of her was just as sweet, too, dressed in a black skirt and black heels. Let me tell you, Ava Gardner didn't have nothing on her. I thought she was the prettiest woman I ever saw. I'd been dreaming of a woman just like her.

I was making little passes at her, right up there from the stage, giving her a look. Later she told me it felt like I was staring a hole right through her and it really bothered her and made her nervous. I couldn't help that. See, I had to keep looking at her to make sure she was real and I wasn't dreaming.

She got me so mixed up in the head I kept forgetting the words to the songs. I was a mess. Carter was giving me a hard time. Carter always liked to get something on me. This time he had me. I was fouling things up, even on my banjo breaks, and I couldn't help it. The sight of Jimmi wouldn't let me. When I saw her, I fell hard. She was the right woman for me; I knew she was what I'd been looking for all my life.

Like I already told you, I'd been married before, but there wasn't anything much good about it. Neither of us were satisfied and it wasn't meant to be. I believe a lot in predestination, like a lot of the old Baptists believe. Some things just ain't meant to be. Some things are. Like Jimmi and me.

Now, I want to tell you who Jimmi was and what she was doing at the Ken-Mill that night. If you're wondering about her name, well, that's her given name right there on her birth certificate. Her daddy, James Crabtree, had been a-wanting a boy and had the name James picked out, and when she showed up, well, she got the name Jimmi. Her family originally hailed from Kentucky and had always been Stanley Brothers fans and they played our records at the house. When she was little, Jimmi and her brother would playact and sing along to the records. He'd be Carter and she'd be me. When her grandma listened to the Stanley Brothers' gospel records, she'd get to shouting like she was in church, and she'd say, "That's the best blessing I ever had."

Later on, when Jimmi was in her teens, she liked the rock 'n' roll, Elvis and so forth, same as a lot of kids growing up in the fifties. But she always kept a place in her heart for the Stanley Brothers. Deep down, she was always a fan of the old-time music. Every year on June 30, her family would request a Stanley Brothers record, "Memories of Mother," on Wayne Raney's all-night show on Cincinnati's WCKY, the song with the line "Mother's at rest in a lonesome old graveyard." Wayne would play the record as a special dedication in memory of Jimmi's mother, who got killed in a car wreck on that date.

Jimmi's older sister, Louise, and her husband, Duane, was always getting on her to come down to the Ken-Mill to see us play. For years Jimmi wouldn't go, until that night she finally gave in and went with them. She figured she was twenty-one years old and she was ready to go to a bar for the first time and she'd finally get to see the Stanley Brothers in person.

She didn't drink and she wasn't looking to meet nobody. She came for one reason, and that was to hear Carter and me sing.

She enjoyed our show fine, but she was really bothered by the look I was giving her. Said she could feel my eyes going up and down from her head to her toes. I reckon it was the only way I knew how to make little passes at her while we was playing our songs, just to let her know she'd caught my eye. I didn't know that in her mind she was thinking, "Why, Lord, have mercy, I wouldn't fool with him." She'd try to turn sideways but could feel my stare on her. She got so bothered she told her sister she wanted to leave.

"You couldn't get Duane out of here with a stick of dynamite," Louise told her. "You like their music, don't you?"

"Yeah, they're good singers, all right," Jimmi said. "But that Ralph Stanley fella is staring a hole into me."

Well, they stayed until the end of the show, and afterwards I went down to the table and talked to them. I done the best I could to be polite, held my hat in my hands, sort of awkward-like. But Jimmi didn't say a word and kept looking away. Duane and Louise were the fans you always want to have. They loved the music and were just as nice and friendly as could be.

Duane finally shook my hand and said, "I'll see you at the show tomorrow night, buddy." I could see that he was giving me a chance to give it another shot.

"You'll be with them?" I said to Jimmi. "Won't you?"

She answered right fast: "No, I won't be there."

I could tell she'd already made up her mind. And she walked out of there like she meant it. I figured that was that. I was wondering if there were any other girls like her in Cincinnati. Sure wasn't none like her in Dickenson County or Bristol or anywhere else I'd been to. That night, driving back to the motel, I couldn't get her out of my mind. I started singing a new version of that old ballad "Pretty Polly":

Jimmi, pretty Jimmi, won't you go away with me?

Carter was laughing. He thought it was funny. Not just the way I'd put a change on "Pretty Polly" but the whole night, with me acting a fool over this brown-eyed girl. I mean, this was the man who wrote "How Mountain Girls Can Love." He knew a thing or two in that department.

"Little Brother," he said. "I believe this woman has got your number."

Now it was Jimmi's turn to have a vision. That night she dreamed we were together after the show and I kissed her gentle on the mouth. And that was her undoing right there. It was the sort of thing that put her mind at ease after all the staring, because it made her think to herself, "Well, at least he's a gentleman." That stayed with her all the next day, and when Louise and Duane asked her if she was going to the show, she told them about her dream and said, "Well, he *was* a gentleman, at least." So she put on a red dress and went with them to the show.

That night, they were at the same table and Jimmi looked even sweeter than before. I tried to do a little less staring and a little more singing and playing. One thing I noticed from the stage was a fellow at the bar kept trying to buy her a drink. I knew from last night she didn't drink, and it was another reason I liked her. She just had a bottle of cola the whole time.

After the show, I asked Duane if I could walk Jimmi to the car and give her an autographed photo. He said it'd be fine. The real reason I invited her to come get a picture was to get her out there alone so I could kiss her.

On the way out, the fellow from the bar headed over to make one more try. It's always some tough competition when pretty women are involved. But the fellow realized that she was leaving with me and she wasn't up for grabs, so he kindly tipped his hat to me and said in a good-natured way, "Why, how you doing, Tex?" and then he eased his way back to the bar, like he was just another fan come by to say hello.

I'm glad I didn't have to fight for her, because I'm not a fighting man, but I believe I would have.

Out in the parking lot, I guess you could say that was our first date. She said she wasn't interested in dating anyone, but then she told me about the dream and how I'd put a spell on her. I said I was trying my best to do just that but she was the one who done the spells; she'd bewitched me. We got in the backseat of the car, and I gave her an autographed photo of me and Carter. I leaned over to give her a kiss on the mouth, but she turned her head to the side, and she told me, "Now, don't try to get cute." So all I could get was a little peck on the cheek. It wasn't as good as the dream kiss, I don't reckon, but it was a start anyhow. So right from there, we were stuck with each other.

I had seen a lot of different girls on the road, but she had something none of the rest had. She was pretty, sure, but she wasn't a fast girl or smart-alecky or nothing. No come-on about her, I could tell she was down-home. She seemed to be the country girl I was always looking for, and it turned out she was. I liked that Jimmi wasn't the flirting type. She wasn't easy. She was the only woman that I had ever had to work at, and I had to work at her for a long time. It took years. I started sending her letters and photos and Stanley Brothers albums. Free records. Now that's the way to a woman's heart, if she's a music lover.

After we met, we stayed in touch. I would call her every time we played in Cincinnati, and we'd try to see each other whenever we could. But it was a tough situation. I was a professional musician on the road nearly all the time, and there was women always hanging around. I was just hardly making a living and I didn't want to give her that kind of life.

It wasn't just me who wasn't ready. She was of the same mind as me. She had no illusions about how the grind would be on a young wife. She knew all the temptations and all the pitfalls. One time she came to a show and saw me there with another woman, and she walked out of the club. We had some big blowups. She wasn't sure she could trust me. Later, she told me she was thinking, "I can't sit around at home, and all those women going after him. No telling what he'd be doing." She figured it was too much heartache down the road.

But we really were stuck on each other. We couldn't live with each other, couldn't hardly live without each other. I was busy trying to keep the band going, with Carter getting weaker and weaker, so I concentrated on business. Had to, so we could survive. I know it was harder on her than it was on me, but I couldn't do anything to change the way things were.

When she did finally fall in love with me, she fell hard.

She was really in some deep misery. She wrote a song about all she was feeling, "I Only Exist," which I later recorded on my first solo album. Jimmi said the words came to her all at once when she was driving north on Interstate 75 from Cincinnati to Warwick. That's how it is with the good songs; they come to you all at once, and all you can do is try to get the words down on paper before you forget.

Jimmi has written some others I recorded, like "I Bid You Adieu," and she has lots more she wrote and never did finish all the way. One's called "The Tide's Turned and You're the One That Went Under." Another's called "You're Always Leaving But You Never Took the Time to Pack."

There's a song I wrote for her, "My Darling Brown Eyes," that I'm right proud of, but I think her song "I Only Exist" is better. A real sad song is usually better than a love song. Sad songs go deeper, I think. Lots of fans come up to me at shows and tell me that it's their favorite Ralph Stanley record, maybe because so many people have felt the way Jimmi did. Her words can tell you better than I can what she was going through:

No, I'm not living, I only exist
How much longer can I go on like this?
You broke my heart and tortured my mind
I've lost you, darling, you're long gone this time
My home is broken, you wrecked my young life
You left me here alone to cry
These tears that are flowing will soon dry away
And someday, darling, I know you will pay
I knew you were no good right from the start
My friends all told me you'd break my heart
When your roaming and rambling days are through
You'll pray for a love like I had for you

Now that's a true-life song if there ever was. I'm sorry it took so much misery to make the song. And I wish she and I both didn't have to suffer through so much, but it couldn't be helped at the time. I know it was a lot more my fault than it was hers, but I done the best I could with the hand dealt to me.

During this time, Carter was always a big fan of Jimmi's. They was real close. Part of it was their personalities. They both liked to talk and laugh, and they enjoyed people a lot more than I do. Carter knew Jimmi was the one for me, and he always said she was my one true love and everything would work out in the end.

At the time, it didn't seem as easy as that. I don't reckon neither Jimmi nor me could rightly believe Carter, much as we wanted to.

"Jim, you love him and he loves you," he'd tell her. "You and my little brother will be married."

"No way," Jimmi'd say.

Carter would smile and tell her, "It's a big world, Jim," his way of saying anything can happen.

"Ain't that big, Carter."

"You'll see, and when you get a baby, name him after me."

Well, Carter was right again. Only it took a while, and he never did get to see it happen. Not long after he died, I took Jimmi to Smith Ridge to meet my mother. Took her the rough way up the mountain to the old home place, and she couldn't hardly believe how far back in the mountains it was. She didn't say nothing about being scared, but I knew she was. Later she told me she was thinking, "Where in the world are you taking me?" She wondered what she'd gotten herself into.

She liked my mother fine, but she didn't much care for the deep, rolling hills of home. She hadn't seen anything like these mountains round here, not in Kentucky where she was born, or anywhere else. When we first fell for each other, she always told me, "I'd go live in a cave under a big rock cliff with you," and I believe she really did mean it. But after seeing where she'd be living and raising a family and spending the rest of her life, she said, "I thought the rock cliff would be nearer to my home in Cincinnati, not way out here in Dickenson County." She was laughing when she said it, but it really was a big change and it was hard going there for a while.

Well, she finally decided the Clinch Mountains would have to suit her. She was stuck with me, I reckon. On July 2, 1968, seven-and-a-half years after we met, Jimmi and I got married. We didn't make a big fuss about it. We had the ceremony in a little grocery store not far from the old home place. When we made up our mind to get hitched, we did it pretty quick. I went up to Ohio and got Jimmi and brought her down to Virginia. We didn't tell nobody what we were doing. Some things you just have to do your own way.

We got a preacher, Joe Johnson, to do the vows. He was a Free Will Baptist, and he had a way of preaching that was near to the preachers I had heard growing up. I didn't care what kind of church he preached at, just so he could marry us. We got Preacher Joe because he lived close by, just down the road, and the store was handy for us, too. It was called Atkins General Store, down past the old Spraddle Creek bridge near where you hit the hardtop road after you go down the hill.

It was what you call an old-time country wedding. There wasn't anybody there except us. Just me, Jimmi and the preacher. It was about as private as you could get, except for the man running the store and a few customers coming in and out of the place. But they didn't pay no attention, and that's how we liked it; we didn't want a big fuss.

Before we took the vows, Jimmi had to find a place she could change into the wedding dress she'd bought up in Cincinnati. It was a pretty blue, lacy-like dress. Preacher Joe was waiting on us, so Jimmi said she'd change clothes right there at the store to save us time. She ducked into a storage room down in the basement. There was dust and thick cobwebs hanging down and all kind of things crawling around in the dark, and she kept thinking a big spider might bite her. I don't believe any bride-to-be has ever gotten into her wedding gown as fast as Jimmi did. She told me later the room wasn't fit for a dog. I reckon she was wondering what she'd got herself into, coming all the way down from Cincinnati to get hitched in a general store way out in the sticks, cobwebs on her dress.

But you know, Jimmi's a Kentucky mountain girl at heart. She's not one to pout and she didn't let the situation get her sour. When she came up those creaky old stairs, she was beaming a big smile like she'd just stepped out of a fancy dressing room.

We stood in front of a Pepsi machine and Preacher Joe started in on the wedding vows. Only problem was, he couldn't speak plain; he had a speech impediment. And he had a big wad of chewing tobacco in his mouth, too. I was used to it because I'd known him for years, but it was hard for Jimmi to understand what he was saying. To top it off, when we were exchanging our vows, a big summer storm came blowing in off the mountain and the sky got black as midnight. Then come the thunder and lightning, and the Pepsi machine got to blinking and the power went off. So we had to finish the vows in the dark.

I believe the whole thing cost $20; that's what I pulled out of my wallet and paid Preacher Joe. He put the money in his pocket and pulled the chaw out of his mouth and wished us good luck and happiness together. Now, that's the smart way to finance your holy matrimony, I think. You hear about $20,000 weddings today, and it makes me wonder how long it'll last when the money runs out. I reckon $20 is a pretty good deal for forty-one years with Jimmi.

So we walked out of the Atkins store as husband and wife, right smack into the worst thunderstorm Dickenson County had seen since the Flood of '57. And that was the easy part. The hard part was another bit of business we had to take care of. Something I'd been dreading ever since we'd decided to get hitched. We had to tell my mother.

We drove over to the home place to give her the news. We hadn't told her a thing, so she was surprised when I just walked in and said, "Me and Jimmi got married." First thing she said was "Well, where's the license?" I don't think she could quite believe we'd really done it. So I went out to the car and got the marriage license, and that satisfied her. My first marriage didn't really count in her book. And not in mine, neither. I had to go through the bad marriage to be ready for a woman like Jimmi, I reckon. This time it was real, and it hit my mother hard, and she threw me a frown.

I didn't have time to hash it out just then, because me and Jimmi were on a tight schedule. That night we stayed at Buck's Motel down in Clintwood, and two days later we were in Ohio, where I was playing some show dates for Fourth of July weekend. We headed on the road and went right to work. That was our honeymoon.

Having Jimmi travel with us was good for me, but it was awful rough on her. It was some hard driving, me and Jimmi and the band all crammed into a station wagon, like going back to the forties when five Clinch Mountain Boys squeezed into a Chevy sedan. I had tried to tell her how it was going to be and maybe she should stay home, but she wouldn't hear it. "I'm your wife now and I'm a-coming with you," she said, and she meant it. In a way, I welcomed her tagging along, to tell the truth. With Carter gone, I'd been drinking more than was good for me, and she was worried about that. On the road, she could keep an eye on me, whether it come to drinking or tomcatting around. She kept me honest, let me tell you.

The fans accepted Jimmi right off. They'd come up to us at shows and festivals and thank her right to her face and hug her. I believe they wanted to make sure she was real. They'd tell her she was a gift for me and she'd help me stay strong, and they were right. After Carter died, I couldn't have made it without her.

Some said Jimmi must have been God-sent because they'd never seen me smile hardly at all until she came along. A lot of fans figured I must have wrote "Hemlock and Primroses," the real old-timey song from my first solo album, about Jimmi because the singer has a dream of a fair maiden with dark brown hair. Well, I wish I'd a-wrote the song but I didn't; it's been a real audience favorite through the years, and I get a lot of requests for it even today.

Jimmi was a hit with the people, but it took a while for my mother to warm up to her. She could see Jimmi and me were in love and we were going to last. But instead of that making her happy, she felt hurt. Now she'd lost the only son she had left. Not only that. As much as she loved me and Carter both, I was always her favorite, because I stayed with her and helped her around the house after my dad left, when Carter was out running wild with his friends. And she was always grateful, and she wanted me for herself, even though I was a grown man.

My marriage to Jimmi was only making her sad. She was alone now in a way she'd never felt before, and it stirred up all the bad old memories of when Lee deserted her and when Carter died. She was feeling abandoned, and she took it out on Jimmi.

I tried to explain things to Jimmi about why my mom was mistreating her. She'd lost me, she was getting up in years, set in her ways. I told Jimmi it wasn't all my mother's fault. It was mine, too. I told Jimmi I was sorry for the way my mother was treating her, but I couldn't do much. I maybe should have tried, but I didn't want to hurt my mother any more than she was already hurt.

We had a road trip out through the Midwest with long, hard all-night drives. Somehow we got lost in Iowa and almost missed a show. The station wagon wasn't made to carry a whole band around the country. Jimmi was pregnant and she really had no business being out traveling like that, but she wanted us to be together. One day she was feeling sick and we stopped at a motel, and she had a miscarriage. She was in some awful pain, and that night she had a dream where Carter came to her and said, "Jim, you'll soon be with me." She took it as a warning that she was going to die.

Heading back home, Jimmi got to hemorrhaging. She was thinking about the dream, about Carter and what he'd said; she decided her time was up and she said she wanted to go home. We finally made it back to Virginia and she went straight into the hospital. She was laid up in intensive care for a week, and when they finally let her come to Smith Ridge, my mother wasn't too welcoming.

"Well, I seen you made it back to life," she told her.

I explained to my mother about the medicine and fluids that Jimmi had to take to get her strength and her weight back, a half teaspoon every few hours and so forth, eating little bites in between doses.

"Well, you know," she said, "we eat three meals a day here."

Then I really got sharp with her. I believe it was the only time I talked that way to my mother.

"I don't care how many meals," I said. "We got to feed her just like the doctor ordered and get her stomach stretched out. She is a sick woman and needs rest and care."

Jimmi got better, but later she suffered through another miscarriage, and she finally went to the doctor about it. He said don't worry, it will be all right. I was worried, though. I figured it was my fault, for taking Jimmi on the road when she wasn't well enough. All my mother saw was my worrying, not the pain and suffering Jimmi was going through. My mother was not very comforting when Jimmi got home, and she laid into her. She was blaming Jimmi for everything, including the miscarriages.

"You'll never carry a baby for Ralph," she told her.

This hurt Jimmi worse than a slap in the face. She was crying. Then she let loose like I never seen her. She turned to my mother and said, "Me or you, neither one of us know what I'll have or I won't have. It's only the Man Upstairs knows." Then she slammed the door and stormed out of the house. My mother didn't say another word about it.

But things got better later, after we had our daughters, Lisa and Tonya Carletta. My mother took to being a grandma. I reckon it gave her a place back in the family that she thought she'd lost. There was a big change in her. She got to see the girls a lot when they were just toddlers. We got a double-wide trailer and lived in that, beside my mother's house, and then we built the house down the road where we live now, and she would come over to our new place and rock Lisa to sleep in her chair. She said they was some of her happiest days when those baby girls were running around Smith Ridge.

The best thing was, she and Jimmi became real close. They both had suffered a lot in their lives. My mother losing every man she ever loved, and Jimmi losing her father when she was nine, then her mother in the car wreck when she was thirteen. They understood each other.

When I went on the road, they kept each other company, and they turned to each other for comfort. My mother would pour her heart out to Jimmi. It gave her a friend she needed and a daughter-in-law she loved. All those years later, it was Lee leaving that weighed on her mind, and she told Jimmi all the things she had held inside for so long.

Jimmi used to tell me how much her heart would bleed for my mother. But it really did help my mother to talk with Jimmi. She got to telling her about when Lee came back to Smith Ridge demanding some things after running off with the younger woman, and how furious he got when he found out she'd sold off his team of horses.

Jimmi said it took a lot of nerve for Lee to ask for anything after what he'd done to her. Jimmi said, "You know what I'd have done when he come back to get the rest of what you had here? I'd a-just got me a double-barreled shotgun, and I'd a-put it in his hind end. I wouldn't a-killed him, though. I would have just made him think a little bit." My mother laughed and said, "You know, Jimmi, I shoulda done that." Getting my mother to find humor in that old hurt, it took some doing, and it was some medicine my mother had been needing for years.

Over the years, I've come to realize just how blessed I was that night at the Ken-Mill. The vision I saw turned out more real than I could've dreamed. What's most real is what's true, and Jimmi's always been true to me.

Lots of musicians I've known, they didn't have a good woman behind them, and it hurt 'em bad. They never had that support. No tender-hearted love, no home cooking, no nothing. In this business, it's tough to survive on your own. I've seen so many go down by the wayside because they didn't have anyone when things get rough. When I was on the road, which was most of the time, Jimmi stayed at home and took care of the kids. I know she got lonely there, and at first I promised her I'd never leave for longer than a few days. But the kids needed to be in school and the road trips got to be longer and longer. It had to be that way, I'd tell her. It was the only way we could make a living. And hard as it was on her, she understood that those show dates all over the country was what I had to do.

A lot of times, I'd come home from playing shows way late at night or in the wee hours of the morning, and when I came into the bedroom, I always saw her laying right there in that bed, waiting for me. I never did have to worry about seeing an empty bed like some have to. And that's a good feeling.

Like I've already told you, I'm pretty bad to trade. I've traded cars and cattle and horses and swapped just about anything you can think of, but there's something I'm always gonna keep, and that's Jimmi. I wouldn't trade her for nothing.

Jimmi has never stopped having dreams and visions and premonitions.

She takes 'em as signs. One night, she had a dream we'd be living on a house on top of a hill sloping down to a bend in the road, and when she saw a place nearby on Sandy Ridge, she knew that was it, and that's where we live today. She's had so many over the years, it'd take a whole 'nother book.

Now, of course, there's some dreams that never come true and never change, neither; they just haunt you and they won't ever leave you be. Jimmi has a dream like that, one been bothering her for years. It always starts out happy and hopeful; she hears the Stanley Brothers singing somewhere off in the distance, and she can hear that it's Carter and me playing together again at a show, but she can't find where the show's at. She can hear us singing and it's always a sacred song; it comes and goes as she gets closer or farther, and she don't know which way to go. She runs around asking people for directions to the show. But she can never find out where the sounds are coming from, and at the end she's always at a gas station, the sound of the Stanley Brothers hymns drifting from somewhere down the road, and then she wakes up.

I've dreamed of Carter a lot, too, in the years since he died. I always dream about when we were playing together at places we used to play in the early days.

In the dream, we're getting ready to go on stage. We're fixing to put on our hats and strapping our instruments on. It's showtime; everything's in order and everyone's waiting for us to go on. And the announcer says, "Friends and neighbors, now I'd like you to meet the stars of the show, two fellas you've heard on records and radio throughout the nation. We'd like for you to get together and make them welcome here today, Carter and Ralph, the Stanley Brothers!" It's a dream but it seems so real.

We're ready to put on a show like we always done, but something always happens and we can't make it to the stage. Every time, it's the same, and we never reach the stage to start the show and get to sing together.

Then I wake up, and I realize it's the same old dream again. I'll tell you, it's one of them dreams make you feel funny. Not a good funny, neither. There's no name for a feeling like that. It's a hurt that don't go away. I reckon it's a dream that won't ever go away, either.

Chapter Eighteen

The Stanley Sound

"Ralph Stanley has worked hard in the last few years to reestablish a hardrock center in his music, based on the almost primitive stock of things that never change—anguish, loneliness, wild joy and a faith that consists of accepting what is and building with it something that is better. Stanley has assembled a group of musicians and singers who have the understanding and ability to produce the sounds he hears."

—from a review in *Muleskinner News*, 1971

I told you about how I found my wife, Jimmi, in a bar in Ohio. Well, I found my best lead singer—the best I had after Carter, anyhow—in a bar in Ohio, too. I reckon I owe a lot to the state of Ohio for that.

With Jimmi, I knew from the moment I laid eyes on her that she was the one for me. With Roy Lee Centers, it was a little different. It took a while for me to warm up to him. A couple of years, to tell you the truth. Don't rightly know why it took that long. Maybe it proves the only thing harder than finding a good wife is finding a good lead singer. I know one thing for sure. I misjudged Roy Lee at first, and I was glad that I got the chance later to make up for that.

You'd be surprised how looks can play a part in whether a musician gets a job or not, even in a hillbilly band. Not whether a fellow is handsome or ugly, exactly. Just the looks of him. I've heard of a man not getting a job because somebody in the band just didn't like his face. They said he was a hateful-looking fellow and thought he might scare people in the crowd, so they hired someone who looked better onstage. More friendly and smiling and so forth.

It was a little bit like that with Roy Lee at first. I just wasn't all the way satisfied he was the right man to front the band. Now, I knew nobody could compare with the way Carter's smile could light up the stage, no matter how give-out he was feeling inside. But it wasn't so much how Roy Lee looked as it was how he'd come up in music, knocking around in the bars and the taverns.

I've got nothing against the bluegrass bars up that way, because I played in many a one myself, and they loved the mountain music about as much as anybody I've ever played for. But they also liked to drink and fight right along with the music. What I'm saying is that you really have to be on your guard. Playing six nights a week in these places might turn a fellow mean just to survive.

Carter and me played shows in the Dayton area quite a bit, especially in the last few years he was alive, and it sure didn't help his health any. Anyhow, we had a lot of supporters in Dayton, people like Jack Lynch, who would help us out on bass and later helped carry Carter's coffin up to the cemetery on Smith Ridge. Roy Lee Centers played with Lynch for a while, and then he and another fellow had a little group together. They called themselves the Lee Brothers. They weren't brothers, but they played some of the best bluegrass in Dayton. Roy Lee played a fine banjo and sang even better, and he was trying his level best to make a living in bars like Tom's Tavern.

Like I told you before, I'd known about Roy Lee for a long time from the club scene. And the thing was, I studied about Roy Lee even before I hired Larry Sparks. And I liked his singing actually better than Larry's at that time. Roy Lee was in his mid-twenties and was already a fully developed singer; he didn't need the work that Larry did, being as young he was.

But the age and experience Roy Lee had was what worried me. Now, you might think this is strange, because age and experience is usually what you look for in a musician. But in this case, I thought maybe he'd had a little too much seasoning, so to speak. I was afraid that with Roy

Lee playing in all them rough Dayton bars all the time, the lifestyle might have rubbed off on him. I thought he might be a drunk or tough or what have you, and I was afraid to take a chance on him. Goes to show how wrong you can be.

After Larry Sparks left to go out on his own, I was finally ready to take Roy Lee into the band. I knew he was ready, that he was licking his chops and he was hungry. Jack Lynch and some others in Dayton vouched for him, and that was good enough for me. They said there wasn't a nicer fellow I could find, and there wasn't any more hardworking musician in town. So I called and said, "Roy, we need a lead singer and I think you're the man." He didn't hesitate; he'd been waiting to get that call. He played our next show and he didn't miss a show for us in almost four years, not even with a fever and flu that would have knocked most men out for a week.

There was something special about Roy Lee. When I say he was the best lead singer I've had, I mean he came the closest to replacing Carter. A lot of times his voice sounded so close to Carter's I'd swear Carter was standing right there onstage. It used to make me feel funny to hear it sometimes. It was eerie. But it sounded good.

Now, I don't know whether he tried to sound like Carter or not, but he'd do a song exactly like Carter. It just seemed like it fell into place. And it wasn't only his singing that reminded me of Carter sometimes. There were so many things in Roy's actions and just in the way that he'd do something. He was a lot more soft-spoken and he wasn't such a big talker or prankster, but he was game for most anything, just like Carter. I don't know why it was. I guess a lot of things are meant to be.

Roy Lee told me that years ago the Stanley Brothers played at his school in Jackson, Kentucky. That's way back in the mountains, a place called Breathitt County. He was just a little boy, eleven or twelve years old, and he was there at his first Stanley Brothers show. He was sitting in the front row, and we took a break for intermission. Carter stepped off the stage and took his guitar off and laid it around Roy Lee's neck, picked him out of all the people sitting in the seats there, like it was something meant to be. Carter told him, "Son, hold my guitar till I get back." Roy Lee said he held that guitar so tight his hands hurt.

Through the years, I've heard from so many musicians who saw the Stanley Brothers at shows when they were kids, just like Roy Lee. One time in the early 1990s, Dolly Parton invited my wife, Jimmi, and me down to Dollywood, the theme park she built in Pigeon Forge, Tennessee. She had put my name on the Walkway of Stars there, which was a big honor; the only bluegrass musicians with their names on the walkway are Bill Monroe and myself. Jimmi and me spent a whole weekend at the park. Dolly treated us real nice and she gave us a personal tour. She told me when she was twelve years old she saw the Stanley Brothers play at her high school in Sevierville, Tennessee. She said it really meant a lot to her, and she said it helped inspire her to write her own songs about growing up in her Tennessee mountain home.

It was like that for Roy Lee, too. Getting singled out by Carter from the crowd, he just figured it was a sign. It stayed with him, and he became a die-hard fan of our music, singing along to our records and pretending he was Carter. Later on, Roy Lee moved up to Ohio, like so many mountain people who came north for jobs, and he followed the musical path that started back at the Stanley Brothers show in East Kentucky. He would come to see us whenever we played in Dayton, and he told me later that he admired Carter and he considered him the greatest lead singer that had ever been.

Predestination is something I believe in. I believe that God knows everything that is and will be, and that He knows every hair on your head. So Roy Lee taking Carter's place made perfect sense to me. And I wonder if Carter himself didn't know something when he handed his guitar to little Roy Lee. Sometimes it really did seem like Carter knew things most of us don't know, like he was privy to things of this world most of us aren't.

When Roy Lee joined the band, I took him off the banjo and put him on rhythm guitar. Now, good as he was on banjo, he couldn't be beat on rhythm guitar. So that was a better fit for us; instead of Larry playing lead guitar, we had Roy Lee singing lead and playing rhythm like Carter did. And Roy Lee was a number one rhythm guitar player; he really had a gift for it, like he did with his singing.

Not long after Roy Lee came on board, sometime in 1970, we were booked at a club across the Big Sandy River from Louisa, Kentucky. It was a little bar in Fort Gay, West Virginia, a place we played pretty regular. On the way there, we had a flat and we got held up for a good while waiting to get the tire fixed.

I can count on my hand all the times we've ever been late for a show. There's nothing I hate worse. It's bad for business. If you don't make the show, you don't get paid and that's a bad way to make a living. I always tell my band, "Better to be four hours early than ten minutes late," and I mean it. Most of the time we get to the club a few hours before showtime. I want the people to see my bus parked there when they come to the place. That's the way I do things, and it's worked pretty well.

See, it's even more than bad business. It's embarrassing. The club owner's waiting on you, the crowd is waiting on you, and all you can do is call ahead and say, "Just hold on, we'll be there as soon as we can." The fans, they don't care about why you might be late. They don't care if it's a blown tire or a killer tornado. All they know is, they paid to see you play and you're not there. They don't like it one bit and I don't blame them. Being late ain't professional.

When we finally did get to Fort Gay, we were forty-five minutes late and I was in a bad mood. The parking lot was full, and I knew every one of those cars meant fans inside waiting on us. I was walking across the lot just steaming inside. Someone opened the front door ahead of me, and I heard music coming out of the club that sounded familiar. It was the Stanley Brothers. I figured somebody had the jukebox playing our old records.

When I went inside, I saw it wasn't no jukebox. It was too young gentlemen, standing onstage with a fiddle and a guitar, singing Stanley Brothers songs. They was just boys, not even old enough to start shaving yet. But they could pick like nobody's business and they were singing their hearts out. They sounded just like me and Carter in the early days, every song was Stanley Brothers.

I didn't know what to think, but I liked what I heard. So I pulled up a bar stool and sat down to listen for a few songs. They sounded identical to the way me and Carter sounded when we first started. These teenagers did it even better, I'd say, and they knew more of the old Stanley Brothers songs than I did.

The one boy playing fiddle was a shaggy-haired, round-faced fellow. The other one, playing guitar, had a crew cut and big thick horn-rimmed glasses. I thought he looked just like a young Harry Truman. This is how I first discovered Ricky Skaggs and Keith Whitley.

Later I found out how they'd worked it that night. They'd only been playing a short while together. Keith and his brother Dwight had a band called the East Kentucky Mountain Boys. They played a local square dance in Ezel, Kentucky, and that's where Keith met up with Ricky, down in the dressing room after a show. Turns out both of them loved the Stanley Brothers and they started singing our songs, and their voices just fit together, like the way Carter and mine did.

Ricky and Keith started their own band, the Lonesome Mountain Boys. That's what they called themselves when we come that night to Fort Gay. They got to the club early to hear us play, and when we didn't show up on time, well, the owner knew they played Stanley Brothers. So he told the boys to grab their instruments from the car and go on stage and hold the crowd until we got there.

And that's just what they did for a half hour, until I walked in the door. They played songs me and Carter had done that even I'd forgot about, and they ran through one of our Mercury albums note for note. And after the set, I cheered right along with the crowd. They went wild over these "Junior Stanley Brothers."

There was a little dressing room there, and they were packing up their instruments while we was hurrying up to get ready for our show. They were very polite boys, you could tell they had been raised up right. They were sort of sheepish about all the fuss they'd caused. They even apologized, saying that they didn't mean to be in our way and all.

"Don't worry about a thing," I told them. "You boys did a fine job, and you brought back a lot of old memories of when I was first coming along. It was really something special." We went on stage and did a set.

The crowd was really behind us, but they missed Ricky and Keith. Some were hollering to get them "Junior Stanley Brothers" to come on again.

I thought they deserved an encore, not only for playing so well, but for keeping the crowd happy until we made it to the club. "Those boys were awful good, don't you think so?" I said to the crowd and they went wild again. "So how 'bout we get them back up here to play for you during the intermission?" And Ricky and Keith unpacked their instruments, climbed back on stage and just about raised the roof on that little club. It was really something, and it got me thinking.

After the show, we got to talking. I asked Ricky if he played anything besides fiddle. He said his favorite instrument was mandolin and that he had played with me before when he was a little kid, back when his dad, Hobart, brought him to Stanley Brothers shows in Prestonburg and Olive Hill. Well, that rang a bell, the little boy with a mandolin. And I got to thinking. Ricky and Keith were both barely fifteen, but these boys had some talent you don't find that often. The most important thing to me was their determination. It reminded me of Carter and me, back when we first made up our minds it was going to be music or nothing.

They told me how bad they wanted to get started in the music business. I could see their talent and I was thinking about how loud the crowd had cheered for them. They had a gift, both of them. I figured I could help them and they could help me, too. They had the drive, so I figured they deserved a chance. Part of it was selfish, too. I was proud of the Stanley Sound that Carter and me had made from scratch. And I wanted to show people that here were these boys who could do that kind of singing. I wanted to see the tradition carried on, and these boys knew how to do it the right way. I wanted to help them, and I wanted to see the music go on, too.

I told them, "Why, if there's ever anything I could help you out with, you let me know," and they said, "Okay." I had already made up my mind that if they were willing, I'd try them out and take them on the road with me. The thing was, I already had a full band then, and they made seven, but I wanted them on board anyway.

A couple weeks later, Keith's dad, Elmer, called up and we set up a date to meet and talk it over. The Whitleys and the Skaggs all came up to my house in Dickenson County. Everybody was ready to give it a go. First, I wanted to see how the fans took to them.

"We've got a big festival coming up in Reidsville, North Carolina," I said. "We're going to do a salute to the Stanley Brothers, and I want to use you two. So let's see how that goes."

That was the plan. If everything went well, the boys could join up with the band when school let out. I said right up front I couldn't pay them much, and they understood that this was more about getting experience than it was about getting rich. They said they'd have done it for free, and I couldn't have been happier, because even though they were just teenagers they had the talent of five or six men.

They traveled with us to the Reidsville bluegrass festival and they did a little set of Stanley Brothers songs, and they got two encores. The crowd took to them just like they did in that little club where I first saw them. They were a big hit. They stayed with us permanent after they graduated from high school the next year.

Ricky lived only a few miles from Keith, so Ricky's dad, Hobart, would drop him off at Keith's, where we would come by to pick them up for a road trip. Sometimes we would set for a spell at Keith's place, and I got to know his parents real well. The Whitleys were good country people, the best you could ever hope to meet.

Keith's dad, Elmer, was a master electrician and a regular handyman, which I always admired because I can't hardly hang a picture myself. He'd lost most of his left hand when he was in the service, but he didn't let that stop him. Keith's mother, Faye, reminded me of my mother when she was younger, just real down-home country and nice as could be. She told me her dad had played banjo at old-time square dances, and she cooked with lard the old-time way. I liked how she really doted on Keith, fixing up his favorite dish, chocolate gravy with biscuits. I could tell he was a mama's boy just like I was.

The Whitleys lived outside Sandy Hook, way out in the sticks past Laurel Gorge. It's a little crossroads town in Elliot County, which is the next county over from Pike County, where Curly Ray lived. The Whitleys had a double-wide mobile home after their house had burned down a few years before. They couldn't afford to build a new two-story house like the one they'd had, but they loved that little spot of land too much to move. So Elmo bought a couple new trailers and pushed 'em together and made a peaked roof over top and they were able to stay put. They were just making do the best they could, like a lot of people in eastern Kentucky.

It was a big boost having Ricky and Keith in the band. I done everything I could to get the boys exposure. They were just kids but I saw potential there. And I'm very proud that I took them into the band, because they both done so well for themselves and made great careers on their own.

Having them along was like a trip down memory lane; they brought back a lot of old material I hadn't performed since Carter was alive, songs like "The White Dove," "Will You Miss Me" and "The Angels Are Singing (in Heaven Tonight.)" I started featuring Ricky and Keith for a little set of Stanley Brothers songs. For a lot of fans, it was a special treat. When they'd step up to do their bit, the crowd would catch fire. They really added a lot to the show, and I wanted to give them a chance to shine. A lot of bandleaders don't want to share the spotlight, they feel threatened by that. But I just wanted to turn 'em loose and let 'em do all they could.

On some songs we all pitched in. Keith would sing lead on one verse and Roy Lee would sing lead on the second. Then I'd sing tenor on the chorus and Ricky would sing tenor on the second verse. We all knew where the other men were; we got to trust each other, and the way we could harmonize really got to the crowd. They hung with us all the way, and it meant the world to me that they believed in what we were doing.

Writer Robert Cantwell was in the audience for some shows when Keith and Ricky first joined up, and he described how we sounded onstage in his book *Bluegrass Breakdown:*

"The performance of this group became a kind of séance, annealing the vocal sounds of the Stanley Brothers' career into a single audial image: the ethereal harmonies of the young duet, the repining voice of the dead

Carter Stanley, eerily lodged in the throat of his replacement, Roy Lee Centers, and finally the voice of the surviving brother, the cry of a vendor of sorrows."

To my way of thinking, it was a way to give fans more show for the money. But I was also making a statement. Bluegrass was getting too slick, I thought, and it was getting too far from its roots. A lot of the new young pickers were more interested in flashy solos than anything else. They wanted to show off how much they knew instead of getting across what they felt. This music isn't about just the notes you play, but the emotions you have. The bluegrass festivals started to seem more like contests to see who could outpick the competition. Ricky and Keith were living proof you could be young, hot pickers and still play the old-time style. After a show, Ricky could jam all night and outpick anybody in the parking lot, but he knew there was a time and place for everything. He and Keith knew where they fit in with our band, and they respected it.

Now, just because we dressed like we was going to a funeral didn't mean we didn't have some fun. Keith brought a lot of comedy to our show. He used to really get the crowds lathered up with his Lester Flatt imitation. Lester was his hero, and he could not only sing just like him, he had his way of talking down perfect. After a medley, he'd do a little skit, Lester talking with Keith's Lester.

Not long after Keith joined our band, we were playing a festival, and Lester was one of the headliners. Keith had never met him in person, and I knew he was too shy to go up and introduce himself. I decided to pull a prank on him.

"Keith," I said. "Would you go on over to Lester Flatt's bus and see if he could play my Memorial Day festival? It'd sure be nice to have him down to the old home place."

So Keith went over there and straightaway knocks on the door of the bus. He was excited to finally get to meet the great Lester Flatt. What he didn't know was, I had Lester waiting on him. Lester was sitting in the bus, poker face, like to be half-asleep.

"Mr. Flatt?" said Keith, as polite as could be. "I'm Keith Whitley, one of the new boys in Ralph's band. He sent me over to ask if you could come and play at his festival down at Smith Ridge this Memorial Day weekend."

Now, Lester had the best deadpan delivery of any man alive. He didn't let on nothing. "Well, son, let me see now," he said. "What day does Memorial Day come on this year?"

Well, that got Keith flustered. Lester just sat there, picking his teeth. About all Keith could finally say was, "Don't it come on the same day every year?"

Another time I had Lester hide in the bus, and when Keith was doing his imitation, Lester popped out from behind and surprised him.

Keith was a good sport about it. He could take a joke just fine and he could hand them out even better. The one who Keith liked to pull pranks on the most was Curly Ray. It tells you how much Curly Ray loved Keith, because Curly Ray was like me, he didn't like to be the butt of no man's jokes. I still don't rightly know how Keith got away with some of the things him and Ricky did to poor ole Curly Ray. Nobody else in the band would have dared to do it, but they could. Partly it was because they were so young, and partly because Keith and Curly just took to each other.

One time, Curly was asleep on the bus and we were headed to a festival. This was in the summer, and it could get hotter than blazes on the bus. The AC was always broke or barely working; we had enough trouble keeping the engine running good enough to make it to shows. There was Curly snoring, just as peaceful as could be in his seat, not bothering nobody. Keith and Ricky took a notion for an ambush. They wrapped an old wool army blanket around him so he couldn't escape. Then they started stuffing a loaf of bread down him. Now Curly woke up and got to eating for his very life. There was sweat pouring off his head, the only part of him outside that blanket. He couldn't holler because his mouth was full of bread, and he couldn't fight back with that blanket around him. They'd about choked him to death if Curly wasn't such a good eater.

It was something awful, but Curly didn't mind even that. No matter what they'd pull, he'd always enjoy it and have just as much fun. He laughed right along with 'em.

Curly, of course, I already told you a little about and you'll hear a lot more about later. Ten years before, Carter and me couldn't even afford to have a fiddler. Now I had a fiddler who could entertain a crowd and keep me entertained between shows.

And someone else joined up, and he was real important to the band, and still is to this day. That was our bass man, Jack Cooke. He was from Norton, and he first played with the Stanley Brothers when he was seventeen years old, just helping us out from time to time. He started with me regular in 1970, and he was my bass player until the doctors grounded him this past year for health reasons. Bass ain't all he can play. He can play rhythm guitar like he done for Bill Monroe for a short spell, he can sing tenor or baritone both, and he can do some comedy in the show. He can drive, too. He's a real handyman, Jack is.

I finally had me the band I'd always wanted. They believed in me, and I believed in them. And the most important thing was, they got me believing in myself.

Chapter Nineteen

Rebel Yell

"For a quarter-century now the name Stanley has been synonymous with the finest in old-time gospel music. Although his current audiences have extended far beyond the Appalachian bible belt that produced this remarkable man, hymns remain as popular as ever with Ralph Stanley fans. This album is abundant proof why. It's truly an exciting experience, yet it's more than that, for it inaugurates some very significant firsts for him."

—Review of *Cry from the Cross* album,
Bluegrass Unlimited magazine, 1971

I was sitting in a creek somewhere down in Georgia. It was summer of 1970 and I was playing at a bluegrass festival. I'm hazy on the details, but I do recall it was hotter than blazes. There aren't many places hotter than a bluegrass festival in Georgia in the middle of July. I was taking a breather, sitting on some rocks in the cool rushing creek water. I was there with a fellow named Dick Freeland. There was music from the festival stage drifting through the big shade trees hanging over the banks. We were talking business to the sound of the banjos and the bullfrogs.

Freeland wasn't the suit-and-tie type of record executive you have to meet in an office. The creek was fine by him. He wasn't a flashy wheeler-dealer, just a plain, self-made man, which is the kind of businessman I like best. He was an independent, like my dad was. Freeland was the man behind Rebel Records, the bluegrass label he ran out of his basement in Washington, D.C. I had approached him and told him maybe we could work something out. Rebel was a small independent label with its own way of doing things, still fairly new at the time. It was doing pretty good, so I decided I'd just as soon give it a try.

Faster than you'd get a bite on a fishing line, I shook Dick Freeland's hand and signed up with Rebel. It took us maybe thirty minutes to close the deal, and I stayed with Rebel for the next thirty years and recorded thirty-five albums. That was a time when about all you needed was a man's word.

Now you may be wondering why I would join up with Rebel, a one-man basement operation. First off, there was no major labels interested in me. And second, Rebel was giving me the freedom to record as I pleased. When you were playing bluegrass back then, you weren't getting rich; you could make just enough for a decent living. So what really mattered was your freedom. And Rebel was ready to let me make my music exactly the way I wanted to.

Rebel may have been small, but it was really the premier bluegrass label, after Nashville had turned its back on traditional country. Rebel had some of the finest bluegrass bands around, bands like the Country Gentlemen and Seldom Scene that started as fans of the Stanley Brothers and Bill Monroe.

Freeland was a fan of the old-time sounds, too. He was in his early thirties, so he had the energy it takes to survive as a one-man business. I liked what he told me about how he got started in distribution. It was a lot different from the days when Hobe Stanton peddled 78s out of the trunk of his car in our little corner of Appalachia. You had to go national to make a go of it, and that's what Freeland did. He headed to the Library of Congress in Washington, D.C., and he scoured through all the phone books state by state and got all the mailing addresses of record shops and radio staions and jukebox operators from all around the country. And back then, there were thousands. He went down the list and sent out postcards to the record stores telling about the bluegrass artists Rebel had to offer. That's how he started selling to the stores direct and got the distribution to compete with the major labels. It took some pluck, and I admired his determination.

Before he got into the record business, Freeland was a land surveyor, so he knew all about hard work. He was Pennsylvania-raised and knew his way around. I liked doing business with him because he got right to the point. He didn't waffle, and he really loved the music. So above everyhing else, he had one goal, to make the best records he could.

Freeland was sort of a throwback like I was. He went for the old-time in everything from music to whiskey. He did like Canadian Mist over Jack Daniel's, but I forgave him for that. He loved the Stanley Brothers, and he liked what I'd been doing on my own. He said he respected me because I had the guts to do my own thing, no matter what was commercial or not.

This was a strange time for bluegrass. What they called the counterculture and what I called hippies, they started showing up at the festivals. They were long-haired and barefoot, the ones in the crowd and the ones onstage, too. The hippie types didn't know any better; they really thought they was playing bluegrass. You'd hear a solo on electric banjo and like to murder the man a-playing it, just to get the noise to stop. There was New Grass Revival and Bluegrass Alliance and about a million others, and you could be sure if they had the word "bluegrass" in their name they didn't sound nothing like bluegrass, to my way of thinking.

And it wasn't just the young hippie crowd. Even Earl Scruggs started playing electrified music, with his sons Randy and Gary, amplifiers turned way up so you could hardly hear his banjo in all the noise. I felt bad for Earl; I thought his sons should be following his style of music and not the other way around. The Country Gentlemen were using drums on some of their records. Jimmy Martin brought a drum kit on stage at the festivals. He figured if you can't beat 'em you might as well join 'em.

There was an interview with Lester Flatt around this time, and he took a stand. "I would never use electric help in my music because that just wouldn't be bluegrass," Lester said. "Besides, I just don't like it. And most people at festivals don't want to hear electric music. They're looking for a more honest, simple sound. So we'll never use electric instruments. It just doesn't go with our style of music. To be real, and to be like we were down through the years, I certainly wouldn't want it in my outfit."

Not in my outfit either. Lester and I always got along fine through the years, and this was another thing we saw eye to eye on. I never liked electric music, and I never will. It don't much matter if it's what you call bluegrass or what I call old-time mountain music. It don't mix well with modern ingredients, and it spoils the dish.

And it wasn't just the sound; the songs had changed, too. Everybody was wanting to prove they could do bluegrass on any song. Even some Rebel bands, the Country Gentlemen and the Seldom Scene, were covering pop singers like John Denver and James Taylor. The most popular bluegrass song around was "Fox on the Run," which was originally done by a bunch of British rock 'n' rollers. It never entered my mind to try to do that sort of foolishness.

At the festivals, the Seldom Scene and the new bands were starting to get a younger crowd that liked hearing those songs. They had the new fans, but we had our old fans, and that was enough for me.

All the newgrass and progressive foolishness and such didn't worry me a bit. I just stuck to my old style that had done good for me. I saw no reason to try to be something different. That wasn't me.

I had all the show dates I could handle. I didn't need to try to get more commercial with my music. I just wanted to keep my tradition alive and make it grow. I know there was grumbling from some people. They said I was stuck in the past, and I couldn't cut the mustard anymore. But my real fans stayed with me all the way. At the festivals, they'd come up and tell me, "Stick to your roots, Ralph, you're the only one doing it the old way. You're the only one we've got left."

Freeland didn't want me to try to change with the times, neither. He wanted me to be Ralph Stanley. At the same time, he didn't want to bring back the past. He told me my best music was ahead of me, and together we were going make the best music Ralph Stanley could make. I believed him, and I was lucky he believed in me.

Here's what's sort of funny. At forty-three years old, playing old-time music, I was considered too old for the major labels. It took until I was seventy-five years old before I signed up with a major label again, and I reckon I wasn't too old then. That was when the *O Brother* thing hit Nashville like a ton of bricks, and I will tell you more about that later. It just goes to show that you ain't never too old as long as somebody thinks you can sell. You have to just keep working, so when they come a-knocking you're ready. Just do your work. That's all you can do in this life.

Anyhow, back in 1970, I didn't feel old. I didn't even feel middle-aged, though I reckon that's what some folks would call it. Uncle Dave Macon was well past fifty when he cut his first records, and he'd been a mule driver most of his working days, and he wasn't a bit tired. Listen to his records and you've never heard music with so much pep. But that was back in the 1920s, when the country music business was just starting and it was still wide open. They didn't care how bent your back or how long your beard.

First TV, and then rock 'n' roll, changed everything. Musicians had to be pretty instead of just being able to play pretty. Looks got to be more important than the licks you could make on your instrument.

But I didn't pay no mind to what Nashville wanted or not. Forty-three years old felt to me like twenty-three, and the boys in the band made me feel even younger. They kept the music sounding fresh. I was in my prime and I had my best band and I was ready to make music, and Rebel was ready to help me do it. In the next year, I made four long-playing albums. I don't know if that's a world record, but I'd say it was doing something.

The very first thing I did for Rebel was something I'd been wanting to do for a long time. A gospel record. Not your standard gospel album, but a real old-timer like you'd hear in one of the Primitive Baptist churches where I grew up. Something old, but for most people, it'd be something completely new.

You have to remember when this was, in 1971. If a man had tried this in Nashville, they'd have run him out of town. Freeland was the opposite. There was no big fuss about it at all. He was ready for something different. I did sort of keep it low-key, though. I didn't say anything to anybody about what I had planned. I sent Freeland a rehearsal tape we'd worked up, just a preview of what I was wanting to record. He heard it once and he was sold. "I love it," he said. "Sounds like real Ralph Stanley music to me. When can you come by and cut the songs?" That was all I needed to hear.

The album was called *Cry from the Cross*, and we recorded the whole thing in a two-day session in February '71, at the basement studio of a man named Roy Homer. Got so much in the can we had enough material for another record. And that's pretty much the way it went. We did seven albums for Rebel in two years.

When we first pulled up to Roy Homer's place, I wasn't sure if I'd made the right decision. It was a little split-level ranch house in Clinton, Maryland, not far from the district line. It was still country out there then, some chickens scratching around in the yard next door, but not the country we was used to. Hard to explain, just different.

Roy worked for the government for his day job. On the side, he was a fine engineer and a big-time bluegrass fan and he had converted his basement into a first-class studio. It ended up that, for our type of music, you couldn't have asked for a better setup than Roy Homer's basement.

Before Roy, Rebel had recorded bands in all sorts of places, wherever they could rent out studio time and sometimes just wherever they could find a place to record, period. In 1965, the Country Gentlemen had the label's first big hit, "Bringing Mary Home," which a college student fan cut on portable equipment at a recording lab at Syracuse University.

As the Rebel roster grew, Freeland needed a base of operations near his place in Mount Rainier, outside Washington. Roy Homer lived nearby in Clinton and he had his own studio he'd custom-designed himself. Soundwise, it was as good as any studio you'd find anywhere, even if it was in his basement. The Country Gentlemen had cut some fine gospel tunes there, old-timers like "A Beautiful Life" that Carter and me had done back in the fifties. Roy had all the right equipment to get that deep, booming sound you need on those hymns.

So Roy was ready for us. The studio wasn't a very big room, but it was big enough for what we needed to do. Roy repaired radio equipment for the U.S. Weather Bureau, and he had the touch with all things mechanical. If anybody could fix it, Roy could. And he was a real go-getter and a do-it-yourselfer. If there was a piece of equipment his studio needed, by God, he would get it, even if he had to do it himself. Roy wanted one of those big echo chambers that all the fancy studios had, and it was too expensive to buy. So he went down to the U.S. Patent Office in Washington, D.C., and got a copy of the drawing for it, and came home and built one for himself off that design. An echo chamber gives some real depth to what you're recording, and it came in real handy for the gospel songs on *Cry from the Cross.*

The ones I chose for the a cappella arrangements were old favorites of mine. We did "Gloryland" and "Sinner Man" and "Bright Morning Star," which is a favorite at mountain funerals to this day. Those were the highlights, and then we redid some old Stanley Brothers numbers, like the title song.

The man who really stepped up was Roy Lee. I give him a lot of credit. As a singer I'd a-put him up against anyone in bluegrass, and on the gospel songs he was as good as any I ever heard. Take a listen to "Stairway to Heaven," and you hear a singer coming into his own, finding his voice. You know, a lot of people told me I could find a replacement for Carter easier than he could have found a singer to replace me. And that may be true, because I've always been able to find others to sing with through the years.

Like I told you before, I led Carter with my tenor, and that styled it natural. I never could follow another man's lead. For that reason, all the lead singers that have sung with me, from Roy Lee on down, they have to follow me, so that holds the style. Roy Lee understood this by instinct; I never had to say a word about it.

Going a cappella, it was a gamble, but it paid off. *Cry from the Cross* got the best reviews I'd had in the years since I'd been without Carter. And the thing was, the reviewers saved their highest praise for the a cappella singing. They understood what I was trying to do. "This is unquestionably the best bluegrass gospel album of the year," reported *Muleskinner News*. "This is real old-time bluegrass gospel singing at its best—durable mountain music with guts, integrity and truth. There is no finer music anywhere."

"For the first time on a Stanley record, possibly the first time on any bluegrass gospel record, a capella singing (no instruments) appears, and the effect is unbelievably beautiful," wrote the reviewer for *Bluegrass Unlimited*. "A tremendous LP, and a moving testimonial from one of the great pioneers of traditional music. This album is indispensable."

It was good to get the positive notices, but the real test was to find out how the fans would take to it. There's some people think the old-time Baptist singing is too gloomy. They want gospel music to lift their spirits up and they say the Primitive style brings them down. There are some who live in my area, and they will tell you they won't walk across the road to hear it. To them, it's too depressing. Even Carter didn't care for it much at all.

So I knew there'd be some who believed that type of music should stay in the church where it belongs. Same way they don't bring any instruments into the church, maybe the singing should stay inside, too. But I didn't hold to that. I figured there was a lot of people like me who love the sound and the feeling it gets across. It's just pure singing what gives it the power it has. All you need is the voices together and you don't need any instruments to go with it. It'd take away from the purity that makes it special.

The one thing I did was to make it fit better for my type of music. In the church I was raised in, the whole congregation sang together. There would usually be a group of men and a group of women, and the women would come in higher, just an octave higher, and it really blended well. But everyone sang lead, like one big voice. The change I made was to set it for a quartet. So we used the tenor and the baritone and the parts of harmony singing you hear in bluegrass.

That's the main difference, and the other is the timing. My way is phrased different. The way they sing it in church, they drag it out longer than I do. I sing my words a little bit faster, more in time to the music, put a rhythm to it and shorten it up some. They hold it for a while until they go on to the next verse. They go on for seven or eight or ten minutes or more, because they're singing to God alone and they ain't worried about nothing else. But that's too long to hold an audience. So I do the same hymn in about half that time. I just change to fit my style, but other than that, it's the same singing I learned to do in church.

I did have to teach the band to follow me on the a cappella numbers. I had to line it out for them, just like the preacher does. None of the boys knew much about it. They'd heard about it but never sung it themselves. They didn't have to be raised up Primitive Baptist to get the style right; they were from the mountains and that was enough. All the boys needed was me leading, and Roy Lee chording his guitar at the end of the chorus, to keep everybody on pitch.

The biggest reason I went back to the a cappella style was simple. It was who I was, as a singer and as a believer, too. I reckon it was the old Primitive Baptist in me, I just grew up singing like that, and I wanted to hear it again. I like to sing the old-time way and I believe in those old-time hymns. We were raised in a Christian home and taught to go to church and sing that way. So it was just a matter of staying true to my music and my beliefs.

I still didn't know how the people would take to it. We never did do any a cappella singing with the Stanley Brothers. This was something new. Ever since Carter passed away, I'd been advised by a lot of people to do more lead singing. I held back some, I guess. And I stayed pretty close to the tenor singing. But when I started the a cappella gospel, it was a chance to do more solo lead on my own. It was time to really step out and show what I could do, as my own singer and my own man. I figured the true fans would be behind me, and my hunch was right. Once we started singing a cappella at shows, the fans took to it in a big way, right from the start. They'd get real quiet, and listen real close, and they loved it. It always seems to touch a lot of people that never heard it before. At the festivals, fans in the crowd started requesting the a cappella numbers, and all the other bands took notice of that as well. Pretty soon there was a lot of others started to add that type of singing to their performances. As far as I know, I was the first one to do the a cappella singing in bluegrass music, so I'm proud to say I was the one that got the ball rolling, and it ain't stopped yet.

Even today, everywhere I go, that's what people want to hear, especially after my a cappella version of "O Death" from the *O Brother* sound track. It could be New York City or anywhere, the people ask for that more than anything else. In fact, they demand it. Especially the young people. We've played Bonnaroo rock festival several times now, and that's always what the fans there want. They'd be half-naked and painted all over, but you'd hear them holler out, "A cappella, we want the a cappella!" and they'd clap so loud for it, it'd make your head hurt.

It makes me proud that they love the old Baptist hymns done the old way. It makes me think of the people back in the church at McClure. They still don't allow instruments in that church. The members will buy every CD and album and tape I make, but they won't have it in the church. I respect that tradition and I'm proud to have taken the old-time Baptist way of singing all over the world. I don't reckon they'd have ever believed those old hymns would be sung in these places like Bonnaroo, in front of thousands of screaming kids. I know I wouldn't have believed it until I done it myself. Just like Carter used to always say, "It's a big world out there."

And it all started with the *Cry from the Cross* record. A lot of people have asked me about the cover shot we done for *Cry from the Cross*. At that time, most gospel albums had a photo of a little country church on a hill, or maybe the band standing in choir robes around the altar and whatnot. I had done quite a few of those myself. That was sort of the standard for the time.

The cover for *Cry from the Cross* was different, as different as the music on the album. It shows the Clinch Mountain Boys high on a ridge in front of a big iron cross, as tall and wide as a goalpost at a football stadium. It's a formal group shot; we've got our stage clothes on, like we'd just stopped off the road on the way back from a show. Which is what we did. Not a smile in the bunch. Just business.

We used to pass by this roadside cross on Lee Highway in Northern

Virginia, not far from the Big K radio station where Tomcat Reeder was the disc jockey for so many years. We used to play a club up the highway, Partners II, close by Centreville, so we'd see that cross a lot. It was one of those sights you always look for when you're traveling, like a signpost. After a while, it's like an old friend. The cross stood high in a cemetery on top of a hill, and it was rigged up with electricity so at night it was lit up like a Christmas tree.

You see roadside crosses everywhere, especially out through the mountains where I live. Out near Bristol, on Interstate 81, there's one of the biggest I've ever seen, a hundred-foot-tall cross made of iron beams and painted bright white. And there's many a one we see on our road trips, little homemade jobs, just a couple of plain boards nailed together and hammered down in the ground. There is a fellow in West Virginia who built hundreds of crosses all over Appalachia. He always had three wood-pole crosses set in groups along the roads, one in the middle painted gold and the others painted blue. He said the Holy Spirit came to him in a vision and told him to build the crosses.

There was something about the big steel cross in the cemetery on Lee Highway, especially the way it lit up at night. It was a powerful sight. Told you more than any billboard ever could. Dick Freeland thought it was a good idea to photograph the band on the hill under that cross. Make a statement that our new album was a landmark, just like the cross on the hill. Around in late February we climbed up on the hill and took a photo. It was cold as the dickens on top of that hill, wind whipping off the Blue Ridge.

We still pass through that area often on the way to shows. Out of habit, I find myself sometimes looking out the window, checking on that cross. You know, there's not much that lasts in this world. I hope our music lasts as long as the steel cross on the hill.

Freeland made things happen. One thing he did right off was get us a tour in Japan. The only bluegrass act that had traveled over there was Flatt and Scruggs. That was in 1968, and the Japanese fans were hungry to see traditional American country musicians in person. Thanks to a distribution deal Freeman had set up, our records were sold over there, so I was a very well-known figure in Japan. Not as big as Elvis, mind you, but more popular than I was in a lot of the United States.

I may have said this before, but I'll say it again. In all my travels, I've never found a better place for fans of my music than the state of Kentucky. They were there when the Stanley Brothers started out, and they've stayed behind me all the years I've been on my own. I can go to Ohio or Michigan or Maryland or Pennsylvania and I'll hear people going crazy, and nine times out of ten they'll wind up being from eastern Kentucky or somewhere back in those mountains.

Australia's another place you can't beat. There's a group of fans over there that used to call me on my birthday, every twenty-fifth of February. They used to hold a festival every year on that day and play my music and even put a statue of me on stage. They say I'll always be welcome in Australia, thousands of miles away and as friendly as your next-door neighbor. They tell me to bring some personal items to sell if I want to. They say just bring anything, it don't matter what, a box of matches or a hair comb that I've touched and I'll get a hundred dollars for it or whatever I ask, just so I've touched it. I think that may be going a bit overboard, but those are some good fans.

Even with the supporters I have in Kentucky and Australia, Japan has 'em all beat. They love our music over there and they love bluegrass musicians, and somehow I've become one of their favorites. They ain't afraid to show it, too. They bow to you; I mean, they really lay it down. When we went there, I was treated like I was President of the United States. It was a ten-day, five-show tour all around the country, and they couldn't get enough of us, no matter where we went.

The cities we played were Tokyo, Osaka, Kyoto and Fukuoka, so we got to see the big cities and some smaller towns, too. It didn't matter where we went, the people came out to cheer us on. You hear how people are very formal in Japan, and they are about things that matter. They love ceremonies and they take it real serious.

But with music, they don't hold back their feelings. They want you to know how they feel, in their own way. In Tokyo, a nice woman named Kayko Shimada came out on stage and gave me a big bouquet of flowers.

She was the local representative of the Ralph Stanley International Fan Club. Japan had more club members than any other country outside the United States.

Being a fan over there really means something, and they buy every one of your records to show their appreciation. The meet-and-greets we did after the shows could get pretty wild. One time, we were sitting at the record tables, signing the programs and the handbills and records, and the line got backed up. Freeland had printed up a souvenir program, and I mean this was deluxe. It had song lyrics and bios and discographies and big portraits of the band members from the *Cry from the Cross* photo shoot. That program like to be as thick as the Dickenson County phone book, and every fan seemed to have one for every Clinch Mountain Boy to sign.

A lot of fans had armfuls of LPs, and they wanted every one of those records autographed, and they usually wanted to get a photograph, too. It was taking a while to get all the record signing and picture taking done, and it got to be too many people packed into the room. The crowd sort of surged forward and shoved the tables back. It happened fast, and we got pinned back against the wall. We almost got crushed, and we were lucky to get out of there alive.

The best thing was how much they appreciated the music. Not just loved it, but really appreciated it. There's a difference, and when you're onstage you can hear the difference from that crowd. We played some big halls and packed 'em, too, with eight to ten thousand. When I'd be talking in between songs, it was so quiet you could hear a mouse's heartbeat. Then, when we'd be playing a song and one of the Clinch Mountain Boys would take a fiddle solo or a guitar break, why, they'd let out a roar like to tear the roof off.

The Japanese fans knew all our songs inside and out. They didn't know English and it didn't matter a bit. They didn't have a clue what the words meant, but they knew the words to every song. They'd holler out requests all night, and they'd sing right along to every verse right through to the encore. What they understood was the feeling behind the songs, and that's all music really is when you get down to it.

I don't know why we're so popular in Japan, but I believe part of the reason is the deep respect they have for tradition; they honor their old folks the same way we honored ours when we were growing up. Lots of the fans were college kids and they held us in high reverence.

Now, the Japanese are very respectful people and they expect you to show them respect in return. In all the towns we played, there were always one or two local bluegrass bands. Over there, people really enjoy playing the music for themselves, and let me tell you they can play bluegrass. After the show and all the signing was done, we'd head over to one of these little beer joints where a bluegrass band was playing. We'd stick around for a while and join them on the stage for a medley or two. The crowd loved it. It was an honor for that band to be onstage with the Clinch Mountain Boys, and it was a way for us to give back the respect they gave us. I would stay for a while just to make an appearance, then head back to the hotel to get some sleep, because that was a tough tour and I needed my rest.

Roy Lee and Jack Cooke and Dick Freeland and some of the others would stay real late and close the place down. It gave Roy Lee a chance to have fun with his banjo, and they really had a time, and it was much appreciated by the fans. It showed that we respected them as much as they respected us.

The tour in Japan was something special. Course, just when you get puffed up, there's always something to bring you back down to earth. For me, it was local politics. The people back home in Dickenson County didn't care how big I was in Japan, and I found out the hard way. We could sell out shows halfway around the world, but I couldn't get elected to office in my own county. You might think it was jealousy or something; mostly it was just dirty, crooked politics.

Here is what happened. Maybe it will be a lesson for anyone thinking politics for a career. Watch out, because there's no nastier business around. Except maybe for the music business. I'd always been interested in politics, and I still am. I like what some politicians try to do for the poor man, and I enjoy following the campaigns and elections because I like a good horse race as much as the next man. Politics is about all I follow outside music; I don't follow sports and I don't have hobbies.

So I liked politics and I figured I'd throw my hat in the ring and give it a shot. I thought to myself, "I can run for office as good as anybody. I ain't no ways a speech maker, but I got some name recognition and some supporters." The first time, I ran for circuit court clerk; that's an eight-year job and a very important position. I ran against a man named Teddy Bailey. He was the most popular Republican in Dickenson County. He had served one term when I took him on. I ran as a Democrat; I've been a Democrat ever since I voted in my first election in '48, when I cast my ballot for Harry Truman. It's the poor man's party, at least the nearest to one I've ever seen.

Well, Teddy beat me by about ninety-nine votes. He come up to me after the results came in and he said, "Now, Ralph, you know and I know you're the most popular man in the county, but when you're in politics you're out the window."

What happened was, the party swapped me out; they used my popularity and money to elect somebody else. I was done dirty. Let me tell you how they do the swapping. What they do is, there are three or four hundred of them in Clintwood on that swapping. The Republicans and the Democrats get together, and they say, "You vote for my man and I'll vote for yours."

They get on the telephone and change the outcome. Here's how they work it. Clintwood is the county seat, and in order to win, you've got to go into the Clintwood precinct with more than five hundred majority votes, and I could never go into Clintwood with more than five hundred majority. That's how they fouled me up, they swapped me out that many votes. My own party done it to me.

The same thing happened when I ran for commissioner of revenue, and they did it again when I ran for treasurer. On that last try, I don't think it helped my cause when we misspelled my campaign bumper stickers: "Ralph Stanley for County Tresuer," but it didn't much matter with both parties stacked against me. I was pretty sore at the dirty stuff they pulled on me in Clintwood. It was a low blow and it stayed with me for a while. At the merchandise tables at our shows, we sell a lot of "Ralph Stanley for President" bumper stickers. It's one of our bestselling items, and it has been for years. Well I'd say I'd come nearer to being elected President of the United States or the governor of Virginia than I could winning a county office here in Dickenson.

It wasn't long after I had got swapped out in one of these elections when I made an appearance on *Hee Haw*. One of the most popular routines on the show was the Kornfield Kounty Salute to the guest performer's hometown. You'd call out your hometown and population, and then all the *Hee Haw* cast members, Grandpa Jones and Junior Samples and all the rest, they'd all together pop out of the cornfield and take off their straw hats and holler out, "SAAAAA-LUTE!"

Course, it was corny as all get-out. It was meant to be funny, but it was also a tribute to all the little towns so many big-name country performers come from. The show's producers knew that most of their audience out there in TV land lived in those same country towns where the stars were born and raised. So really, the Kornfield Kounty Salute was a salute to the people who watched *Hee Haw* and made it such a hit.

Well, I had a sort of a problem when it came to choosing a town to salute. I was raised way out in the sticks—first down in a hollow and then up on a ridge. There were four or five places I could have named. My truest hometown was probably Stratton, Virginia, the name of the post office down by Big Spraddle Creek, where I was born, but there was no more Stratton by this time because the post office had closed down. Then when I moved to Smith Ridge, the nearest town was probably McClure, the little logging camp. But my new house sits atop Sandy Ridge, in between Coeburn and McClure and a long ways from Clintwood. I was still only a few miles from Spraddle, where I was born, and Smith Ridge, where I was raised, but being from the country, I had any number of towns I could have said and still be telling it right.

In past years, Carter would usually introduce us onstage as being from Clintwood, it being the county seat and biggest town in Dickenson. But that was in the days of the Stanley Brothers, before I was on my own, and before the gang in Clintwood had traded me off and cost me getting elected.

So I made up my mind. I went on *Hee Haw* and I jumped out of that cornfield and I waved my hat and I saluted Coeburn as my hometown. Like you might expect, that didn't go over too well in Clintwood. *Hee Haw* was the most popular TV show for country music fans. Every Saturday it had a huge national audience, and nobody in these mountains missed an episode. So when the folks in Clintwood saw me make my salute to Coeburn, they took it as a big slap in the face. I reckon it was, because I was still sore at the way I'd been swapped out in the elections.

Right after that happened on *Hee Haw*, I had to go down to Clintwood on some business. I was at the courthouse to pay for my dog tags, and I went into the treasurer's office, and he was a friend of mine. Naturally, he'd seen me on *Hee Haw*, and he congratulated me and he sort of joked with me about all the trouble it stirred up, especially with people at the courthouse. He said some of the big shots were hopping mad after I saluted Coeburn as my hometown. "Ralph, they aren't real pleased with what you did," he told me. "Judge Phillips said to tell you when I saw you that he was going to disown you because you didn't salute Clintwood."

"You know and Judge Phillips knows exactly why I did that," I said. "And you can tell him I'll never salute Clintwood. Not only that, but you can also tell him I'll salute Coeburn the next time, too." And I meant what I said. At least I did at the time. I even swore to myself not to set foot in Clintwood again unless I absolutely had to.

Today all that bad blood seems so long ago. Things change. You get older, and realize what's important. I guess you could say I forgave Clintwood and Clintwood forgave me. Now Clintwood is where my museum is, right on Main Street, in the old funeral home where Carter was laid out.

It's called the Ralph Stanley Museum and Traditional Mountain Music Center, and it opened in 2004. It's a $2 million museum in a renovated Victorian mansion, and all the exhibits and everything in there are first class, a real professional job. It goes all the way back to my boyhood days on Spraddle and Smith Ridge, and it has exhibits on the Clinch Mountain Boys. If you want to get the whole history of the Stanley Brothers and Ralph Stanley and the Clinch Mountain Boys, you can go to the museum and make a whole day of it. Sometimes I drive down there from home and spend a morning or afternoon in a rocking chair on the porch. I talk to people who visit and reminisce. They come from all over the world, from England and Japan and Australia and Germany and many other countries, and I'm glad to have them.

That's something I'm real proud of, and I'm thankful to the folks in Clintwood for that. I never expected such an honor, not in my lifetime, anyhow. I was real tickled and pleased when that happened. And I was surprised, too. Most people are dead and gone before they get their own museum. Now when I look back at what happened when I tried politics, I don't feel as sore about it anymore. I know that it wasn't meant to be. Maybe I was getting too big for my britches, maybe it was the Man Upstairs telling me to stick with what I knew best—music.

I'm proud of the museum, and I'm also proud of another way I've brought business to Dickenson County. It's the Memorial Festival in honor of Carter that we've held almost every year since 1970.

It was an idea I had not long after he died, but it took a while to get off the ground. Memorial Day weekend seemed like the right time to gather folks together and pay respects to those who've gone on. It's always been a special holiday for people in the mountains and still is. A lot of old-timers still call it Decoration Day, from an old Southern tradition when you would go to the family graveyards and lay down flowers and remember.

The main reason was, I just wanted it as a memorial and to keep Carter's name alive. It was a way to teach some of the new bands coming up, and others too young to know, the history, so they could understand how much he did to lay the groundwork. He and Bill Monroe and a few others had kept it going during the lean years; they believed in it. Carter had worked and sacrificed to pave the way for everyone who come after. He died a poor man, and he never got to see all he had helped get started. Having a big festival on Smith Ridge seemed the best way to honor him and show the love and respect he deserved. I thought the old home place would be magic, the key to it being a good draw. It would give a lot of people a chance to come see where Carter and me were raised and where Carter was buried and where I'll be buried someday.

There weren't too many festivals back then. There was Bean Blossom, the festival Bill Monroe had in Indiana, and a few others. I got busy trying to publicize the festival, because you have to put the word out for an event like that or you won't get enough people to come. That's what happened at the first multiday bluegrass festival Carlton Haney ran at Fincastle, Virginia, in 1965. It was awful far from the cities and so it had poor attendance.

Now, I knew that my festival was even farther out in the sticks than Haney's was, and I gave early notice in the winter edition of the Ralph Stanley International Fan Club publication the *Stanley Standard:* "I will be promoting The Carter Stanley Memorial Festival on the old home place where the Stanley Brothers were born and spent our boyhood life, where I still make my home when not travelling. This will be Memorial Day Weekend, May 28, 29, and 30th. There will be several leading bands and bluegrass artists at the festival. Their names will be published later, along with a map and complete directions of how to find the place. It is about four miles from McClure, Virginia. I would like for every one of my club members to be there."

It's one thing to decide you're going to have a festival. It's another thing to do it. And it took some doing, let me tell you. I had a place for a stage picked out, down in a little ravine below the cemetery. The hillside made a natural amphitheater better than any bulldozer could, a steep slope where people could sit and get a good view of the music. I was lucky to have a lot of help, because I sure couldn't have done it on my own.

Keith's dad, Elmer, being an electrician, helped wire everything, and Ricky's dad, Hobart, was handy with carpentry work. Everybody in the band got a hammer and pitched in. It was like an old-time barn raising, was what it was, only this time it was a music stage we were raising.

We had a big crowd the first year. It snowed, and snow in May is rare. I took it for a good sign. Like the way it snowed for Carter's funeral. The snow sort of turned to ice when it hit the ground, and then it turned into a muddy mess. I didn't like having to play in the cold, but the fans didn't seem to mind, they was too busy enjoying the music. They slid around in the snow and mud and had a real good time.

We built a new stage, with a lot of volunteer help just like the first time. I was helping out on the construction, right along with everybody else. Course, I'm not as good with a hammer as I am with the five-string. I remember nailing down floorboards and I whacked myself good, right on my left index finger. I smashed it something awful, and somebody commented on the fact that I didn't holler out and cuss up a storm like most would. I just squeezed it tight and rocked back and forth and winced out the pain till I could get back to work.

I don't know why I hold things inside me. I think I got that from my mother. I let out my feelings in my music; I reckon it's the only way I know how. Whether that's good or bad, I ain't rightly sure, but it's too late to change now. Anyhow, my finger was black-and-blue for a while, but I just bandaged it up and played as good as I always have.

The music part of the festival was never a problem. I could always get the best entertainers in the business. Bill Monroe was there every year from the start. We swapped out on that; I would always play his Bean Blossom festival and he would always play my Memorial Festival. Once you get Bill, you can get anybody to come.

No, the hard part was getting the fans up the mountain and getting them back down. Most people weren't used to driving those winding back roads. From Coeburn, it's a good fourteen miles along a fairly treacherous two-laner. That road's just about all curves, climbing from the bottom at Tom's Creek up all the way to the top of the ridge. Back then it was still dirt, too. I know a lot of them had never seen such sights as the heaps of slag and the strip-mine benches cut into those hillsides. Maybe it done 'em some good, to see where the energy for their electric heat comes from.

The worst was after the festival was over and the fans tried to leave Smith Ridge and head home. The road's a might easier going down, so that wasn't so bad. All the trouble was on account of the police. The state troopers were real bad there for a year or two. They really gave us some trouble. They tried to say we had too many people. They didn't like the big crowds we drew for the festival. They always harassed our fans and gave me a lot of grief. You'd have folks pulled over and arrested for every sort of infraction.

One year, I had to get up on stage and say something to help the fans. I said, "Anybody want to stay on this mountain tonight, you're welcome to do that. You just wait it out up here and get you down safe tomorrow morning. They won't bother you none then." It was only thing I could do. The police were out to shut me down. It was no secret. Many a festival, you'd have the Wise County jail filled up with people who never been in trouble with the law in their lives. Only thing they done to get locked up was try to enjoy the festival.

It was mostly political, I believe. The Republicans went to the judge over at the county seat in Clintwood and tried to get the judge to order the festival closed down. But the judge was a Democrat and a fan of mine. He wanted to know why, and he was told, "Too many people to take care of, crowds are too big for the police to manage." What they were really saying was my festival was too popular and they didn't like that.

There was opposition to the festival all the way up the ladder. Even the state government didn't do nothing to help, and they were Democrats. I know a thousand or more wrote to Governor Chuck Robb, telling him about what was happening, and he never did do nothing about it. I'd say it got even worse. The police got so bad that people started getting too afraid to come, and attendance dropped off. I finally just had to stop having the festival for a while. It got to be too much.

But politics can get you out of jam just as easy as it gets you into one. The last festival we had before shutting down, the lieutenant governor called and said, "If you ever get ready to have another one, you let me know, and you won't have no trouble at all." So he got to be governor and he was behind me all the way. I had some more friends to help me, too. Rick Boucher, the congressman here in the ninth district, is a fan and a friend. I played shows for him when he was campaigning and helped get him elected.

A few months before the festival, I called Rick and told him we were going to give it another shot. "Don't you worry about a thing," he said. "As soon as we hang up, I'll call the governor and take care of it." And he stood up to his word. I haven't had any more trouble from the authorities.

The festival is the biggest event in Dickenson County, and we're going to keep having it as long as the people want to come. A lot of old, former Cinch Mountain Boys join us on stage and it's like a big family reunion. What we do now is rig up a speaker at Carter's grave. It plays Stanley Brothers songs for the whole festival, day and night. People come by and get their picture taken there; they lay wreathes for him. I think he'd be proud of his little brother that we kept the festival going.

Course, there are always some nasty types that enjoy making sport of other people's sorrows. You run into them once in a while, even up at the Hills of Home Cemetery. They don't want to let nobody rest in peace if they can help it. One of these is a well-known entertainer. Years ago, he came to Smith Ridge to play at Carter's Memorial Festival. He was talking to some of the musicians and he said the real reason he agreed to perform was to get revenge. "I just came here so I could get the chance to piss on Carter's grave" is what he told them.

This fellow was holding a grudge against Carter for something that happened a long time ago. Of course, it was over money. You remember how my daddy used to do the booking for Carter and me back in the WCYB days. Well, this entertainer, he was just starting out like we were, and he went on the station, singing for two or three weeks. But he couldn't book a show; he wasn't getting the invitations for personal appearances like we was. Then some of his band left him and he was having a rough time.

So my dad felt bad for him and said he'd get him some bookings while he was working the station in Bristol. He figured while he was out booking us shows, he'd get this entertainer some shows, too. And my dad got him booked solid for a few weeks, and the fellow got some steady show dates. My dad had told him he'd do it for 15 percent, which was the booking fee rate back then, but the singer wouldn't pay him a dime. So my dad was about to get into it with this entertainer, and it almost came to blows, but Carter stepped in between them. "Dad, you don't need to mess with him," said Carter. "I can handle this." They didn't do no fighting. Carter just stood him down and it was a standoff; the man never did pay what he owed to my dad.

And that was all there was to it. The fellow's grudge against Carter all went back to that. He had kept his hate burning inside for years after Carter's death. I hear he still tells that story about wanting to piss on Carter's grave to anybody who will listen, and when he does he snickers like a smart-aleck kid who thinks he got away with something. Well, he'll never get the chance to do it again, because he's never been invited back to Smith Ridge.

I believe some of the grudge was jealousy. My brother had his weaknesses like anybody else, but he had no time for getting even, he was too busy getting on so we could survive. You couldn't be mean and petty and sing like Carter. I believe that is what's eating at this entertainer; he knows he couldn't touch people's hearts the way Carter could.

Carter was the only singer I've ever known that could make a studio man cry. You can hear the song for yourself, "Sweeter Than the Flowers," that we made for King Records in 1962. I remember the A & R man over in the control booth broke down crying. You can hear Carter's voice break on the line *Mama, when I passed by your coffin, I didn't want to remember you dead.* Any words in a song about mother, well, that would really get hold of Carter.

I've felt it like that, too. Many's the time I've been singing and I've had tears running down, and I see people in the audience doing the same.

The name of this entertainer ain't important. But I'll tell you he's part of the Nashville crowd that's never had much use for the Stanley Brothers because we always did things our way. Carter and I never had handouts or favors given to us. No mentors or friends in high places. We never had managers, excepting our dad for a while in the early days. What we had, we earned.

Some have told me it's my own fault because I never made the move to Nashville and learned to play the game. I don't have a thing against Nashville as a place to make records and play some shows. I play the *Opry* once in a while and I'm happy and honored to do it. I just never felt the need to move my family there and change my life around to fit into Nashville's way of living. I've done just fine staying here in Dickenson County, where I was borned and raised. Right here near the old home place. There's many who agree that I'd be crazy not to stay right here.

There was a man in our area, a fellow who lived not far from here, in a place called Jervis Fork. He was a tough biker type, and he got into drugs and motorcycles and the outlaw life pretty heavy and he finally died of an overdose. He was a regular at my festival, and the one thing that could always bring a tear to his eye was the view from the cemetery on Smith Ridge. He told his wife and everybody he knew, it was the prettiest spot on the planet. Said he wanted to be buried here. So he was.

The first we knew of all this was when all these fellows on motorcycles come by the house, a whole gang of Harleys roaring up Smith Ridge, asking my wife, Jimmi, could they bury the man in the cemetery like he'd always wanted. I wasn't home at the time because we were working show dates out on the West Coast. It so happened I was on the phone with Jimmi when they knocked on the door. It sounded like a sad story, so I told her to tell them it was all right, and to put him off to one corner of the cemetery. They were real polite and thanked Jimmi for the permission. I figured that was the end of it.

But they didn't give him no ordinary funeral. The night before the burial service, all those bikers brought his body up to the cemetery. They didn't need a hearse with all them Harleys. Then they had a kind of get-together right there in the graveyard. It was the wildest wake ever seen around here. Some of our neighbors saw it happen. Along about four in the morning, the dead fellow's biker buddies got kind of carried away and opened up the coffin. They pulled his body out and gave him a shot of this dope they had. Then they rode him around on the motorcycles for a time. I believe they thought they could bring him back.

Anyhow, they finally did put him in the ground. About a year later, the fellow's son died of an overdose, and they done the same with him. He's buried next to his daddy.

There is something I am real thankful for, which is that my mother got the chance to enjoy the Memorial Festival a few times before she died. I knew it meant the world to her, seeing all the people come to pay their respects to Carter and listen to my music. She could see that her boys had made good, and I know it made her awful proud. At the last festival she attended, we had to carry her down the hill in a chair so she could get close enough to see the bands. She had broke her hip and couldn't walk too good. Later I moved the stage because it was too hard for old people like her to get down to it.

She had her health problems in the last few years of her life, but even so she felt better about how things had come to pass. She got to be a grandmother to our little baby girls, Lisa Joy and Tonya Carletta. She had her family around her at the old home place, she had her garden, and she finally knew some peace after so many years of care and worries.

She always said she hoped she'd live to see the day the girls would be old enough to walk over to her house and knock on her front door. We were still living in the double-wide down the road from the old home place; Jimmi would watch Lisa Joy back down the steps of our trailer and take her little toddler steps over to my mother's and crawl up and knock on the door. My mother would let Lisa in the house and they'd have lunch together, and Jimmi would check on them later and they'd be taking a nap in her bed. My mother told me those granddaughters made her the happiest she'd been in years.

The broken hip was her downfall, really. She fell and broke her hip and she went into the hospital and she took pneumonia from laying on her back in bed. It was the pneumonia that finally killed her. Doctor said her heart was good and she'd a-lived to be a hundred or more if she hadn't fell. Anyhow, she never did walk anymore and was laid up at the hospital, and in her mind she was ready. Back then, they didn't do too much at the end, I don't guess. I think a lot of old people are like that; they don't care too much about hanging on with tubes and machines and whatnot. I believe they feel that way, the suffering's too much and they're ready to go.

When she died in May of 1973, my mother was eighty-six years old and she'd lived every bit of it. We laid her to rest next to Carter in the Hills of Home Cemetery. The Primitive Baptists did her funeral; the preachers were Landon Colley and Stuart Owens, same ones who done Carter's. I was too broke up to sing. After all those years, what I dreaded the most had come to pass, like Carter wrote in his song "Memories of Mother":

Mother's at rest in a lonesome old graveyard
With the grass covered o'er it seems so neglected
When the spring season comes sweet flowers will bloom
I'll never forget the love Mother gave us
As children we played around our old home
I know her reward is a mansion in heaven
While children on earth are scattered and gone

She was gone, but I kept her memory alive as much as I could. It's hard to even talk about what my mother meant to me. I wouldn't have been worth much if I hadn't had Jimmi to help me get through it.

Funny how the past sneaks up on you as you get older. Memories come to me when it's late at night and I'm on the road, going down the highway in our bus and can't get to sleep. You get to staring out the window, and your mind just drifts along with that engine and you start to see things. Hear things, too. Memories in the passing lane. Now it's way past midnight and way before daylight.

Seems like it's always that time when I'm on the road, pitch black outside the bus windows, when a bump on the highway wakes me up. It used to be I'd get my bearings and head down the aisle to tell my old bus driver, E. C. French, that it felt like we were about halfway between Lexington and Winchester. Just like the Louvins said, *Kentucky, the dearest land outside of heaven,* and I say, a lot of nice rest stops on the highway.

E.C. would just nod his head. He'd seen me do it many a time, just bolt up out of sleep and holler out a town or county or stretch of interstate. And it's almost always where we are. It's just something I developed after so many years traveling these highways, something you can feel in your bones. Probably only a truck-driving man knows what this is like, a knack you can't get from any map.

Now I can't do it as much; I wake up and don't know where in the world we are.

The road's been good to me, it's how I've made my living. It's wore me down but it hasn't wore me out. I respect the road because I've seen it break many a good man. There wouldn't be any way I could travel like I do at my age if it wasn't for my Prevo bus.

I've had some buses in my day, enough to fill a Greyhound parking lot. The first one I bought was what they call a Silverside, and she gave us her best years until the engine blew up. Then I had a few Eagles, but all these buses were used and wore out when I first got 'em. This Prevost is top of the line, like a Cadillac is to a Chevrolet, the last bus I'll ever need. I got it brand-new just a few years ago around 2003, I believe, straight out of the factory. I took the shell and had her customized at Star City Coach in Roanoke.

I had it partitioned off into rooms. I got myself a private room with a queen bed and a bath and everything, and the boys got one for themselves. By the time all the custom work was finished, the bus cost half a million, and it's been worth every penny. She's carried us nearly 500,000 miles and it's still like a home away from home.

You can watch TV or play cards or whatever you want to do. Get up and walk around when you need to stretch. Get up and go to the bathroom when you have to, don't need to make any pit stops like the old days. Most of the Clinch Mountain Boys that's with me now say they can sleep better on the bus than they can at home.

Usually I can, too, but tonight I'm restless. Can't sleep a wink, even with the rthym of the engine humming all the rest of the boys to sweet dreams. In the old days, I'd likely go on up to keep the driver company, maybe sing a few hymns. But here in my room, with the dark countryside outside my window and me, I'm alone and well satisfied. The room on this bus is as good as any motel room we ever stayed in back in the Stanley Brothers' heyday.

Ernest Tubb died on his bus, and maybe I will, too. Wouldn't be a bad place to go, either. Tonight I'm thinking about Carter, how much he would've enjoyed rolling down the road in this Prevost.

On the night he died, he was talking about how we were finally going to get a bus we'd always planned on. That was the way Carter was, even when he was hemorrhaging on his hospital bed, he wasn't going to give up or give in.

Carter had his heart set on a bus for years. Nothing fancy, mind you. He just wanted something like the one that some of the other bands had. I believe it was Don Reno and Red Smiley that was the first bluegrass act to have their own bus, even before Flatt and Scruggs got theirs.

It's no wonder Reno and Smiley were the first to go for a bus. Don Reno had been in a real bad car accident back in 1952 in West Virginia. When he was recovering in the hospital, he got inspired to write his gospel song "I'm Using My Bible for a Road Map," which was their first big hit. Which goes to show how you can get a good song out of a bad situation.

Anyhow, about '62 I think it was, we played a show with Reno and Smiley somewhere up North. Carter was good friends with both Don and Red, and they let him ride in their bus back South. He slept on the bus, got him some real good rest like he could never get crammed into our car, and ever since that trip he was eager to get a bus for us. Of course, he died talking about getting the bus that would turn it all around for us and put us on the road to success. Well, Carter, we finally got that bus.

Chapter Twenty

Bloody Breathitt and the Boy from Sandy Hook

"Mathie struck the very first blow, it hurt Lord Arnold sore;
Arnold struck the very next one, left Mathie laying dead in his door
He turned his eyes to his wife on her bed, the rage and the hate saw she,
'Who do you like best now?' he said, 'Little Mathie Grove or me?'"

—"Little Mathie Grove," Ralph Stanley

Around seven o'clock on the morning of May 2, 1974, the phone rang by my bedside and I picked it up. The voice of a child came over the line. It was Lennie Centers, Roy Lee's son.

"My daddy's been killed," he said. "A fellow shot him last night when I was with him. Mama said to tell you."

What can you say to a scared twelve-year-old boy who's just seen his daddy shot down? I don't remember what all I tried to say, only that I told him to sit tight and we'd be on our way just as soon as we could.

Down through the years, there's a lot been said about the murder of Roy Lee. A lot of it is just hearsay, you know. Somebody will tell you one thing and somebody will tell you another, and the story gets different every time. Then it gets to where you're nowhere near what's the truth.

I heard that Roy Lee and another fellow were at a party and they played music and whatnot. Of course, there was some drinking involved, and they somehow fell out that night, and whether it was jealousy or the drinking, I was told he was taking Roy Lee home from the party and he took him out and shot him down.

I ain't here to set any record straight because I don't rightly know for sure what did happen. What I do know is that Roy Lee was a good man and a great singer, one of the best Clinch Mountain Boys there ever was—and that the fellow who killed him got away with murder. I want to tell you what I know and what I heard from folks who were there. I believe Roy Lee would have wanted it that way, and so would so many of his fans through the years who've wondered about what led up to his death and what come after.

We had just flown from a tour of the West Coast. All the boys had gone back home to rest up for a few days until our show the next week. Roy Lee went to Jackson in Breathitt County, Kentucky, where he'd been born and raised. Now, Jackson is the county seat of Breathitt, which has got the name "Bloody" Breathitt because of the feuds they've had there down through the years.

This ain't just legends and such, but a lot of killings. There was a long history to it; you'd hear old-timers say Breathitt is as dangerous as a meat-ax. It was a place you'd hear about a lot from anyone who'd been there, to watch out if you ever go through there. If you were an outsider, you were a rank stranger and you weren't welcome.

On the country station in Jackson, there was a local song that got a lot of airplay, "There'll Be No Hippies in Heaven," not the kind of record you'd ever hear out of Nashville. The title of that song tells you pretty well how people in Breathitt County saw things in those days. The man who wrote and sang it, Cager Farler, recorded other songs, like "Black Lung Cadillac," that told how life was in Breathitt. It was a place where working in a coal mine could make you feel safe from all the bootlegging and feuding and shooting going on.

Cager was what you call a go-getter. He had a record store and a restaurant in Jackson and ran a popular bluegrass festival outside of town. The summer before Roy Lee's murder, we played at the festival along with Jim and Jesse, Lester Flatt and Bill Monroe and a lot of other top acts. It rained right through the whole five-day event and still drew twelve thousand people, which shows how much the fans down there love their bluegrass. Now, we always had a good time at Cager's festival. We played many a time in the Jackson area, and we never had problems I can recall. Musicians maybe get special treatment there, at least bluegrass musicians do.

Most of the trouble in Breathitt is strictly between the folks who live there, amongst themselves. And that's what happened to Roy Lee. He was shot down by a man he knew well, a neighbor and fellow musician who was supposed to be a friend.

Roy Lee was like a lot of professional musicians. Even when he was off the job, he was still always ready to go play for fun. I can understand that, because music really does gets in your blood and it's hard to just leave it alone. Seems like there's always somebody wanting to play. But I never went in for picking parties and campfire jams and whatnot. Even at the festivals, when I finished my show I'd always head off for bed when a lot of people like Roy Lee would stay up all night playing. I've taken care of myself and I believe that's why my health has been as good as it has. I play for my living. I don't play for free, and when I go home, I go to get some rest and get away from music. I don't even want to see my banjo, and I don't want to hear somebody else play one, either.

Anyhow, Roy Lee got invited to a birthday party at a farm near his place. He said he was too tired, but his buddies pressed him and he finally gave in. He said he didn't want to hurt their feelings. Since he'd been singing lead in my band, Roy Lee was a celebrity around the area. Mostly that was good, being a Clinch Mountain Boy, but there's always some that's jealous, maybe want to take you down a notch or two.

Roy Lee didn't act like a big shot and he didn't put on airs. He'd moved back to Jackson after spending all those years working a factory job and playing the bars in Dayton. He'd come home to raise his family in the place he was raised, the mountains of eastern Kentucky. Said he wanted his kids to grow up where he did.

He was a hometown boy made good, but he was humble about his success. He didn't need a mansion on a hill to prove he'd made it. He and his wife, Lucille, and their young sons lived in a trailer park on Quicksand

Road near the Jaxon Drive-in Theater. He still drove his old '63 Chevy Nova. He did like to dress sharp when he could, though. On our trip to California, he bought a nice leather buckskin jacket with fringes. He got a matching jacket for his wife, Lucille, too.

Like I said, Roy Lee went to the party just to be a good sport. He didn't want to let his friends down who'd promised that he'd be there. So he put on a blue velvet vest and his new buckskin jacket and told Lucille he was taking Lennie, who was already a fine picker for a boy, and they wouldn't stay late. He grabbed his guitar and banjo, and they got in the Nova and headed out.

The party went the way most parties do when there gets to be drinking and carrying on. There was some drinking and playing music, a fight or two, and more playing and more drinking. After a while, of course, they're all of them drunk. Somebody said Lennie caught some heat for outpicking another man's boy. By all accounts, Roy Lee was feeling fine and rolling with it. They said right before he left the party he stood on the tailgate of a pickup truck and sang "Stairway to Heaven," a gospel song we done on the *Cry from the Cross* album. Probably somebody made a request and Roy Lee didn't want to say no. And he always did love doing gospel, didn't matter when or where. I can see him now, reaching out to the sky, fringe hanging down from that buckskin jacket, head reared back and singing his heart out:

There's a place at the top of the stairway
Where we'll rest when we're all safely there
And friends that believe, someday we will meet
In our homes at the top of the stairs

When the party broke up, it was late, well past two o'clock in the morning. Roy Lee's Chevy Nova was nearly out of gas, so he stopped to get some at the house of a man named Billy Joe Hurst who'd been at the party and lived close by. This is where the trouble started. He and Roy Lee were well acquainted and had known each other for years. This fellow came from one of the rich families of Jackson; they had friends in high places. They were local real estate developers, owned a lot of land, and they'd built the Hurst Shopping Center, which had the area's first supermarket.

Hurst was a fan of Roy Lee, from what they said, and he was am amateur musician, one of those boys like to play wherever there's people around. But he and Roy Lee had been known to argue about their sons, bragging about which boy was a better guitar picker. Maybe he felt like if he couldn't be as good a musician as Roy Lee, his son could be better than Lennie was. That's a mistake, thinking that maybe you can just practice up and will it and you'll be good. You know, that's one thing about music, it tends to run in families, like a good line of dogs, and there ain't nothing you can do to change that.

Roy Lee and Hurst had played together at the party, and that was when those strong words were exchanged over Lennie being a better picker than Hurst's son.

Somehow they fell out that night after something happened in the house. We'll never know why because the half hour Roy Lee was in the house was the only time in the whole night that Lennie wasn't with him. He was waiting in the car outside.

Hurst later said Roy Lee came inside the house for a beer and he was as drunk as a skunk. Said he flirted with Hurst's girlfriend in some way or the other and exposed himself and peed in a planter right there in the foyer. Next thing you know, there was a scuffle and a pistol shot and Roy Lee was running out of the house, his buckskin jacket torn and falling off him.

Hurst was a bonded deputy, and he come out waving his pistol, shouting and pointing. He told Roy Lee he was under arrest and he was taking him to jail. He's armed and dangerous and ain't much use arguing with him. So Hurst ordered Roy Lee and Lennie into his pickup truck and off they go. They headed way out into the boondocks off Highway 30 there, and then he changed routes.

"That's the wrong road there," Roy Lee said. "Where you going?"

"I'm going to take you out here and kill you," said Hurst.

He turned off onto a dead-end road down by a creek way back in the woods. All along the way, he was beating and punching on Roy Lee as they drove. A lot of people have asked how come Roy Lee didn't fight back after he knew what the man was fixing to do. Well, he did. He leaned over and slammed his foot down on the gas pedal and floored it while he grabbed the steering wheel, and yanked it over to make the truck go into a ditch.

But Hurst was still running things, because he had the gun. He told Roy Lee to get out of the truck, and he shoved him down the hill to the creek and they started scuffling. Now, Roy Lee was no pushover. He was a strapping fellow who could hold his own in a fistfight. Friends will tell you he was the type of man who'd beat the tar out of you and then help clean you up and laugh about it.

But Roy Lee knew this was no joke. He was fighting for his life, and for Lennie's, too. He hollered out for Lennie to run for it and that's what Lennie did. Now, Roy Lee may have been unarmed, but he wasn't about to be whipped, so he gave back everything he was getting. Roy Lee finally broke away and ended up catching his breath on a rock in the middle of Cane Creek. Hurst ran back to the truck to grab the gun and headed straight back to where Roy Lee was resting on the rock.

"I'm going to silence that golden voice forever," he said, and he shot him right in the mouth, then two more times in the head. Then he turned around and took the butt of the pistol and beat him all to pieces, and left him to die facedown in the creek.

All this is what Lennie said he saw. He'd run off when his daddy shouted for him to, and he saw the whole thing from a hiding place in the woods.

Roy Lee didn't have what you'd call enemies. He was one of the most well-liked fellows I've ever known. It goes to show that all it takes is one man who don't like you. Now, I don't know all that happened. Most of what I know come from Lennie, who saw the killing happen. But there was the part that happened inside the man's house, when Roy Lee stopped for gasoline and Lennie was out waiting in the car.

I have to believe it was jealousy. Jealousy over Roy Lee and his fame and talent as a musician. Jealousy over the woman, maybe, too. All that jealousy come to a head. Whatever happened back at the house we'll never know for sure. Maybe Roy Lee did flirt with Hurst's girlfriend. Only Hurst knows. But I don't think the killing happened all on account of a woman. Some would rather cut your throat than admit you're a better guitar picker. After Hurst shot Roy Lee, he pistol-whipped him so bad he flattened the trigger ring of that pistol out. That takes some doing. That takes some rage.

Bad as it was, a killing that rough ain't nothing new. The old songs are full of such things, even worse. You got songs like "Little Mathie Grove" I recorded a few years ago. It's hundreds of years old, and probably did happen, in England. Mathie goes out with Lord Arnold's wife and takes her away. He's just a farm boy, really, not from royalty or nothing high, but she loves him all the way. Mathie takes her and shacks up with her all night. Lord Arnold comes in the next morning and catches them in bed. He kills Mathie in a sword fight, then he goes after his wife, too. He cuts her head off and kicks it against the wall.

That's pretty rough, but those songs are about things that did happen and that's why they're still around. They come from things that happen to people. I reckon with a lot of the old songs—"Little Mathie Grove," "Barbara Allen," "Omie Wise," "Banks of the Ohio" and so many others—those things actually did happen and they got turned into songs, and those songs are still living long after the people in the songs are dead and gone. The songs don't die.

And people back in the country here, especially back in the mountains, when they have disputes and arguments, it often leads to a killing. It's not much different from anywhere else. The difference is that in cities you heard about it through newspapers and whatnot. Back in the mountains, where I was raised and where Roy Lee was raised, you heard about it through songs.

Don't matter if it's Breathitt County in the 1970s or England in the 1600s. People don't change that much. Still living and fighting and loving and dying over the same things. You got Mathie Groves and you got Roy Lee Centers, they're the ones maybe with the talent and the ones the women fall for. Then you've got Lord Arnold and Billy Hurst, and they've got everything in the way of money and power, but they ain't got what Mathie and Roy Lee got.

Roy Lee dying like that was rough. I'd have never dreamed something like that would happen to him. He had survived all those years playing the rough beer joints of Dayton, and all it took was a jealous-hearted man to cut him down back in his hometown. Everybody thought the world of Roy Lee. All it takes is one who don't.

Roy Lee was a good lead singer for me and I liked him as a man, too. I never did have a cross word with him all the years we were together. I think he was well satisfied to have his job in the Clinch Mountain Boys, and I was always well satisfied with the job he done. He did his job the best he knew, more than I could ever ask of him. He was always dependable and he was always there when I needed him. He was always on time and he never let the band down. I couldn't have asked for a better lead singer or a better man.

I reckon the drinking got him into trouble the night he died, but in all the years he was with my band, it was never a problem and he never let it interfere with his job. He may have drank a little, but he did it in late hours, on his own time after the show, never when he was with me. Roy Lee had a good character and he was a gentleman. He was always the same in his temperament, meaning you could count on him, and that's important on the road. That's why it hurt so much to lose him and it hurt to lose him from the band. Now I was out a lead singer, the best I'd had since Carter.

We went down to the funeral in Jackson. Roy Lee's family was getting death threats and they were scared that something else bad might happen. Somebody would call the house and tell Lucille that they were going to get Lennie, even if they had to get him at the graveyard. They didn't want him testifying at the trial.

The memorial service was held in the local high school gymnasium, the same gym where Carter had draped his guitar strap around Roy Lee's neck when he was just a little boy seeing his first Stanley Brothers show. The crowd packed the gym to pay their respects, and it was mighty tough to get through the service. The sheriff sat in front of Lennie, close by the casket, in case the threats turned out to be the real thing. We sang "Gloryland" and "Stairway to Heaven," Roy Lee's favorite, the one he sang just before he left the party the night he was killed.

Keith Whitley was singing with us there at the service, and it was good to see him again. He wasn't doing much with music at the time. He was working at a restaurant back home in Sandy Hook, washing dishes. He had come to the funeral with his daddy, Elmer, and his mother, Faye, and we talked about family and about this and that. I always thought they was good people, just as down-home as they come.

We got through with the funeral, and I admit it crossed my mind that Keith might be interested in joining the band. But I didn't mention a thing about the job. It didn't seem the proper place or time to be bringing it up, and I reckon Keith felt the same way. So we said our good-byes and parted ways.

As we were leaving Jackson after the funeral, we stopped off at a restaurant downtown to get us something to eat, and Keith and his parents were in there, too. They invited me over to sit in their booth and I slid in the seat there with the family. That's when Elmer spoke up, because I believe Keith was too shy to say anything on his own behalf.

"Ralph," said Elmer. "I just want you to know that if you ever need a lead singer, I know where you can get one."

All the while Elmer was looking over at Keith, who was just staring at his plate of fried chicken there on the table.

"Well, I need one right now," I said. "Keith, you can start helping me as soon as you can."

Keith looked up with that big Keith Whitley grin and he said he'd be well pleased to do that. So I hired him right there in the diner and he stayed with me for four years.

Before we leave Breathitt County behind, though, I want to tell you how they handled things back then in "Bloody" Breathitt. Lennie testified at the trial, and it took some courage to take the witness stand. The death threats kept coming, but he didn't let that stop him. He'd seen too much to keep quiet. He told how he'd watched his daddy get pistol-whipped and gunned down at point-blank range.

Hurst said Roy Lee had tried to seduce his girlfriend, that's how the whole thing started. And when they were down by the creek out in the woods, he said he shot Roy Lee in self-defense. Said he was in fear of his life when Roy Lee come at him with a rock. The jury believed Lennie and sentenced Billy Joe Hurst to ten years in prison for voluntary manslaughter. That should have done it, but this being Breathitt County where they did things different back then, he served only a month in jail.

I wanted to tell some of this to do some justice to Roy Lee's life. It happened so long ago now, but the stories always kept a-growing. Sometimes you'd hear Roy Lee got himself killed in a drunken brawl like it was somehow his fault. Maybe he was drunk and maybe there was a brawl, but that don't get anywhere near the truth.

He was in the wrong place at the wrong time. About the only thing I know for sure is, Roy Lee was willing to give his own life to save his son. His music lives on, and so does his memory for anyone who knew him. Another thing: I believe Roy Lee got some revenge on the coward who killed him. Lennie went on to become a fine bluegrass musician, and he has passed down the music to another generation, his son Roy Lee II.

Roy Lee's funeral was on a Sunday. We had a show on the coming Saturday down in Mississippi and Keith played with us. So I didn't miss a show without a lead singer. Keith was right there. That's been very fortunate for me. Somebody's been ready to step in every time, even when there was no time to even release or properly warm up the new man on the job. Like with Keith.

Before Keith started back with me, I had some other business to take care of that couldn't wait and couldn't be rescheduled. I had to take my Shriner's degree in Roanoke. It was something I'd set my sights on for a long while. I had joined the Masons in 1970 when I became a member of the Clintwood Lodge. It was something I wanted to do on my own. My daddy and his daddy and all the way back, none of 'em ever fooled with it that I know of.

But I was interested. I knew it was a good organization that did good things for people. A friend had advised me on that and I listened to him and I thought it was the right thing to do. Of course, the Masonry is a secret organization, and you can't let none of it out. I can't talk much about what all we do, but it's from the Bible, a lot of it. If you live as a third-degree Mason, it's as good as any church you ever walked into. If you live it.

A Mason's a third degree, and you have to go through twenty-nine more degrees, like I did, to get the Shriner's degree. The highest degree you can make as a Shriner is a thirty-third degree. You can't get that one here; you've got to go overseas to get that degree. You've really got to be somebody for that. Harry Truman and Colonel Sanders, those are two I know of who got the thirty-third degree. There aren't many. When you're a Shriner, you're part of a brotherhood, and it's a lot to live up to. It sets you apart from the herd, I reckon. I belong to the Kazim Temple of the Shriners in Roanoke, and I'm an honorary member of the Wise County Shriners, too. We do whatever it takes to help the cause with charities and fund-raisers and so forth, and I'm proud to be a Shriner.

The same Saturday we had the show in Mississippi, I drove to Roanoke to take my Shriner's degree at Kazim Temple. They let me out a little early from the initiation ceremony so I could catch a plane south. Keith and the boys in the band had already left and went on. They were waiting for me at the festival. I landed at the airport and rode by car as fast as we could go. Made it about fifteen minutes before we were supposed to go on. I hustled up to the stage like a man late to his own wedding; the boys had their instruments and we barely had time to tune up.

For some reason I've never been able to draw much of a crowd on my own in Mississippi. When it's a festival along with other performers, I do all right down there. I wasn't a bit afraid of how we'd do with Keith, because he knew everything we done in the band. But I could tell that he was nervous. Other than the hymns at Roy Lee's funeral, it had been more than two years since we'd sung together.

We hadn't had time to rehearse because of my initiation. I could see Keith eyeing the musicians gathered around the stage, waiting to see how he was going to make it as my new lead singer. Before, when he and Ricky came on board, he was just a kid along for the ride, and now he was in the spotlight, and he was feeling the pressure.

We got ready to go on stage, but there was still some time while another band finished their show. Keith gave me a worried look.

"Ralph," he said. "Don't you reckon we maybe oughta run over a few songs?"

I didn't even look at him. Just made it seem like a silly question to even ask. I wanted him to know I had faith in him, so I downplayed the whole thing.

"No," I told him. "We'll just go out and sing like we always done." And that's just what happened, and he done a great job, like he always did for me. Keith was a natural, a rare one. A singer like him only comes along once in a good long while.

With Keith coming back as lead singer, that was really when I finally established my own sound. Roy Lee sang so much like Carter that sometimes it was too much. But with Keith, we had our own sound that wasn't as much bluegrass. And I could get my tenor out in front now and get that mountain sound more than I could with Carter or even with Roy Lee. Anyhow, for several years there, I hadn't been able to let it out like I wanted to. I would hold back a little. I reckon I finally felt freed up to get it all out. That was when I took the lead singing a little bit more back in the mountains than ever before.

Another thing that helped the band was, we got a new lead guitar player, Ricky Lee, who was seasoned and ready to go. He grew up in the mountains of North Carolina and had a bluegrass band called the Carolina Tarheels. Roy Lee was the first to recognize Ricky's talent but it took a while to get him on board. He knew all the Stanley Brothers records by heart and he'd seen our new lineup at festivals, so he fit right in with our sound; he could play just like I sang. When you listen to Ricky Lee lay down the melody line on the Carter Family's "Gold Watch and Chain" from my album *A Man and His Music*, you can understand why bluegrass pickers still talk about his playing even today.

Ricky Lee was not only a reliable guitar man, he was like a big brother to Keith, who needed some guidance and strong helping hand, because it wasn't easy for Keith in the early years he was my lead singer. A lot of fans missed Roy Lee just like they missed Carter, and some took a while to warm up to Keith's way of singing. He was interested in all kinds of country music beyond bluegrass, and he could do all styles from Lester Flatt to Lefty Frizzell to Hank Williams Sr. Ricky Lee gave Keith a lot of encouragement and kept him from getting down on himself, and I later heard that many a time he had to lift a plumb worn-out and passed-out Keith up into his bunk bed on the bus after they'd be out all night playing music and drinking at jam sessions.

That summer Keith turned twenty years old. We were on the road when his birthday came and I remember thinking how much he'd grown up. His voice was getting deeper and more like some of his honky-tonk heroes, like Lefty Frizzell. And he could talk even closer to Lester Flatt than Lester.

He had come to be real good buddies with Lester Flatt. He loved him to death and he admired him even more. Lester had mellowed a lot since the early days, and it seemed like just about everyone back then thought the world of him. Lester used to get Keith to do his imitations so he could enjoy Keith doing Lester right there in person.

And Keith took a liking to Lester's old guitar, too. He got to wanting that guitar real bad, until he just had to have it. Part of the reason was, Keith was tired of the guitar he'd been using. It was a piece of dead-sounding, modern junk. Lester's guitar was one of them old beauties, an antique herringbone Martin. But Keith also wanted that guitar out of love for Lester. When you admire someone that much, you want to have something of theirs, maybe the apprentice wanting the master's sword, or whatnot.

A story got around about how Lester just flat-out gave Keith the guitar for a present. I think someone in Nashville started that story, and I believe Keith just let it keep going because it sounded good, and he never bothered to tell all what really happened. Like a lot of times, the truth makes an even better story than the one everybody believes, so here is what really happened.

We were at Bean Blossom, the big bluegrass festival Bill Monroe had every September in Indiana. Earlier in the summer, we'd played at another bluegrass festival, and Keith had finally got up the nerve to ask Lester if he could buy his guitar. Lester surprised him by saying that'd be just fine. They struck up a handshake deal, which was that Keith would pay him $1,200. It was a decent price, because even back then a vintage Martin was fetching big bucks. Lester didn't need the money nohow and had more than one old guitar he used, but he wasn't going to just give one away, neither. But he thought the world of Keith and loved his impersonations and he just wanted Keith to have it for a fair price.

Keith was too scared to go to Lester's bus alone. He was about as nervous as the other time I had sent him over to ask about the Memorial Day Festival. So he got Ricky Lee to go with him, sort of keep him calm and just have a buddy close by. Ricky Lee says Keith was as nervous as could be walking to the bus, with the check for $1,200 in his pocket. You'd have thought he was a teenager going to see his girlfriend's daddy to get his permission to ask her out on a date. The thing was, Keith was afraid Lester was going to back out of the deal at the last second and maybe make it into a big joke.

So Keith and Ricky got into the bus, and they took a seat next to Lester and his road manager. Lester was playing it low-key and letting it drag out. I think he may have wanted Keith to sweat it out a little bit. After a good while, they finally got around to talking about the guitar and the deal they had. Keith just grinned and sort of blushed and pulled the folded check out of his shirt pocket and handed it over to Lester. Well, Lester opened up that check, and he looked it over all squinty-eyed.

"Now, hold it a second, son," he finally said. "Do you reckon there's twelve hundred dollars in all of Sandy Hook, Kentucky?"

Keith couldn't hardly say a word, just grinning from ear to ear, his face as red as a tomato. Lester handed over the guitar, and far as I know,

Keith had that Martin until the day he died. The rest of the time he spent with us, he carried it with him all the time. For years after, Lester would sneak up behind Keith backstage when he'd have the guitar strapped on, and he'd say, "Lester, how long you had that ole gee-tar?" They had a lot of fun with that, Lester doing his best Lester imitation.

Some of my fans say they can hear my style of music become my own about the same time my hairstyle changed, and my hair changed because of Keith, too. What happened was, my hair got more wavy, and I would be trying to tame it before the shows, and one time Keith come over and fixed it up for me and done a good job.

"I reckon I wouldn't mind too much to have this done every day," I said. I was sort of half-joking, but I really did like the hairstyle the way he'd fixed it.

"I'll do it," he said.

After that, Keith would fix my hair up nice before I'd go on stage. He done it just for me, not for nobody else in the band, because he knew it helped me out. Knew I had a lot of things on my mind besides my hair—booking shows and keeping payroll and maintaining the motor home we traveled in and whatnot. Now there was one less thing I had to worry about. That's how Keith was. He just liked to make people happy, and he'd do anything you asked.

The funny thing is, when Keith gave notice that he was leaving to go with J. D. Crowe, he came up and said, "Ralph, I reckon it's time for me to move on. I feel like I need to let my hair down." I was fine with his decision and told him so and wished him all the best. He really did let his hair down, too—it got real long and shaggy.

One of the last songs me and Keith did together was the duet on "O Death." We traded off the verses and he sang, *O Death, You're stiffening my limbs and making me cold / Taking my body from my soul.* For a kid barely in his twenties, he sang like he'd suffered more than most men in a lifetime.

Death finally did get hold of him: I would have never dreamed that Keith would be gone so soon. He died of an alcohol overdose in 1989, just when he was finding commercial success in Nashville. His song "I'm

No Stranger to the Rain" went to number one on the country charts a week after his death. He had so much talent, he could have done anything. He was only thirty-three years old, and his best days were ahead of him, same as Carter and Roy Lee, too.

It hurt me bad when I found out he was gone, but I was proud of what he had been able to do in the few years he had. And I'm just glad I had a little something to do with getting him started in the business.

Before we head out of this sad chapter about Roy Lee and Keith, I want to tell you a little story about Keith and his pranking. Around about 1975, I had a dream of mine come true. I got to go back to school, but I didn't have to take classes or do homework. All I had to do was play music and talk about playing music. I wish school had been more like that when I was coming along. It was at Lincoln Memorial University, in Harrogate, Tennessee. They had some professors there, and they loved my style of mountain music. They held a seminar on the Stanley Sound.

I hadn't been in a classroom since 1945. I never really did like school and I especially didn't much like Ervinton High School. Back then, it was eighth grade through eleventh and that was the end of your schooling. Mine was the last class to graduate after eleventh; after that, they went to twelfth grade. Even with a year less, I was pretty lucky to graduate at all, because my heart was never in it.

In those high school years, I was always busy helping my mother on Smith Ridge. There was always something to do, so I was kind of bad for missing classes. I'd either be too tired or some chore would keep me from going. I had a good friend named Alice Nunley who helped me out. Now, Alice was one who liked to talk in class, and I would be listening more than talking, but we'd both get in trouble. The teacher would punish us both. We'd have to write five hundred times, "I will not talk in school." And Alice would write hers and she'd write mine, too. Her handwriting was close to mine, so the teacher never knew the difference.

Alice felt sorry for me having to miss school to help out with chores. So if I missed a day, when I'd come back to class, I'd find all my lessons in order and turned in to the teacher just like I was there. I have to thank her now, because she's the one that got me through school. Without her help, I don't know how I would have made it.

The only subject that I took a liking to was agriculture and farming. I had a teacher named Orville Deel, who taught the agricultural class at Ervinton, and he was one of the best I ever had. He got me interested in veterinary medicine, and I was figuring on making a career of that if the music didn't work out. I was full of notions back then. Every summer, as part of our grade, we had to do a summer project for the Future Farmers of America, and mine was a pig.

I thought it was something I could do well, caring for cows and livestock and such, since I'd been around them all my life. I thought it would be a good career because I liked pigs and cows, and if I was a veterinarian I could doctor to them. If someone's dairy cow, like our milk cow, Pied, took down with something, I'd be able to help. I was a good student in Mr. Deel's class because it was something I cared about. I liked learning about all the different breeds, hogs especially.

Well, I was getting good marks and everything until we had to go out in the field. For a class project we had to go out and work on some sick animals. It wasn't what I thought it was going to be like. I thought a vet would maybe tend to a calf or check on a lame horse. There was some of that, but it was a lot more. I learned to castrate hogs and I had to castrate a few bulls, too. I didn't think much of that.

So after my earlier struggle in school, I was happy when they asked me to teach a class at Lincoln Memorial University. The man who made it happen was Dr. Douglas Gordon, a professor in the English Department. He was a fan of my music and he believed in my style; he thought it was worth something for students to learn about. Dr. Gordon called me and asked if I would come down and lead the classes.

I didn't hesitate at all. I was thinking about what the principal at Ervinton High School had told Carter and me when were first starting out. "Why don't you boys throw down that music and get you a real education so you can make a living?" Well, I reckon the music had done me better than most jobs could have. And now here was a university asking me to teach my music. I told Dr. Gordon I would bring the Clinch Mountain Boys and we'd be raring to go.

Lincoln Memorial University was an easy drive from Dickenson County, a little ways south of Johnson City in eastern Tennessee, at the Cumberland Gap. We drove down in the Winnebago for the first seminar in December 1975.

When we got there on the campus, though, I sort of wondered what I'd got myself into. All the big stone buildings and professors walking around, carrying their briefcases full of lecture notes; they'd all wrote books and whatnot. I was a musician, but I didn't think I was much of a teacher. I told Dr. Gordon I would teach all that I knew. But I could have told the students in ten minutes all I knew. I wasn't sure what I was going to say. I didn't know nothing. Except playing music.

The university had advertised about the class, and there was forty or fifty students from all over the East Coast; a few came down from New York. Me and the band stood at the head of the class, and the students sat at their desks, waiting to learn about the Stanley style of music. I thought to myself, "This is supposed to be a four-day course, and I'm not rightly sure how we're going to get through the first day." I looked over at Curly Ray. He was the man who could win over any crowd, but he was as nervous as I was. Curly had got his schooling in the coal mines; he could barely write his own name. He must have felt like me: "What in blazes are we doing here?"

Well, Dr. Gordon made it work. What we did was play music and tell stories. Now, that was something we could do, and the whole thing worked out fine. Curly did win over those students, just like he could win over a crowd of mean-looking, hard-drinking miners on a Saturday night. He showed how you don't have to be a scholar to be a gentleman. And when he showed off a few tricks he liked to pull on "Orange Blossom Special," those students got a lesson in showmanship.

I told them I considered myself a singer more than a banjo player. Banjo pickers are a dime a dozen, but a singer can carry a band, which was what I'd been doing ever since Carter died. "Singing is what keeps me going," I said. "It's what I was borned to do. It would suit me to lay the banjo down and just sing."

Of course, I knew that a lot of them had come to hear my banjo, and I didn't want to let them down. One thing I thought might be useful to them was to show how my banjo was just an instrument, it wasn't much different from any other. Nothing tricked up. I told them how in the early days, back in the fifties, when I first got that 1923 Gibson Mastertone, I'd take it apart every once in a while and sand it down. Clean it up and keep the chrome from rusting out. "You've got to loosen the strings a little and take the bridge out and sand it down," I said. "That'll give you a sharper, better tone." It was a way to keep it in good shape like you would any tool you might use a lot; I think my maintenance helped keep that bright tone.

I said it was best to keep it simple, right down to the strings you use. I never was much at changing strings on my banjo. I've had the same strings on a banjo for over a year. I'd just play 'em till they broke or till they got that dead sound. After you play the same strings for a while, they will eventually go dead on you. The trick a lot of people don't know is when one string breaks, you need to change them all. But you don't need to be worrying about new strings. I never was real rough on my strings like some banjo players, so the strings last me a long time and sound good the whole while.

I'd play a few numbers and slow it down to show them some of the fingering. Help 'em see how you worked the fretboard and such. I did "Clinch Mountain Backstep" and a few others. I told them songwriting, especially when it comes to instrumentals, is something I didn't understand much myself and I wish I could share some tips on how to do it but I didn't rightly know. The songs I've done pretty much wrote themselves. They come to you and you try to work them out and remember how they go before they get away from you. All the best banjo tunes out of the fifteen or twenty I wrote were the simplest.

"The only way I can explain it is to tell you to try to keep it simple," I said. "It sounds crazy but it's true. All the songs I write are real simple. They're so simple that a good musician can't even play them, hard as they try. I've had the best banjo players around tell me that a lot. They couldn't play the tune because it was too simple."

The next year, the university had another seminar in Harrogate. At the end of the classes, they presented me with an honorary doctoral degree in music. On the same day I got my college degree, I got a bill I wasn't expecting. It was a strange thing that happened, and I wasn't even involved. Now that classes were over, the Clinch Mountain Boys had got a notion to have some fun. I was at the campus, accepting my award from the university officials. Meanwhile, they were back at the motel room, raising holy hell.

From what I heard of what happened, it all started with Curly Ray. He was the instigator and the main agitator. And Curly Ray had a lot of help from Keith Whitley. Which didn't surpise me, since the horseplay always started with those two.

The deal was, Keith got hold of some firecrackers, and he and Curly decided to celebrate the end of classes right there in the room. So they got to lighting the firecrackers and busting them on Curley Lambert's head. If you're having trouble keeping track of your Curlys, well, Curly Ray was the big one with curly hair and Curley Lambert was the bald-headed one we sometimes called Goat. Curley was mostly bald and had him a big wide forehead, so it was a good place to throw the firecrackers.

The thing was, Curley was helping them as best he could. He was sitting still on the bed to give them a good target. Well, some hit the bull's-eye and some didn't. Curley was all right, the firecrackers didn't do him any damage, but they tore the hell out of the motel room. It was a big mess, burn marks and everything all sooty and trashed.

The room was in my name and I got the call from the motel manager. He was going to charge me to get the room fixed and redone the way it was. It was a couple hundred dollars. I called the band together and had a big talk with them. I was ready to set things straight. That wasn't the way I expected the Clinch Mountain Boys to behave. But when they got to talking about the fireworks popping off Curley's head, I started laughing right along with 'em. They shouldn't have done it, but they were just letting off steam and having fun. I couldn't say much about it, because they had such a good time and I had a good laugh, too. When you're on the road, you need some laughs to pass the time. So to me it was worth the money. I paid the bill and that was the end of it.

Getting the honorary degree in music, though, I took that awful serious. It meant a lot to me. I remembered again what the principal at Ervinton High School had said to Carter and me. It always stuck in my mind. I wonder what he would have thought of me earning my music degree at a university. He was wrong that you can't do good with music. That's how I got the title "Doctor" without ever even making it to veterinary school. And I'm real proud of it.

And you know, playing in my band has given many a musician a pretty good education down through the years, even if you don't get a college degree. There's been so many, Larry Sparks and Ricky Skaggs and Keith Whitley and others, who found success on their own, and they've done me proud. And Keith should have been the biggest success of all.

Now, with Keith, I have to tell you I knew he had a problem with drinking. It went back to his teenage years, I think. But he didn't let it interfere with his music, at least not when he was a Clinch Mountain Boy. It was a personal problem, maybe, but not a professional problem at that time. He may have done it after hours and when he stayed up late playing and drinking after shows, but he never did it around me, except for one time.

It was on the last tour with us. We were playing some shows in California, and he got to hanging out with a movie star he knew, a buddy of his. Keith was real fond of motorcycles. He loved his Harley, and he was always riding back home in Sandy Hook when he'd lay off from music. This movie star was also a motorcycle rider, and he was shooting a movie about bikers, and Keith went to visit him on the set. They were filming the movie close to where we were playing in Los Angeles, and Keith got connected with him and he got drunk, really drunk, and he barely made it back before showtime.

He showed up on stage just a mess. He was in no shape to get anywhere near a microphone. I wasn't so much mad as I was disappointed. Keith was the kind of person you couldn't get mad at.

"I can't use you on this show," I told him. "You go out in the audience now and sit and watch us play. Just sit tight and try to sober up for the second show."

He looked at me sad; he was ashamed of himself. He didn't get defiant or belligerent like some drunks will do. "I'm sorry" was all he said. Keith was like that. He felt bad. He knew he'd let the band down. I knew he didn't mean no harm. He'd just got himself carried away with the motorcycle star shooting the movie.

So Keith went and sat in the audience and we put on the show while they poured coffee down him. And by the night show, he'd sobered up and he was ready and he done fine. You'd a-never known the shape he was in that afternoon, the way he straightened out and sang his heart out, too.

Keith was a nice boy. What hurt me so bad was, Keith was really getting ready to do something when it happened. He was getting popular in Nashville, and finding success on the charts, and I was proud of him and so glad for him, too. He'd worked hard to make his own style. He'd come out of bluegrass, but he found his own kind of country, from not only his East Kentucky mountain tradition but the honky-tonk tradition of sad ballads like Lefty Frizzell and George Jones done so well. Nobody sounded like Keith. When you heard him on the radio, you knew who it was.

If he had lived, he would have been one of the greatest singers Nashville ever saw. But he had something deep down inside him that wouldn't let him alone.

Chapter Twenty-one

The Old Kentucky Foxhunter

"Hello, Friends and Neighbors. This is Curly Ray Cline, the fiddle player with Ralph Stanley. We're looking forward to seeing all you nice people in Japan. So you all come out and be with us and we will try and put you on a nice show."

—from the Official Souvenir Program Book for Ralph Stanley and the Clinch Mountain Boys on Japan Tour, April–May 1971

I told you earlier how my kind of music needs a fiddle to make it sound right. I've always liked to feature the fiddle in my band, and I try to have a fiddle on every song I can. That's how I first heard music when I was a boy. Just a fiddle and a banjo. It sounds right to me, the way mountain music should sound.

Fiddlers are a different breed than you or me. There have been so many good fiddlers in my bands through the years, and I've enjoyed them all. Some are a lot better than others. But one stood above all the rest, and he was a good bit wider than most of them, too, much as he liked to eat. The fiddler I'm talking about was Curly Ray Cline. He was my fiddle player longer than any other, and he was probably my favorite entertainer of all time. We were together twenty-six-and-a-half years, through thick and thin, the good times and the bad. He was with me more years than I was with Carter.

The hardest thing I ever had to do was to let Curly go. Healthwise, he got to be where he wasn't able. But I'm getting ahead of myself.

When I started writing this book, I decided right off that Curly was going to get his own chapter. The same way he always got his own part of the show, when he'd cut loose with his fiddle and do his little Curly Ray dance and whip up the crowd when they needed whipping up. Nobody could work a crowd like Curly; it didn't matter if the crowd was in Kyoto, Japan, or Jackson, Kentucky, he could win their hearts. All over the world, people loved Curly. Whenever the show was dragging, I could always count on Curly Ray to get things moving. Seems like that's where we are now in the book, at a good place for Curly to get some time in the spotlight.

First, let me start with a little story. Curly wasn't only a fiddler. He was a foxhunter. He loved foxhunting as much as he loved fiddling. Maybe more. Now, for me, foxhunting is one of those things I can take or leave. Most times, you don't get the fox and that's not the purpose anyhow. When you go foxhunting, you're mostly just out there to hear the dogs bark. You listen to the dogs get to running that fox for as long as the chase lasts, and the fox goes into a hole, and that's the end of it. It lasts a couple of hours.

That's what Curly liked best about it. It was more of a pastime than a sport for him. It was more about the dogs than it was about the fox. Curly would go out in the woods under the tall trees and build him a big fire and sit and listen to the dogs run and he'd make a whole night of it.

I'll take coon hunting any day. There's more action to it and more of a point to it. Most of the time you get the coon. If you've got a good dog, he'll tree it and you have more of a payoff to my mind.

So I was out on a foxhunt with Curly Ray. It was in the woods where he lived in Rockhouse, which is farm country in Pike County, Kentucky. It was in the late fall, a real cold, wet night where you wouldn't even want to be outside unless you had to be. Curly had his best dogs out there; he spoiled those hounds rotten, he really loved them. The chase hadn't even started yet, and it was hard to tell who was more excited, Curly or the dogs. I felt cold and tired, but I went along because it meant a lot to him to have me along.

The dogs jumped the fox and they were running it down the mountain, barking every breath, and Curly was really enjoying all the commotion. He was just beside himself, smiling his big piano smile like he'd get during a fiddle break onstage. Up ahead of us ran the pack of hound dogs. By the sound of it, they was gaining on that poor ole fox. It was dark, so we couldn't see the dogs, but we could hear 'em fine, barking so loud it like to split your ears.

Curly Ray stopped to catch his breath and rest up a while and then he pulled on my arm. "Lord, won't you listen to that music?"

"Well," I said, "I don't hear nothing but them dogs a-barking." But it was music to his ears.

Onstage, I always introduced Curly Ray as "the old Kentucky foxhunter from Rockhouse, Kentucky," and I know that made him proud. It really does describe Curly as good as anything. Outside of music and his wife, Verdie, Curly loved foxhunting more than anything in the world, and what he loved most about foxhunting was his dogs.

When we were on the road, people would always come by after the shows and they would give Curly all kinds of hunting dogs, from the finest purebreds to the sorriest mutts you ever saw. Mostly, they'd give him just about any kind of foxhound you could think of. Whether they was any good or not, Curly didn't care. They'd put the dog off on Curly Ray, and he never did refuse one that I know of. It didn't matter what dog it was, he treated it like it was worth thousands of dollars.

One time we played a pretty good joke on Curly Ray. A fan gave him a real fine-looking foxhound, and we were carrying the dog with us on the bus. Now, we'd done this many a time, but this hound turned out to be a real whiner, and of course he wasn't housebroke. The bus wasn't made to be a kennel, and the dog was getting on my nerves.

After a few days with the hound riding along, we had a show date at a club where I dreaded to play every year. I never could stand the MC who ran things there. He liked to push people around, and he talked big but he didn't make a bit of sense. He was what you call a fool. We were at the parking lot before the show, and he was saying this and that, and none of it didn't amount to nothing, when I heard Curly Ray's hound dog a-barking from the bus. It gave me an idea. Kill two birds with one stone.

I went back over to the bus and called two of the Clinch Mountain Boys, I won't tell you which of them they was, and I told them what I was fixing to do. With the boys in my band, I don't need to do a lot of explaining, Don't matter if it's about how to play a song or how to pull a prank, they usually get my point pretty quick. That's why I hire them, not only because they can play my music but because they understand the way I think.

"Boys," I said. "There's Curly's dog, and there's that fella's pickup truck. You know what to do."

They went to our bus and came back with the dog.

"That's a nice leash on that dog," I said. "When you finish the job, I want the leash."

They took the dog and did exactly what I told them. The MC had a topper on his pickup and he'd left it unlocked. They put the dog in the back and came back with the leash. I set the leash in the bus back where Curly could find it.

After the show, we made sure to watch the MC pull out of the parking lot, with the dog in the back of his truck. We never did find out how far down the road he got before he heard any barking. Then Curly came back to the bus with some scraps, but he didn't have no dog no more. It was just the leash. Curly didn't know for sure who done it to him. He always suspected it was the band pulling a prank on him, but he never could prove it. For a long time after that, he tried to get it out of us, but we didn't say nothing.

Not that long after that, another of Curly's dogs went missing. This time we were somewhere near Memphis, heading back home from a tour out West. Curly had got him another dog, and we'd made it near a thousand miles with the hound taking up two seats in our bus. This dog I took a liking to. He reminded me of a coon dog Carter once had. He was what you call mellow—as long as there was no fox or squirrel or coon around.

We stopped at a restaurant, and Curly tied the dog up right outside the front door. It was crowded in there, and the waitress put us in a booth way in back, where Curly couldn't keep an eye on the door. We ate our dinner and forgot all about it. When we came out, the dog was gone. This time the leash was gone, too. Curly was sure one of us done it. But we were all innocent this time. Somebody stole the dog. He always believed one of the Clinch Mountain Boys done it. But it was a real dog-napping.

Curly never did change his ways about his dogs. When he got old and feeble, Curly finally quit foxhunting because he couldn't get around too good anymore, but he still kept his dogs, till they all got old like him, you know. And some of 'em would get in poor health, but he wouldn't sell 'em or give 'em to nobody. If he got hold of a hound, it was for life, and that dog had a home until it died. That's the way Curly Ray was.

The same loyalty he gave to his dogs he gave to me. I believe if I'd told Curly to jump off a cliff, he would've jumped. He was that loyal and he was that dedicated to me. He gave twenty-six-and-a-half years of honest and dependable service. I couldn't have found a better man or a better fiddle player. He respected me all the way.

The truth of it was, I needed Curly as much as he needed me. When I started on my own in 1966, after Carter passed away, I had two ways to go, up or down, and Curly was the man who helped me go up. He was in there for me day or night, whenever I needed him. He was the life of the show, and he was my right-hand man and my first lieutenant, and he done such a good job for so many years.

He was a wonderful fellow to travel with. He was a good man to keep things humorous after Carter was gone. It didn't matter if he was on the stage or not. There was always something going on. He helped make all them hard miles we rode together go by a lot easier. When we were on the bus, let me tell you, Curly had the floor. He kept us well entertained. Curly wasn't a comedian, not the kind that tells jokes and one-liners. He was just funny, whether he meant to be or not. He would say things and do things. He came across as funny, he was just natural that way.

Now, Curly liked to have his fun, but he was a hard worker all the way. I've never had a man more dependable than he was. He was never, ever late, and in the whole time while he was with me, he never missed a show that I know of. I remember when his mother passed away, we took him by there for the viewing and he saw her laid out, and right after the funeral, he went on with us to a show that night. He was grieving, but he knew it was his job and he had to do it no matter what. He was as dedicated as they come.

Curly used to tell the story of how he won a fiddlers' contest when he was barely thirteen years old. This was back in the 1940s, when fiddle players had big followings, the way wrestlers and football stars did. Curly entered a big competition in West Virginia and he was up against some of the best players around. There was Georgia Slim and Skeets Williams and the most famous of all, Fiddlin' Arthur Smith. Fiddlin' Arthur was the man Leslie Keith played to a draw at a contest in Bluefield.

All these fiddlers were famous. They were older, they were better, and they had more experience. But Curly had something on 'em, and that was good old-fashioned showmanship. He got up on that stage and played "Orange Blossom Special," and he grinned his piano smile and he laughed and he danced and he pulled every stunt he could think of to win over the crowd. He took top prize, and the other fiddlers were mad as hornets about this chubby kid clowning his way to an upset.

Arthur Smith hated trick fiddling worse than anyone. He could play a solo for half hour or more and never repeat himself. He took his fiddle playing serious. Arthur was a real long-faced, lean fellow, sort of the way Stan Laurel looked. Well, he stormed over and he yelled right in Curly's grinning face, "You ought to be shot!"

Fiddlin' Arthur was a better musician, but Curly knew one of the secrets of show business. Life is sad and people want to forget their troubles for a while and laugh and be entertained. Curly was born happy and his gift was to make other people happy, at least for a little while.

Many a time I seen Curly save a show from dying. He would take his fiddle bow and wave it around like it was a magic wand. That's when even the deadest crowd would come to life. Curly'd be waving his bow, sweat pouring down his face, and he'd take a handkerchief and dry himself off, and keep waving the bow until he heard the crowd make some noise. It was like he was saying, "Come on and join me, I'm having fun up here, come with me." And the people always did come with him.

It wasn't just a stage act, though. The man you saw onstage was the same man you got in person. And that's why Curly was one of the finest salesmen I've ever seen. Selling is something people don't always understand, especially nowadays. Selling got a bad reputation somehow, like when you hear a fellow is bound to "sell out" and not be true to his talent. I'm talking about old-time selling, which is moving merchandise off a table and making customers feel good. Curly was so good, he sold his records to people who didn't even own a record player.

At the festivals, you'd see Curly set up his record table, and there'd be all these well-known fiddle players nearby sitting at their record tables. They'd be working hard to push their stuff, but it didn't come off natural. Too much of a hard sell. Like they weren't enjoying it. So you'd have hardly any fans coming up to buy their records. And these were the best fiddlers in the business.

Then you'd see the people lined up at Curly Ray's table. He's smiling, they're smiling, everybody's happy. And I'd be standing there, right next to these other fiddle players sitting there glum while Curly would just work that crowd and peddle them records. A great fiddle player once told me he'd given up trying to compete with Curly, while we stood there and watched him work the table.

"Lord have mercy," this fiddle player said. "How in the world does he do it?"

"Personality," I told him. "You don't have it. I don't have it. There's not many have it. Carter had it, and Curly Ray's got it, too."

Curly Ray sold souvenir key chains along with his records. The key chain was a real cheaply made thing, with a little blurry black-and-white photo of Curly Ray on the side, like a booth prize at a county fair. He sold so many of these key chains, there was one company did their biggest business from Curly, made more of his key chains than any other product. There weren't many times when Curly didn't talk a fan wanting a record into getting a souvenir key chain along with it.

It was a cash-only business back then, selling records and souvenirs at the shows. Curly Ray would come back from road trips flush with every denomination from one-dollar bills to one-hundred-dollar bills, and everything in between. He'd have so many loose bills on him, just wads sticking out of pockets and whatnot, it got to be comical to watch him try to handle his earnings. Keith and Ricky would always be asking how much money he had from selling his records that day. They bothered him no end. So Curly finally started hiring out Keith and Ricky to count his money. He'd charge them each a dollar to count it all out. They thought it was fun, handling those big stacks of bills like they'd robbed a bank. Only Curly could pull off something like that. Get them boys to count it for him and make another dollar off each of them.

Curly didn't believe much in banks. He didn't have a checking account and he paid all his bills in cash. He had his own way to deposit what he earned. Ricky Lee got to see how he done it. Ricky was handy with construction work, and Curly somehow talked him into helping dig the top off his septic tank at his place in Rockhouse, Kentucky. After they were done with the septic tank job, Curly Ray took him down in the basement. Had something he wanted to show him.

Ricky Lee said he could hardly believe it. There were quart Mason jars lined up on shelves, like what you'd use for moonshine or preserves. Instead of liquor or strawberry jam, Curly had filled the jars with cash money from all his record and souvenir sales. Some jars had 100 one-dollar bills. Then there were jars with 100 five-dollar bills, and jars with 100 ten-dollar bills, twenty, fifty and so on. Curly Ray had rolled up the bills and stuffed them into the jars. That was his bank. And he said there were plenty more jars buried out in the yard.

There were lots of old-time country musicians that did the same as Curly with their money. Stringbean got killed because of it. Stringbean's real name was Dave Akeman, and he was the man playing the banjo the first time I saw Bill Monroe when I was a boy. I always liked Stringbean's frailing banjo, and he was also one of the best comedians in the business. He was tall and skinny with a long, sad face, and he wore a shirt that hung down to his knees. He could be funny just standing onstage and not saying a word. In his later years, Stringbean worked on the *Grand Ole Opry* and *Hee Haw,* just like Grandpa Jones did.

For years, you used to hear how Stringbean kept money stashed in his cabin outside Nashville. In 1973, a couple of robbers went out to the cabin and hid in there, waiting for Stringbean and his wife, Estelle, after String finished his Saturday night show at the *Opry*. The robbers couldn't find the money and shot Stringbean after he wouldn't tell 'em where he hid it. Then they killed Estelle, too. All they ended up stealing was some guns and a chain saw. It was Grandpa Jones who found the bodies. The thing was, Stringbean really did have money stashed in his cabin. They found $20,000 in cash behind a brick in the chimney. But the bills had rotted, so it wasn't worth nothing.

Old-timers like Curly and Stringbean came up in the Depression years when people lost everything, and they didn't trust banks to hold their savings. They wanted to make sure they knew where their money was. I know how that is. I'm awful tight with my money, too. But Curly was real close with his money. In plain old words, he was tighter with a dollar than any man I ever knew.

One time we had all the Clinch Mountain Boys sitting together at a restaurant out near Dulles Airport in Northern Virginia. It wasn't a fancy place, but the prices seemed a mite too steep for Curly's liking. Everybody at the table ordered a regular meal, but when the waitress asked for Curly's order, he told her he wanted a spaghetti dinner from the children's menu. She looked at him real stern. "Sir, you're too old to order from the children's menu," she said. "But we have an adult spaghetti dinner at an adult price."

Well, Curly was having no part of it. He had to have the children's spaghetti dinner at the discount price. Somehow he won the waitress over, and she went from being mad at him to feeling sorry for him. And Curly wasn't trying to be difficult or deceitful. He was just being Curly. He finally did get her to bring him what he wanted.

He'd squeeze every nickel into a quarter. It got to where the boys in the band would throw change on the ground and get him thinking he'd dropped some of his own coins. They'd really have him worried he had holes in his pockets and was losing money.

It took some real doing to talk Curly Ray into recording his own solo albums, because he didn't think there was any money in it. He'd done so well working the table and selling my records, I figured he should sell his own albums. I finally tried to talk him into recording on his own and making some extra cash. He was afraid to risk it. In plain old words, he was just too tight to put up the money to record his own album.

I figured he'd do better than well and the people would take to it. I finally told him to go ahead and record an album and make five hundred copies and sell 'em at shows. See how it goes. I said he didn't have to put up a dime, I would cover all the costs, because I believed in him. "Don't worry about the money," I said. "If it don't work out, you don't owe me nothing." That was the only way I could get him to record.

He gave in, and I think he was well satisfied he did. I was, too, because I didn't have to pay. He done fine with those records. People wanted to hear Curly Ray as his own man, doing songs he liked to do. I helped him on his albums, and I was glad to do it. He was a good singer, and I liked to sing with him. I could sing a whole lot better with him than I could with a certain fellow who traveled with us awhile and was supposed to be our lead singer. I could feel it a lot more with Curly Ray.

Curly's albums are in a class by themselves. I believe his first one for Rebel was called *They Cut Down the Old Pine Tree*, from around 1971, and then he just kept making records until he ran out of material. Early on Curly realized the more goofy he got, the more records he sold. He had album titles like *Boar Hog* and *Chicken Reel* and *Who's Gonna Mow My Grass?,* full of the silliest novelty songs. He usually cut 'em in a couple of hours, with a few Clinch Mountain Boys there to help him out. I'd usually play on a few cuts, too; we'd do the songs in one take, and sometimes we couldn't get through a tune without busting out laughing, and we'd leave it just like it was.

Curly Ray spent more time working on the album covers than he did making the record. He had an album called *Fishin' for Another Hit*. Course, he'd never had anything close to a hit, but he liked that for a title. On the cover, he's standing in knee-high wading boots by the side of a lake, and he's showing off his big catch on the end of a fishing pole. Well, I'm here to tell you what he done was, he found a dead catfish on the bank there, and he stuck that smelly old thing on the hook. If that ain't low-budget, I don't know what is.

For the cover of *Why Me, Ralph?* Curly's poking his head out of a coal mine. You'd think he was trapped in there and trying to escape. Now, that wasn't all made up; there was some truth in that. Curly did work in a coal mine for a while before he went full-time with me. See, he worked in them West Virginia mines where if a man died, they'd lay him over in the corner of the mine shaft and finish out the shift. It was some tough times. Curly was always grateful I helped get him out of the mines and found him a permanent job in music.

But he never lost his coal miner's loyalty; he was a company man whether he was working in the mines or playing in my band; that's why he was such a good lieutenant for me. You see, his hero was John L. Lewis, head of the United Mine Workers, who did a lot to make life better for the miners. Lewis would get locked up, and the mine workers would put in money and raise funds and bail him out. And Curly was as loyal to me and the Clinch Mountain Boys as he was to John L. Lewis and the UMW.

Anyhow, the *Why Me, Ralph?* album cover is good, but the cover he did for *Chicken Reel* is probably my favorite. Curly's got a rooster by the legs, upside down, and he's got a big smile on his face, like he's fixing to make dinner. Well, you can be sure he didn't kill the rooster. He just borrowed it for a while from the neighbors of Roy Homer, who had the basement studio in Clinton, Maryland, where we recorded for Rebel. The neighbors was Roy's in-laws, and they kept chickens in their backyard, and it gave Curly the idea to take a photo with the rooster.

Curly had a lot of fun making his records, and there's a lot of fine music besides the silliness. He always liked to have some pretty gospel tunes on his records, and he was a good singer when he wanted to be. He could get serious when he got the notion.

Once Curly came home from the road and found one of his huntings dogs dead. Name of Trail. He'd jumped a fence while he was tied to the doghouse, and he'd got tangled in the leash and he hung himself. It really shook up Curly and he was sad for weeks. Curly grieved it out with a song, and he recorded it on his album *Smarter Than Your Average Idiot*. It was called "A-Hanging" and it was set to the tune of John Anderson's number one country hit, "Swinging," from 1982.

Rod was on the sofa eating rhubarb pie
Verdie was in the kitchen cutting possum up to fry
I went to feed old Trail and he was still tied to his chain
He's jumped across the fence and now he's howlin' in the rain
He's just a-hanging, just a-hanging
When I looked at Trail, I made myself a nervous wreck
He'd forgot that he was tied and now he's broke his ignorant neck
He's just a-hanging

The song really helped Curly. Those dogs meant the world to him, and to lose Trail weighed on him. Singing about what happened was Curly's way to mourn it out.

Verdie was Curly Ray's wife, his "blue-eyed Verdie," a Pike County girl he married when they was real young. That's how Curly ended up living in Rockhouse, next to where Verdie was raised. Her daddy was Flem Jones, a big man around Pike County.

So he was what you'd call an adopted son of Kentucky, but you ought to know he was originally a West Virginia boy, and he was playing music long before he ever met up with me. He was from a little coal town called Gilbert in Mingo County, West Virginia, wedged way back in there not far from Pike County, just across the Kentucky state line and over the mountain, near Williamson and Bluefield. It was a lot like where I come from. About the only work was coal mining. Curly's dad lost his legs in the mines from poisoning. Curly said when he was a boy he once worked in the mines two weeks straight without a day off. And those were ten-hour days, too.

His dad played some fiddle when he wasn't in the mines, and Curly learned his first tunes from him. Music was just a hobby for his dad, but for Curly it became his way out of the mines. He was playing for tips when he was five or six years old, standing on a chair and dancing with a cup. He was sixteen when he was on his first radio program and playing pie suppers and candy shows. He cut his first records for RCA back in the early fifties, with the Lonesome Pine Fiddlers, his brother Charlie and his cousin Ezra. Those were some records. He played with just about everybody and I first saw him play with the Lonesome Pine Fiddlers at a show in Princeton, West Virginia, in the mid-1950s when he was just a skinny kid with a mop of curly hair.

When country went uptown in the 1960s, Curly found himself back in the mines. It happened with a lot of musicians after the Elvis years. They quit the business because they couldn't survive.

When Curly Ray finally went full-time with me, it made a really good match. His fiddle was the kind I liked best, which was the kind that played the song. A lot of fiddlers try to beat dance around the melody. Curly could play the breakdowns as good as anybody. But when he played behind my singing, he stuck right with the tune. He played it real simple, which ain't easy to do. He didn't fool with what I call the "hot stuff." I don't care for that. When I play the banjo, I do my very best to make the strings sound just exactly the way I'm singing the song. And Curly Ray played the fiddle like I play the banjo. He followed my lead singing just as close as a man could. Then on his hoedowns, he'd break out and play it just like he wanted to. That was his right. He played it the way he felt it, but he tried to play it as near to the melody as he could. The fans loved him for this as much as I did. I seen people walk up to him at a show and ask for a certain tune, and they'd say, "Curly, we heard somebody play this but he left this and that out, and we want to hear you play it right, because when you play the song, you play every note of it."

Curly was a fixture in the show, and you could always count on him to pick up your spirits, not just in the crowd but for us boys in the band, too. Curly had a really good ear, and that's what a man in my style of music needs more than anything. You have to listen to the band to be able to find out where your spot is.

Good as he was as a musician, Curly did eventually let his showmanship get in the way of his playing. In the later years, Curly got a little lazy with his fiddle on the stage. Sometimes he was more worried about selling his records and his key chains than he was about playing the right part. If somebody in the band would complain, I'd always speak up for him. "Don't you be concerned about Curly Ray," I said. "He can play when he sets his mind to it." I knew it was partly my fault, because I had got him to make those records. And I knew it was a lot of work to do his job pleasing the crowd. And for that he always gave 110 percent. He was the one to get the crowd awake. It's hard to be a perfectionist musician up there onstage at the same time you're trying to wake up the crowd.

One show out on the West Coast, Curly got carried away, hawking his stuff a little too hard, so me and the other Clinch Mountain Boys decided to play a trick on him. Just to learn him a lesson that it wasn't all the Curly Ray Show. He ripped into one of his selling routines and we all sort of eased our way off the stage, one by one, leaving Curly out there by himself. He started into a fiddle medley to hold the crowd until we got back on stage. But we didn't come back. We waited out in the wings and just watched until Curly run out of tunes and was standing there, a fiddle player with nobody to play with. We put him on the spot and let him sweat it out. Just to remind him he was in a band.

I've already told you Curly didn't like to be the butt of any jokes, unless it was Keith Whitley who done it to him. But he was a pretty good sport with me, too. He used to call me "Sherm," for General Sherman, meaning William Tecumseh Sherman, the Union general who tore up the South during the Civil War. I ran a pretty tight ship; you had to be on time and well dressed and on good behavior. I didn't like the nickname much, and Curly was only one who could get away with calling me Sherm to my face. The other Clinch Mountain Boys had to do it behind my back.

I got to calling Curly "Hitler" to see if I could get his goat. I just thought up the name and hung it on him and it stuck for a while. It was about the worst nickname I could come up with. On my album, *Stanley Sound Today,* you can hear me yelling out, "Take it away, Hitler!" right before Curly goes into a fiddle break. It was a funny nickname to us, because his personality was about the most opposite from Hitler there ever was. Curly didn't have a mean bone in his body. I could use that nickname, but nobody else could. One time a fan hollered, real friendly like, "How ya' doing, Hitler?" and Curly Ray got hopping mad: "You don't know me well that well, buddy," he said. "Don't you call me that."

When I tell you Curly was natural, I mean that in the best way. Sometimes, though, he was just a bit too natural and he'd forget who he was with. Sometimes, Curly Ray just being himself wasn't proper, and you'd have to remind him. One time we were in a promoter's Cadillac Seville, driving through the desert from a show in Sante Fe, New Mexico. Some of the band was packed into the backseat as tight as sardines, and Curly Ray cut loose with a real greaser; I mean to tell you, this was one for the ages. Well, Curly and a few of the boys grinning like mules eating sawbriers, but I was sitting up front with the promoter, and I could tell by the look on his face that it wasn't a bit funny to him. Not to me, either. After we got out of the car and breathed in some fresh desert air, I called the band together, which I always hated to do. I didn't look at Curly, but everyone knew who I was talking about when I said, "Boys, when we're out here among the public, we have to hold ourselves up." Curly didn't whimper or complain or say a word, and he got the message loud and clear.

Most times, Curly would help out any way he could; it was his way. One summer, as we drove back out of California into Kentucky, I had on my Shriner's ring, and we stopped in a store and went inside to get some crackers and supplies to take back to the bus. It was so hot in there and my finger was sweating bad, so I asked Curly to wear my ring for me so I wouldn't lose it. Of course, he shoved it on his finger.

I told you how the Shriners are a secret society and they've got secret words and codes and whatnot. When you're a Shriner, I can tell you this much, somebody'll say, "I see you're traveling EAST" and that's a secret word; I can't tell you what it means, but anyhow the owner of the store must have been a Shriner, because he walked up to Curly Ray and he said, "I see you're traveling EAST." And Curly said, "No we're just playing a show over here in town." The Shriner didn't know what to say, and I was standing there getting a kick out of the whole exchange.

You hear about how so many musicians get to drinking and drugging and it does them in. I've seen it many a time. There are so many temptations on the road. But with Curly, it wasn't alcohol or pills that was his downfall. It was eating too much. I'd say food was Curly's worst enemy. He got to where he was eating out of habit instead of when he was hungry. He just couldn't stop. I believe he just about ate himself to death.

Curly would clean his plate, then clean all of our plates, too. All the Clinch Mountain Boys, and later, when we got a full-time bus driver, he'd finish off his plate, too. Now, he was polite about it. He'd eat his meal and wait for us to leave some crumbs. For Curly it was nothing to eat a half-dozen foot-long hot dogs. I saw him do it many a time on a bet, but it wasn't really a fair bet because everybody knew he could do it.

People used to bring food to Curly when we were at shows. Like they brought the hunting dogs. They knew he liked to foxhunt and they knew he liked to eat. There was a fan of ours, Clyde was his name. He was a trucker, a big bald-headed heavyset fella with a real deep voice. He'd always bring ham sandwiches for Curly and for all the Clinch Mountain Boys. He'd get out the bread and tomatoes and ham and make us some sandwiches. It was real good salty country ham and we got to calling him Ole Salty Bald Head.

One time, we were packing up the ham Ole Salty Bald Head left with us, and of course Curly was still hungry like he always was. So I cut up some of that ham, and Keith Whitley wanted to play a joke on Curly. He slipped some salt on the ham, and this ham's already real salty to start with, you know. Keith put salt on there about a half-inch thick.

And Curly bit into those sandwiches and got to laughing so hard, knowing this way too salty even for Ole Salty Bald Head's ham. But he was so hungry he just kept on eating, and he was laughing and his face got redder than you ever saw on a man, but still he was breathing, shoving that salty ham into his mouth. I don't know how in the world he was able to eat that ham. He knew it was Keith who'd tricked him, but he couldn't stop eating the ham anyhow.

Because it was Curly, you didn't think of his weight as a problem. The way he carried it seemed natural. And when he played his fiddle and did his dance, all those extra pounds moved along with the music, and it added to the show and kept the crowd lively. The fans loved to see Curly move and enjoy himself. He was as fun to watch as he was to listen to, two for the price of one. Just like our comedian Henry "Pap" Dockery, from the early sixties, used to say, "I always did get a terrible charge out of seeing a fat man fiddle or a fat woman laugh. Seems like there's so much of 'em a-having a good time!"

For a long while, it was fun with Curly and his eating. It was an amusement for us, just having a good time to pass the miles out on the road. He always kept us well entertained, and I think that may have done him wrong somehow, because it got to be like Carter got with his drinking, it started to do Curly bad. He looked at food as a pastime and it got to where his eating led to all sorts of ailments and got to where he couldn't put his shoes on because his feet swelled up so bad.

It finally got to where Curly couldn't do his job anymore because of his health. He'd get confused about where he was. He used to make the thirty-mile drive from Pike County across the Kentucky state line to meet me in Coeburn. We kept the bus parked behind the Food City grocery store, which is where we always keep it gassed up and ready for the long road to this very day. I used to get calls from the state police about Curly. They said he was getting dangerous about how he drove when he was coming to Coeburn. He was all over the road, swerving this way and that; one time he ended up driving off the highway through somebody's yard. The police told me I needed to do something about it, because he was going to have an accident and kill himself, or kill somebody else.

Where it really got bad was onstage, in front of the public. He'd stand there and just look around a lot, like he was out of it. He'd forget to take his break when it came his time, he'd be waving the fiddle instead of playing. During a song, I'd be looking over to see how he was doing and he'd be looking at me like he needed help. He wasn't himself no more. The Curly Ray we knew was fading right there in front of us. Every show we played, seemed like a part of him was left back there.

Well, I knew I was going to have to do what I dreaded most, and that was let Curly go. He wasn't the type of man to retire. He was like me and a lot of other entertainers. Music was his whole life. And he wasn't in his right mind to even make a decision like that on his own.

I've had to fire some musicians, but only a very few. In the Stanley Brothers days, it was Carter who did the firing. I couldn't handle it. He didn't like it either. Once Carter had to fire our fiddler Paul Mullins, but not over his playing. He had a bad case of stage fright. He'd rehearse with us and do just fine. Then he'd get out there in front of a crowd and he just couldn't cut it. The pressure got to him, and he'd just go to pieces.

What made it extra hard for Carter was, he and Paul were good buddies. They hunted coons together. It was more mutual than it was a firing, because Paul had told us he was sorry it wasn't working out. But it was still tough for Carter when he let him go. He was crying and everything. Sometimes you have to look at music like a business, even when you know it's personal.

With Curly Ray, it was even worse. We'd been together so long, he'd done so good for me, always done whatever I asked of him. And in the last few years, he'd cry on a dime. He'd got to where he'd cry when we gave him an award or cited him onstage. He was a mess with his emotions and that was part of his health problems.

In 1986, I gave Curly a trophy at the Memorial Festival at the old home place on Smith Ridge. It was something I'd been meaning to do, but I could never find the right time to do it. Well, that time finally came, and I told the crowd I had a special announcement.

"I can't stand here and take all the credit and all the awards without giving Curly something," I said. "I was going to present it but I don't think I can, so would somebody backstage bring out something, and let's make Curly Ray smile or cry. I'd say he'll do a little of both." The trophy was for "20 Years of Dedicated Service." When they gave it to him, Curly just broke down, and so did everybody else on the stage, and lots of people in the crowd, too.

I'm glad we had the chance to give Curly some recognition while he was still with us. So many times, it doesn't happen. It's like the song I recorded with Curly, *Won't you give me my flowers while I'm still living and let me enjoy them while I can/Please don't wait till I'm ready to be buried and then slip some lilies in my hand.* Well, Curly got to have him some flowers.

He got so heavy in his last years, and he got feeble in his mind. His weight and his age just caught up with him and he wasn't able anymore. He really stayed on the road too long, but I didn't have the nerve to let him go. I loved the man too much. So he hung on with us for a few more years, until 1993, when I finally done it. Told him he had to step down. He looked at me strange, like he didn't really understand, so I had to tell him I was letting him go from the band. And then he just broke down and he cried and he couldn't stop. It hurt for me to do it. It was the hardest thing I ever had to do. Curly Ray was as close to me as anyone. I didn't want to hurt him, but I believe it broke his heart.

He spent his last few years in a nursing home near Rockhouse. Ralph II would go visit him. I never could handle it. I wanted to remember him like I knew him in the old days, that big piano smile and doing his Curly Ray dance, setting the stage on fire.

Curly Ray died in 1997. He was seventy-four years old. They had a memorial service for him at the United Free Will Baptist Church in Pikeville. I couldn't make it to the funeral because of some show dates we had, but I was wanting to say a few words at the service, to try to say how much Curly Ray meant to me. Tell some of the things I told in this chapter. The funny things Curly did to help all those miles go by better. All those shows we played, from the Morgan Theater in Grundy to the *Grand Ole Opry* and *Hee Haw* and the Smithsonian Institute. And everywhere we played, Curly won that crowd over.

I got to the podium and couldn't hardly get a word out. It was too much for me, I just couldn't do it. I would have told them Curly Ray was a fine fiddler, one of the best I ever heard. As far as old-time fiddling goes, he couldn't be beat. He was at the top of the heap. But he was as fine a person as he was a musician. And there's not many you can say that about. He was a good, honest man and a wonderful friend to have.

But I wasn't able to get those words out. I was as close to breaking down as I could be, so I finally just did all you can do for an old Clinch Mountain Boy who gave everything he had for the music.

"Friends," I said. "There are so many things I could say about this man, but I'm real tenderhearted. So we'll just go ahead and sing."

So me and the band sung "Gloryland," the same gospel song we done at Roy Lee's funeral:

If you have friends in Gloryland, who left because of pain
Thank God up there, they'll die no more, they'll suffer not again
Then weep not, friends, I'm goin' home, up there we'll die no more
No coffins will be made up there, no graves on that bright shore

I had trouble finishing that hymn. My throat got lumped up, and my voice almost choked me up, and I almost couldn't get it all out. It was too emotional, and like I said, I'm real tenderhearted.

It's always hard singing at funerals, and I've sung at so many. There's usually an old-time preacher at the funeral, and they say things that touch you, so I don't like to go if I don't have to. The singing always comes hard no matter how many times you do it. So to tell you the truth, I don't really like to do it. I find a way to get through it, but a lot of times the singing's not good. It's too emotional and you feel it too much, and your singing gets off-key. It's embarrassing when that happens, because singing is my job, and it's real hard to do a good job. I'd rather sing before ten thousand people than I would in front of twenty people at a funeral. But you feel like you owe it to them when you're asked to, and I've been asked a lot. Most times, I've been busy with show dates, and if there's any way I can make an excuse, I will. You know, it's a pity, really, but I still try my best do it when I'm able to. It's something you're glad you done when it's over with.

I remember when we sang at the funeral of Hillard Blankenship, the man who drove the bus for me for so many years. I was singing and Ralph II was singing and Jack Cooke was singing. And they both broke down and had to quit and I carried it on by myself because they couldn't handle it. I know just how they felt.

For my funeral, let them sing a couple of Baptist hymns and maybe preach a little bit, just the old-time way. That's the way Carter's funeral was.

Losing Curly was hard to take. What made it so sad was how much he loved being alive, more than anyone I ever met. He just enjoyed life, everything about it. He could have more fun drinking a cup of coffee than a lot of people could have in a month. He appreciated little everyday things that most of us take for granted.

I remember we'd be driving through the mountains of eastern Kentucky close by his home, and we'd be traveling down the same roads we'd always travel back and forth to shows. Now, to me, that can get old fast. Even the prettiest country in the world can look pretty tired after a while. Same hills, same trees, same sky. Not for Curly Ray.

He'd be looking out the window and he'd say, "Ain't it awful that we have to leave this pretty place?"

"Yeah, Curly," I'd say. "I reckon so."

To me, it was just a road we'd seen a thousand times before. Not to him, though. For Curly, every back country road and cow pasture and old barn along the way was something special, and he felt blessed to be alive to enjoy it. I don't think Curly was scared of dying. It was just that he loved this world so much. To him, this place was so wonderful that he just thought it was the saddest thing that we're all gonna have to leave it behind someday. For Curly Ray, this was heaven right here.

Chapter Twenty-Two

Professionals and Amateurs

*"**Bluegrass:** Lawrence Welk with a tenor banjo*
***Hard Core Bluegrass:** Recent Osborne Brothers*
***Hard Hard Core Bluegrass:** Bill Monroe*
***Hard Hard Hard Core Bluegrass:** Ralph Stanley, alone, on a mountain top in a blizzard"*

—"How to Read Bluegrass Reviews and Covers," *Bluegrass Unlimited* magazine, December 1974

If you ask me what kind of music I play, I'd rather not say a thing. I'd rather just play and sing and let you decide. But I know that for this book, I can't let my music do the talking for me anymore. So if I have to give a name to my music, I'd call it the Stanley Sound. Not to brag, but I think it's an altogether different sound to anything that's ever come out.

I don't play bluegrass. I never have, really. I think the only true bluegrass is Bill Monroe, and maybe a very few others along with him. That's his music. There was only one Bill Monroe, and I never wanted to sound like Bill. His music comes from where he's from, way out in the bluegrass country of western Kentucky. He's not from the mountains. Neither was Earl Scruggs or Lester Flatt, or Red Smiley or Don Reno. They were all lowlanders, too, from mill towns from the piedmont.

Bill was the first for this type of music—ain't no one can argue otherwise. But it wasn't called bluegrass back in the early days. It was just called old-time hillbilly music. Around 1965, when they started doing the big bluegrass festivals, everybody got together to come up with a name to call the show. They decided that since Bill was the first, and he was the oldest man, and he was from the bluegrass state of Kentucky and he had the Bluegrass Boys, they'd call the music "bluegrass." They hung the name on the music and it stuck.

Bluegrass the way Bill and Earl and Lester done it has its own timing. It fits their style of playing, which is more about the picking than the singing. Bluegrass the way Bill Monroe done it is supposed to have more of a drive to it. Don't get me wrong. I like bluegrass just fine when it's done right. But bluegrass is a little more polished and it's got a whole different timing to it than the type of singing I do.

I come from the mountains. I was singing my music long before there was such as thing as bluegrass. Mine has more of a down-to-earth feeling. I couldn't play it any other way, because it's been bred into me. The Stanley Sound comes from way back yonder on that steep hillside on Smith Ridge, *where the mountain meets the sky*. Some might say it's more lonesome, but I'd say it's just played more simple.

So I never have felt that it's proper to call my music bluegrass. Bill Monroe, Flatt and Scruggs, Reno and Smiley. That's bluegrass to me. Mine has always been different from theirs. If you press me on it, I'll tell you the same thing I always tell the crowd at a show: "Old-time mountain style of what-they-call-bluegrass music." It's a mouthful, I reckon, but it's about the best I can come up with.

I don't know about a lot of music they're calling bluegrass, but it don't sound like it to me. What they call bluegrass has changed so much that I'm a lot closer to Bill's bluegrass than I am to all the new kinds out there. There are all sorts of music that people will call bluegrass but it ain't. Just because there's a banjo in a band don't mean it's bluegrass.

Newgrass was what they called it back in the 1970s. A lot of the younger musicians couldn't play the old way, so they started to change it up. You can't blame them, really. They were just doing what they could. There's not too many people left that can play the old-time way. You've got to feel the old-time way to play it. There's a lot of people don't feel it anymore. Bluegrass done the right way is as rare as hen's teeth these days. And that's because if it's done right, sung right and with the proper feeling, it's the hardest music to play in the world.

It was at the first big bluegrass festival, at Fincastle, Virginia, where I first noticed the difference between the old and the new, what they started to call the progressive style. There had been some one-day festivals, but Fincastle was first to spread out the music over three days. It was held on Labor Day weekend in 1965, at Cantrell's Horse Farm outside Roanoke, and all the big acts were there together: Bill Monroe, Jimmy Martin, Mac Wiseman, the Osborne Brothers, Don Reno, Red Smiley. That was an important event. It really got the festival circuit started, and that was the savior of our music for a lot of years. Otherwise, I think bluegrass might have faded out, because we couldn't have survived on record sales. Fincastle was the start of how we could make it financially.

Carlton Haney was the organizer and the man that started it all. He was one of the best promoters in the business, a fellow with some real horse sense. He had done a lot of bookings for Reno and Smiley and Bill Monroe. He saw how the fans of bluegrass and old-time country had thinned out in the Elvis years. He got the idea to bring all the fans together by bringing all the different bands together. Get the Bill Monroe fans, get the Ralph Stanley fans, get the Reno and Smiley fans, the Jimmy Martin fans. Put all that together for a big reunion, so we could all help each other instead of fighting against each other.

First, a lot of the feuds had to be resolved. There used to be a lot of jealousy and grudges involved in bluegrass. But Haney managed to smooth out the disputes. He told the bands we had to either come all together and stay alive or we were all going to go down our separate ways. Playing the bars and taverns and little schoolhouses couldn't pay the bills no more.

Well, it worked out pretty well. The first Fincastle festival really was like a big family reunion. A lot of former Bluegrass Boys got on stage with Bill, and a lot of hard feelings just sort of faded away. There was some funny stuff, too. Carter and George pulled a prank on Jimmy Martin.

They slipped Jimmy some Ex-Lax before he went to play his show. This festival was a big deal for Jimmy, because he was really making a name for himself. Somehow he made it through the set, and then he knew he had to go, fast. Right after he finished, he ran off the stage looking for a Port-O-John, but he couldn't find one close by, and last we saw of him he was headed out into the woods, pulling his britches off as he was running.

At the Saturday night show, there were like to be thousands of moths swarming the stage lights. They were bombing the hell out of those bare lightbulbs Haney had put up, which was real close to the microphones.

Now, we were used to bugs and gnats and whatnot from playing so many drive-in theaters and outdoor country music parks. You'd never think birds could ruin a show, but we had some robins make so much noise from a nest onstage at a fair in Edinburg, Virginia, that we could barely hear ourselves sing. The reason was, the little baby robins was hungry, and they made such a racket we had to cut the show short.

We'd get everything from bats to bees and anything with wings and something to bite you with. Most times, we'd just keep right on playing like nothing was the matter.

I remember when we had to fend off an attack of yellow jackets at New River Ranch in Rising Sun, Maryland. There was a hive tucked in the roof of the stage. Somehow, around the time I played "Clinch Mountain Backstep," that old forward roll on the banjo got 'em all stirred up and they started swarming. Now, yellow jackets, they don't let up until you're out of their territory, and they'll sting the tar out of you. They want to see you run, and they kept trying to run us off the stage during the show. I finally set down my banjo and hollered out, "Get the DDT and let's burn 'em out!" We had to stop the show for a while and clear the hive out.

Another time, I got choked up during a song I was leading on, and had to stop to try to clear my throat. Carter wanted to know what all was wrong. He just asked me over the microphone, like it was part of the show.

All it was, I reckon, was a gnat or mosquito; I never did find out exactly what it was. But I couldn't get it out, either by swallowing or coughing. So I got on my mic and told Carter something was crawling down my throat. Carter asked if I wanted him to get me a drink of water. "No, but thank you kindly anyway," I said. "I believe I'll just let him walk down on his own." You had to make jokes, otherwise you'd go crazy.

Anyhow, this swarm of moths at Fincastle was about the worst we'd ever seen. I mean the splotchy milky white moths, big, ugly-looking boogers that don't quit for nothing when there's light around. Carter was singing and somehow he swallowed one, and he had to stand there and cough the moth out, mid-song. Carter would never let a chance for a good joke go by, so he got on the mic and told the crowd, "Well, I reckon them chocolate bugs are all right, but I can't hardly stand the taste of them vanillers."

Fincastle was the first big festival, but moneywise it was a failure. The problem was the location. A horse farm in southwest Virginia was too far away from the big cities. The crowd just didn't show up like Haney was counting on. There was only about three hundred people there, and that wasn't enough. Haney just about lost his shirt, and he didn't pay everybody what was promised. Carter called Haney "Shorty," and he spoke up for all the bands. "Shorty," he said. "I know you didn't make much, but everybody's got to eat." We ended up getting a bad check and somehow worked it out later on.

Fincastle was a start, and that meant something. But that festival also opened the door to what I call the amateurs. When you swing the barn door open, everybody wants to come inside. That's only to be expected. But letting so many inside maybe hurt the bluegrass a bit in the long run.

What happened was, they had a banjo contest at Fincastle, and I was one of the judges. Bill Emerson of the Country Gentlemen was the other judge. Bill was still fairly young at the time, but he didn't try to show off like a lot of the younger generation did then. And that was exactly what was wrong with this banjo talent contest. There was too much showing off, and way too many notes. That was only part of the problem. I remember listening to a lot of the young pickers; they were slick and they knew how to play, but I could tell a lot of them had learned banjo from a book.

A young fellow would play "Old Joe Clark" and he'd start out fine and then he'd go off on his own and leave "Old Joe Clark" behind. The song wasn't enough. He was trying to be better than the song. But you can't compete against the song you're playing. That's not music, that's a sport. They're the ones that later on started playing the newgrass and the progressive style. It got to be hard to tell one from the other. They knew the licks they learned from reading, but they didn't know the feeling. They couldn't get the tone or nothing, just a bunch of fancy notes.

Tone is everything with banjo playing. No two people get the same tone out of an instrument. That's something I was always blessed with, getting a good tone on the banjo. You get your tone from the way you hit those strings, and that's all about feel. I've had people play my banjo and they can't get the sound like I could get out of it. Same with Monroe and his mandolin. There's never been a mandolin player I've ever heard that could get the tone that Bill Monroe got. Labels like "bluegrass" and "newgrass" don't mean nothing except to the people selling. The musicians are playing music, and the good ones don't sound like nobody but themselves.

Jim and Jesse McReynolds were borned and raised just a few miles from Carter and me. In fact, Jim and me were borned only two weeks apart back in February 1927. They were from a little coal-mining town named Carfax, outside Coeburn. But Jim and Jesse never sounded like the Stanley Brothers. Not even close. And they were living down the road. They developed their own way, and we developed ours. It's like horses you have borned in the same stable. Some horses trot and some horses walk, right from the start. It's in their nature, and they're true to their nature.

All the best country performers had their own sound. The Carter Family sounded like the Carter Family. Flatt and Scruggs sounded like

Flatt and Scruggs. A million pickers have tried to duplicate Earl Scruggs on the banjo and they can't get near the real thing. I know I never could sound like Earl, so I never did try. I pick a different banjo from anybody else. It may not be as good or fancy as Earl, but you can always tell who it is.

I've always liked plain and simple picking the best. I think you ought to play every note like the song calls for. No more and no less.

There are a lot of musicians and entertainers who will notice you more if you throw in a lot of hot, fancy licks and play all around the melody. I don't like it and I never did try to play like that. I've heard a lot of good banjo players, and they'll pick maybe a couple lines of a tune and play it exactly right, and then they'll mess it up in the last line or two. What I call messing up is they get away from the tune and they just go wild with it, and I don't care for that.

Now, those hot licks will get you a lot of attention and compliments from other banjo players maybe. But I never cared much as to what other musicians want to hear. They're not the ones who pay to come see the show. See, I don't make any money from the musicians and all them bands out there. I've made my money from the fans who pay to see me do it my way.

I've heard people say they can pull into the parking lot at a festival and if I'm onstage, they can tell it's me from more than a mile away. "Sounds like Ralph Stanley, don't it?" That's the important thing for a musician, to have his own style. Something that stands out from the rest. You have to be your own man instead of trying to be somebody you're not.

Singing is the weak spot in the younger bluegrass bands. To me, the hot playing is a way to cover up bad singing. They can pick the notes, but they can't sing worth beans, not the way I like to hear singing.

Ever since I started out in music, it was the singing I cared about most. That's what I worked on the hardest, and same with the Stanley Brothers. Carter agreed with me on that. "Mandolin players, fiddle players, guitar players, they're a dime a dozen," he'd always say. "You've got to get that sweet harmony singing in there if you're going to make a go of it." That sweet harmony is the secret ingredient to the Stanley Sound. You can have all the blends of different voices you want as long as you get that harmony right. I try for that every song I do.

That's why I've always thought I was more a singer than a banjo man. I like singing more than anything in music. I feature singing more than I do the instruments. A banjo or a fiddle or a guitar, they're just there to help you along, to bolster up the singing. It's the singing that puts a song over. It's the singing that goes to your heart.

I think people want to hear the song, not just my banjo. Now, it's good to have some instruments behind you to take a break, but the song is what people are interested in. There's nothing like a voice a-singing out. That's the way most people listen to music, I think, and I play music for people, not just for myself. Otherwise, you may as well set home and sing by yourself.

When it come to the old Primitive Baptist hymns, well, that's how me and Carter were different. He never cared for the a cappella singing and the real old-timey sound of that. He liked to experiment more than I did and modernize a bit. Try different styles and singing arrangements. So since I've been on my own, I've found my own sound I couldn't get with the Stanley Brothers. It's one of those things you make on your own when you have to, when it's only yourself left. I like it just as lonesome as you can get, like the old church singing.

One thing some people don't understand is how serious we professional musicians take our business. When it's your job and your living depends on it, you treat it with all the respect you can. I never have got lazy about my music. I would never let down a crowd. I don't care if there are ten people in the seats or ten thousand. I do my best every time out. And that means looking your best, too.

That was another thing I didn't like about the newer bands. You started to see a lot of jeans and T-shirts and long hair. It looked sloppy to me, and it was as sloppy as their playing. It was amateurish, and I didn't like it at all.

The Clinch Mountain Boys were different, and we were proud to be different. Proud to be professional musicians, paid for what we do. And that means looking professional, onstage and off. We had a dress code always in place. I never had to say a word about it, and nobody ever asked why. It was just understood. We always tried to look our best, didn't matter if we played a beer joint or a political rally. We always had on our matching suits, no matter how hot it was onstage. Carter had always been very strict about that, and I was, too. If you respect the music, you need to look like a professional, and if you're onstage looking sloppy, that's a slap against the music.

It was Bill Monroe taught us that. Like I told you before, he always looked as sharp as his music sounded. He dressed neat and formal as a Kentucky colonel. Jodhpurs and pressed britches. He wore a hat and he was always shaved and he always held his head high. It means a lot in this kind of music to look good and put forward your best appearance before your audience.

Now, I've rambled on a ways about professionals and amateurs, and the ways they're different, in playing right and dressing right, too. But there's even something worse to my way of thinking, and that's musicians behaving amateurish in the way they do things. If something is not up to par, if it's not up to the right standard, I call it amateur. You see amateurs all the time. You might have a band making all kind of noise backstage, when you're up there finishing your show. They're back there hitting on their instruments, warming up and whatnot, and that feeds through and messes things up for the band that's doing their show. That's amateurish. Or you might have some boys who get on stage half drunk and loud and laughing too hard at their own jokes, making fools of themselves in front of their fans. That's amateurish.

Now, there's something that's worse than just being amateurish. And that's being dumb and stupid. This happened some, and most times I would let it go and not pay no mind to it. But sometimes it would get under your skin and really get to you. There was one musician I want to call out on that: John Duffey.

I didn't have any problems with Duffey as a musician. I know he was a big fan of the Stanley Brothers. We'd see him in the audience a lot in the late fifties and early sixties. He used to travel for hundreds of miles to record our shows. He'd be there with a tape recorder right by the stage. That was how he learned a lot of our songs that ended up on those early Country Gentlemen albums.

His tenor could hardly be beat. I remember when he came by the studio in the early seventies. We were going to do a new version of Carter's "Lonesome River," which was Duffey's favorite Stanley Brothers song. He was very polite and sincere; he wanted to sing with me on that song. We were going to do the high trio arrangement like we'd done it on the Columbia record from 1948.

Duffey told me it was a real honor and so on. Now, he was a well-built fellow with broad shoulders and a flattop crew cut like a Marine sergeant, and he was used to doing things his way. This was different. He was nervous to do this song with me.

"Ralph," he said, "do you want me to play what I want to play on the mandolin, or should I play it like Pee Wee did on the record?"

"The record would be just fine," I said.

And so Duffey done it just like I told him. On the mandolin part he done fine. That was the easy part. It was the singing part that give him trouble. It was mentioned that we had to get it all straight as to the key we'd be singing, and somebody said, "What key do we want to do it in?"

Duffey was confident about his singing, and he had a right to be. He thought he could handle whatever we threw at him. Now he was ready to prove he was up to par.

"Whatever you want," he said sort of smart-alecky. "It won't matter to me."

On the high trio arrangement, Roy Lee was lead singer, and I was tenor, and Duffey was high baritone. That was Pee Wee's part, and that meant Duffey had to go higher than Roy Lee and me. I wanted to show him that this wasn't as easy as he figured it might be. I wanted to test him a little bit, to see if he had what it took to really do the old Stanley Brothers style the way it could be done. I just sort of nodded over to Roy Lee and we threw it up about two keys higher than we'd ever done it. Me and Roy Lee Centers were really pushing him, and Duffey couldn't quite make it to the high baritone he was supposed to. We got our parts fine but Duffey failed on his. We had to lower it down a notch for him so we could get through the song.

A lot of people love the version we did of "Lonesome River," but everybody in the studio knew Duffey's voice had let him down. And Duffey knew it more than anybody, and I know it embarrassed him a little. I don't know if he held that against me or not. He never did mention anything about it, but I sometimes wonder.

Speaking of "Lonesome River," one of the best versions of that song was one me and Bob Dylan sung together. We done it for the *Clinch Mountain Country* album, and it was the only time we ever got together. He just came down to Nashville and there was a big storm that day. It was a-raining and a-thundering outside, and he walked into the studio and we shook hands and we talked a little bit. He's good fun. He's a little bit shy, same as me, but he's number one in my book. He said singing with me was the highlight of his career. That kind of swells your head a little bit.

Well, "Lonesome River" was the song Bob wanted to do. But he wanted to do it as a duet instead of the trio, and I respected him for that. He was smart enough to know there was no way you could top the way me and Carter and Pee Wee did it on the original. We ran over the song a couple of times, and then we recorded it twice. He did the lead and I sang a part that matched him. We didn't have a bit of trouble and Bob done his part just fine. My wife, Jimmi, said it was her favorite song on the album.

That shows you what kind of singer Bob is. He knows what he can handle and what he can't. And that's the way he's always been, right from the start. He recorded "Man of Constant Sorrow" on his first album for Columbia, when he was just nineteen years old. Young as he was, he done it his own way, and that's how a singer ought to go about things. He sung it like Bob Dylan, not like Ralph Stanley or anybody else. That's how I am. I couldn't imitate anybody if I tried.

Anyhow, I ain't out to run down Duffey, just let you know he wasn't always as smart as he thought he was. I give him a lot of credit; he done a lot for bluegrass. Both of his bands, the Country Gentlemen and the Seldom Scene, helped bring our music to new fans, people who loved Bob Dylan and the Beatles. He helped all of us bluegrass players earn more than we did before. He drove a hard bargain with promoters, and I admired that. I was used to just taking what was out there and be grateful there was any work at all. Not Duffey. He'd book the Seldom Scene to work a college show and he'd get $1,800 at a time when most of us couldn't get half that much.

This may sound strange but it was as a businessman that I most admired Duffey. Let me tell you, he was tough. His attitude was "Here's my price. If you don't want to meet it, I don't need the job that bad, so the hell with you." In the 1970s, the Seldom Scene was the hottest thing going for a while, so he could afford to get the price he wanted. And that made it easier for a lot of us to get a better deal. He opened the door for a lot of bluegrass groups to start making some decent money.

Not just moneywise, either. He helped get more respect for bluegrass outside the country music crowd, with the college fans and the city people. I know he loved and honored the music as much as anybody who ever played it. Where he fell short was the way he treated the people who made the music. I don't know what was at the bottom of it. I just never liked the way he did some of the musicians.

It was just the way he was, I reckon. As a man, Duffey could be as mean as a striped snake. Now, a lot of people might call that just his way of being funny. He liked pulling pranks, like a lot of the musicians, but his pranks had a cruel streak about a mile wide. If you ask me, he did all kinds of things that I think was just plain wrong.

One time, Duffey pulled a prank on Jimmy Martin. I reckon he probably thought it was the slickest stunt he'd ever done. I thought it was one of the worst things I've ever seen, and I've seen a lot. I once had a turd thrown in my bus. I believe it was from one of them long-haired hippie bands, but I never could prove it. That turd smelled bad but it didn't bother me none. You get all kinds of pranks in bluegrass, but I'm talking about a stunt where you humiliate a man in public. And that's what Duffey done to Jimmy Martin.

I always liked Jimmy, and he liked me, too. I'd say I got along with him better than anybody in the business. We were so different in our personalities, and maybe that's why we got along so well. Jimmy was one of the friendliest fellows you'd ever meet, but some people thought he was full of bull and just couldn't handle him. It's true he talked too much and he cried too much and he laughed too loud. It was always about Jimmy. And a lot of what he said didn't amount to much, but he had a good heart.

If Jimmy wanted to talk, I'd let him do it. When he got to talking crazy, I'd just not pay him any mind. I'd just agree with him and go on about my business. He'd cry on a dime if he got to drinking or his feelings got hurt, and he had a temper. Large and loud as he was, he never did grow up from being that little barefoot boy from Sneedville, Tennessee. He was like a lot of us born with nothing way back in the sticks, in the deep mountains. Music was all we ever had and all we could ever really count on.

With Jimmy, every ounce of pride came from being a musician. I'll tell you a story about how serious Jimmy took his music. Jimmy was a pro; when it came to making a record, he was all business. I recorded an album with Jimmy for King Records in the late sixties. Singing with Jimmy was always easy; he knew his part and I knew mine. We cut the album in a just a few hours and the King studio people were surprised we done it so quick. Jimmy said, "Well, I reckon it pays to have somebody that knows what they're doing." He took a ton of pride in doing his job right.

That's why what Duffey done to him was such a crummy thing. It happened at a festival down in North Carolina. Jimmy had his bus parked way out in a field. Jimmy's band was called the Sunny Mountain Boys, after his big hit, "The Sunny Side of the Mountain." That was his signature song. He had the band name painted on both sides of the bus; it was in big fancy lettering. It must have cost him a lot, and he was tight with his money. Everybody knew how proud Jimmy was of his bus and of his band.

Well, Duffey and some of his buddies got a notion to have a little fun at Jimmy's expense. They waited until Jimmy was onstage playing. Then they snuck out across the field to the bus, where nobody was around. Duffy was a good artist, and he changed one letter on both sides of the bus. He did it up right, too. It was a real professional job.

When Jimmy finished his show, he went on back to the bus to rest up. Then he saw what Duffey had done. On both sides of the bus was "Jimmy Martin and the Funny Mountain Boys." Well, you never seen a face get redder than Jimmy's did when he saw that. He didn't see nothing funny in it. It hurt his feelings. All the fans and musicians saw the prank and Jimmy saw them looking and laughing. Duffey and his helpers were laughing from behind him.

That was the thing about Duffey. You were never sure if he was laughing with you or if he was laughing at you. I'd say most of the time he was laughing at people, especially at country people. He was a city boy and he was a real smart-aleck. He'd grown up with money, outside Washington, D.C., and his dad was an opera singer, and from what I heard, he never approved of Duffey playing bluegrass. It took some guts to follow his dreams, I give Duffey that. You knew he loved bluegrass music, but you never knew how much he really cared about the bluegrass musicians. We came up hard in a way he never did. For some reason, this made him have resentment.

I remember sitting in our motor home one time, and the Seldom Scene were onstage and Duffey was getting into his real raunchy jokes. This was at a festival, kids in the audience. I didn't believe in that. Now, I don't wish anything bad on nobody. I've always believed that in our business there's room for everybody, all different kinds of musicians.

But there were times like that I would think to myself: "I wish Duffey and them Seldom Scenes would starve to death." Of course, it ain't right to think that, but you can't help it sometimes.

I didn't like what Duffey done to Jimmy, and I didn't like all the other dirty stunts he pulled. He tried to joke with me some. There was a time I heard he got to calling my band "Ralph and the Rip-offs." He mostly left me alone as far as anything the fans could see.

After all these years, it still leaves a bad taste. Duffey's dead and gone, but I still don't like all them mean, amateurish pranks he done. When I heard he died, I thought maybe the bad feeling would die away, too, but it was still there. There are some things you just can't ever forget.

On the stage and behind the microphone, Duffey was a fine professional musician, but offstage he could be an amateur, at least to my way of thinking.

But Duffey wasn't the only one, not by a long shot. There's plenty of 'em you can find at shows and festivals. I've had some in my own band behaving amateurish now and then, and I've had to make my point. I haven't had to do it too often, because the Clinch Mountain Boys usually know how to handle themselves. But there's been times I've had to make things more clear.

Now, there's nothing I hate worse than having to tell a man how to do his job. It puts me in a bad mood and I reckon it doesn't help with his mood neither. In some situations, I don't have to say a thing. Years ago, if I'd notice a Clinch Mountain Boy's whiskers getting long, I might just walk to the back of the bus and hold up a shaving kit to remind everybody what it was for.

That's fine to get a fellow to make sure he's clean-cut, but there are other things even more important in our line of work. If I had to boil it down, I'd say it's about looking a certain way on the stage and behaving a certain way off the stage, but that really don't nail it. Like a lot of things, it's easier to explain what I'm driving at by telling you what ain't up to par, instead of what is.

To me, being a professional comes down to a few plain and simple don'ts. They go something like this:

Don't be rude to the fans. It don't matter if there's just cause or not. The fans are what made what you're doing possible. You have to treat them with respect no matter what.

Don't get on stage dressed in your street clothes, or what Curly Ray used to call "riding clothes," which is whatever you wore to get to the show. Don't ever get on stage with a beer in your hand, or a cigarette or toothpick in your mouth. This ain't a jam session; it's a show with an audience who paid to see you. You've got work to do and you need to give it your full attention.

Don't walk around in public, at the venue or festival grounds, with a woman you're not serious about. This is probably the toughest rule to follow, but there are a lot of good reasons for it.

Don't drink in front of the public.

Don't be late to a show. Like I already said earlier in the book, nothing gets me more irate than being late. I'd rather be fifteen years early than five minutes late. Many a time we went onstage in place of a local amateur bluegrass band who were late for the show, and they lived just a few miles from the festival. That's one of the reasons they're amateurs and not professionals. If any young musicians are reading this, I will tell you this: If you abide by these rules, I don't care if you're playing Carnegie Hall or the corner beer joint for tips, in my book, you're a professional.

Chapter Twenty-Three

Gloryland

"The road's been rough and rocky that I travel day by day
But I feel at the end of my journey, I'll see the great Milky Way
I cannot sing like an angel and I cannot preach like Paul
But Lord, when You get ready, I'll try to answer the call"

—"I'll Answer the Call," Ralph Stanley

There comes a time when you have to take a stand for what you believe in. You don't know when or where it will come. You don't know what you're going to do or how things will end up. That time came for me when I wanted to sing gospel songs at a bar on a Saturday night. And so I did. The management tried to stop me and pulled the plug. There like to been a riot. But the riot was on my side.

I wasn't looking for trouble that night. You know by now that I'm not one for confrontations. I don't go spoiling for a fight. I try to turn the other cheek and back my way out of a jam. Call me a coward if you want. It don't bother me. Maybe that's how I've been able to last so long in the business.

In all my years playing music for the public, and that's sixty-odd years and counting, I don't change my show for nobody or nothing. It don't matter if it's a junky little nightclub or the nicest concert hall you ever saw, I always sing a few hymns. That's how I was raised up. I enjoy singing sacred music everywhere I play.

And as an entertainer, I believe it makes for a better show. "Pretty Polly" has a place in the show, but you can't be doing murder ballads all night long. You need "Gloryland" or "I'll Wear a White Robe" or "A Robin Built a Nest on Daddy's Grave." You need some hope. It don't matter whether you believe or not; it don't hurt to get you some Sunday morning on a Saturday night, or any other night.

I've only been challenged on this one time, and that was enough. We were booked into this bar, The County Palace, in Columbus, Ohio. This was a popular venue, always packed with people from our home territory who'd moved north for work and were homesick for mountain music. It was a long gray cinder-block building in a run-down section of town. Not much of a palace. The dressing area was an old storage room.

It was a local bluegrass organization that put on the show. Some diehard fans who loved bluegrass hosted bands like us and helped us make a living. This was the 1980s, years before *O Brother* hit, and we needed shows like this to survive; it was our bread and butter outside the festival circuit.

The fellow who owned the club was not part of this group. Somehow or another he got word we did some religious numbers and he wasn't happy about it. After we pulled up in the bus, he came out and gave us a warning. "We don't want none of that church music in here," he said. "There'll be no gospel songs sung in my building."

He didn't say much as to why. He may have been a nonbeliever, I never did find out. I think the the main reason behind it was money. He wanted to keep the show going with fast bluegrass songs to keep everybody buying drinks. He figured us singing all them sad, slow hymns would maybe spoil the mood and cost him at the cash register.

But that was none of my concern. No man can tell me what songs I can play. Never could, never will be able to. I've done a few thousand shows in my career, and I've always done whatever I felt at the moment. Never fooled with a set list. Never needed one. I play whatever fits my mood. That's what keeps it interesting. Otherwise, I would have quit a long time ago. There're other ways to bore yourself to death.

The club owner caught me at a bad time. I was tired from the long drive north. I was in no frame of mind to be standing in a parking lot negotiating about what kind of music was allowed and what kind was not. He was pushing me and I pushed right back.

"I never have put on a show yet where I didn't do some old-time gospel songs," I said. "I do a few hymns every night."

Then he got right into my face. "I don't care what you do in other places," he says. "Don't do none of your gospel in my club."

"I'm gonna do some old-time gospel hymns here tonight," I said. "And I'm gonna dedicate one to you."

He turned heel and went inside the club and I didn't press the matter no further. Me and the boys commenced setting up to go on stage. I thought I'd taken care of the situation, standing up to him like that. I was well satisfied with myself. I was going to do what I wanted. Only problem was, that wasn't the end of it. He was ready for me.

The way the club owner done it was pretty sneaky. He wasn't around for the show, at least I never did see him that night. He had his brother do the dirty work for him. The club owner was pretty short like me, just a squirrely little fella, and I was no ways scared of him. But his brother was another deal. He was a big, fearsome-looking ole boy with great big arms and long ratty hair. We had a good nickname for him. He called him Dick the Bruiser, after the pro wrestler from back in the fifties and sixties. Back home, that's what they call any big, mean bully. This Dick the Bruiser was working the sound system for his brother, standing at the back of the club.

We were having one of those good nights where everything goes smooth. No hitches at all. Now, you can do that all night long and there's nothing wrong with that. But I want to take people to another place. I want 'em to feel like I did when I first saw Bill Monroe play at our school back in the mountains. That's when I want the music to shift gears. That's the time when I feel like digging deep into the hymnbook.

I did "Rank Stranger" and the crowd went wild. So many of them must have felt like that, being from the mountains in Kentucky and Tennessee and Virginia and trying to make a new life in places up North like Ohio and Michigan. You feel a stranger in the place you moved to and you feel a stranger in your old place where you come from. That song always stirs up a crowd and hits the spot.

Then we did our a cappella favorite, "Gloryland" from the *Cry from the Cross* album. And you know there are a lot of moments of silence in those a cappella hymns. And Dick the Bruiser started hollering during those long pauses in between the verses: "Quit doing that graveyard music!"

This was something I didn't expect. I'd never seen anything like it in all my years. I've seen shootings and fistfights and heart attacks out in the crowd, you name it. But this here was an inside job. You had the club owner's brother, working the PA system, the man whose job is to give me the best sound he can do, and he's shouting me down in the middle of a song.

When you're an entertainer, that stage is yours and yours alone. You can't let nobody in the crowd take it away or the show's over. It's sacred ground. Now it was a battleground, and it was me against Dick the Bruiser. I wasn't no ways going to let him win that stage from me.

After the song, I got hold of the microphone and I looked right through the crowd to the back of the room. I was staring down Dick the Brusier, and I didn't give a rat's ass what he thought anymore.

"I've been in the music business for forty years, and I've always done gospel songs in my show," I said. "And I'm going to do them now. Right over this here PA system."

There was a big roar from the crowd. I knew they were on my side. That gave me some courage. We went straight into another gospel song, I believe it was "Children, Go Where I Send Thee."

A few verses in, Dick the Bruiser pulled the plug on the sound system and the microphones went stone dead. He had some troublemakers on his side, and they were yelling for us to shut down the show and get off the stage. But we didn't let that stop us. The crowd was still on our side, and we just kept right on singing and finished out the song like we weren't bothered at all. Like we were in a war, and we wasn't ready to surrender.

We went ahead and ended the set like we always did with an up-tempo gospel song, "Traveling the Highway Home." We didn't need a sound system to get our music across to the crowd. I looked right at Dick the Bruiser and his gang standing in the back, and I sang out, "One of these days, YOU'LL be traveling the highway home." When the song ended, I said, "I reckon that's all we're going to get to play for you tonight."

By now the crowd was getting as mad as I was. They were hollering for Dick the Bruiser to turn the power back on so we could get on with the show. They'd paid good money to see the show, and here was the promoters stopping the music. There were some tussles going on out on the floor, and we realized we'd better just clear out of there.

Most of the Clinch Mountain Boys, we just bolted out a side door. Charlie Sizemore, my lead singer, headed towards the front, carrying a cup of coffee, making his way through the ruckus. Up ahead, one of my fans was in a pushing match with Dick the Bruiser, and when Charlie walked by, he stopped to check on things. Dick the Bruiser turned on him and knocked the coffee out of Charlie's hand.

Now, understand this. Charlie comes from eastern Kentucky, and he took that as a challenge. He was born fighting, and when things get rough, he don't back down. This Dick the Bruiser fellow had sabotaged our show and now he'd done this. It was enough. Charlie punched him square in the jaw, and all hell broke loose. Like I told you, it was like to be a riot, and I wanted no part of it, so I got out of there fast.

From what I heard later, Charlie got blindsided by one of the club bouncers. He took a hard cheap shot direct in his face and that set off a whole new round of brawling. A bunch of fans ganged up on Dick the Bruiser, a woman as old as me smacking him good with her purse. Next thing was, Dick the Bruiser's laid out on the floor, and Charlie's kicking on that old boy like there's no tomorrow. Charlie had on a pair of cowboy boots, so it must have hurt bad.

By then, the police had shown up, and they got things under control. Charlie was escorted out by a nice female officer who I reckon took pity on a man who was paid to play music, not to defend his honor. She told him to stay out of the building and there wouldn't be no trouble. Charlie said he was dazed and shaken up, but somehow he found me out by the bus. He looked rough, his nose bleeding and eyes all swelled up.

"Ralph," he said. "I really knocked the snot out of him, didn't I? I really put the shoe leather to him, like to break his ribs. He deserved it, though, didn't he? Ruining the show like he done."

I ain't much for showing my feelings, unless it's when I'm singing a song. It's just not my way. Can't help it and can't hardly change. All I could do was pat him on the knee.

"You done fine, Charlie," I said. "I guess you're for me, ain't you?" And I knew he was.

Shut down for playing gospel. That may have been the first time in music history, and I hope it was the last. I'd never thought I'd see the day. Thing was, it only made me more determined.

Sometimes you need something like that to wake you up. Let you know where you stand. I reckon I took it for granted that I could play any music I wanted wherever I wanted. Sing any songs I felt like singing. Well, this set me thinking. I was well blessed to be doing this.

I reckon I'm a gospel singer as much as anything these days. Don't get me wrong. I will always sing "Pretty Polly" and "Little Maggie" and "Man of Constant Sorrow." Them old ballads will always follow me wherever I go. But I always want to sing different songs, and the sacred material adds something. It makes my show more entertaining.

One of the greatest showmen ever, Uncle Dave Macon, was like that. He'd sing gospel right along with his gutbucket songs wherever he went. You'd hear him sing "I Keep My Skillet Good and Greasy," sticking out his tongue and twirling his banjo between his legs. Then he'd switch up and hit you with the gospel tune "Walking in the Sunshine," and you'd believe he was leading you straight into Gloryland.

I believe Uncle Dave knew just about every song that ever existed, all the way back to the Civil War days. There were hundreds and hundreds, and the words would just roll out of him. And he didn't think you needed to play perfect, either. Just play it loose and natural, like you're feeling it.

I didn't know him too well, but I met Uncle Dave and saw him play a few shows back in the forties. He was a self-made man if there ever was, a real character. He'd take fresh-cured ham with him on the road, and he'd get the restaurants to fry it up for him. With his food and hygiene, he was very particular. He carried his own slop jar with him, too. He was afraid of the germs he might get from public restrooms, and he was always worried about getting something contagious. "You're pretty," he'd tell the waitress. "I'd kiss you, but I'm afraid of catching that ole bad disease."

Uncle Dave always carried whiskey with him, and he'd charge a man for a drink off that bottle, least I heard he did. He carried some honey along with him, too. His own personal stash. He was still on the road into his eighties, and he used it to keep his voice. I keep honey with me on the road, too. I put the honey in my coffee, and it really helps get my voice ready for a show when my throat's feeling rough.

Anyhow, Uncle Dave liked to show off and carry on and clown it up, but he sang the sacred numbers like he meant every word.

Gospel songs are different. The words mean more, I think, because they talk about higher things. They need every bit of feeling you've got, and I believe I put more feeling into the sacred numbers. They deserve everything you've got inside you, to put those songs over. The older you get, the better the hymns sound, too. When you get past eighty, you start to really pay attention to what they're saying. You start to realize the sacred songs are talking to you.

I've been blessed to write some of own through the years. It usually comes when you're worried and troubled. Something may be bothering you and the song is a way to set you right.

I can wake up of a night in the wee hours, and that's one of my most lonesomest times. That's when I feel down and out. I can't get back to sleep because my mind gets to worrying and I start to think of so many bad or sad things that could happen, or good things that might not happen. In the dark hour, you've got nobody to talk to, and you just feel alone. You get down about your life. You think of everything happening to you and you just look at it wrong, you're negative about it.

And that to me is the darkest hour, just before dawn, when you have all them bad feelings. You're unsure of yourself and what you should do. Then when it gets daylight and you get up to start the day and everything, why, you're all right. In the morning, you start fresh and you forget all about it.

One night I woke up singing. It was about four o'clock in the morning and I wrote four gospel songs before I knew what had happened. Songs like that just come to you. If it don't happen, you can't do it. It's a gift from the Man Up Above. I actually woke up singing after I had dreamed the melody and some of the words for one song. I got up and grabbed some paper and wrote it down so I wouldn't forget in the morning. It just came to me out of the real lonely feeling. I reckon I must have been sad about something. It was "The Darkest Hour Is Just Before Dawn":

The darkest hour is just before dawn, the narrow way leads home
Lay down your soul at Jesus' feet, the darkest hour is just before dawn

Some of my favorite gospel songs are the ones I heard when I was a boy, like "Village Churchyard." I told you how my dad used to lead a lot of hymns at the McClure church. Sometimes, he'd get some help from his brother, Jim Henry Stanley. He worked for my dad at the sawmill business; he used to drive a team of horses out in the woods. They would lead on "Village Churchyard" on Sunday mornings, and it was one of the saddest hymns I ever heard.

You never know where you're going to get a good gospel song. Sometimes you find one in an old hymnbook. Sometimes you hear one, and there's something in the words and melody that pulls you in and won't let go. You know it's the right song.

I learned "Jacob's Vision" and "Turn Back" from Enoch Rose, a Free

Will Baptist preacher at Rugby Church on Caney Ridge. Enoch and his wife, Mattie Rose, sang a lot together and recorded some albums, and they also taught children at school on the ridge. Enoch never tried to soften the message in his songs; he wrote it like he felt it from the Bible. When you hear "Turn Back," which I've done several times through the years, you hear a hymn that don't take the easy way out.

There are many preachers all the time sending me songs. I reckon I've got a thousand or more buried around the house I'll never get to look at. They're every kind you can think of. Maybe a hit song in there, just waiting to see the light of day. There's so many songs, it's hard to know.

There's a local preacher named Franklin Viers, and he's given me many a hymn, and he sold me many a car through the years, too. Now, that's what you call a bargain. Frank worked as a salesman at Turner Chevrolet in Haysi, and he says he sold me 101 cars down through the-years, and I don't doubt it. I'm bad for swapping cars. The dealership closed after the owner, Larky Turner, crashed his car off a mountain road and burned to death. Frank's seventy-five and retired now, but he still preaches and officiates funerals all around the area, from Lick Creek to Fletcher's Ridge.

Frank knows all the old-time Baptist hymns from the Goble book, and he finds ones that fit my voice. He found me "Jerusalem My Happy Home," which I recorded in the 1980s. And he writes some good ones, too; he gave me "If I Could Crown You, Mother," and he's got a new one he says he's been meaning to sing to me over the phone: "Hold On to Your Rose." He can sing in the good old-time way, too, Frank can.

Some of the finest gospel songs come from where you least expect. A fellow who's given me some beautiful hymns has been in prison for most of his life. His name is John Brenton Preston, from Macgoffin County, in the eastern Kentucky coalfields. Back in the sixties, he got in trouble with the law over thirty dollars. Robbed a bootlegger and it put him behind bars.

Once when Preston was out on parole, we took him on the road with us, but he acted up a little bit. He was riding on the bus, and we pulled into a truck stop near Baltimore. He tried to get out of the store with a pair of boots and they caught him and locked him up. Somehow or other, he got out of jail pretty quick, because he just about beat us home the next day. By the time we made it back to Coeburn, he was already in Kentucky. But it wasn't long before he was back behind bars. He always gets in trouble and gets himself locked up again. He just can't seem to get along with people out in the world. To tell you the truth, I think he likes it in the pen. That's where he's spent most of his life. He feels more at home there, I reckon.

He's presently doing time in the East Kentucky Correctional Complex in West Liberty. If you write him, he will write you back, you can count on that. The man's got things to say. When he's not writing petitions and filing appeals, he writes gospel songs. Hundreds and hundreds. When you're facing a life sentence, it can set your mind to bigger things beyond, and I reckon that's what happened with Preston. His gospel songs are something else. They have a power that no court of law can deny.

He wrote a song called "I've Just Seen the Rock of Ages." It's about a vision the singer's mother has on her deathbed. She's a-dying, she's got a raging fever and in her final agony, but she's the one who's comforting everyone around her. Telling them it's going to be all right.

I knew it was a classic the first time I heard it. I recorded it back in the 1970s, and ever since, it's been one of my most requested numbers. You always hear somebody holler for it. Larry Sparks cut a fine version, too, and so have a lot of bluegrass groups. It's one of those songs that you hear it and you think it must have been around forever. Like something out of the Scriptures.

Preston was in solitary confinement when the song hit him like a lightning bolt, and he didn't have a pen or nothing to write with. The only thing he could find was a piece of rock and he scratched out all the words on the concrete floor.

You might be asking: How does a jailbird get on the receiving end of something like that? That tells you something about the power of the sacred songs. No steel bars can stop the inspiration getting through.

I remember back in the fifties, we heard a gospel group called the Willow Branch Quartet. They played around the Bristol area, and they were like a lot of gospel groups that only played at church programs and on Sunday morning radio shows and never made any records. These little quartets had some of the prettiest singing you'd hear and they never wanted to make any money at it. All they wanted to do was sing to glorify God.

We were driving to a show, listening to the radio, when we heard the Willow Branch Quartet doing a song called "Rank Stranger." There was something there that grabbed Carter and me. We'd never heard that term "Rank Stranger" before. The song was all about feeling a stranger in this world, even with your own family and friends and neighbors, and how the next world would make all that right.

The Willow Branch Quartet did a good job on that, but we wanted to make it different. Carter and me worked out a whole new arrangement that had my tenor coming in solo out of nowhere on the chorus. A lot of people tell me when my voice comes in that first time, they get chills running up and down their spine. We wanted it to be like somebody surprising you from behind. Like somebody waking you up and everything seems different and you don't know if you're awake or still dreaming.

I reckon it became the most popular song the Stanley Brothers ever sung. They holler for it everywhere I've ever played, with Carter and without Carter. I don't care where we've been in the world, if I mention "Rank Stranger" on the stage, you're going to hear from the crowd.

I never heard a thing about the Willow Grove Quartet since we heard them sing that Sunday morning, but "Rank Stranger" keeps on going. It's one of those songs you know will always be sung somewhere, by somebody. I'm proud Carter and me somehow helped it from dying out. I know for a fact the song has helped many people when they've been down and hurting.

I ain't one to preach, but back when I was a boy, I used to have the urge to preach the Gospel. I don't know exactly why. It was a feeling I got. Must have been seeing my uncle John Smith at the McClure church, the way he done his preaching, the way he moved people, the feeling from that.

Don Reno was another one who almost became a minister. He told me how when he was a young man he felt the calling and he studied the Bible and he was close to joining the ministry. But music always came first, and he told me he hoped the Lord didn't hold it against him that he didn't follow through on that. I said he done just fine preaching through his music, because he wrote some fine gospel songs. Everybody knows how good a banjo player he was, but Don had a way with hymns made you glad he stuck with music instead of the ministry.

Don said his sacred songs came from what they call divine inspiration. It sounds like what happened with me. He'd wake up late at night and set himself down at the kitchen table and write a bunch of gospel songs. In the morning, he'd look at the paper and could hardly believe what he'd written. He'd have the whole thing all laid out, no mess-ups or words scratched out, all the verses to "Some Beautiful Day" or "A Rose on God's Shore" and so many other classic hymns.

He said God deserved songwriting credit with him, because he was just taking down the words what come through him. Whether God was helping him or not, Don deserves to be better remembered. In 1979, a year after Don died, I recorded one he wrote, "Oak Grove Church," that put me in mind of those days singing with my mother and dad at the McClure church:

There's an old church so dear, standing lonesome and still
But in memory it's still to me
A place still so sweet where I heard as a boy
An old hymn, "Nearer My God to Thee"
There I heard Mother sing and I heard Daddy pray
With the tears running down their face
Many now have passed on whose souls there were saved
While we all sang "Amazing Grace"

Bluegrass lost one of the all-time greats when Don passed on, and I lost a good friend. He was only fifty-eight years old, and he gave all he had to music. I don't believe I ever had a cross word with Don, and I knew him for more than thirty years. He was always ready to lend a helping hand and share the stage to get you more exposure with the fans. Around 1956, he invited the Stanley Brothers as guests on the TV show he had in Roanoke. We done a twin banjo tune and then we sung the gospel song "Over in Gloryland," with Carter on lead, me on tenor, Don on baritone and Red Smiley on bass. That was some quartet.

One time, we traded banjos onstage; he played my 1923 Gibson and I played his 1934 Gibson. They were both arch-tops anyhow, so it was easy playing the other man's instrument. We just always got along perfect. He was a good-natured fellow and always jolly. Mostly, we'd just joke around with each other, and he'd pull a monkey face at me.

The thing is, as easygoing as he was, I know Don would have made a fine Baptist preacher. If you ever heard his recitations on "The Lord's Last Supper" and "The True Meaning of Christmas," you know he could get across the Scriptures. It was Don who did the first recitation in bluegrass, "Someone Will Love Me in Heaven," way back in 1954. He could make the Bible come alive and he didn't shove it at you, neither.

I know something about the calling to preach that Don felt. It never really does leave you. I have preached to myself, driving late at night to a show. I used to preach up a storm, nothing but me and the night and all those miles. I reckon I was mostly just trying to stay awake. And there was many a time when the old-time hymns and some good old whiskey kept us awake on the road back in the early years. Now some might say the gospel and liquor don't go together, but they can work fine if you know the proper amounts.

This was back in the sixties, and we'd have 500-mile drives from one show to the next. I've always been able to hang in there pretty good on the all-night driving, but sometimes it took a little help from the hymns and Jack Daniel's. I never did go for coffee, because it didn't set well with my system, and I never took pills or dope.

George Shuffler and me, what we'd do is, we had maybe a half pint bottle of whiskey laying between us in the front seat. And we'd just take barely a sip maybe once an hour or so, just enough to give us that little boost, to pep us up so we wouldn't doze off. And we'd sing some of them old gospel songs and trade off taking nips on that bottle until morning broke and we'd made it safe to the next show. The singing and the sipping set us right, and I reckon it probably saved us from many a car wreck. Never did fall asleep at the wheel, and I've made a million miles or more. I reckon the Man Upstairs was taking care of us.

My job is to sing the best I can, and I try to tell it in the music. You have all them people in the audience and they're looking at you, listening to you, a-hanging on every word. You need to give them something that's worth their attention. That's the part of music that's doing the job right.

Now, I ain't a bit ashamed saying I'm a Christian, but I'm there to sing for the people. And you've got believers and nonbelievers in the crowd. You've got Methodist, you've got Holiness, you've got Baptist, you've got every kind of believer. So I sing Holiness songs, I sing Baptist songs, I sing 'em all. A lot of the hymns I do come out of the African-American churches, and I love to sing those as well. One of my favorites is "Go Down Moses," which I always do as a trio.

You sing the hymns people know and love, but you do it your own style. Like the way I sing "Amazing Grace." It started out as a Methodist hymn two hundred years ago, and everybody seems to take that song to heart. Now, most performers do it the same standard way, but I line it out like the Primitive Baptists do. It's still "Amazing Grace," but it's done my way. I respect the song but I put my stamp on it.

My gift is singing, not preaching. I've had a lot of the old Baptist preachers tell me that they got more out of my singing than any preaching they ever heard. Well, now, if you know what I'm getting at, I sort of preach my songs out. And I'm hoping that's the gift I'm supposed to do, and take that out to the people.

Carter used his music to preach, too. When he died, the local paper ran a headline, "Famed Gospel Singer Stanley Buried in Native

Dickenson." Now, that's as good a job description as he could have asked for. Carter could have been a fine preacher if he hadn't been a singer. We'd be on the road, and he'd be sitting up front, and the feeling would hit him, and he'd start preaching up a storm. Sometimes, we'd read the Bible in the motel, to shore us up when we were feeling low.

Course, for us, it always came back to the singing. I believe it runs in families, this feeling for gospel music. When my son Ralph II was just a little boy, maybe three or four years old, he used to cry when he heard me sing them lonesome old hymns. This was way before he even knew what the words meant, it was just the sound of the gospel music that touched his heart. My grandson Nathan has the same love for the sacred music we do. He recorded a gospel album before he was old enough to drive.

Carter and me were always most proud of our sacred records. For our last big session for Syd Nathan and King Records in 1965, we recorded a whole bunch of sacred numbers. Most were originals. Near the end of his life, Carter was writing more gospel songs than anything else. King pressed up the album and called it *The Greatest Country and Western Show on Earth*. It burned me up. It was just plain wrong to call the album that. I gave Syd some guff and he said he was sorry and fixed it. The later pressings gave it a proper title: *A Collection of Original Gospel and Sacred Songs*.

Right from the start, we always worked hard on our gospel songs. In the early days, a lot of Stanley Brothers fans wouldn't come to hear us in the bars where we played. They were strict Christian people and they wouldn't come in any place where they sold beer and liquor. They didn't want to be seen in a place like that.

I'd have a lot say to me, "Would you like to be doing something like playing music in a bar when Jesus comes? You wouldn't want to be caught in a place like that, would you?"

"No, I wouldn't want that if I could help it," I'd say. "But that's my job."

See, there's another side to it. Just because you play music in a place where they sell beer and people get wild, don't mean you have to indulge in it. The bar won't do you any harm if you don't let it.

I've had just as many Christians who thanked me for playing a beer joint where they saw me. They say, "I got saved" or "I saw the light in a certain bar you played in. You sang a hymn that changed me." That makes you feel like you done good to be in the bar that night. Like you were meant to be there, to help someone. I believe you need to be doing work where there's work needs to be done, not just preaching to the choir.

The gospel songs can do things a preacher can't do with a sermon. That's where music has a purpose. I've seen it many a time. I've had people write and tell me they've had a bottle in their pocket, and then they heard me singing gospel, and they'd throw the bottle away and go to church. These are people who'd spent their whole paycheck on drinks and not got their family what they needed, and they tell me, "Your songs changed that. I'm a different person now." I think a hymn can make better people out of worse people.

I've had so many people tell me they were saved by my singing, in bars and everywhere else. We might not have sold as many records as the top country stars, but maybe we changed a lot of people's lives in the bargain. I've got to thinking I need to do another album of sacred songs. I've been running it through my mind that I might do me one more CD. If I do, it'll be gospel. And it'll be the last one.

There used to be a saying that when you heard a Stanley Brothers record, you'd either want to get drunk or go to church and get saved. In some of them bars we played back then, you'd want to do both. We sang to a lot of drunks in a lot of clubs, and you would see the music work on some people, whether they was half-lit or stone sober. I've seen people holler out, get up and shout when we were singing a hymn. They'd let the music carry them right out of their seat like they was in church on Sunday morning.

I remember when we used to play a TV show down in Jacksonville, Florida, back in the late fifties. That was when we first started doing "Rank Stranger," which became one of our most requested songs. So we began featuring that on our show and got a lot of mail on that. The two that was bringing more letters than any was "Rank Stranger" and "Man of Constant Sorrow."

I got a letter from a lady who lived there, and her letter always stuck with me. I can just about remember it word for word: "My husband has always been a drunk and he's been mean to me and mean to the children. He's always bought whiskey and brought the bottle in and set it in the refrigerator, and that was all he cared about. If he had any money left he bought food, and if he didn't have any left, we didn't have no food. But we saw you singing some gospel songs on the TV the other day, and he began crying and couldn't stop. He had a fifth of liquor right there and he went to the sink and poured out the liquor, and he's never drank another drop. He's an altogether different man after he heard you singing."

Lot of the time, though, it was the women who would get the most excited from the gospel songs. It would be in a bar or some place, but they'd get to carrying on like they was in church. I saw it happen out in the audience, during the shows. I'd see women get up out of their seats and get to shouting when I'd do a hymn. I haven't seen any shouting for a while now, but I see a lot of tears. It means the music is getting through somehow. That's when you're feeling something, feeling the spirit, and I'm proud that I can help them feel that. I give all the credit to my mother and dad for taking me to church. I believe it helped me to sing a hymn in church when I was a little boy.

I don't play in bars too much now. We mostly play in auditoriums and big halls. But I still have people say things like that to me. They come up after the show, and they tell me they were saved by my singing. At least they were for that night, anyhow. It makes me feel good to hear that, when people tell me, "You're God-sent," or something like that. I feel like I've not wasted all those years playing music, like maybe I'm doing some good and helping people.

After a time, though, I started realizing I was helping everybody but myself when it come to the sacred songs. I started to wonder if I wasn't too busy singing the hymns to really hear what the words were saying. It started to work on me, and I started to see myself out in that crowd during hymn time. I'd have tears in my eyes singing those sacred songs, just like they did. I was like them, hurting and hungry for the Gospel. I know how a lot of these people felt. I know how bad they must have been hurting.

I felt something like they did until I finally got myself baptized. I'm talking about the old-time way like it used to be when I was a boy and everybody was river-baptized. I remember seeing my mother baptized in the river. Most of the times, you're an adult when you get baptized in our church. They're pretty strict about that; they want you to be mature, and you're supposed to have an experience with God to show you're fit to be properly baptized and be in the church.

And I'd never got around to it. Something had been holding me back all those years. I knew what it was, and I ain't ashamed to tell you now; I was too afraid to go through with it.

I've had the belief all through the years. Getting baptized was something I'd been fixing to do. I had even written a song about it, "I'll Answer the Call," back in the 1980s. I sang the words and I believed the song, but I didn't follow through.

All those years I just dodged it. I didn't know whether I could live it or not. I didn't want to be a hypocrite. I wanted it to be real, and I wanted to be sure. There are so many temptations on the road, so many wrong turns and distractions from the right way. I was doing some things I knew I'd better quit doing.

What happened was, I got a sign, when my daughter Lisa Joy was pregnant with twins and the doctor told her that one wasn't getting the nourishment she needed to survive. I was real scared for her, that she wouldn't be able to carry both babies to term. But Lisa's a lot like her mother Jimmi in her faith and she wouldn't give up. And she went home and her friends came by to pray with her and lay hands on her belly and two weeks later she went back for more tests and the baby had gained 14 ounces. The doctor said he couldn't explain it. Ashley Hope and Alexis Faith were borned premature, but they were both healthy baby girls and it got me thinking a lot about the miracle-working power of God. Doctors are good but they don't have the final say.

This stayed on my mind, and I think it helped prepare me to be ready to answer the call. Like the way you get a field plowed and it's ready to take the seed. All I can tell you is, it finally did hit me that it was time. I believe God gets ahold of you and shows you what to do. I was seventy-three years old. If I wasn't ready now, I might never be ready. Then it would be too late.

It had been knocking at my door for so many years, and I finally gave in. When I got to wanting to go in the water, I knew I was ready. What finally done it was a dream. It was a dream I had that showed me what to do. Not just one dream, it was a series of dreams that were all part of the same vision.

The first time, I dreamed one night I was out walking and I met a preacher. I didn't know his name. He reached down and we shook hands. He gave me a cold handshake. I went on a little farther and met another preacher. He reached down and hugged me. His name was Landon Colley. He's the one who preached my mother's funeral and Carter's funeral. That stayed with me. I couldn't sleep, it hit me so hard. It was more than a dream, you know. It was a vision.

Round about this time, summer of 2000, I had started going to a little country church to hear this preacher, Ezra Davis Jr., Brother Junior. He's half my age, but he preaches the old-time way and he's been doing it since he was sixteen years old. I liked his tone and the sound he had in his delivery. It grabbed me the same way those old Baptist hymns grabbed me when I was a boy.

Our church believes the Lord finds you, and I guess that's what happened with me. I had gone to see Brother Junior preach at his little church, the Slate Creek Primitive Baptist Church, over in Buchanan County. After we left the church-house, two ladies were going to be baptized that day. The Clinch River runs by there, and that's where Brother Junior done the baptizing. I thought that was a pretty spot on a bend of the river, pretty shade trees on the water. And the place stayed with me. From then on, it wouldn't let me go.

Then came the second dream, over and over again. I began to dream about that pretty place of baptizing. I would see the bend on the river, and I'd be standing on that beautiful spot under the shade trees, with the water going by, and then I would wake up. I believe that was telling me where to go get baptized. In the next few weeks, I must have dreamed of that place seven or eight times. I believe it was calling me.

One night I couldn't sleep at all. I laid in bed and rolled around, worried and bothered. It was 4:30 A.M. of a Sunday morning, but I had to do something to get it off my mind. So I called up Brother Junior. I told him I was sorry to bother him but I wanted to be baptized there in the Clinch River that day. He said, "That's the best news I ever heard in my life."

So I made the arrangements right then. That's the way it happens with a lot of us in our church. It hits you and it don't matter when, it's always the right time. I've heard people say they had to break the ice in the river to get baptized. It hits you and you go. There's a song I recorded, "These Men of God," that puts in words how it works on you:

Go down to the river, God told Lazarus
Dip yourself in Jordan, wash your spots away
Lazarus did obey, his spots were washed away

I woke up Jimmi and told her I was sorry for anything I'd ever done to hurt her. There had been a lot I'd done in the past. Many a time I'd done her wrong, and I was needing her forgiveness before I could do what I had to do. I asked her to come with me to get baptized down by the river at that spot that had been haunting me. She said she would and she told me my face was a-shining in the darkness.

That very day, we went down to Brother Junior's church. And after the service, we went down to that place on the river bend and I got baptized by Brother Junior and Landon Colley. My daughter Lisa said I looked like an angel when they brought me up out of the river. People could see the change.

One way to tell you how it feels: It's a lot like the words to "Two Coats," a hymn on the *Cry from the Cross* album: "I took off the old coat and put on the new." I sang the song in 1971, and now I could finally live the words.

I don't like to tell people what to believe, and I don't much like to talk about what I believe. I think it's between yourself and God. But I will tell you that the faith I was raised up in, and the faith I believe in today, it has never changed. It was the same before I went to the river, and it will be the same when that river runs dry.

We believe that Jesus died on the cross and died for the whole entire family of Adam. He done the saving for everybody when he died on the cross. Some of the other Baptist churches believe so many people were born for heaven and so many people were born for hell. Our church, which is the Primitive Baptist Universalist faith, is different from that. I think we have a little more hope.

I'm not much on quoting the Scripture, line and verse. But there's a few places in the Bible that says it all, as far as my beliefs and the beliefs of the old-time Baptists. One line says, "Christ came to seek and to save that which was lost." And the other is just as important, and it goes right alongside that verse. Before he died on the Cross, Jesus looked up toward his Father and said, "I have finished the work which Thou gavest me to do."

That puts it all together, I reckon; there's not much more that can be said. I believe in this and try to live by it the best I know. Living it is harder than believing it.

I'm now a member in good standing of the Slate Creek Primitive Baptist Church in Buchanan County, Virginia. Times is busy, but whenever we can, Jimmi and me go there to hear Brother Junior preach. There are plenty of Primitive Baptist churches near where I live, and a lot of people ask me, "Why don't you go to church around here?"

I tell them I can't get the feeling at other churches that I get at Slate Creek. It's worth it to me to drive that extra distance one county over, because I get more out of it. I have to go where it feels right.

Some of you may be wondering, "Does the baptism really change a man?" Well, that isn't for me to say. I believe I came out of the river a new man. I hope a better man, too. Jimmi says I'm a better man, and that's good enough for me. If my wife, Jimmi, says something is so, you can take it to the bank.

And there's something else, too. You know that beautiful place I dreamed about, that shady bend of the river? After I was baptized, I haven't dreamed about it since.

CHAPTER TWENTY-FOUR

Clinch Mountain Country

"I especially want to thank The Clinch Mountain Boys, both past and present, for always being there when I needed them and for their many contributions to the Stanley Sound."

—Ralph Stanley, the 33rd Annual Memorial Bluegrass Festival Souvenir Program, 2003

I've traveled to shows in just about every vehicle you can think of ever made in Detroit. I've had a black 1937 Chevrolet sedan, a white '39 Cadillac, '46 Packard, a Buick LeSabre, a Mercury Monterey, a Pontiac Bonneville station wagon, a Winnebago, a '48 Silverside MCI bus, and a broke-down camper, to name just a few.

Enough cars, campers, motor homes and buses to fill a whole parking lot. No matter what's carried me in, I've always carried my own band, the Clinch Mountain Boys, with me. Once, when the camper broke down, I had to put some of boys in the back of a rented U-Haul and get to the show that way. They was a little banged up from the ride, and they scared some fans when they came crawling out of there at the festival parking lot, but they still put on a good show.

I don't care how good the lead man is. You need sidemen who can do the same. I've always kept men who could do the job. I owe them a lot, because they've helped me keep the Stanley Sound going all these years. If they didn't play the music right, I didn't keep them.

That's why I don't believe in pickup bands. I never have. Neither did Carter. With the Stanley Brothers, we decided from the start to travel with the men who played with us every day. We believed in our music, and we wanted our fans to believe in it, too. We wanted the same sound onstage that people heard on our records. We wanted to give our fans the quality they'd come to expect from us.

And that's the way I kept on, no matter how many men have come and gone. All the way through good times and bad. Like I told you earlier in the book, I've sold cattle to keep my band together, and I'd do it again. I've always believed the people paying to see the show deserve to hear the same band you have on your latest record. Or at least as close to that band as you can bring. Anything else is false advertising.

There's many entertainers who work by themselves and for themselves. They believe in every man for himself and the hell with the rest. They like to haul into the bluegrass festivals in a shiny new car with a girl sitting up front. They hustle backstage to find a bunch of local pickers, trying to learn the songs an hour before the show. Sometimes they get a good band, sometimes they don't. With these entertainers, it's every man for himself and everything for hire, the band and the girl, too. The ones who operate this way are selling their fans short.

It's not easy keeping a band together. It's not cheap, either. That's why so many do it with pickup bands, because the money's better. The local bands don't get hardly nothing, whereas the man who hired 'em gets the whole till to himself. Then he heads to the next festival to play a show with another bunch of strangers. The money's good but the music's not, and that's why I don't believe in that way.

But it's not just for the fans that I bring my own band. I do it for myself. I like to play music with the Clinch Mountain Boys. Whoever's in my band, well, they're my favorite musicians in the world as long as they're playing with me.

Probably only Bill Monroe had more men in his band than I've had in mine through the years. A whole lot of Bluegrass Boys came from close to where I'm from. Kenny Baker was Bill's favorite fiddler for close to twenty years, and he was from Jenkins, the tiny coal town where I saw families in the soup line when I was a little boy during the Depression. Kenny worked as a miner and a hog farmer before he joined Bill, so he knew what "hard raising" was. And he could play many styles besides bluegrass and old-time. He could do western swing so good you'd swear he was from Texas.

That was how Bill was different from me as a bandleader and recruiter. He experimented more than I did. People forget that early on, Bill carried an accordion player in his band, and that his girlfriend Bessie Lee played bass for a while. He hired sidemen like Kenny, who could play anything on the jukebox, and he hired a lot of musicians from all over the country.

Some of the best Bluegrass Boys came from places thousands of miles from Western Kentucky, where Bill is from. He had a banjo player from up in Boston and a fiddle player from out in California. And they were some of the finest Bluegrass Boys that Bill ever had. He went with talent whenever he heard it and didn't care where the talent come from. Now, Bill made them learn to play his way, but they brought something new to his sound he wanted.

That's not my way. All my men are from my area and play my style of music. I don't train anyone, not like the way Bill did. He would mold his men into Bluegrass Boys, whereas mine come in already knowing the Stanley Sound. Nothing against the North, but I've never had any Yankees in my band and I don't plan to. I've had some fill in on a show when I was short a man and they done fine, but I've never hired any permanent. I like to play shows in Boston and New York and a lot of places up North, where we have some of our best fans, but you couldn't find a Clinch Mountain Boy up there if you spent the rest of your life looking.

All my men, even as far back as the days of the Stanley Brothers, come from pretty close by where I'm from and still live. It's worked out well, so I've seen no need to change that. I've always been able to find all the talent I need from within five hundred miles from Dicksenson County. And they've always been lining up once word gets out somebody's leaving the band. I've never needed to do any job searches, and I've never had to play a show a man short, unless it was during the lean years when we couldn't afford a full band. I've been lucky that way.

There's probably been near a hundred Clinch Mountain Boys. I reckon most have come from Virginia, Kentucky, West Virginia, North Carolina, Tennessee, and Ohio. That's a guesstimate, but it's probably pretty close. It don't matter what state, really. They was all raised on the Stanley Sound. Clinch Mountain Country.

Some people have asked me about that. There are a lot of reasons I do it. There was one guitar player who tried for a long time to get a job with me. He played a good lead guitar, one of the best in the business, and he knew the Stanley style very well. But he was from up North and I'd always turn him down.

Somebody asked me, "Ralph, why didn't you ever hire that boy? He's really good and you know it."

"I know he's good," I said. "I just didn't figure he was my kind of people."

Now, that ain't a bit fair, but that's the way it is. The fellow didn't talk like us and he didn't walk like us and he had a different way of doing things. The Clinch Mountain Boys have a lot of hard road to travel, and it's already tough enough for everybody trying to get along. I think it helps when there's a certain understanding about things, when there's already a common ground.

I don't say my way is right or better. Only that it works for me. As the band leader, that's the way I run things.

It's not just ones from the North that don't fit in. It's anywhere outside Clinch Mountain Country. With a man from another area of the country, well, he wouldn't speak his words like we do. He wouldn't phrase things the same way, and so he wouldn't be as easy to play with, and music's tough enough as it is.

Now, there are exceptions to this. One of the best singers we ever had in the Clinch Mountain Boys didn't talk a bit like us. This was Curley Lambert; he was from Virginia but he wasn't from the mountains. We found him back in the 1950s playing in a band in the eastern part of Virginia near Lynchburg. That was close to where he was from in the Piedmont area near Broadnax, down between Richmond and South Hill.

It's flat land out that ways and Curley had that strange way of talking like they do in East Virginia. They've got a little something to their words that we don't have down in the mountains where I'm from. To give you an example, instead of "house," he'd say what sounded like "hoose" to us, and he'd say so many words different than us.

So we thought Curley talked funny, and we had a lot of fun with him. We'd laugh at him as he was talking and that would get him to stuttering. That would make it worse, so we couldn't understand a thing he was saying, and that would make us laugh even harder. He'd get real nervous and that would make it more fun for us. That may sound mean, but Goat enjoyed it right along with us. He could take anything you could throw at him, and he'd end up laughing harder than anybody else. He could not only take a joke, he was a good driver for the long trips, too. He was a good man for the band.

And the thing was, as different as he talked, Curley sang like we did. You'd've thought he came straight from the mountains. He sang like we'd known him all our lives. Outside of George Shuffler, he was about the best man to sing with of all the Clinch Mountain Boys.

He was a good baritone singer, and he really added something special to our quartet singing. He had a blend that we needed. Another thing was, he followed my tenor as close as anybody ever has. He had a knack for knowing where I was going when I didn't even know myself. That's not easy. I've had many say I was the hardest man to sing with. Curley was just like a natural when it come to harmony.

I mentioned earlier how I nicknamed Curley "Goat" when he first joined up with us. He was like me, not the best-looking man in the world. He'd already lost most of his hair before he was thirty and his face reminded me of a billy goat. So I saddled the name Goat on him. And he started calling me Rabbit and then Fluffo, which was a kind of lard you could buy, because I was on the heavy side back then. My nicknames didn't stick, but Goat did. He carried that on, he really wore the name well.

I wish right here I could do that old Kornfield Kounty Salute to the Clinch Mountain Boys, at least the ones I can remember, and name every one for you on the page. Some you've heard a lot about, some not at all, but they've all been down the road with me these past sixty-two years. But there's been so many, and I don't want to leave any out.

A couple or few Clinch Mountain Boys do come to mind, not for any other reason than I'm old and things come to me and I've learned just to pay heed before they drift away from me and fade back into the past. There was this young, fast-talking, fair-haired boy out of Emory Gap, Tennessee, Frank Wakefield; he played mandolin for us a stretch in the fifties. I believe he's the only one I can recall that up and quit the Stanley Brothers in so short a time.

Now, Frank was a mandolin whiz; he could play anything from Bill Monroe to Bach, and he had a funny way of talking backwards sometimes, sort of like pig latin, hillbilly-style. The day he started with us, he showed up and it turned out he was holding Pee Wee Lambert's mandolin, which he'd got from a Dayton pawnshop after Pee Wee had broke it accidentally and thrown it in the trash.

Frank was an odd character for sure, but he done fine for us. What run Frank off had nothing to do with music or not getting along; it was that our traveling schedule just plumb wore him out, and he was a man who'd played the Dayton bars for years, so he knew the hard life. Well, he made it two weeks with us, and after a show in Baltimore, he said thank you but he'd had enough and he was headed home to get some rest. "This is too much like a real job," Frank told us. "This is too dang much like work and I'll tell you plain, I like to have a little more fun!"

I reckon Frank had a point, about needing to have some good times. It's just that Carter and me never looked at music in that way. For us, it *was* a job, and that meant hard, hard work. That's the way we felt about it. It's just like a man going to punch a clock and do his eight-hour shift: You do your job and you do it right.

We never did do music for fun, but for a living. That don't mean we couldn't have fun doing it, but that wasn't and still ain't the reason behind it. Now I've stayed on the road fifty years since Frank quit us, and I still feel that way about what I do. Music's been good to me and I wouldn't abuse the music profession and the privilege of playing music for nothing in the world. Because I respect music more than anything; everything I've got come through music.

This story about hard work and what it means puts me in mind of another Clinch Mountain Boy from the early days. It's Joe Meadows, a fiddler we had back in the Mercury years, and on the *Farm and Fun Time* show. I remember looking in a room at the WCYB studio, and I'd always see Joe in there practicing fiddle. I mean this was hours before we went on the air and hours after we were off the air. He'd be there alone, facing the wall, sawing away on that fiddle. He had a dedication to improving himself that you don't see too often. It paid off, too, when his fiddling on "Orange Blossom Special" helped us win Instrumental of the Year from *Country & Western Jamboree* magazine in 1955.

I've had a few Clinch Mountain Boys who had trouble toeing the line, as far as playing my music and acting the proper way. There was one boy from Ohio who was a fine picker but he had an attitude problem. Thought he knew more than anybody else in the band. Once he came to a show without his hat, and that really burned me up; it was lucky for him I had an extra hat he could wear or I wouldn't have let him go on-stage. Another time, I heard him carrying on about how great Ricky Skaggs sounded on the gospel song "Drifting Too Far from the Shore," and he didn't know Ricky was just doing it the same way he heard from an old Stanley Brothers record. So I said, "You oughta brush up a little bit on the history of this music." This same Ohio boy was always trying to add his own fancy licks when we played our shows, and I finally had to tell him, "Listen, you can't be out here playing 'Boogie John' one minute and then be playing my music the next." I finally had to let him go.

On the lighter side, I'd like to make mention of the fact that some Clinch Mountain Boys aren't as bright as some other ones, and the dim bulbs are just as important as the others, because they keep things interesting. We had a nickname for these fellows, which was Hook 'n' Beans. Nothing can hurt a band's morale more than boredom on the road, and having a Hook 'n' Beans fellow on board can help the situation. The name come like this: There used to be a couple of boys who didn't maybe know as much as some people did. They'd call a pork chop a "buck chop" or instead of pork 'n' beans, they'd call 'em "hook 'n' beans." These boys might misname things sometimes, and maybe they couldn't talk plain and couldn't say things right. They were slow and not blessed with everything up top. Well, without a Hook 'n' Beans around, you probably couldn't make too many road trips without going crazy from lack of amusement.

Instead of trying to remember every Clinch Mountain Boy from Pee Wee to my grandson Nathan, I'd rather try to explain to you what I think it means to me to be a Clinch Mountain Boy. Now, I've had some men that have worked out fine. Most of them have. They've all been good musicians, or I wouldn't have hired them. But they've all had to be good men, too.

When I hire a man to be in my band, I have to know his character. The way I judge a man, I want to know if he's a man we can travel with. The playing is only part of the job. I expect him to play his part right and play well, but then I expect him to be a good man along with his playing. I never would keep one that didn't do the right thing off the stage as much as on the stage.

But everybody makes some mistakes. I had one musician who got in trouble with the law. Bad trouble. I can't say all that it was, only that when he was arrested, it caused me a lot of embarrassment. When it hit the news, they put my picture on TV and reported the arrest of one of Ralph Stanley's Clinch Mountain Boys.

I didn't support what the man did, which was something awful. But I still supported the man, right up until he went in jail. You don't condemn the sinner, just the sin. We played a show to support his legal expenses. He did his jail time, he paid the price. He has since started his own band, and he's been welcomed to the Memorial Festival at the old home place on Smith Ridge.

A lot of people didn't think I should have stayed behind him when he was in trouble. They said it wouldn't look good for me. It would hurt my reputation. Well, I did what I thought was right, and I'd do it all over again the same way.

Speaking of the legal system, Charlie Sizemore was a good man to have around. Charlie's not only a bluegrass musician, he's also a lawyer.

Charlie was my lead singer for nine years, and he was one of the best. Not just as a musician but as a man. He's from down near Salyersville, Kentucky. He saw the Stanley Brothers play in his hometown when he was a little boy. He says he still has the autographs we did for him; our bass man at the time, Melvin Goins, says he remembers the show well because we got paid in $2 bills.

Charlie's daddy, Henry Clay Sizemore, was a principal in the local school system back then, and he booked some of our shows in the schoolhouses. Sometimes we went and stayed with the Sizemores to save us from paying for a motel room. Charlie was just a little boy then, not more than five or six years old. He was so small that he'd sit in Curly Ray's lap and try to play on his fiddle.

Charlie played rhythm guitar and sang lead, and he also did a lot of the business for me when I was too busy or feeling bad or what have you. He was the one who done my hair when we were out on the road. Helped style my hair before show dates, like the way Keith Whitley used to do. Done a good job on that, like with everything he did. Once he even helped kill me a chicken for dinner, when I stayed over at his place.

Charlie has a law practice in Nashville and he can write as good as he can sing. He wrote about the time he got me the chicken, when his uncle Boone lent him a hand just when he needed one. It's one of those things that happened a long time ago and he remembers it a lot better than I do, so I thought it'd be a nice break in the book to let Charlie tell you how it happened. Being a lawyer and all, he typed up this little recollection years ago and filed it away and he dug it out for me. Knowing how hazy and faded my memory has gotten about most things after 1980 or so, he figured I'd need a little help for my book, so here is a little gift courtesy of Charlie, and I reckon it's as close as you'll get to how it really happened:

Dr. Ralph was serious. Typical of him. But he was more than usual this time. He was standing at my kitchen sink in my house trailer. He had a knife, or perhaps a fork, or maybe a knife and a fork in one hand and a dead chicken in the other. All bloody. But it was clear to me that the doctor was attempting an operation that he had not heretofore performed: picking little metal balls out of what was to be our dinner.

His bus was parked out front. I had told Ralph that he and any of the Clinch Mountain Boys were welcome to stay at my place anytime. I lived alone then, except for my drunk uncle who'd been living there with me. My brother, or my brother's wife, had kicked him out of their house, and he ended up on my doorstep with nowhere else to go.

This day he earned his keep. As I recall, Ralph and the band were on their way to somewhere up North, and for whatever reason Ralph took me up on my rather flippant "stay at my place" offer. Only once.

When Ralph and the boys pulled up and got out of the bus, I figured they'd be hungry. I informed them that I didn't have much to eat around the place, but I did have some chickens I'd be happy to kill if they would fix them.

My grandfather had raised and sold game roosters. They were for fighting, not eating. And I don't remember how I came about owning game chickens, unless one of my brothers had left them there at my place. But there they were. Not fit for eating and hard to kill. Ralph seemed interested in this proposition.

"Kill me a couple," he said, "and I'll fix 'em."

Wishing I had ordered a pizza, I retrieved a .38-caliber Smith & Wesson that I'd picked up in a trade at a truck stop. I wasn't a bad shot, but I'd never even picked up the habit of hunting after I discovered when I was twelve years old that I was unable to kill a squirrel. In fact, I'd never killed anything bigger than a fly in my life. But I grit my teeth and took dead aim at one of those poor critters in my yard, locked my elbow and squeezed the trigger. Whether due to a poor aim or a weak stomach, I was unable to kill or even mortally wound, although I did succeed in shooting the comb off the object of my bloodlust. The poultry then vanished, along with the rooster's chance of a merciful death.

Then here came Uncle Boone. Drunk. Happy and wild-eyed. True to his given name, which was Daniel Boone, he shot a chicken and the wounded rooster in rapid succession. His judgment was better than mine—

he used my Iver Johnson twelve-gauge shotgun instead of a pistol—but his aim was off. He shot the creatures full in the side, filling the edible parts with steel balls not much larger than grains of sand.

Feeling a little embarrassed, I picked them up and handed them to Ralph. Acting no different than when I'd see him introducing a band member or a song, he said, "Charlie, get me some hot water and a knife."

Well, I'm here to tell you the chicken tasted just fine to my recollection, and I do appreciate all the trouble Charlie and his uncle Boone took to get us dinner.

Charlie is the only Clinch Mountain Boy to ever earn a law degree. He stays busy with his lawyering, but in the last few years, he went back part-time as a professional musician too. He's got his own band and he's made some fine records on his own. I sang with him on one, and it was like meeting up with an old friend. We just fell right back into it.

Through the years, there's been many a Clinch Mountain Boy that's bounced back and forth between playing music and working other jobs. Music is a tough business, and sometimes you need to fall back on other means. And sometimes, you find a job that gives you more pleasure than music. Leastwise, until the music calls you back.

For a long time our fiddler Art Stamper ran a barbershop in Louisville. He had graduated from cosmetology school and he was a fine hairdresser, but he kept playing fiddle on the side right up until he died. I remember when Art came back to help me out in the early nineties after Curly Ray left the band. You might find this hard to believe, but Art was to my ears a much better fiddle player with us the second time than in the early days, when he was a teenager playing with the Stanley Brothers in the early fifties.

I know for a while in the late 1960s, Curley Lambert got burned out on bluegrass, sold his mandolin and worked for a time as an orderly at a mental hospital in Richmond, Virginia. He told me it was one of the best jobs he ever had because he knew what he was doing made a difference for people. Not long after that, though, Curley joined back up with me and pulled another stint as a Clinch Mountain Boy in the 1970s. It made four stints with the Stanley Brothers and two stints with me, and that may be a record. I reckon it's like a lot of marriages—can't live with 'em, can't live without 'em. With a singer as fine as Curley, I was always glad to take him back whenever he was willing and able.

Like I said, the business is hard, so a lot of great musicians had to find steady income doing factory work or whatever they could find. But just because they didn't play music for a living anymore don't mean they weren't still professionals in my book.

Pee Wee Lambert, the very first Clinch Mountain Boy, the one who laid the foundation for all the ones who come after, the one who could sing so high and lonesome, had to leave us early on because he had a young family. He walked away from the music business, but he never did quit playing music. He worked a day job as a road engineer and played the bluegrass bars in Dayton at night, right up until he died of a heart attack in 1965 when he was only forty.

Years later, Pee Wee's widow, Hazel, found something in his wallet he'd never told her about. Behind some photos of his children was a little folded piece of paper, four creases, he'd carefully tucked away who knows when. When she unfolded the paper, Hazel discovered it was the label from the Rich-R'-Tone record of "Molly and Tenbrooks," the Bill Monroe song that Pee Wee had sung lead on for us back in 1947. He'd peeled the label off the old phonograph record and carried it close to him all those years and preserved it as a keepsake of a time when we was young and starting out and our music was everything. When she told me about it, Hazel laughed and said, "You know, Ralph, I think Pee Wee done a better job on it than Bill."

The thing about Pee Wee, as good as he was a musician, he was even better as a man. You never heard a thing said against him, and I never heard him say nothing against anybody else. He lived by the Golden Rule, and there's very few I've known been able to pull that off. And that's the most important thing for a Clinch Mountain Boy, in my book: to be as good a man as you are a musician.

CHAPTER TWENTY-FIVE

My Friend Bill

"All the good times are passed and gone
All the good times are o'er
All the good times are passed and gone
Little darling don't you weep no more"

—"ALL THE GOOD TIMES ARE PASSED AND GONE,"
RALPH STANLEY

All the time you hear how things ain't like they used to be, whether it's music or movies or cars or what have you. A lot of people my age complain about that, and I've done my share of complaining, too. Seems like not much is as good as it once was. I reckon that's why they call 'em the good old days.

Well, I don't know. If you had ever tried to drive them two-lane back country roads full of potholes and curves like we did back in the forties and fifties, you'd give thanks for the straight, smooth highways we've got now. I do every day, because I still make more than 100,000 miles on the road every year.

Things are are a lot better than when I was young. As far as the comforts of life and modern conveniences for a lot of people, anyhow. It's still way too hard out there for the workingman. Right here around Dickenson County, young people leave every day because there ain't no jobs. Rich get richer and the poor get poorer. I don't know if that will ever change.

But I will tell you, I do miss some things about the old days. Things like good country ham and my friend Bill Monroe. They don't make men like Bill Monroe anymore, and they don't make music like Bill made. And the world's a poorer place without Bill and his music. I know we can still listen to his records. It's about the only music I can stand to hear. But Lord knows, how I miss the man. Now, let me tell you what kind of man was Bill Monroe.

A while back, I was at a bluegrass festival, talking with Bill Monroe and some other friends. I think Don Reno was there, too, making monkey faces at me like he usually did. I was complaining you couldn't find a decent country ham nowhere. That was something I took for granted growing up in the Clinch Mountains, a country ham. Back then, we butchered our own and there weren't a Thanksgiving I can remember didn't have a hog killing. So I was complaining about how nobody was curing their own ham anymore and what they sold in the store was pretty much garbage as far as I could tell.

Well, not that long after that, I got a call from Bill. He was passing through my area on the way to a show, and he was in Norton, on a pay phone.

"I've got something for you," he told me. "So come on down and meet me on the bus."

Bill never said more than what he needed to say. He didn't tell me what it was and I didn't ask. I drove from Coeburn twenty-five miles to the intersection of Highway 58 and Route 23, where Bill's silver and red bus was parked there at the motel.

I climbed in the bus, wondering what was so important to get me to drive all the way out here on my day off. Bill didn't say nothing. He just shook my hand and said there was a special present all for me. In the back of the bus was a whole hog salted down, just waiting for me to take back home. He'd killed a hog and cured it himself and brought it to me. Two hams, two shoulders, two middlings. That was some good eatings, I'll tell you. That lasted me awhile.

This was the Bill Monroe I knew. He was the Father of Bluegrass, but he was a lot more than that. I'm proud to say he was a good friend of mine, and that's just one way he showed it to me. There aren't many who will bring you a hog when all you maybe wanted was a slice or two of a good country ham.

When Carter and I were boys, Bill was an idol for us. Years later, I was lucky enough to be his friend.

In the early days, we went down a rocky road with Bill there for a few years, Carter and me did. Back in the late forties, after we put out our record of "Molly and Tenbrooks" before he did, he was sore at us, and he let us know it. Those were the Bristol days, when the *Farm and Fun Time* program made us the hottest thing going. Bill came through the area and played a show nearby, in Elizabethton, Tennessee, and we went to see him. It was me and Carter and Pee Wee Lambert and Leslie Keith.

During the show, Bill dedicated a number to Leslie out there in the audience. "This one's for a real fine old-timer and a good friend, Leslie Keith." That was his way of saluting Leslie, who had been in the music business a good while and knew Bill from the thirties. But it was also a slap in the face against the rest of us. Bill saw us sitting right next to Leslie, and he made a point of ignoring us.

After the song, Benny Martin, who was playing fiddle for Bill at the time, stepped up to the microphone and he got a few strong words in before Bill could stop him. "Yeah," said Benny. "I've got a couple good friends sitting out there, too, Ralph and Carter Stanley." When he said that, the crowd let loose with a big cheer. This was really our territory Bill was playing in that night. There was more of our fans in that crowd than Bill's fans.

It was nice of Benny to do that and it took some guts, too. I know Bill wasn't happy with what Benny done. When Benny called us out to the crowd, he was standing up to his boss in public. A few years after that, Benny helped us out on fiddle for some of our best Mercury records. We always were grateful to him, and he was always a good friend of the Stanley Brothers.

Bill really took it hard when he felt he'd been done wrong. A year or so after that happened, he got sore when we signed with Columbia. He left for Decca right after that, and it was a good long while before he'd even talk to us. I remember when we were booked in Greenville, South Carolina, when the Bluegrass Boys were there on a show, too. We were downtown, just window-shopping and killing time, and we looked down the street and here come Bill walking our way, along with his girlfriend, Bessie Maudlin, who played bass for Bill sometimes. About a block or so away, they looked up and saw us and they crossed to the other side of the street so they wouldn't have to pass us on the sidewalk.

With Bill, though, at times all it took was some time for him to come around. And we buried the hatchet, and all the bad feelings were forgotten, when Carter joined up with him in 1951, and they became the best of friends, and Bill and I did, too.

I never had a better friend than Bill. Especially in the later years, we were real close. Neither of us were big talkers. I can explain something in four or five words as good as most people can talking all day. Well, Bill could do it in even less than me. With Bill, you didn't need to use a lot of words. We had a lot in common, on not only how we were raised but what we believed in. Hard work and doing right and living up to your word. All the things that matter the most, we saw eye to eye. So we never did need to say much to each other.

When we did, we never talked too much about music. I remember at a festival one time we was watching a young band play with amplified instruments, so loud we could barely hear each other, and he said, "Many a good bluegrass band's been ruined by an electric bass." We both agreed our music was never meant to be electrified. It ruins the feeling you get from acoustic music. You lose the tone.

Most of the time, me and Bill talked about how we were raised up hard in the country and all the things we used to do. Bill would tell how when he was a boy working the fields, he'd holler out songs like "Old Joe Clark" when nobody else was around. He was afraid somebody'd make fun of his singing. Out by himself, he could sing as loud as he wanted. He'd say how lonely he was growing up. I told him I felt a lot like that after Carter had gone into the service.

Mostly me and Bill talked about farming and raising livestock. We were just like a couple of farm boys all growed up. Once I went and stayed at his place out in the country where he lived outside Nashville. We rode horses all day and the next day. He had close to three hundred acres, some of the prettiest farmland you ever saw, and he was proud of it. We took two days to ride all over his farm and see all he wanted me to see. He had certain places we'd ride to and he would tell me about things that he remembered and that he wanted to point out. When we came up on a place, maybe a big oak tree or a forked creek, he'd say that this was where he done this work, or this happened out here. He was just explaining his farm to me and wanted to show me the land. I believe Bill knew about every inch of those three hundred acres. If he didn't, I guarantee you his horse did.

Bill was a throwback in most everything; it was how he lived and it all came out in his music. He kept a bunch of mules and horses to do all his farmwork. He never did get modern with any of that. He never did buy a tractor or a gasoline-powered mowing machine. He'd bale his hay the old-time way, and he'd plow the fields with a team of horses using a harness just like when he was a boy. He kept in shape right up until his stroke by plowing and baling and working. And in the early days, he made some of the Bluegrass Boys do up the heavy farmwork right alongside him.

Bill was old-time in most everything he did. He used the old-fashioned soap and mug and brush to shave with, and the straight razor instead of the safety razor. And he would shave in ice-cold water. Me, I didn't like that ice-cold water, and I never had much use for a straight razor myself; if you miss, you get nicked up bad. It's not easy to do. But that's the way Bill done everything, the hard way. He could shave with that straight blade and never bat an eye. He had a razor strap, a long thin piece of leather; he'd hang it on the wall and sharpen the blade with that. He didn't believe in beards or mustaches, neither. I'm pretty much the same as far as that goes.

There were other things that set Bill apart from most musicians and most men, too. He didn't smoke and he didn't drink, far as I know. He just didn't fool with a lot of the habits that can bring a man down. His big weakness, if you want to call it that, was women. He had girlfriends all through the years. They gave him a lot of joy and a lot of grief, too. Trouble with women gave him some heartache, but he got some great songs out of that heartache.

One time we were at a festival and Bill had one of his girlfriends staying with him in his camper. Carter got the idea to pull a prank with some Ex-Lax. He didn't do it to Bill, though. He waited for the Bluegrass Boys to take the stage and he slipped some of the Ex-Lax to the woman. Well, after the show, Bill came back to the camper, ready to settle in with his girlfriend for the night. But the Ex-Lax kept her busy in the bathroom all night when Bill wanted to be alone with her. I don't think Bill ever did find out what Carter had done.

Back in the sixties when we were living down in Live Oak, Florida, Bill came down and played a few shows with us. Bill stayed at my house there for a couple or three nights. I had brought some country ham down with me that I had cured at the old home place in Virginia.

The first morning he was there, Bill come down for breakfast with us. I fried a big batch of country ham and some eggs and Bill ate a big country-style breakfast with us. He was sitting at the table, looking at me hunched over the skillet, and he said, "I never would have thought that one day Ralph Stanley would ever cook me my breakfast."

Thinking back on that now, I reckon the hog he gave me wasn't only on account of my complaining about store-bought ham. It was his way of thanking me for cooking him breakfast down in Florida. But he never did come out and say why he did bring the hog. It wasn't Bill's way to make a lot of explanations. In that way, he was a lot like me. He wasn't much of a talker, either.

Bill's word carried a lot of weight. When he talked, people listened. And he would always stick up for me when I needed him. He wasn't too big to help a man when he was down. One time at his festival at Bean Blossom, Indiana, Bill came to my defense when I got my banjo stolen.

You need to keep up with your instrument all the time, because you never know when someone will pick it up and walk away. I usually keep a close eye on my banjo. But this time I let my guard down. Bill and me and a few others had been playing some music in the dressing room behind the stage. We went to take a dinner break and left our instruments laying there. We figured we wouldn't be too long.

When we got back, there was Bill's mandolin sitting with the other instruments, and none of them were touched, just like we left 'em. The only thing missing was my banjo. Somebody had stole it. Now, this was my good old Gibson Mastertone. I could never replace it.

I'd had that banjo for more than twenty years and it was my favorite. It was the banjo I used on most of the King Records and for all of my Rebel years. It had the sharpest sound I ever got from a banjo. I had traded for it when the Stanley Brothers were on tour in 1962 in California. There was a fellow I met there and he was originally from Tennessee, down in Laurel Bloom near Mountain City, and he'd moved out to Sacramento. He was a fan and we got to talking at the show.

"I've got an old five-string I bought a while back," he said. "Seemed too pretty to play it. So I just put it under the bed and left it there. Got an inch of dust on the case."

He said it was a '29 Gibson. I told him I'd check it out. I was always on the lookout for a better-sounding banjo.

"Would you trade for it?" I said. "For this one I'm playing?"

"Yeah," he said.

So we went over to his place, and he pulled it out from under the bed. The case was all dusty just like he said it was. Inside was the banjo. It was a beauty. And it sounded as good as it looked. At the time, I was playing a 1923 Gibson flat-head. But the kind I've always liked was the arch-top, like this one. I think the arch-top has more of a brighter, cleaner, crisper sound to it. A lot of the flat-head banjos have a dull sound, and I don't much like it.

I like the tone of my banjo sharp and crisp, and I knew from the first note I hit on this banjo, it was a keeper.

"Do you want to trade even for it?" I said.

"Yeah," he said.

Those are the swaps that are the best. They're quick and right to the point and both sides feel like they got a good deal. I know it was probably the best swap I ever did.

Anyhow, this banjo, what they call a 1929 Style 5 Wreath Gibson Mastertone, this was the banjo that was missing.

When the show started back up, Bill went on the stage and he made a pretty strong deal about it. He got on the microphone and told everybody in the place what had happened. "Somebody walked off with a banjo belonging to Ralph Stanley," he said. "He's a good friend of mine and I want to get it back. This is some dirty business and I won't have it at my festival. Whoever is guilty or knows anything about it needs to step forward, and that banjo better show up."

You know, something like that had happened to Bill when his mandolin got destroyed and nearly totaled. Somebody went into his house and just broke his mandolin all to pieces, and he had to get it all put back together. That 1923 F-5 Gibson mandolin, that was Bill's sound, just like that Gibson banjo was my sound, one of the things that set us apart from everybody else. Bill knew what it was like to lose your instrument. That's a serious crime against a musician, and it doesn't happen too much. So Bill made it plain to the crowd, and word got out about my banjo.

The next night, Bill got home from the festival and the phone rang. A man from Indiana, about fifty miles north from Bean Blossom, was on the line. He said. "I've got Ralph Stanley's banjo."

It took a while to get to the bottom of it. Here's what happened. This teenage boy had been at the festival and he came home all excited and shows his dad a banjo. He said he'd been hitchhiking on the highway back from Bean Blossom and a car came along and the people driving picked him up and they had this banjo and sold it to him. Sounded far-fetched. Then the father saw my name etched on the shoulder strap. He was a fan of mine and knew the boy was lying and had just made up that tale about buying the banjo while he was hitchhiking.

The man got on the phone to Bill and told him what had happened. Bill called me up and said, "This fella's boy got your banjo and he feels real bad," and he gave me the phone number. I called him, and the poor man told me the whole story and said he was sorry for everything.

"Now, where you want him to bring you that banjo?" he said.

"My boy's going to bring you that banjo in person. I'm gonna make him do it."

"Well, the best way is to let him fly into Bristol," I said. "I'll meet him there and pick it up."

The next day, the boy flew into Bristol airport and I met him right there at the gate. He said he was sorry for what he done and I accepted his apology, and he told me his father was so mad with him that he beat him nearly half to death, and I have to say the boy looked awful banged up so I knew he wasn't lying about it. I felt bad he had to get a whipping over it, but it sure beat having to do any jail time. Then he handed over the banjo. By the time I had my good ole Gibson safe in my car and was heading back to Dickenson, I wasn't even sore about it no more. I was just happy to get it back safe and sound. I didn't have to pay no ransom or nothing. It didn't cost me a penny. Just had to drive to Bristol to get it. The whole mess turned out pretty good, if you ask me. That banjo was worth millions of dollars to me. And I owe a lot to Bill for helping to get it back in one piece.

I've heard a lot of musicians say that maybe Bill was hard to work with. All I can say about that is, Bill Monroe put music above everything else, and he wanted to do it right. He just wanted each man to get in there and do his part like he was supposed to and that's the way it should be. If you didn't do it like the way he told you to, you didn't stay with him very long. You can't blame a man for that. He wanted to do his music the right way, the Bill Monroe way. That was his whole life, that and his farming. He was a musician first and a farmer second.

I believe the strength and power of Bill's music came from the land. He was raised in the country and stayed close to the land his whole life. He sang about what he knew and what he loved best.

You'd hear people say that Bill kept a lot of groups and singers off the *Grand Ole Opry*. A lot of that was true. He was a hard man in some ways. In the early days, he had a lot of enemies and he looked at other bands as competition. When Flatt and Scruggs left him to start the Foggy Mountain Boys, he told his band, "I don't you talking to *any* of them Foggies," and he meant it. That's the way everybody was back then. It was a cut-throat business, not near as big as it got later. There weren't many openings on the *Opry*, and you had to look out for yourself.

I'll tell you a little story that Bill told me. When Earl Scruggs first joined up with Bill in 1946, they hadn't heard much of that style of banjo playing in Nashville, or anywhere else. Earl took the banjo and made it a star instrument, and he played serious. At that time, Uncle Dave Macon, he was it at the *Grand Ole Opry*. He was the main attraction, but he was more a clown for acting up and working the crowd than he was a musician and his banjo was mostly a prop; he used it for comedy as much as he did to carry a tune. He didn't care what sound he got out of it.

Bill told me that the first time Earl played the *Opry* with him, he set the Ryman on fire. The people had never heard anything like it. Earl was shooting notes off his banjo like a tommy gun. And off to the side of the stage is Uncle Dave, looking like he'd been shot.

Well, they went back in the dressing room later that night, and Bill called Uncle Dave in there to see Earl play up close. So he sidles in there, and Uncle Dave is past seventy-seven at this point and he's made his living for years having fun with the banjo, and making people laugh. And here's Earl, twenty-two years young, just poker-faced and playing the hell out of "Cumberland Gap," nothing moving except his fingers.

Bill got a big grin and Uncle Dave looked like he was gonna be sick, and he didn't say a word. Now, here was a picture worth taking, where you had Bill Monroe smiling and Uncle Dave Macon scowling.

"Well," said Bill, "what do you thing about that banjo playing now?"

"Well, I'll tell you," said Uncle Dave. "He's a pretty good banjo player, but he ain't a damn bit funny."

Competition. That's the way most musicians looked at each other back then, and Bill was the same way. The way he looked at it was pure survival. Bill didn't think there was room on the *Opry* for any other bands playing his type of music. The better they were, the more he hated 'em. He kept Flatt and Scruggs off the *Opry* for a long time. And a lot of others, too. Carter and me never did get to play together on the *Opry*, and I think Bill had something to do with that.

I know that Jimmy Martin died a-wanting to get on the *Opry* and he'd never made it. That really hurt him. It was his life's goal, to join the *Opry* and play there regular like his hero Bill Monroe, and it just never happened. Now, I don't think that was Bill's doing. I think it was more Jimmy's fault, really. He was his own worst enemy. He would always say things and do things to get him in trouble. There was no doubt Jimmy had enough talent to be a member of the *Opry*. He would have been a plus, talentwise, but he wasn't dependable and they knew it. He was too out of control, and he wouldn't have helped the *Opry* after they added it all up, the good and the bad.

For a long time, I played the *Opry* as a guest but I never did join.

When I got to thinking harder about it, I had some people in Nashville work on it in my corner. They told me I had paid my dues years ago, and not to worry. Bill made the loudest noise. It was all his doing. I didn't have to say a word to him. Bill told them they needed me on the *Opry* and that was all it would have took. This was in 1993. Hal Durham was running it back then, and Harold told me, "You're the only man that Bill's ever asked for them to put on the *Opry*." Bill wouldn't even put in a word for his own son, James, to get into the *Opry*.

With Bill behind me, I could have gone on the *Opry* full-time, but I just never did follow that up at the time. It was a big commitment back then. It used to be you had to commit for most of the year, at least twenty-six weeks, every Saturday night. My schedule wouldn't allow that. I was on the road with my band, and they counted on me for a paycheck.

Later, the *Opry* eased up on how often you had to play. That's when I was interested in making it official and joining. By then Bill was gone, and I had Porter Wagoner on my side. Porter was a big man and host at the *Opry*, which he'd first joined back in 1957, and he helped me a lot. He worked on my behalf for several years, talking to the people behind the scenes who could make it happen. It was in 2000 when I officially became a member of the *Grand Ole Opry*. Porter was there with Patty Loveless, and they brought me out on stage to induct me into what they call country music's most "elite club."

I know Carter would have been proud, and I'm sure Bill would have been, too. It felt like it had been a long time coming. I could only think of a little kid back in the mountains of Virginia, sitting there and listening to the *Opry* every Saturday night on the battery-operated Philco radio. It had been a long, hard climb to the stage at the Ryman Auditorium, but it had been worth every heartache and setback to finally make it. I accepted my membership and I made a little speech. "I'll carry the name of the *Grand Ole Opry* out everywhere I go," I said. "I'll always respect it, and I'll never let it down."

After Bill's death, Porter was the closest of my friends from the old days. He probably knew how much I was missing Bill, and he was at the Memorial Festival the last two years he was alive. He was ailing the last time, but he still made it down to the old home place on Smith Ridge. He was another who always wanted to see the hills where Carter and me were raised. He told me the first song he ever sung was "The White Dove." Porter and his brother learned the words to that old Stanley Brothers 78-rpm record on Columbia.

Porter and me were almost the same age, just a few months apart, and he came from the country and he was raised up hard like I was, and we really got along. He was a wonderful fellow, friendly and sincere; the same man offstage as he was in the spotlight. He was genuine and that's very rare. If he had any enemies, I didn't know about it. We became real close in the last years, and country music lost a lot when he passed on.

In his last few years, me and Bill got even closer. We might only see each other a few times a year in person, at festivals and whatnot, but we'd talk to each other a lot on the phone. He'd call me a lot and he confided in me. Even then, he wouldn't get too personal about anything. That wasn't his way. When his daughter Melissa died in 1990, he called me. She was young, only fifty-four, and Bill took it real hard. No parent wants to survive their children.

He was private about most of his life, same as me. He did talk a little about one girlfriend. Not the one who said Bill hit her with a Bible after she was making him swear on it that he wasn't cheating on her. There were a lot of different women in Bill's life, sometimes at the same time.

The woman I'm talking about he was real fond of. He was really taken by her. He told me he went into the bedroom and he found her sleeping with an entertainer. This entertainer was a real good friend of Bill's, at least he was supposed to have been a good friend. Bill was real bothered about that. He considered that was about the worst thing you could do to somebody. To him, that was more than just fooling around, it was a betrayal.

And I think that's part of the reason he always had trouble when somebody left his band. He took it as betrayal and desertion. He never could abide that, ever since the early days when Flatt and Scruggs left to start their own group. It took Bill a long time to forgive them. When Lester and Earl and the Foggy Mountain Boys were working the *Opry* in the early sixties, Bill still refused to even speak with his old bandmates after all those years. And he wanted his Bluegrass Boys to give the same silent treatment he did. Course, the Bluegrass Boys just did it behind Bill's back.

But for the most part, Bill finally did try to make up with people and settle those old feuds that festered for so many years. I remember the year he made up with Lester Flatt. Not long before Lester died in 1979, he finally did get up onstage to sing with Bill at Bean Blossom. They were each as stubborn as the other, but they were both just country boys, and at the end they got tired being mad at each other.

People forget how much Bill mellowed in his later years. He made amends for a lot of things he'd done. And that takes a big man to do that.

Most of the time, Bill would ask me some advice on everyday things like you would with any friend. He'd usually want to know about some new modern gadget he was fixing to get. He would ask me because he knew I wasn't much for new things, either. Bill was about the only man left who was more of an old-timer than I was.

"Ralph," he'd say, "I'm thinking about putting heat in my house."

Whatever old woodstove unit he had in his log house wasn't doing the job to keep him warm come winter, and he asked me what kind of heat I had.

"Central heat, Bill," I said.

He asked if I was well satisfied with it and would I recommend it.

"It does me fine and it will you, too."

I advised him to get the central heating system installed and he finally did. He was very suspicious of any newfangled things. He always figured oldest was usually the best. But with the central heat, he gave in and he was glad he did. He called me back and thanked me for advising him on that.

As the years went on, most of the time when Bill called we didn't have a happy conversation. Mostly it was sad news about an old-timer in Nashville who'd died. Bill was always the first one to call and tell me somebody we'd known or played with through the years had passed on. Especially if it was somebody that was a close friend of ours. He thought it would be better for him to tell me than for me to find out on the news or some other way. That was another little kindness that people probably didn't know about Bill.

Bill had come by to sing with me for the *Saturday Night & Sunday Morning* album in 1963. The song we did together was "I'll Meet You in Church Sunday Morning." Bill had cut that back in 1964. And he could really get up there in those days, his tenor couldn't be beat. But now his voice was failing him. He could get the falsetto better than he could his natural singing voice, but this was a song he didn't need to go high on, so he just used his natural voice, and he was little flat on his part.

When I sung the second verse, I put a phrase in there he wasn't expecting. I put a little extra feeling in it. When the song was over, Bill grabbed his arm and started scratching. "I wish I had recorded that the way you just done it," he said. "There's chill bumps on my arm."

Bill wasn't never one for compliments, and that meant the world to me. He gave me the same sort of sensation the first time Carter and me saw him play the show at our school in 1940. I reckon it was finally my turn to pay him back. When your boyhood idol tells you something like that, why, you know you've really done something.

Bill played music right up until he was eighty-four years old. His voice failed him some near the end, but he always gave it his best onstage. He really stayed with it and stayed on the road as long as he was able. In his last year a stroke laid him down. His last days at a nursing home gave him the chance to say good-bye to a lot of friends and old Bluegrass Boys. He died in 1996. When I heard he passed, I knew I'd lost the best friend I had left in the world.

They had a memorial service at the Ryman Auditorium, where Bill had first tore up the *Grand Ole Opry* in 1939. All the big country stars came to pay their respects. I was there helping with the singing. Bill wanted "Wayfaring Stranger" to be sung because that was one he'd sung at so many funerals through the years. Then they had some Scottish bagpipes play "Amazing Grace."

The funeral was in Rosine, Kentucky, where he was borned and raised, and he was buried on his eighty-fifth birthday. They had the burial at the little Methodist church there, and I sang a cappella at the graveside. I laid my hand on his casket and I told him, "Bill, thirty years ago, you sang this for Carter, and I'm doing it for you." Then I did an a cappella version of the old spiritual "Swing Low, Sweet Chariot," the same one he sung over Carter that cold winter day in 1966. Instead of saying good-bye, I said, "We'll meet again," the same words Bill said over Carter's coffin. I believe we will.

Bill was such a strong man, like to be made of granite, and you know, they gave Bill a twenty-five-foot tombstone, and if anyone deserved it, he did. He's still the man I measure myself against. I'd like to keep going with my music, and I'll play as long as I'm able to, but I doubt I can last as long as Bill. I doubt I'm as tough as he was.

The world hasn't been the same to me since Bill's been gone. It was like losing a great big oak tree on a hill that you always thought would be there forever. It was where you went for shade and to get some strength to get you through the storms.

Even today I listen to Bill Monroe's music more than anything else, except for the Stanley Brothers. Sometimes I'll listen to Jimmy Martin and some of Doyle Lawson's a cappella gospel and George Jones's old records, especially the duets he done with Melba Montgomery, but Bill Monroe is what I always go back to.

The songs I like best by him I've recorded through the years. "On and

On" was one he wrote from his own life. He called 'em his true-life songs, and it's in those songs where you find out how he was inside. That's why nobody could sing a bluegrass song like Bill. It was the only way he could cry out and let the world know what he felt but couldn't find the words to say.

Well, I've tried to tell you a little bit about the man I knew, but to tell the truth, anything you really need to know about Bill Monroe, you can find in his songs.

CHAPTER TWENTY-SIX

O Brother

"Little birdie, won't you sing to me your song?
Got a short time to stay here and a long time to be gone"

—"LITTLE BIRDIE," RALPH STANLEY

If you'd told me I'd become famous in my seventies from singing in a comedy movie, I'd have said you were the biggest liar I ever heard. If you'd told me I'd win the Grammy for singing "O Death" a cappella style like they do in my church back in the mountains, I'd have said you're not only a liar, you're crazy, too. It just goes to show you can never tell what's going to happen. Like Carter used to say, "It's a big world out there." Big and crazy, too.

I didn't know much about the project, to tell you the truth. T-Bone Burnett called me up and said he was working on a sound track of old-time music and he wanted me to help out. I went up to Nashville and met with him and we talked about it. Now, T-Bone, I liked him right off. He's from Texas, and he's one of the tallest musicians I ever worked with. I believe he's every bit of six-foot-seven. Hawkshaw Hawkins may have had an inch or two on him, when he had on his cowboy hat.

Me and T-Bone got along great. I'd heard he was a Christian, but we didn't talk about religion, just music. He said he'd been a fan of my music since he heard Stanley Brothers records when he was growing up in Fort Worth. But he didn't want to make copies of the old records. He wanted something new that had the old-time sound. That's why he called me.

T-Bone is one of those musicians who live and breathe music. It's not just a job. He hears things regular people don't hear, the way dogs hear sounds we can't hear. He thinks hard about what he's doing, too. I reckon he's more like a philosopher than just a producer. But he doesn't act like a big shot. He'll tell you all he's trying to do is make good records.

There was something T-Bone told me I've never forgot. He said he understood what I'd been doing all these years, sticking with my old-time mountain music when everybody else was going uptown. I told him it wasn't a strategy. More like an instinct. It was just the way I felt I had to go after Carter died. I didn't want to follow the herd. I said I felt like an old moonshiner who heads way back up the creek to the head of the hollow. Where there ain't nobody to bother him.

"I think you were right to do that," said T-Bone. "You had to go backward to go forward." When I heard him say that, I knew we were going to get along fine. That was his statement, not mine, and I've used it ever since.

T-Bone was telling me more about the project. It was called *O Brother, Where Art Thou?* and it wasn't like the usual Hollywood movie. It was set back in the Depression, so the sound track had to fit that time period. They hired T-Bone because the movie was music-driven, Model T–style, and he was the man to steer the whole thing. He loved the warmth of the old-time sounds, the brother harmony duets and the family singing and such. The movie was about the early days of commercial country radio, back when Carter and me were little boys and first heard our calling on the shows broadcast on our old battery-powered Philco.

Usually a sound track like that will feature records from that era, and T-Bone had picked a few radio hits from the thirties, like the Carter Family's "Keep on the Sunny Side." But he wanted to do more. He wanted to re-create the feel of the old-time music, same as when you make a piece of antique-style furniture using all the materials and tools and techniques from bygone days: It's new but it's done the old way. Handcrafted. His idea was to get his favorite country artists to cover old-time songs like the way those bands performed natural on the radio programs they had during the Depression, back when it sounded like the musicians were right there in your living room, singing and playing.

T-Bone was under the gun to get the music done. The sound track had to be finished before they could start shooting the movie. The old-time music was going to help tell the story and set the mood for the scenes, like another character in the movie.

We talked about what songs would be right for my voice. T-Bone had already got some younger musicians like Alison Krauss and Gillian Welch to do some old country songs. And he already had a Stanley Brothers song picked out. He wanted to use "Angel Band" over the final credits.

But something was missing. The last piece of the puzzle. What T-Bone wanted was something in the old-time lonesome style. Most of the movie was going to be a comedy, but parts of it were going to be serious. What T-Bone needed was the music for the movie's big dramatic scene; he didn't say what it was, just that it was different than the rest of the movie, so the music had to be different, too. Something that would really stand out. A showstopper.

The song T-Bone wanted for that scene was "O Death," and he thought I was the man to do it. He wanted me to play it solo and real backwoods. Just me and my banjo, the way Dock Boggs done it back in the twenties. T-Bone hates the word "bluegrass," and he don't like much of what they call bluegrass, and he don't care for bluegrass-style banjo, except the way I play it. He wanted me to play the old-time clawhammer style.

I didn't know the Dock Boggs record. I'd already done "O Death" a few times in my career. First with Carter back in the fifties. Then I sung it with Keith Whitley in the seventies. We always did it as a duet. I said I'd try to help any way I could, so he sent me a copy of the Dock Boggs record, and I worked it out just like Dock done it. Then I got my banjo and went up to Nashville and auditioned for T-Bone.

There must have been two dozen musicians in the studio for rehearsals. I mean, it was a crowd, and when I walked in the room, everybody hushed up fast. Nobody said a word, and I didn't know what to say, either. I reckon some of them thought I was dead and had come back to life. That's about the worst situation for someone like me, who don't mix well in a roomful of people.

The older I get, the more people take me for a legend. I guess if there is such a thing, I'm one of them. I'd rather be a living legend than a dead one. But I'm not much to look at for a legend. I'm just a plain old hillbilly, been lucky enough to hang in there all these years and still get work that pays. People are taking you for a legend, but you're just a man come to do a job.

T-Bone knew what to do."Welcome, Dr. Stanley," he said. "Happy to have you here. What do you say we play some music?"

Well, that hit the spot, T-Bone calling me "Doctor." He knew that I took the title pretty serious, and I broke a big, wide grin. For me, even a little grin is a lot, so when everyone saw me smiling, that broke the ice, and things went fine after that.

T-Bone had an interesting setup, just like the record studios used to do it back in the old days. He had one microphone a few feet away from the musicians, and then what they called a "tree mic" a little farther back to get the whole sound of the music in the room. He wanted to get the feel of a live performance on tape.

I strapped on my banjo and played "O Death" in the Dock Boggs style. I done two takes and it went over well. "Yeah, that'll be fine," said T-Bone. "That's what I was looking for."

Sometimes you have to speak up or you lose your chance. I didn't much care for doing it like Dock Boggs. It was old-timey, but it didn't have the right feel to it. I didn't think the song needed a banjo. It was getting in the way of the words and the meaning. I wanted to take that song back even farther than Dock took it. I wanted to give it the old Primitive Baptist treatment.

"T-Bone," I said. "Would you listen to it the way I'd like to do it?"

"Yeah," he said. "I would."

"Why don't I just sing this without the banjo?"

"That sounds like a great idea."

He'd been thinking the very same thing back in the control booth. That's what I admire about T-Bone. He ain't like a lot of record producers. They already have their minds made up about everything before they go into the studio. They're businessmen first and producers second. T-Bone was a musician first. He'd worked with Bob Dylan, and he was used to thinking different and taking chances. For T-Bone, a recording studio isn't a factory, it's a room where you make music. So he was ready for anything.

I laid my banjo down and stood up to the microphone. I stuck my hands in my pockets and I sang him about three verses in the a cappella style from my church. It's where you worry out the lines so every word means something. Where you can stretch that melody out. When I don't have my banjo, I can focus more on my singing. I put my crooks and turns on the words:

O Death, won't you spare me over 'til another year
Well, what is this that I can't see with ice-cold hands taking hold of me
"Well, I am Death, none can excel, I'll open the door to heaven or hell."
"O Death," someone would pray, "could you wait to call me another day"

I didn't even need to get through the song. T-Bone knew what I was after, and he was all for it. He's a real quiet man, like a lot of tall fellas tend to be it seems like, but this got him real excited.

"That's it!" he said. "That's the way I want it!"

When you leave the voice alone, it brings the song out better. It lets you hear the words and the melody, where you can't do that when you're competing with a banjo and a guitar and whatnot. With "O Death," the song is about everything you've got being taken away:

I'll fix your feet till you can't walk
I'll lock your jaw till you can't talk

I'll close your eyes so you can't see
This very hair, come and go with me

Put a banjo or guitar on top of that and it sounds like you're cheating. I was glad I got to do it my way, but I had no idea that it would be so popular.

Strange thing. Not a one of us would have dreamed *O Brother* would hit big the way it did. T-Bone said everybody done good and he said it was worth the effort. But he didn't have a clue, either. That's one of the good things about the music business. Like politics. It can be nasty and it can be mean, but you never know what's going to happen.

A lot of people don't know this, but *O Brother, Where Art Thou?* wasn't my first movie. Years before, in the early seventies, I was in a movie called *Musical Holdouts*. It's a documentary by John Cohen. He's the banjo player in the New Lost City Ramblers, but he's a filmmaker and a photographer, too. The movie features me and the Clinch Mountain Boys, along with other musicians, including Comanche and Cheyenne performers, black singers from the South Carolina Sea Islands, a guitar-playing cowboy from Arkansas, string-band musicians from a nudist colony and hippie commune in California, and old-time mountain banjo player Roscoe Holcomb of Kentucky.

Now, you may be wondering what in the world these musicians have to do with each other. John wanted to show how some traditional American groups stayed faithful to the old style handed down through the generations. At the beginning of the movie, he explains what he means by the title, *Musical Holdouts,* the ones like me who'd rather stick with their roots instead of changing with the times.

"Throughout America there are isolated groups who have maintained their separate identities. These can be heard in their music. The melting-pot idea has not come true and a homogeneous America does not exist for them. However, the mass media, network TV and pop culture are an insistent challenge to the continued existence of these groups, for they present a daily reminder of their separation from mainstream America.

This film celebrates the fact of their existence, that their glory might not disappear."

John was a lot like T-Bone. He understood what I was trying to do with my music. He had already made a documentary about bluegrass called *High Lonesome,* but he knew mine was an altogether different music from bluegrass. He knew it was about a particular place more than anything else—the Clinch Mountains of Virginia where I was borned and raised and lived.

So John traveled down to Dickenson County for a visit, and he filmed me and the band and my family, too. He didn't go for posed shots or formal sit-down interviews. He wanted to give the spirit of the place that made my music what it was, so he filmed everyday things, like when we all pitched in to build a new stage for the Memorial Festival on Smith Ridge. Then he filmed the Clinch Mountain Boys playing on that stage for the crowd at the festival. He was making the point that here at the old home place you could still find music made by hand, played at a venue built by the same people who played it.

Musical Holdouts is different than any film you'll ever see. It's like a home movie John made on the road, a home movie about other's people's homes in the swampland and backwater islands and the Indian reservations, places you don't see much of anymore. The film is not easy to find. It's mostly shown in schools and colleges. I had never seen it myself until doing some research for this book. For Jimmi and me, it really was a lot like seeing old home movies you didn't even know about, especially when John talked to her while she was in the kitchen of our newly built house on Sandy Ridge, standing by the stove and cooking up beans. Of course, we were both young and just starting our family then, and watching the movie brought back a lot of good memories.

There is a scene that I'd forgot about that says a lot about where bluegrass was when the movie was filmed. I tell an old bluegrass joke: "It used to be pride was about all a bluegrass musician had, but you know, you can't live on pride."

Around the time John made his movie, I was interviewed about all the progressive bluegrass that was coming out, and I was very clear that I was staying true to my roots, even though it wasn't commercial at the time. I said there was a lot of good bands coming on now, but in my opinion there wasn't enough of the young ones doing the old-time traditional bluegrass. I said I believed the ones playing the old sound in years to come would reap a better harvest.

Well, the harvest came when *O Brother* hit. It took twenty-five years, but it was worth the wait. I hadn't changed my music at all since John had come to visit. I was still the same musical holdout I ever was. The change came in the people; they were ready for this music now. The people in mainstream America and the mass media. The ones who didn't even know this kind of music existed. The people were ready for the old-time clawhammer banjo and the a cappella gospel singing. I believe they'd been waiting around for it.

For the *O Brother* movie, I didn't know how they were going to use "O Death." I had no idea what they had done with it until I sat there watching the movie in the theater. I was a little surprised to see they had my voice singing in a Klan leader's outfit. I wasn't expecting that, and nobody had told me they were going to do that. People have asked me how I felt about it.

Well, I have to tell you, as much as it surprised me, it really didn't bother me none. I didn't pay much attention to it, because it wasn't really me in that suit, just my voice coming out of his mouth. It didn't matter whose voice it was, it worked, and that's all that matters. I thought it was powerful the way they used the song. It fit the scene real well, and they needed that for some drama, I reckon, because that's the most serious scene in that movie. There's nothing funny about a bunch of Klansmen burning a cross, and there's nothing funny about "O Death," either. So that song fit what you're seeing on the screen.

Anyhow, it's just a movie, and I don't think anybody's fool enough to think that's really me under that Klansman's hood. Just like anybody knows that's not really George Clooney singing "Man of Constant Sorrow" with his band in the movie, the Soggy Bottom Boys.

I'd say it was a good comedy, most of it. And people enjoyed it, too. But it wasn't the movie that caused the big stir. It was the music that got people talking and buying that sound track. Which is very unusual, for the sound track to be more popular than the movie. The album went to number one on the country charts, even though country radio wouldn't touch it because it was too country. The video of "Man of Constant Sorrow" got so popular that it was a hit with no advertising, just by word of mouth.

That's another thing that really helped me. Having "Man of Constant Sorrow" on the *O Brother* sound track was a big boost for me. Because you know, I reckon I'm the real Man of Constant Sorrow. I've been singing that song for sixty years now, and I think I'm the one that kept it alive. That song would have died out, I believe, if we hadn't recorded it and played it down through the years.

It's like what Mother Maybelle Carter said about "Wildwood Flower," She was talking about how the Carter Family record in 1928 kept it alive and out before the public. It would have died out, but they took that old song and rearranged it. Maybelle said her mother and her mother's mother had sung that song around the house. Just an old parlor song, but it always stuck in her mind. So Maybelle and A.P. took that old song and rearranged it with Maybelle's guitar carrying the melody, and it's been a classic of country music ever since.

A song like "Man of Constant Sorrow" is as old as dirt. It was already old when I learned it from my dad. The record company found the family of a blind singer from Kentucky who printed up the words in a song booklet in 1913 and they paid out something. I think the man's family was as poor as could be and needed every penny, so I'm glad for that. But I don't think they will ever know who really did write it.

I'll tell you, though. I sure wish I'd written that one. I'd have been rich off it if I had. But I was real fortunate, too, because the arrangement they used for *O Brother* was one me and Carter did in the fifties. Carter liked to experiment, and he got the idea to add that jingle, that catchy refrain to the chorus. That's the one the Soggy Mountain

Boys do in the movie, and the man who did it, Dan Tyminski, who was the singing voice of George Clooney, I think he done it good, in his own style.

Then we got word I'd been nominated for the Grammy for Best Male Vocal for Country. I'd been to the Grammys once before, back in 1993. I was nominated along with Dwight Yoakam for best country collaboration for our duet on "Miner's Prayer." Dwight grew up in in Floyd County in eastern Kentucky, near Pikeville. He wrote that for his grandpa, Luther Tibbs, who was a coal miner from Pikeville.

Dwight's a country boy, a wonderful fellow and he's a good friend. Dwight likes the Stanley style of music. I didn't know he was as much a fan as he was, until he played a show in Ohio and he asked me if I would come up onstage and sing a couple songs with him. I said that'd be fine because I was off that Sunday, and so I went up and did that and really enjoyed it. When I was on tour in California, where he lives now, he came out and sang with me for a few shows, so I got to know him real well. We finally got to sing together in the studio on the "Miner's Prayer" for the *Saturday Night & Sunday Morning* album.

That year the awards ceremony was held in New York, but me and Dwight didn't win. So I was happy just to be nominated again, but I didn't expect much. Nashville had never cared to honor the Stanley Brothers in our career, except for one time, and it wasn't for our singing. Like I mentioned to you before, in 1955, a magazine called *Country & Western Jamboree* had voted us Best Instrumental New Group, even though we'd already been in the business for nearly ten years. We won for my banjo instrumental "Hard Times" and for "Orange Blossom Special."

For the Grammy Awards ceremony, Jimmi and me went out to Los Angeles. For the Best Male Vocal award, I was up against big stars like Johnny Cash, Willie Nelson, and Tim McGraw. I didn't think I had a chance. Nobody my age had ever won, and nobody doing my kind of old-time country had ever won. That seemed like reason enough that it wasn't bound to happen.

I told Jimmi not to get her hopes up.

"It ain't gonna happen," I said. "Not for this old-timer."

"Don't ever say no," she said.

That's the way Jimmi is. She always sees the positive.

We woke up the morning of the awards ceremony at a motel outside Los Angeles. Two days before, I had turned seventy-five years old, and I was feeling every bit of it. I was thinking to myself, "Why come all the way out here to another awards ceremony to watch some other fellow win?"

But Jimmi woke up in a real cheerful mood, as is her way. She heard something outside the window, and she went over and opened it up. It was a little bird out on the ledge, singing out. She got all excited and pulled me over there to point it out. She said the bird was a good omen. It's a feeling she gets about some things.

"Ralph," she said. "Listen to that pretty little bird singing so sweetly. It's telling you that you're going to win tonight. That's a sign."

I was looking at the bird; never seen one like it in Dickenson County. So I was asking her what kind it could be. Jimmi didn't know and she didn't care; she was starting to hum along.

"I reckon we're just lucky it ain't a big black crow," I said. "Now, that wouldn't be so good, would it?"

"Don't matter what kind it is," she said. "That little bird knows something you don't know. I believe it's telling us you're going to get the Grammy."

The bird kept right on singing, and it got me thinking about the song "Little Birdie" my mother taught me when I was first learning banjo. That's the only sign I needed; my mother would sure be proud I'd got this far from our little hollow in Big Spraddle Creek, and wouldn't it be something if I did win?

"I'm hopeful," I said. "But I'm still doubtful."

That night at the awards show, they called my name for the Best Country Male Vocal award. I was as surprised as anybody. Jimmi had to give me a poke to get me to move. That's when I knew I'd really won. I reckon she and her little birdie knew something I didn't know. I gave her a big hug and headed down the aisle to the stage to get the Grammy.

Winning the Grammy just felt so good I can't hardly tell you. When I won that night, I had to sing "O Death" for the audience, not just the thousands in the auditorium but for all the millions at home watching on live TV and probably wondering who was this little white-haired man and how in the world did he wander out on this stage without security getting properly notified? There I was, Lucy Smith Stanley's backwards little boy, standing in the spotlight all by myself, no musicians or nothing to back me up. You can't see nothing for all the glare.

And, you know, I wasn't a bit nervous. I reckon I'd come a long way since I was a scared kid leading a hymn at the Point Truth Primitive Baptist Church in Nickelsville, Virginia. I was an old man with an old man's voice, and I just sang it natural and it came out just right. Bob Dylan told me it was the highlight of his career when he sang with me on "Lonesome River." I'd have to say the highlight of my career was singing "O Death" on national TV.

I didn't feel alone on that stage. I had my memories of my mother and of Carter to keep me company and of so many others who passed on but paved the way. That Grammy wasn't for me, but for all them old-time country musicians who never got their proper recognition. A lot of people felt that way about it, and they told me so. People like George Jones and some of them folks that Nashville set aside, well, it tickled them to death when I won the Grammy. That's all I need to feel justified. When you've got George Jones on your side, you know you're doing all right. You don't have to apologize to nobody.

I've been through it all and I believe my music is better for it. I think you've got to go through the hard times to make music that's worth it.

What kept us going in the hard times was we always had hopes and dreams that things would get better. We put all that into our singing and playing. I think some of that would be good for the young performers. Maybe it would help their music sound better.

Some of the younger crowd would rather us old-timers go under the wheels of our tour buses and be done with it. They've got no respect for their elders, and they don't even pretend to.

Back when I was their age, I didn't treat old folks that way. Like when we took Fiddlin' Powers on the road with us. We was barely in our twenties and he was old as our granddad and he hadn't had a record out for years, but we were happy to have him. We knew what Cowan Powers had been at one time. The times passed him by, and we felt maybe in his mind and his heart he wanted to keep playing music for people like he had done. We always wanted to help an old-timer like Cowan who had made it possible for us to make it as musicians. We admired what he'd done with his fiddle; we appreciated him and we wanted to show it.

I remember what Carter said on this subject. He felt strongly on this point. He said just because a horse gets too old to work, you don't take that old horse and shoot him. If he's helped make you a good living or paved the way for you somehow, you show him some gratitude and kindness. You put him on some grassy fields and fresh pastureland and let him graze awhile, and let him enjoy those last years. Well, that's what we done with Fiddlin' Powers. And Cowan appreciated that always. He was grateful and he never went anywhere with anybody except with us.

Winning that Grammy put the icing on the cake for me. It gave me all kind of new fans. It put me in a new category.

The *O Brother* sound track won a bunch of Grammys besides mine. It beat out all the pop and rock 'n' roll groups for Album of the Year. T-Bone got to thinking and said let's take the music out on the road. So we got all the musicians together and did twenty-five cities.

T-Bone Burnett got all the performers from the sound track and we went on the *Down from the Mountain* tour. There was Alison Krauss and Emmylou Harris and John Hartford. It was like the old tent revival shows they used to have with Bill Monroe when he was first starting out back in the thirties, only this time we were playing in big auditoriums and arenas for twenty-five thousand people.

It had been a while since I'd worked any shows without the Clinch Mountain Boys. The last time I'd gone on the road without my band was when I did some shows with the *Masters of the Folk Banjo* tour. It was a bunch of traditional musicians like me, playing folk songs to show how different the banjo is when it's played in different countries. One fellow was from Ireland, he played a tenor banjo. I never did like Irish or Scottish music with all the tin-whistles and bag-pipes and whatnot, and I still don't much care for it.

One musician really stood out from the rest. He was an Ethiopian named Seleshe Damessae, and he's famous in his home country. He played some real old African folk tunes on a six-string instrument with a bowl on the end called a krar, which is sort of an ancient cousin of the banjo as we know it over here. They told me it was kin to an old Hebrew lyre, which they used thousands of years ago, where you read about the Jews hanging up their harps while they were in exile in Babylon.

Seleshe would finger-pick that krar lightning fast, and he'd do some sort of talk-singing, like a recitation in country music. He sang in Aramaic, the language Jesus spoke in. This was the traditional music where he was from. Just like me, he'd learned from his parents, who all the time would play their music while they rode on horses.

We couldn't say much to each other, so we just talked to each other through music. I got a kick out of Seleshe and his krar, and he got a kick out of my clawhammer. He really became my biggest fan.

Every stop on the tour, when I'd go out to do my part of the show, he'd come out on stage and make a bow down to my banjo and sit right there at my feet. When I started playing, why, he would dance around and just have a time. Seleshe would hit the floor every time I played "Shout Little Lulie." He really thought I was *it,* and he would almost do somersaults and such onstage, the music made him so happy.

Watching him dance, I was thinking about Chick Stripling and his Butter Paddle Buck 'n' Wing. Seleshe and Chick would have really put on a show together. There's more than one way to dance to the clawhammer.

For the *Down from the Mountain* tour, I could leave my banjo at home. I was just going to sing, and I was really glad Jimmi was coming along with me.

I've recorded more than two hundred long-play albums and CDs, and that *O Brother* record has done me more good than all those put together. Last I heard, it had sold more than 10 million copies around the world.

I believe that it's proof people are craving our type of country music, and when they get a chance to hear it, they can't hardly get enough of it.

The *O Brother* album got the word out that there were still musicians playing old-time country, and people wanted to see if for themselves.

That tour was really something special. We had a caravan of buses to travel from city to city. It reminded me of the old days when Carter and me would go on package tours with George Jones and Jimmie Skinner and Tex Ritter. You'd really get to know the performers you traveled with.

On the *Down from the Mountain* tour, I made some good new friends, and I especially enjoyed being on the road with John Hartford. I'd known him years before, when we played at bluegrass festivals back in the 1970s. I always got along with him well. He was a real student of old-time music. You could learn a lot listening to him talk about the history of songs. He was one of the rare ones who could do it all. He could play fiddle as good as banjo, and he was a really fine songwriter, too.

John had worked as a riverboat pilot on the Mississippi. He said his music was about the river, and my music was about the mountains. John was the narrator of the concert T-Bone put together, the master of ceremonies. He wore an old pilot's bowler cap and introduced the performers and told little yarns to string it all together.

And the thing was, John really wasn't able, he was sickly and truly ailing on that whole tour. He had cancer pretty bad and he was suffering awful, but somehow he went on with the show. Sometimes we'd have to stop and let him rest up a bit when we were doing a number. But he never let it get him down. He always was ready, he was a real trouper. Watching him work the crowd night after night, it made me think of Carter in the last years, when he'd save all his strength for the stage, and he'd come to life out there. Music is the only thing that kept him going, and I think it did the same for John, too. I'd watch his face light up when he'd play his old-time fiddle tunes. Music is some powerful medicine.

T-Bone had rigged up a special sound system with vintage microphones to make the acoustic music ring out in the big halls and auditoriums. It was close to what we used to do back in the forties and fifties, no amplifiers and no drums, just your basic string instruments. It was a real treat for us old-time country musicians, because it's hard to play our music over the newfangled great big PA systems designed for big, loud rock shows.

Nobody did more than a couple songs per set; T-Bone wanted to feature the songs instead of the performers. He wanted the music to shine. Some way or the other, though, I became the star of the show, when I'd close it out every night with "Amazing Grace."

Being the oldest, I think I stood out from the other musicians. So much of the show was upbeat music and younger performers. The crowd really took a shine to the Peasall Sisters, the little girls in their Sunday dresses. I was starting to feel like I was spoiling the party, like I was Mr. Death out there, in black suit and white hair, singing about people's skin falling off. I got to where I'd introduce "O Death" by warning the crowd, "Now here comes the sad part." At first, we'd been closing the show the same way the movie ends, with "Angel Band." That's a wonderful Stanley Brothers song, but it's a sad one, too.

The mood of it seemed too much like a funeral to my way of thinking. So I got the idea that we could all get together for a big show closer by singing one of my favorite spirituals, "Amazing Grace." I said to T-Bone, "Let's get everybody on stage together, like we used to do for hymn time on Sunday mornings at the bluegrass festivals. So we could give the crowd something hopeful to end the show." T-Bone was all for it.

It worked out beautiful. We gathered all the performers on stage, the whole cast out there together, to stand and hold hands, and join me in singing "Amazing Grace." I'd line out the words like a Primitive Baptist preacher, and they would follow me like the congregation does in church. I'd tell the crowd to stand up and hold hands and join in with us. And the whole crowd would be singing in one voice. Jimmi said it was the most beautiful thing she'd ever seen or heard.

And don't you know the biggest response I believe we got was in Los Angeles. T-Bone lives out there and he said he'd never seen anything like it, the way the people got together on our closing gospel number. "If you can get Los Angeles to hold hands," he told me, "you've done something."

After the show, we were out at the bus in the parking lot behind the concert hall. There were two young boys come looking for me. They were a couple of teenagers with long straggly hair and tattoos all over themselves. I've had a lot of younger fans since *O Brother*. I'm well satisfied to see them, because it means my music has reached them some way or other.

But these two boys were something different than the folks who just want an autograph and a handshake. They came knocking on the door of the bus, asking if they could see me. We don't always let everybody onto the bus, because it gets to be too much traffic and it gets to be a mess sometimes. A sign above the door says "Wipe Your Feet" to let people know to not drag mud and dirt into the bus. It used to get as bad as a hog pen before we put that sign up.

Well, these two would not be denied, and they came staggering down the aisle right to me, both crying, tears just running down their cheeks. I could tell they'd been drinking, and they threw their arms around me and hugged me, just a-sobbing.

But it wasn't anything bad at all. It was good news. Here's what they told me: "When we come to see the show tonight we were nonbelievers, but after we heard you sing 'Amazing Grace,' we wanted to tell you we'll meet you in heaven."

After we done the *Down from the Mountain* tour, I had me a whole new audience. That's the way it's been ever since, and I ain't slowed down yet. I hope my health holds out so I can stay in it a good many more years. I've had a good life in music. I've made a good living and I've learned a lot and I've met a lot of nice people from all around the world. I wouldn't swap it for anything else I could have done. I've been blessed to be able to keep going and I hope it continues. Music keeps me young, and I'm going to keep right on singing until I can't no more.

Chapter Twenty-Seven

Back to the Hills of Home

"I wandered again to my home in the mountains
Where in youth's early dawn I was happy and free
I looked for my friends but I never could find them
I found they were all rank strangers to me"

—"Rank Stranger," the Stanley Brothers

Not too long ago, a stranger came to the mountains near where I live in Dickenson County. Nobody had seen him around these parts before. He was a short fellow with dark sunglasses hiding his eyes and he had curly hair coming out of a hood over his head. He was a man who didn't want to be recognized.

He parked a car with out-of-state license plates down by the McClure River, where there's a roadside historical marker the county put up years ago. It has this engraved in the wood:

"BIRTHPLACE OF DR. RALPH STANLEY. In 1946 Ralph and Carter Stanley, the Stanley Brothers, pioneered the sound of bluegrass music. After Carter's death in 1966, Ralph went on to become a legend in bluegrass."

The stranger took some pictures, and he stopped by a country store close by, asking for directions to my house. The cashier looked him over and told him the way.

"Thank you very much," said the stranger in a raspy voice.

There was a boy stocking items over in the shelves. He saw the whole thing, heard the screen door slam shut as the stranger left the store. He rushed from where he was behind the shelves and ran out of there like the place was on fire. He made it outside as the stranger's car pulled away.

The boy went back in the store, and he looked at the cashier.

"Don't you know who that was?"

"I reckon not," said the cashier.

"That was Bob Dylan."

I heard about Bob's visit from those who would know. They said he was out sightseeing all by himself and he just wanted to get the feel of the land where the Stanley Brothers were borned and raised. It doesn't surprise me Bob would do something like that. He's a searcher, a man who wants to know where things come from. He wants to get to the source.

I never did see Bob for myself on that visit. They said he was too shy to come up and knock on the door. Just wanted to see the home place and go up to Smith Ridge. Stop by Carter's grave I reckon, and get himself a good look around.

Of course, we did meet up back in 1997, when we sang together on "Lonesome River" for the *Clinch Mountain Country* album. Like I told you in the earlier chapter, Bob was sort of shy, the same way I am, but he was just as friendly as could be, and he did a good job on that song. Jimmi says it's her favorite duet on the album.

I was told Bob turned down twenty-two people to record with me. I feel proud he found the time to do that, because I know he stays on the road and his tour schedule is booked a year in advance. Mine is, too, though I don't play near as much as Bob.

As far as touring goes, Bob and me's the same on that. We're musicians, and playing music for people is all we really know how to do. All we're good for, really. I reckon it's why we were both put here, and we were both lucky enough to find out what we were supposed to do with the gifts God gave us.

I know Bob will keep playing shows till he can't no more. I know I will. I still make nearly a hundred show dates a year, and I'm not going to slow down. The road keeps me young, and besides, I've got a band that depends on me. I've had a good life in music. I've learned a lot and I wouldn't trade it for anything else I could have done.

I wanted to tell you another little story about Bob. A lot of people probably haven't heard it, because Bob didn't make a big fuss about it, and I haven't, either. But it says a lot about the kind of person he is and the way he operates.

In 1996, they had a big celebration for me in Nashville in honor of my fiftieth anniversary as a professional musician. There was a fancy reception at the Country Music Hall of Fame, with all kinds of friends from down through the years and former Clinch Mountain Boys there to greet me. Then I played a show with my band at the *Grand Ole Opry*. During the show, *Opry* host Del Reeves announced to the crowd he had a telegram "a special fan" had sent from New York City. The telegram said:

"DEAR DR. RALPH.
THE FIELDS HAVE TURNED BROWN.
NOT FOR YOU, THOUGH.
YOU'LL LIVE FOREVER.
BEST WISHES, BOB DYLAN."

That was something I didn't expect, and it was a wonderful surprise. I know what Bob meant in his message, and it really touched my heart. I know he meant my music would be around long after I'm dead and gone. I believe the music I play will live on. These old mountain songs last. And I'll sing 'em wherever I can and wherever people will listen, because I want 'em to keep on going.

There's something else Bob meant in his telegram, a more important point he was making in those lines where he's talking about Carter's song, "The Fields Have Turned Brown." The singer leaves his home in the mountains to see the world, and years later he gets a letter that tells him his parents are dead, the home place is in ruins, and everything he loves has withered and died.

Now instead of a letter giving bad news, Bob's telegram was reminding me what I had to be thankful for: "THE FIELDS HAVE TURNED BROWN. NOT FOR YOU, THOUGH."

I'm a man who left home to ramble the country, but I've been able to come home and live out my days with all the blessings of family and good fortune. I have my house near the old home place on Smith Ridge, and all my kinfolk around me. I have my wife, Jimmi, and my two daughters and my son and a whole gang of grandchildren, everybody living close by. It gives you peace to be back home and rest up.

I'm glad I stayed right here in Dickenson County. I can make it just as well here as anywhere. So many people have asked me many and many a time, "Why haven't you moved to Nashville or some other big city?" The truth is I don't need to, and I like it right here in the mountains I come from. I get all the work I want to do, and I can stay at home when I'm off the road.

I reckon I could've been a bigger country star or more famous if I'd moved to Nashville, but maybe not. *O Brother* done plenty in the way of fame and success for me. Don't need any more fame.

I'm pretty well centered right here in southwest Virginia. When I want to play the *Grand Ole Opry,* I can be in Nashville in six hours, and that's about as far as I want to go to play a one- or two-nighter. I can get to Washington and the East Coast in a half day's drive. So I've got no reason to move. I can make it just as well here as anywhere.

The main reason is, I don't want to live anywhere else. This is where I was borned and raised and it's where I'll be buried. It's been good to me, and I don't want to leave behind the land I'm from. There's something about these Clinch Mountains. The mountains don't lie to you; they stand for the things that don't change, that stay true to themselves. They've been around a hundred million years and they'll be around for a good while more, I reckon. They keep you humble. They put you in your place. I'm going to see if I can maybe make one hundred years myself. I figure that's what I'll do, and then I'll go right back into the ground that raised me.

I'm grateful to have been blessed with eighty-two years and still be able to do a little something and play my music. Everybody don't have that chance. I've been well blessed and I thank the Good Lord every day for it.

I was past forty when Jimmi and I got married, and I was near fifty when she first started having children, sort of like my mother, who was an older parent, too. So I always wondered whether I'd live to see all my family grown up and having their own families. I used to worry whether I'd live long enough to see all that. Now I've got great-grandchildren, so it's been a gift to live long enough.

And something else, too. For the last few years, I've had three generations of Stanleys on the road together, and that's been an added blessing as well. That's my son Ralph II and my grandson Nathan. Even when I'm away from home, I've still got family right there with me. Sometimes, I get tired and down, because touring isn't easy at my age, even with a nice big bus and the nice modern highways. It gets awful rough on me. These miles get long. Sometimes I may be feeling worn out and don't feel much up to singing, and my son and grandson'll be onstage, just letting it rip. I set back and enjoy them right along with the crowd. When they sound real good, that really peps me up a lot. It makes me proud to hear them playing this kind of music and to see them keep the family tradition going.

I'm well pleased to see Ralph II and Nathan go into music and to help get them started and to give them a decent chance, because it's a tough business for anybody to make it, I don't care who you are.

I don't have to give them instructions. They were both so young when they started working with me, they learned by watching, I reckon, so they know what to do and how to hold themselves in public.

It's pretty rare, having three generations side by side. You don't see it too much in any business. It's been years and years since I first took my son Ralph II on the road with me, and he was onstage with me before he could walk. He became a full-time Clinch Mountain Boy when he was sixteen. He earned that job, and he's been my lead singer ever since. We've played every bit of twenty years and more onstage all over the country, longer than me and Carter were together.

And as I'm writing this, Ralph II has put in his notice that he'll be leaving the band. He's decided to go out on his own and help me out when he can on the side. He's been working to do that one day and it finally came. Everybody has to take a chance and do what's best for him, and I wish him all the best. He's more traditional country, more in the style of Keith Whitley, and I think he'll do fine.

My grandson Nathan plays mandolin and he's a fine singer, too. Back when he was a toddler, he'd crawl on stage and play spoons, keeping time to the music. His time came like Ralph II's time came, and he said, "Pa-Paw, I got to go play music with you," and so he joined us on the road, too. When Nathan started traveling with us, playing shows regular, Jimmi said to him, "You're leaving me, too? That'll be three gone." But she understood Nathan had to go with us, that it was meant to be.

Nathan has always been way ahead of himself, acting older than his age. He's more like a twenty-five-year-old than a sixteen-year-old. He says he wants to carry the music forward like Ralph II, and I'm all for him. A lot of kids his age, they're not thinking about business like that. They're not thinking about their future. Nathan wants to play music and make a career out of this. He's got the ambition and he's got the talent, he's got everything it takes. I guess Carter and me did the same thing at his age, but he's a lot further advanced than we were.

And Nathan's brother Evan, he's got a voice, and he can sing lonesome if he wants to. Back home, there's also my other grandson, Ralph III. I call him Mr. Three. I gave him that nickname because I want him to feel important. I got Mr. Three a Stanleytone banjo for a present, wrote on there for him, "To Ralph III, Love Pa-Paw." I'd like to live long enough to see him use that banjo someday.

My granddaughters, they're into the music, too. Ashley Hope and Alexis Faith, the nine-year-old twins, and little Taylor Brooke who's eight, they like to sing and dance and they're just now getting up the nerve to get onstage and be a part of the show. They all performed together with me at the memorial festival at the old home place this past spring. They done a little dance routine while we played Hannah Montana's "Hoedown Throwdown" and they nearly stole the show.

And my great-granddaughter, that's Makenzie Paige, she's already hooked on the old-time music and she's only three years old. She's pretty stubborn about it, too. She won't listen to anything except her Bubby, which is Nathan, or her Pa-Paw Dad, which is me. In her vehicle, if it's not Pa-Paw Dad's or Bubby's music playing, then it's nobody. That's just the way it is.

One of these days, it won't be long, the roots of bluegrass and old-time music will be gone. The ones who paved the way will be gone, and I think that's going to hurt. I know that things change, but I'm prejudiced to the old-time style, the traditional mountain music. I hope my boys will carry it on the best they can as long as they're able and there's people who want to hear it.

I'd like to be remembered as a musician who stuck to his roots, no matter what. I figured if you're going to stand for something, you might as well go whole hog and not fiddle-faddle around. I'm an old-timer who put the best years of his life into the music business. I've respected the music all the way, on the stage and off the stage, too. I never did like to be out swapping with the public and drinking and rip-rapping and bringing disgrace to the profession. I've always believed a man ought to hold himself up the proper way and respect what he's paid to do; I never disrespected the music, because the music brought me everything I have. I've done what I believed in and I stuck with what I started with.

I'm just about finishing up the book, even though I still have some living to do. How much I have left only the Man Upstairs knows. I know time is catching up on me, especially when I think of all the ones who've passed on. Like I told you when I started telling you the story of my life, I'm about the last of my generation around here. It's been on my mind a lot lately, more than I like it to be.

My bass man, Jack Cooke, took sick a few months back and I figured after he was rested up and feeling better again, he'd be right back on the road with me like always. But now it looks like Jack won't ever be coming back; he's recovering all right, but doctors tell him he probably won't ever be able to perform regular. So he's had to retire from what he loves more than anything. Jack had been with me for forty years, longer than any other Clinch Mountain Boy. I still can't get used to him not being there onstage, thumping away at the dog-house bass and singing "Sitting on Top of the World" and waking up a sleepy crowd the way Curly Ray used to do. But I have to go on, without Jack and all the others who've stepped aside or passed away.

A few Sundays ago, I was at Slate Creek Church, singing some hymns and listening to Brother Junior preach. He had lead on "Amazing Grace" and "Tarry with Me, O My Savior." After the meeting had adjourned, Brother Junior closed the church door; he wanted me to sing a few more for him after the people had left. I sung "Two Coats," and then he wanted me to sing "Man of Constant Sorrow." He just stood and listened there outside the church, under the trees. He loves to hear me do "Man of Constant Sorrow" a cappella, just like my daddy done; maybe I need to do it that way on my next album.

I enjoyed singing for Brother Junior; after all he done for me, it's the least I can do. Slate Creek Church had a split a few years ago; more than half left Junior and went on their own and that cut the church down. Now there are only about twenty-five or thirty people at Slate Creek, and it's like that at a lot of the Primitive Baptist churches here in the mountains. They're losing their members. A lot of the old followers have died and the churches are not as popular. They're dwindling away.

A sad feeling stayed on my mind, thinking about all those empty seats at the Slate Creek Primitive Baptist Church. And that sad feeling came to me again when I played a show with my Clinch Mountain Boys at a nursing home down the road here in Dickenson County.

It's a benefit show we put on every year at a facility for senior citizens in Clintwood. We perform for free to raise money for the residents so they can have presents for Christmas. A lot of them don't have no family left, and the presents are a way they can feel like they haven't been forgotten come Christmastime.

There wasn't a very big turnout for the show, and that didn't surprise me. This past winter I could draw a full house of fifteen hundred in

Rochester, New York, and I could pack a club in Boston close by Harvard University, but I can't barely scare up a crowd to come see me play in Clintwood. Don't matter the venue, a lot of the locals done got tired of Ralph Stanley years ago.

Anyhow, at the nursing home they'd had funerals for three residents who'd passed on that same week, so it was three less that would have attended the show. Looking at the audience, some in wheelchairs and others leaning on their walkers, I knew this wasn't the sort of show to play "O Death." Course, that's the song people want to hear everywhere we go, but it wasn't the time or place for that.

The show was dragging, and I decided to try to pep things up. I did my old clawhammer number, "Shout Little Lulie." Up until then, the only dancing in the place was a few toddlers who got loose from their parents, and they were scooting around like it was playtime. But when I started in on my five-string banjo, don't you know, just like one of the teenagers at the Bonnaroo festival, an old man jumped out from his chair in the front row and hit the floor.

If you never saw old-time mountain buck dancing, well, this man could give you an education. His feet kept time to my banjo and he never missed a beat, even though he got winded fast and looked ready for the emergency room. I looked up and saw it was an old schoolmate of mine from the old days, name of Wallace Sutherland. He wasn't a resident of the nursing facility, he'd just come to the show from his home in Nora, not far from my place.

Wallace had been a friend from the early days when Carter and I first started performing in public and at school plays as the Stanley Brothers, when the principal took us aside and warned us, "Why don't you boys throw down that music and get you an education so you can get you a real job?" After the show, Wallace came by to shake my hand and say how proud he was that I'd made a name for myself and taken the old-time music all around the world. And brought it all the way back to the mountains so he could stretch his legs and feel young again, even just for a little while.

That night, driving through the mountains back home, I got to thinking about Wallace and how few of us old-timers are left. I passed by some boarded-up houses, where the families had left or died off, leaving nobody to take care of the home place. Now they were just dark, empty buildings. I passed by the old McClure Primitive Baptist Church, where we'd sang hymns so many Sunday mornings so many years ago. It was still standing, but it, too, was deserted.

The road I was driving was the same one where I'd walked my horse, Patsy, with my mother riding sidesaddle, down to the church. Past Nora, where it becomes Route 652, the road is now called Ralph Stanley Highway. There are signs all along the way. It goes right past my house all the way down past Tom's Creek to Coeburn. It feels pretty good to live on my own highway.

I started thinking about Wallace buck dancing to "Shout Little Lulie." It made me chuckle to myself, remembering how much fun he was having. I doubted I'd ever see such a thing again. Probably never see Wallace again, either. When you're as old as me, you never know when's the last time for just about anything.

Me and Wallace, we're the last of the Mohicans in our little corner of the mountains. We were the last generation to grow up close to the land, when music was something to get you through the hard times. We take it for granted that we'll always be around somehow, and that the world we knew, at least our memories of it, will be around, too. And then one day, it's all gone, and the mountains bury that world forever.

It set my mind to thinking about things you don't see anymore. Like the chinquapins that used to grow wild up on Smith Ridge. When I was a boy, there was chinquapin bushes all around these parts. One of the first tunes my mother taught me on banjo was the old mountain song "Chinquapin Hunting." Around where I lived, though, you didn't have to hunt for 'em, because they was everywhere.

Most folks have never heard of a chinquapin, so let me tell you a little about them:

They were little round black nuts, something like a chestnut, but smaller and sweeter. At the end was something like a burr, and you could bite into 'em and they were a real treat. They were a taste of heaven for a couple of brothers who had to forage for food many a time when we were hungry on our way to school. I remember Carter and me roaming the hillsides, picking chinquapins and gobbling handfuls down like they was going out of style. And don't you know, they did.

Sometime or the other, chinquapins just died out, for some reason or another, and there ain't a one left on the ridge or hereabouts that I've seen or heard about for years. You just can't find chinquapins anywheres. One day, they were as thick as huckleberries, and the next thing you know, they're all gone like they never was. That's something that will set you thinking.

So I just drove on through the night down the Ralph Stanley Highway, heading home after another show, thinking about chinquapins and some other things that ain't no more.

Acknowledgments

Dr. Ralph Stanley would like to thank: Eddie Dean, for wording out my life story and getting 'er done; all my friends and my family, especially Lisa, for her help on the project; and to the Good Lord, without whom none of this would have been possible.

Eddie Dean would like to thank: Dr. Ralph Stanley, for the music and the memories; Patrick Mulligan and the team at Gotham Books for their hard work and dedication; Gary Reid, foremost expert on the Stanley Brothers, for his invaluable research and assistance beyond the call of duty; my brother, Larry Dean, for his keen editing eye and love of the old-time music; Jimmi Stanley for the Dr. Pepper and good cheer; and all the Clinch Mountain Boys, for sharing their stories. Thanks also to Rebel Records; Bluegrass Unlimited; the Dickenson and Wise County Public Libraries, and the Virginia State Library in Richmond; Fred Campbell and the people of southwest Virginia, for their kindness and hospitality; and finally, to my wife, Maria Allende, and our children, Sophie and Pablo, for their love and support.

WCYB
CARTER
EE WEE